MS-DOS® 6
QuickStart

Que® Development Group

Text and graphics developed by
Suzanne Weixel

Publisher: Lloyd J. Short

Associate Publisher: Rick Ranucci

Operations Manager: Sheila Cunningham

Publishing Plan Manager: Thomas H. Bennett

Acquisitions Editor: Sarah Browning

Title Manager
Walter R. Bruce, III

Product Director
Kathie-Jo Arnoff

Production Editor
Barbara K. Koenig

Editors
J. Christopher Nelson
Heather Northrup

Technical Editor
David Knispel

Book Designer
Scott Cook

Production Team
Jeff Baker
Claudia Bell
Julie Brown
Jodie Cantwell
Paula Carroll
Laurie Casey
Michelle Cleary
Mark Enochs
Heather Kaufman
Bob LaRoche
Jay Lesandrini
Linda Quigley
Linda Seifert
Sandra Shay
Dennis Sheehan
Wil Thebodeau
Susan VandeWalle
Johnna VanHoose
Mary Beth Wakefield
Phil Worthington

Composed in *ITC Garamond* and *MCPdigital* by Que Corporation.

Contents at a Glance

Table of Contents

Introduction

This book describes the connection between personal computer hardware and the disk operating system, and explains to beginning users all the most frequently used DOS commands from the DOS Shell and command line. After you become familiar with DOS's commands and features, you can use the graphics presented here for quick reference.

Making Friends with DOS

DOS is easy! You've heard that statement before. It's the kind of glib remark that might make you wish for an adding machine and ballpoint pen instead of a computer. Maybe you had a personal computer placed on your desk by a manager who "knows you can figure it out."

In a way, that's the worst rub because who wants to admit that you don't know where to begin? After all, your manager might conclude that you are not part of the high-tech generation. He or she might consider you an anachronism in the rapidly changing workplace.

To add to the injury, perhaps everyone's eyes have shifted in your direction, secretly relieved that you—and not they—were chosen for the ordeal. Scanning your surroundings, your eyes focus on the gray cover of a thick book. It's the notorious DOS Manual, that coldly unemotional collection of cryptic commands, disjointed addendums, appendixes, suffixes, prefixes, and file listings.

Making friends with DOS

What is MS-DOS?

What does this book contain?

What hardware do you need to run MS-DOS?

Conventions used in this book

As a young child, I felt ambivalent about trips to the library. This feeling was odd because I enjoyed reading, and I loved the feel of books in my small hands. Seeing row upon row of file cabinets filled with index cards, however, made my stomach tighten.

In time, I grew accustomed to the patronizing stares of bored librarians and the barbs of superiority from schoolmates. Although I long ago mastered the Dewey decimal system, those wooden cabinets still make me a bit edgy.

Not that the system is incoherent or inconsistent: it isn't. In fact, the logic of the library system is remarkable. Nonetheless, the assumption that a logical system will be easy to learn simply because it is coherent and consistent is the ultimate in callousness.

Every day, thousands of intelligent Americans scratch their heads and berate themselves, falling prey to a multibillion-dollar scam. After all, virtually everybody has been inundated by computer advertisements. You see ads in the newspapers, read mailings on sale items, hear about them from friends, and feel guilty about not learning how to use a computer.

Now you have a new computer at your office, or you have decided that a PC will make working at home more efficient. No matter what the reason, you are now face-to-face with DOS.

What Is MS-DOS?

By itself, a computer is just a box and a screen. Ultimately, you are faced with the test of bringing it to life. This means mastering the computer's operating system, which for most of us is MS-DOS.

MS-DOS (or to most PC users, just DOS) is a tool you use to manage the information your computer stores in disk files. DOS is a collection of programs that forms a foundation for you and your programs to work effectively with your computer. DOS is a set of standard routines that your programs use to access the services of the PC.

No matter what anybody tells you, the letters *D-O-S* do not stand for *Disheartening Obtuse Sadist*. To make the most of your PC, you really have to understand its basics. Understanding DOS is required to enhance the enjoyment and productivity of running your microcomputer.

This book is an introduction to the most widely used disk operating system in the world. You will find that the material presented here is written in a unique matter. You won't be patronized with elementary definitions, and you won't be force-fed a litany of cryptic terms.

What Does This Book Contain?

Learning DOS can be enjoyable. *MS-DOS 6 QuickStart* is painless and worth-while reading. Each chapter takes you on a guided tour of a specific part of DOS. You will be introduced to the concept of the MS-DOS Shell and its straightforward, easy-to-use menus. Also, you will be shown how you can type commands that DOS understands by using the command line prompt.

At first you may feel like a spectator, but as you read each chapter, you will find the text fast-moving and the ideas presented in easy-to-understand graphics.

Chapter 1 describes the components of personal computer systems: the display, the keyboard, the system unit, and peripherals. The last part of this chapter traces the way computers handle data.

Chapter 2 covers the fundamental concepts of how an operating system works, including its different parts. You will learn how to start—or boot—the computer in Chapter 3.

Chapter 4 introduces you to the DOS Shell and teaches you how to operate the Shell. You also learn how to customize the Shell.

Chapter 5 teaches you about directories. You learn how to navigate the tree structure of a disk. You use the Shell's Directory Tree area to visualize the concept of directories.

Chapter 6 teaches you how to prepare disks so that you can use them.

In Chapter 7, you learn the fundamentals of copying, moving, deleting, and renaming files. You also learn to copy an entire disk.

One of the functions of DOS is to enable you to start applications. Chapter 8 shows you how to start applications from the Shell. You learn to create and maintain program groups in the Shell.

Chapter 9 introduces you to the command line. You learn how to issue commands and, specifically, how to use the DIR and COPY commands.

Chapter 10 shows you how to protect your PC's data. In this chapter, you learn how to use the DOS Backup program to back up and restore files and how to protect your PC from software viruses.

Chapter 11 introduces you to some of DOS's less-used commands, such as MEM, CHKDSK, and CLS. Although you don't use commands such as these as often as COPY or DEL, they are important to learn.

After you become more comfortable using DOS, you will want to customize DOS for your use. Chapter 12 provides information on how to customize DOS with the PATH and PROMPT commands. You also are introduced to batch files.

Chapter 13 describes the more advanced DOS commands. You learn about redirection and piping, DOS filters, and how to better manage the memory in your computer.

Chapter 14 is an alphabetical command reference. Use this chapter to find the syntax for commands you want to use from the command line.

The final chapter discusses the error messages you may encounter as you use DOS and what action you should take to remedy the situation.

Appendix A covers DOS setup and installation for both floppy and hard disk systems.

Appendix B teaches you how to use the three Windows programs introduced in DOS 6. You learn to use Backup for Windows, Undelete for Windows, and Anti-Virus for Windows.

Finally, a detailed index helps you quickly find the information you need on a specific topic.

What Hardware Do You Need To Run MS-DOS?

The type of computer most likely to use MS-DOS is one that is compatible to a great extent with the International Business Machine Corporation's Personal Computer (IBM PC). COMPAQ, Zenith Data Systems, Gateway, Tandy, Advanced Logic Research, AT&T, AST, EPSON, Wang, NEC, Toshiba, Sharp, Leading Edge, Hewlett-Packard, and many other companies manufacture or market MS-DOS–based personal computers.

Your computer should have at least 256 kilobytes (256K) of system random-access memory (RAM), at least one floppy disk drive, a display (screen), and a keyboard. These suggestions are minimal; most MS-DOS PCs sold today exceed these requirements.

You also need at least 4M of hard disk space to set up DOS 6. To install the three optional programs, you need additional memory: 2M for Anti-Virus for Windows and DOS, 1.7M for Backup for Windows and DOS, and 262K for Undelete for Windows and DOS.

For convenience and processing power, you may want to include a second floppy disk drive, a hard disk with at least 20 megabytes of storage capacity, a printer, and a color graphics display. You cannot use MS-DOS on most computers made by Apple Computer Inc., Commodore (except the new Amiga computers, when equipped with additional hardware), or Atari. These computers use operating systems sometimes referred to as DOS, but their operating systems are not MS-DOS compatible.

Conventions Used in This Book

Certain conventions are used throughout the text and graphics of *MS-DOS 6 QuickStart* to help you better understand the book's subject.

This book uses a symbolic form to describe command syntax. When you enter a command, you substitute real values for the symbolic name. Examples present commands you can enter exactly as shown.

DOS commands can have various forms that are correct. For example, the syntax for the DIR command looks like this if you use symbolic names:

   DIR *d:filename.ext* /W /P

DIR is the command name. *d:filename.ext* is a symbolic example of a disk drive name, including its extension, and a file name. A real command would have actual values instead of symbols.

Some parts of a command are mandatory—required information needed by MS-DOS. Other command parts are optional. In this example, only the **DIR** is mandatory. The rest of the command, *d:filename /W /P*, is optional. When you enter only the mandatory command elements, DOS in many cases uses values already established for the optional parts.

You can type upper- or lowercase letters in commands. DOS reads both as uppercase letters. You must type syntax samples shown in this book letter-for-letter, but you can ignore case. Items shown in lowercase letters are variables. You type the appropriate information for the items shown in lowercase letters.

In the preceding example, the lowercase *d:* identifies the disk drive the command will use for its action. Replace *d:* with A:, B:, or C:. The *filename.ext* stands for the name of a file, including its extension.

Spaces separate some parts of the command line. The slash separates other parts. The separators, or delimiters, are important to DOS because they help DOS break apart the command. For example, typing **DIR A:** is correct, but **DIRA:** is not.

In the numbered steps, the text you must enter is displayed in boldface blue type, and keys are shown as they appear on the keyboard, such as Ctrl or F7 Screen messages appear in this special typeface. The color blue emphasizes some of the more important areas of the graphics illustrations.

MS-DOS 6 QuickStart is your guide to becoming comfortable using DOS on your personal computer.

Understanding Computer Technology

Have you ever wondered why our society has emotional attachments for some machines, but not for others? We love our automobiles, for example, but we don't feel that way about our refrigerators, garbage disposals, or lawn mowers.

This attachment to cars comes from our capacity to develop a very interactive relationship with a mechanical beast. We are social creatures, and not many mechanical contraptions supply us with that give-and-take we seem to need, which may be why we have such love affairs with contraptions that do.

For some people, a personal computer is another machine that provides an abundance of emotional "bang for the buck." Other people, however, may feel disappointment with their first computer purchase. It may appear to be little more than a big, dumb box. If not for the fact that most people must use a personal computer for business, they may have preferred to buy a new television set.

Although you may be anxious about getting started, once you understand something about how the computer works, you will feel a good deal better about learning to use it. This chapter provides a quick, but illuminating, lesson about how personal computers

1

work. Learning about the personal computer, its components, and how all the parts work together is like learning new car controls: displays and keyboards (dashboards), the CPU (engine control unit), peripherals (tires), and disk drives (the cassette player).

Does a computer take you from zero to sixty in six seconds? Even faster: it takes you close to the speed of light. Computers may not yet turn you into an Indy 500 car driver, but you will be able to participate in a drama of your own making.

This chapter explains the components that have become a standard for the IBM PC and compatibles. Do you need to remember every term you read? Not unless you are a college student preparing for a final exam. Nevertheless, this chapter's design will help you enjoy working with your new computer. After all, knowing where the oil goes in your car is always useful. And as cars have their own terminology, so does the personal computer.

Every term defined here is rooted in the English language. These terms are no more mysterious than terms such as *dashboard*, *acceleration*, *mileage*, *pause*, or *reverse*. Computer terms are simple to remember and impressive to use at the office. Knowing them may even get you a raise.

Key Terms Used in This Chapter	
CPU	Stands for *central processing unit*. The processor in which the actual computing takes place. It is the brain of the computer.
Display	The screen or monitor.
Peripheral	Any device, aside from the computer itself, that permits you to do something or shows the results. A good example of a peripheral is your printer.
Disk	A plastic or metal platter used to store files. A *disk drive* records and reads back information on disks. Disks come in two basic sizes and function like the cassettes you place in your tape recorder. The main difference between disks and cassettes is that disks resemble small LP records. Like the arm of a phonograph, the read/write head swings into position over the spinning disk to make data retrieval quick and simple. The disk drive head can swing right to the data you need.

1

Modem	A device for exchanging data between computers through standard telephone lines. A modem is similar to your telephone handset. Just remember that a computer does not have mechanical hands, vocal cords, or ears. All information transfers via computer-generated audio signals.
Input	Any data given to a computer.
Output	Any data transmitted by a computer.
Bit	A binary digit. The smallest discrete representation of a value a computer can manipulate. A computer thinks only in numbers. Several numbers make up a character, such as a word or letter. In short, bits are similar to the dot/dash concept used in Morse code.
Byte	A collection of eight bits that a computer usually stores and manipulates as a full character (letter, number, or symbol). A byte is a character identified by a sequence of numbers.
K (kilobyte)	1,024 bytes, used to show size or capacity in computer systems. Technically, the term *kilo* means thousand, but you must allow the computer revolution its poetic license.
M (megabyte)	1,024 kilobytes.
Data	A broad term meaning words, numbers, symbols, graphics, or sounds. Data is any information stored in computer byte form.
File	A named group of data in electronic form. In word processing, a file can be a letter to a friend. In a database system, a file can be a name-and-address telephone listing.
Network	Two or more computers linked together by cables. They can share data, files, and peripherals.

1 Computer Technology Defined

Until a few years ago, computers were large, expensive machines generally unavailable to individual users. Although the rich could afford them, not many people wanted to fill three rooms of their homes with energy-guzzling electronics that served no practical purpose.

Advances in computer technology led to the engineering of smaller computer parts called *integrated circuits*, more commonly known as *chips*. The actual processing in a personal computer takes place on one of these chips, called the *microprocessor*. The newer, high-capacity chips meant a savings in both space and energy. The ultimate product of chip technology is the *microcomputer* as exemplified by your personal computer.

In 1981, International Business Machines (IBM) introduced the IBM Personal Computer, or PC. Whether or not the PC is the best of the breed is arguable, but IBM did give personal computers respectability in the business community. As a leader in the large business computer market, IBM held an excellent marketing position. IBM's name, sales force, and corporate contacts made the PC today's standard in home and business computing. The arrival of the Personal Computer worked out well. IBM created both a market for PCs and a standard upon which other firms have built.

Today, many manufacturers produce computers that are in many ways superior to the IBM product line. Rapid technical developments in newly created companies are raising microcomputer technology to new heights. Even the venerable IBM uses much of this technology in its newest PCs.

Although the Apple II and Macintosh are also personal computers, the term *PC* has come to mean computers that are made by IBM and other manufacturers and that run the MS-DOS operating system. Originally, PCs by other manufacturers were called *compatibles*, but were only partially compatible with the IBM PC. Today, these personal computers are often called *clones* and, if well-made, operate virtually the same as the equivalent IBM models.

The intense competition among PC manufacturers over the last few years benefits everybody. Never before could you purchase so much computing power at such a reasonable price.

Components of Computer Systems

A computer system is composed of hardware parts that exist in a variety of configurations. All MS-DOS computers operate in essentially the same manner.

Engineers base the size of the computer more on human physiology than on anything else. Designers developed the standard model to be large enough to contain disk drives and other devices. The portable, on the other hand, is small and light, perfect for computing while on the road.

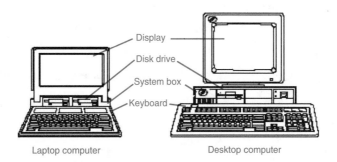

Laptop computer   Desktop computer

Personal computer systems based on the IBM PC are functionally the same, despite the wide variety of configurations available. As long as you have the main components, the shape and size of your computer matters very little. For example, you can find equally powerful machines in the traditional desktop configuration, in floor models, in portable laptop models, or in compact, lunch box–sized computers. The wide variety of PC software operates equally well in any of these cosmetic configurations.

Hardware and software make up the two main segments of a computer system. Both segments must be present for a computer to work. Many texts waste several pages supplying complicated definitions for terms that are simple, but this book won't.

Hardware refers to the physical machine and its peripherals—electronics and moving parts of metal and plastic. A VCR, television, tape deck, CD player, and turntable also are everyday examples of hardware.

Software encompasses the program and data files created, stored, and run by your PC. These records are the equivalent of text books, novels, newspapers, and videotapes. Table 1.1 illustrates the variety of software available for a computer.

Table 1.1
Computer Software

Type of software	Examples
Operating systems	MS-DOS; OS/2; UNIX
Databases	dBASE IV; Paradox; PC-FILE
Spreadsheets	Lotus 1-2-3; Excel; Quattro Pro
Word processors	WordPerfect; Microsoft Word; PC-WRITE
Utilities	Fastback Plus; PC Tools Deluxe; SideKick
Graphics	Harvard Graphics; CorelDRAW; Lotus Freelance
Integrated programs	Symphony; Microsoft Works; Q&A
Games	Flight Simulator; Tetris; SimCity
Home finance	Quicken; Managing Your Money
Desktop publishing	First Publisher; Ventura Publisher; PageMaker

The operating system provides the working base for all other programs by creating a uniform means for programs to gain access to the full resources of the hardware. Operating systems that help programs access disks are called *disk operating systems*, or DOS.

This book covers the common operating system for IBM PC compatibles: MS-DOS. The IBM versions of DOS and the various versions of Microsoft Corporation's DOS are highly compatible. Actually, they are nearly identical, except that IBM calls its version *PC DOS*, whereas Microsoft calls its version *MS-DOS*. For this reason, *DOS* is used in this text as the generic term when referring to both packages.

Text and Graphics Displays

The video *display* (also called the *monitor* or *screen*) describes the part of the computer's hardware that produces visual images. To date, the cathode ray tube (CRT) type of monitor, which operates on the same principle as a television set, provides the most crisp, most easily read image.

```
Volume in drive C has no label
Volume Serial Number is 195F-849A
Directory of C:\DOS

[.]             [..]            DOSSHELL.INI    MOUSE.COM       FORMAT.COM
PKUNZIP.EXE     NLSFUNC.EXE     KEYB.COM        ANSI.SYS        DEBUG.EXE
EXPAND.EXE      BACKUP.EXE      FDISK.EXE       SYS.COM         UNFORMAT.COM
ATTRIB.EXE      CHOICE.COM      DEFRAG.EXE      INTERLNK.EXE    INTERSVR.EXE
MSD.EXE         EDLIN.EXE       POWER.EXE       MIRROR.COM      [TEMP]
DOSSHELL.COM    DOSSWAP.EXE     MODE.COM        SETVER.EXE      SMARTMON.EXE
FASTOPEN.EXE    SHARE.EXE       PRINT.EXE       MEM.EXE         XCOPY.EXE
RECOVER.EXE     DOSHELP.EXE     MSHERC.COM      APPEND.EXE      QBASIC.EXE
COMP.EXE        HELP.COM        EDIT.COM        ASSIGN.COM      CHKDSK.EXE
GRAFTABL.COM    DISKCOMP.COM    DISKCOPY.COM    FC.EXE          FIND.EXE
LABEL.EXE       EXE2BIN.EXE     MORE.COM        JOIN.EXE        RESTORE.EXE
SORT.EXE        GRAPHICS.COM    DOSSHELL.EXE    REPLACE.EXE     TREE.COM
DOSKEY.COM      SUBST.EXE       LOADFIX.COM     UNDELETE.EXE    MWUNDEL.EXE
MWAV.EXE        MWAVTSR.EXE     VSAFE.COM       MSAV.EXE        MEMMAKER.EXE
MWBACKUP.EXE    SIZER.EXE       MSBACKUP.EXE    DBLSPACE.EXE    DELOLDOS.EXE
EMM386.EXE      SMARTDRV.EXE    COMMAND.COM
      78 file(s)      3239145 bytes
                     46635008 bytes free

C:\DOS>_
```

On the display, a blinking symbol (box, underscore, or other character) shows where the next character will appear. This symbol is the *cursor*.

Personal computers are interactive. Interactive means that the PC reacts to any action you take and shows the results on the computer display screen. The video display is the normal, or *default*, location the computer uses to communicate with you.

Manufacturers also incorporate other types of technology into computer displays. For example, to build flatter displays, manufacturers use a technology known as *gas plasma*. Gas plasma displays produce an orange color against a dark background. This type of display is found primarily in portable computers, where a TV-type display would be heavy and cumbersome.

Another technology adapted to computer displays is liquid crystal. *Liquid crystal displays* (LCDs) work on the same principle as today's digital watch displays. Most LCDs produce dark characters against a lighter background. LCDs work well in brightly lit rooms, because the light striking the display increases the contrast of the display image. Some LCDs also use a backlight to increase the display's contrast. This type of display appears primarily on laptop computers.

Regardless of the display type, all computer screens take electrical signals and translate them into patterns of tiny dots, or *pixels*. Pixel is an acronym coined from the phrase *picture element*. You can recognize pixels as characters or figures. The more pixels a display contains, the sharper the visual image. The number of pixels in the image multiplied by the number of lines on the display determines the image's *resolution*.

The higher-resolution image (left) uses four times as many pixels as the low-resolution image (right).

The resolution of the visual image is a function of both the display and the *display adapter*. The display adapter controls the computer display. In some PCs, the display circuitry is a part of the motherboard (see this chapter's section "The System Unit and Peripherals"). The display adapter also can reside on a separate board that fits into a slot in the computer. The display adapter can be a monochrome display adapter (MDA), Hercules monochrome graphics adapter (MGA), color graphics adapter (CGA), enhanced graphics adapter (EGA), video graphics array adapter (VGA), extended graphics array adapter (XGA), super video graphics array (SVGA), or a less common display adapter.

Text Display

When you see letters, numbers, or punctuation on your display, you recognize these images as text. This text comes from your computer's memory where the text has been stored under the standard that most computers recognize, the *American Standard Code for Information Interchange (ASCII)*. Text displays and text display adapters can display only text characters. They cannot display graphics characters.

Each ASCII code represents a letter or a symbol. These codes are sent to the display adapter so that you can see the characters on-screen. The display adapter has a built-in electronic table from which the adapter can take the correct pixel pattern for any letter, number, or punctuation symbol.

Although 128 standard ASCII codes exist, a single computer character can contain 256 different codes. The upper codes are known as IBM *extended ASCII codes*. These additional codes are used for patterns of foreign language letters, mathematical symbols, lines, corners, and special images, such as musical notes.

If a program needs to display a pixel or pattern of pixels not included in the ASCII-to-pixel table, you are out of luck. Text displays and text display adapters cannot generate graphics. Of the various display adapters available, only the monochrome display adapter (MDA) is a text-only display adapter. Because so much software today is graphically oriented, virtually all personal computers sold today have graphics displays.

Graphics Display

Graphics displays can produce any pixel or pattern of pixels. This type of display enables you to view, on-screen, complex figures with curves and fine detail. The computers work harder to create graphics images than text images, however, because images are "painted" on the screen with pixels. To display the correct point on-screen, the display adapter must find the screen coordinate points for each pixel. Unlike the ASCII codes in text mode, no table of predetermined pixels exists for graphics mode.

Graphics displays differ in the number of pixels available. The greater the number of pixels, the finer the detail of the display. Each pixel contains characteristics that describe to the graphics adapter what the color or intensity of the pixel should be. The greater the number of colors and intensities, the more storage space you need in memory. Graphics adapters offer varying combinations of pixel density, number of colors, and intensity.

Table 1.2 lists the most common display adapters, showing the maximum resolution and the colors available with each type of display adapter.

Table 1.2
Resolution and Colors for Display Adapters

Adapter Type	Graphics Mode	Pixel Resolution	Colors Available
CGA	Medium resolution	320 x 200	4
CGA	High resolution	640 x 200	2
EGA	CGA high resolution	640 x 200	16
EGA	EGA high resolution	640 x 350	16
MGA	Monochrome graphics	720 x 348	2
MDA	Text characters only	80 x 25	2
VGA	Monochrome	640 x 480	2
VGA	VGA high resolution	640 x 480	16

continues

Table 1.2 *(Continued)*

Adapter Type	Graphics Mode	Pixel Resolution	Colors Available
VGA	VGA medium resolution	320 x 200	256
Super VGA	Super VGA	800 x 600	256
Super VGA	1024 Super VGA	1024 x 768	256
XGA	Standard mode	1024 x 768	256
XGA	16-bit color	640 x 480	65,536

The number of colors available on the display depends on the program you are using and the amount of memory on the adapter. For example, a Super VGA adapter with 512K of video memory can display 256 colors, but the software might display only 16 colors. A Super VGA adapter with 256K of video memory can display only 16 colors, even if the software can display 256 colors.

Keyboards

The keyboard is the most basic way to enter information into the computer. The computer then converts every character you type into code the machine can understand. The keyboard is therefore an *input device*.

Like a typewriter, a computer keyboard contains all the letters of the alphabet. The numbers, symbols, and punctuation characters are virtually the same. The computer keyboard has the familiar QWERTY layout. The term *QWERTY* comes from the letters found on the left side of the top row of character keys on a standard typewriter. However, a computer keyboard differs from a typewriter keyboard in several important ways.

The most notable differences of the computer keyboard are the extra keys that do not appear on a typewriter. These keys and their standard functions are described in table 1.3. Some of these keys have different functions when used with different programs. Also, depending on the type of computer and keyboard you use, you will see 10 or 12 special *function keys*.

Table 1.3
Special Keys on the Computer Keyboard

1

Key	Name	Function
↵Enter	Enter	Signals the computer to respond to the commands you type. Also functions as a carriage return in programs that simulate the operation of a typewriter.
↑ ↓ ← →	Cursor keys	Changes your location on-screen. Included are the arrow, PgUp, PgDn, Home, and End keys.
◂Backspace	Backspace	Moves the cursor backward one space at a time, deleting any character in that space.
Del	Delete	Deletes, or erases, any character at the location of the cursor.
Ins	Insert	Inserts any character at the location of the cursor.
⇧Shift	Shift	Capitalizes letters when you hold down Shift as you press another letter key. When pressed in combination with another key, Shift can change the standard function of that key.
Caps Lock	Caps Lock	Enables you to enter all capital letters when the key is pressed down in the locked position. Caps Lock doesn't shift the numbered keys, however. To release Caps Lock, press the key again.
Ctrl	Control	Changes the standard function of a key when pressed in combination with another key.
Alt	Alternate	Changes the standard function of a key when pressed in combination with another key.

continues

17

1

Table 1.3 *(Continued)*

Key	Name	Function
`Esc`	Escape	Enables you to escape from a current operation to a previous one in some situations. Sometimes Esc has no effect on the current operation.
`Num Lock`	Number Lock	Changes the numeric keypad from cursor-movement to numeric-function mode.
`PrtSc`	Print Screen	Sends the displayed characters to the printer. This key is provided on Enhanced keyboards.
`Scroll Lock`	Scroll Lock	Locks the scrolling function to the cursor-movement keys so that they scroll the screen instead of moving the cursor.
`Pause`	Pause	Suspends display activity until you press another key. (Not provided with standard keyboards.)
`Break`	Break	Stops a program in progress from running.
`7` `8` `9` `4` `5` `6` `1` `2` `3` `0` `.`	Numeric keypad	A cluster of keys to the right of the standard keyboard. The keypad includes numbered keys from 0 to 9 as well as cursor-movement keys and other special keys.

Many of the function keys are designed for use in combination with other keys (see table 1.4). For example, holding down the Ctrl key as you press the PrtSc key causes DOS to continuously print what you type. Pressing Ctrl and PrtSc a second time turns off the printing. The Break key is not a separate key. With some keyboards, pressing the Ctrl and Scroll Lock keys together causes a break. With other keyboards, pressing the Ctrl and Pause keys together causes a break.

1

Table 1.4
DOS Key Combinations

Key Combination	Function
Ctrl-S	Freezes the display. Pressing any other key restarts the display.
Ctrl-PrtSc	Sends lines to both the screen and to the printer. Pressing this sequence a second time turns off this function.
Ctrl-C or Ctrl-Break	Stops the execution of a program.
Ctrl-Alt-Del	Restarts MS-DOS (system reset).

The function keys are shortcuts or command keys. Not all programs use these keys, and some programs use only a few of them. When used, however, these keys automatically carry out certain operations for you. For example, programs often use the F1 key for *on-line help*. On-line help displays instructions to help you understand a particular operation. The DOS 6 Shell uses the F3 key to cancel the Shell. The F10 key activates the menu.

The original standard keyboard contains the function keys F1 through F10 on the left side. The standard Extended keyboard offers keys F1 through F12, which are located across the top of the standard keyboard. The Extended keyboard must have been designed by programmers. These people are known for being poor typists, and this keyboard layout is the result. On the other hand, the Extended keyboard has a cursor-control keypad separate from the numeric keypad.

AT and Enhanced Keyboards

Many early PC-compatible computers use a standard keyboard design similar to that of the IBM PC. Other machines use a Personal Computer AT-style keyboard. The IBM PS/2 computers and almost all other personal computers today use a 101-key Enhanced keyboard. Some users prefer the layout of the standard keyboard, and others prefer the Enhanced keyboard.

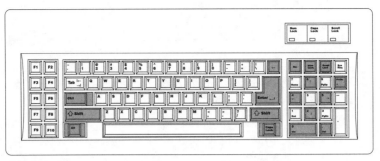

AT keyboard

You can determine whether your computer has a standard keyboard, a Personal Computer AT-style keyboard, or an Enhanced keyboard. You find certain keys only on specific keyboards. For example, you find separate PrtSc and Pause keys only on the Enhanced keyboard. You can, however, simulate these keys by using a combination of keys on the standard keyboard.

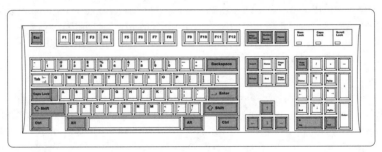

Enhanced keyboard

Special Keyboards

Some new keyboards try to provide the advantages of both the older and the newer keyboards. Such keyboards enable you to change key caps and switch key definitions for the Caps Lock, Ctrl, Esc, and tilde (~) keys. Some keyboards provide the enhanced layout, but locate the function keys on the left side of the keyboard instead of at the top.

Northgate Computer Systems, for example, offers keyboards with the separate cursor keys arranged exactly the same as they are on the numeric keyboard. This arrangement makes the cursor keys easier to use with most software. One keyboard model has a set of functions keys across the top and a second set on the left so that you can choose which set to use.

Keyboards for Portables

Small "lunch box" and laptop portable computers employ nonstandard keyboards, usually to conserve space. A *space-saver keyboard* is small enough to fit in a portable computer, but often the trade-off for its smaller size is fewer keys and less functionality. A few of these computers have so little keyboard space that you may need to add an external numeric keypad for software that manipulates numbers.

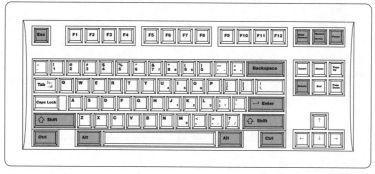

Space-saver keyboard

The System Unit and Peripherals

Industry engineers designed the standard desktop PC around a box-shaped cabinet that connects to all other parts of the computer. This box is called the *system unit*, which includes disk drives and disks. Any devices attached to the system unit are *peripherals*. The system unit and the peripherals complete the hardware portion of the computer system.

The System Unit

The system unit houses all but a few parts of a PC. Included are various circuit boards, the disk drives, a power supply, and even a small speaker.

The system units on today's PCs come in many variations of the original design. Desktop models are smaller to conserve disk space. Larger models with room for larger, multiple hard disks and other peripherals often use a floor-standing tower design that requires no desk space at all.

1

A hypothetical system unit, showing the placement of the hard and floppy disk drives and the system board, also called the motherboard.

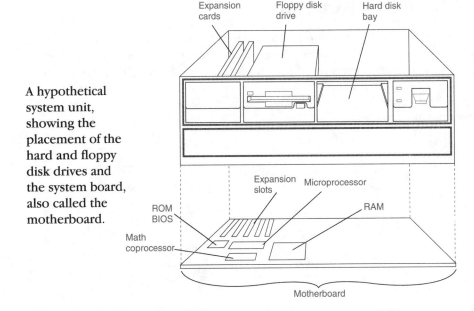

The *motherboard* holds the main electronic components of the computer. The microprocessor, the chips that support it, and various other circuits are the primary parts on the motherboard. The motherboard usually contains electrical sockets in which you can plug various adapter circuit boards. These electrical sockets are called *expansion slots*.

Chips that provide the computer with its memory are located on the motherboard. You can plug additional memory adapter cards into an available expansion slot to increase the system's memory. The number of available expansion slots varies with each PC builder. Most motherboards have a socket for a *math coprocessor*. Math coprocessors help speed up programs that manipulate large volumes of graphics or math equations. Spreadsheet programs and desktop publishing software, for example, benefit from the addition of a math coprocessor chip.

Disk Drives and Disks

Disk drives are complex mechanisms that carry out a fairly simple function: they rotate *disks*, which are circular platters or pieces of plastic that have magnetized surfaces. As the disk rotates, the drive converts electrical signals from the computer and places the information into or retrieves information from magnetic fields on the disk. The storage process is called *writing* data to the disk. Disk drives also recover, or *read*, magnetically stored data and present it to the computer as electrical signals. Magnetically stored data is not lost when you turn off the computer.

The components of a disk drive are similar to those of a phonograph or a CD player. The disk, like a record, rotates. A positioner arm, like a tone arm, moves across the radius of the disk. A head, like a pickup cartridge, translates information into electrical signals. Unlike a record, the disk's surface does not have spiral grooves. The disk's surface is recorded in magnetic, concentric rings, or tracks. The tighter these tracks are packed on the disk, the greater the storage capacity of the disk.

Two types of disks are available, which come in a variety of data storage capacities. Disks are either *floppy* or *hard*. Floppy disks are removable, flexible, slower, and of a lower capacity than hard disks. Hard disks, also called *fixed* disks, are usually high-capacity rigid platters that you cannot remove as you can floppies.

When a computer writes to the disk, it stores groups of data that the operating system identifies as *files*. You can tell that a drive is reading or writing a floppy disk when the small light on the front of the disk drive glows. You should never open a drive door or eject a disk until the light goes out, unless the computer specifically instructs you to do so.

When a hard drive is reading or writing data, a light may glow on the front of the drive or there may be a separate disk-drive light on the front of the system unit.

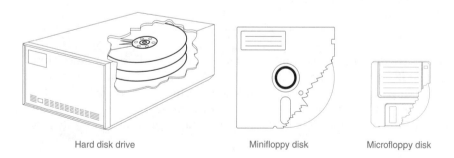

Hard disk drive   Minifloppy disk   Microfloppy disk

Hard disks are sealed inside the hard disk drive. Floppy disks are encased in flexible 5 1/4-inch jackets or in rigid 3 1/2-inch jackets. The 3 1/2-inch disks are often called *diskettes* because with their rigid shells they are no longer floppy.

Floppy Disks

Floppy disks store from 360K to 2.88M bytes of data and come in two common sizes. Originally, the 5 1/4-inch floppy disks were called *minifloppies* to distinguish them from the 8-inch disks used on very early personal computers. The 3 1/2-inch diskettes are sometimes called *microfloppies*. The measurement refers to the size of the disk's jacket. Unless size is important, this book simply refers to both disk types as *floppies*.

In almost all cases, the disk drive uses both sides of a disk for encoding information; therefore, the disk drives and the floppy disks are called *double-sided*.

A drive can handle only one size disk. You cannot read a 5 1/4-inch floppy disk in a 3 1/2-inch disk drive or vice versa. Table 1.5 shows a number of different floppy disk capacities. Only the most common floppy disk types are listed. The disk capacities are in kilobytes (K) or megabytes (M).

Table 1.5
Common Floppy Disk Types

Disk Type	Capacity
5 1/4-inch	
Double density	360K
High density	1.2M
3 1/2-inch	
Double density	720K
High density	1.44M

Make sure that you know your drive's specification before you buy or interchange floppies. Floppies of the same size but with different capacities can be incompatible with a particular disk drive. A high-density disk drive, for example, can format, read, and write to both high-density and double-density floppy disks. A double-density disk drive can use only double-density disks.

Hard Disks

Hard disks often consist of multiple, rigid-disk platters. Each side of each platter has a separate head. The platters spin at 3,600 RPM, much faster than a floppy disk drive spins. As the platters spin within the drive, the head positioners make small, precise movements above the tracks of the disk.

Because of this precision, hard disks can store large quantities of data—from 10M to hundreds of megabytes. Hard disks are reasonably rugged devices. Factory sealing prevents contamination of the housing. With proper care, hard disks can deliver years of trouble-free service.

Peripherals

Besides the display, keyboard, and disk drives, a variety of peripherals can be useful to you. Peripherals such as a mouse, printer, modem, joystick, and digitizer enable you to communicate with your computer easily. For example, using a mouse with a modern computer program—such as a desktop publishing package—takes best advantage of the program's features.

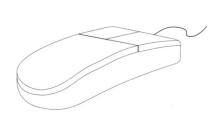

A *mouse* is a computer pointing device whose shape vaguely resembles that of a real mouse. You use a mouse with graphics programs and modern graphical interfaces such as the DOS 6 Shell.

A *joystick* is a popular peripheral in games and is used to enter information into the computer. Sometimes, joysticks are used in place of keyboard operations.

For many users, a *digitizer tablet* feels more natural than using a mouse. When a digitizer's "puck" moves across the tablet, that motion is displayed on-screen. It is used most often in high-end graphics and computer-aided design (CAD) programs.

1

The Mouse

The mouse is a pointing device that you move on the surface of your work space and that causes the computer to correlate this movement to the display. The mouse is shaped to fit comfortably under your hand. The contour of the mouse and the cable that trails from the unit give the vague appearance of a mouse sitting on the table. The mouse has two or three buttons that rest beneath the fingers of your hand.

You use the mouse to move a *mouse pointer* to make menu selections, draw with graphics programs, move the keyboard cursor swiftly, and select sections of your work to manipulate. Not all software supports a mouse, but many popular programs do. Although mouse functions in different programs can vary, the standard mouse techniques are based on Microsoft Windows. These mouse techniques are also found in the DOS Shell.

Printers

Printers accept signals (*input*) from the CPU and convert those signals to characters (*output*), usually imprinted on paper. You can classify printers in the following ways:

- How they receive input from the computer
- How they produce output

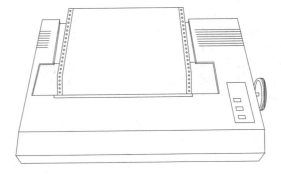

A printer accepts data from the computer and renders it as text and images on paper.

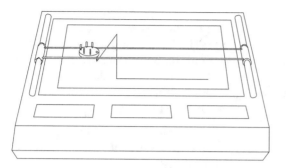

A *plotter* lets you draw with the computer. Unlike the printer, a plotter draws up and down as well as back and forth.

You connect printers to the system unit through a *port*. A port is an electrical doorway through which data flows between the system unit and an outside peripheral. A port has its own expansion adapter or shares an expansion adapter with other ports or circuits, such as a multifunction card.

The terms *parallel* and *serial* describe two types of ports that send output from personal computers to printers. A parallel port continuously sends all the bits of data synchronously, through separate wires in the cable, one byte (character) at a time. Parallel printer connections are more common than serial connections. A serial port delivers the bits of data, one bit after another, in single-file fashion. Although sending one complete byte by using serial communications takes longer, serial ports require fewer wires in the cable. Serial printers also can communicate with the port over longer distances than parallel printers.

All printers have the job of putting their output onto paper. This output often is text, but it also can be graphics images. Four major classifications of printers exist: *dot-matrix*, *laser*, *inkjet*, and *daisywheel*. Each printer type produces characters in unique ways. Printers usually are rated by their printing speed and the quality of the finished print. Some printers print by using all the addressable points on the screen, much as a graphics display adapter does. Some printers even produce color prints.

The most common printer, the dot-matrix, uses a print head that contains a row of pins or wires to produce the characters. A motor moves the print head horizontally across the paper. As the print head moves, a vertical slice of each character forms as the printer's controlling circuits fire the proper pins. The wires press corresponding small dots of the ribbon against the paper, leaving an inked dot impression. After several tiny horizontal steps, the print head leaves the dot image of a complete character. The process continues for each character on the line. Dot-matrix printers are inexpensive. With the print quality close to that of a typewriter, this type of printer is commonly used for internal reports.

1

Laser printers use a technology that closely resembles that of photocopying. Instead of a light-sensitive drum picking up the image of an original, the drum is painted with the light of a laser diode. The image on the drum transfers to the paper in a high dot density output. With high dot density, the printed characters look fully formed. Laser printers also can produce graphics image output. The high-quality text and graphics combination is useful for desktop publishing as well as general business correspondence.

The inkjet printer literally sprays words and graphics on a page in near silence. Moderately priced, the print quality rivals that of a laser printer, and of all the printers, only a laser printer is faster and sharper than this high-resolution printer.

The daisywheel printer steps, or moves incrementally, a print head across the page and produces a complete character for each step. The characters of the alphabet are arranged at the ends of "petals" that resemble spokes on a wheel. The visual effect of this wheel is similar to a daisy's petals arranged around the flower head. Because the daisywheel prints fully-formed characters, the quality of daisywheel printing is about the same as a typewriter. Daisywheel printers are far slower than the other printers and are virtually obsolete.

Modems

A modem is a peripheral that helps your PC communicate with other computers over standard telephone lines. Modems are serial communications peripherals. They send or receive characters or data one bit at a time. Most modems communicate with other modems at speeds from 300 to 9600 bits per second (bps), and speeds up to 19200 bps are not unusual. The most common speed for modems, however, is 2400 bps. Modems need special communications software to coordinate data exchanges with other modems.

You use a modem to send or receive files to another computer, to use a computerized *bulletin board system* (BBS), or to access an on-line service such as Prodigy or CompuServe.

A modem transfers signals between computers by using telephone lines.

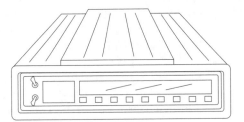

How Computers Work with Data

1

Now that you have learned about the essential parts of the computer system, you are ready for an overview of how all these parts carry out the job of computing. The world inside a computer is a strange place. Fortunately, you do not have to know the details of a computer's operation to produce finished work. If you explore a little bit, however, you will adjust more quickly to using your computer.

Computers perform many useful tasks by accepting data as input, processing it, and releasing it as output. Data is information. It can be a set of numbers, a memo, an arrow key that moves a game symbol, or anything you can imagine.

The computer translates input into electrical signals that move through a set of electronic controls. Output can be thought of in four ways:

* As characters the computer displays on-screen
* As signals the computer holds in its memory
* As codes stored magnetically on disk
* As permanent images and graphics printed on paper

Computers receive and send output in the form of electrical signals. These signals are stable in two states: on and off. Think of these states as you would electricity to a light switch that you can turn on and off. Computers contain millions of electronic switches that can be either on or off. All input and output follows this two-state principle.

Binary, the computer name for the two-state principle, consists of signals that make up true computer language. Computers interpret data as two binary digits, or *bits*—0 and 1. For convenience, computers group eight bits together. This eight-bit grouping, or *byte*, is sometimes packaged in two-, four-, or eight-byte packages when the computer moves information internally.

Computers move bits and bytes across electrical highways called *buses*. Normally, the computer contains three buses: the *control bus*, the *data bus*, and the *address bus*. The microprocessor connects to all three buses and supervises their activity. The CPU uses the data bus to determine what the data should be, the control bus to confirm how the electrical operations should proceed, and the address bus to determine where the data is to be positioned in memory.

Because the microprocessor can call on this memory at any address and in any order, it is called *random-access memory*, or *RAM*. The CPU reads and executes program instructions held in RAM. Resulting computations are stored in RAM.

Some computer information is permanent. This permanent memory, called *read-only memory* (or *ROM*), is useful for holding unalterable instructions in the computer system.

Displaying a word on a computer screen seems simple: you just press keys. However, each time you enter a character, the computer performs a complex series of steps.

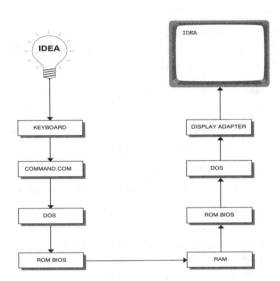

The microprocessor depends on you to give it instructions in the form of a *program*. A program is a set of binary-coded instructions that produce a desired result. The microprocessor decodes the binary information and carries out the instruction from the program.

You can start from scratch and type programs or data into the computer every time you turn on the power. Of course, you don't want to do that if you don't have to. The good news is that the computer stores both instructions and start-up data, usually on a disk. Disks store data in binary form in *files*. To the computer, a file is just a collection of bytes identified by a unique name. This collection of bytes can be a memo, a word processing program, or some other program. A file's function is to hold binary data or programs safely until you type a command from the keyboard to direct the microprocessor to call for that data or program file. When the call comes, the drive reads the file and writes its contents into RAM.

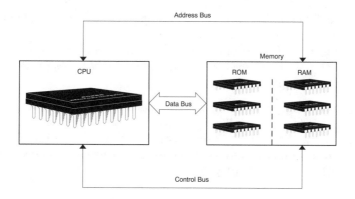

Stand-Alone versus Networked PCs

Until the mid 1980s, most personal computers were *desktop*, or *stand-alone* models, which meant that the software and hardware that comprised each PC was designed for a single user. Today PCs in a corporate environment often are linked by cables into *networks* or *workgroups*. PCs on a network can share data, applications, and peripherals. For a business, that capability translates into increased productivity; it ensures that employees are using the same tools and can communicate easily, and it decreases spending because fewer peripherals and software programs are purchased.

In a PC network, each user still has a PC on his or her desktop. To the individual user, the PC looks and acts like a stand-alone system; however, it may not have all the components of a stand-alone, such as disk drives. The PCs are managed by a more powerful PC called a *server*. The server stores the software and controls the data input and output.

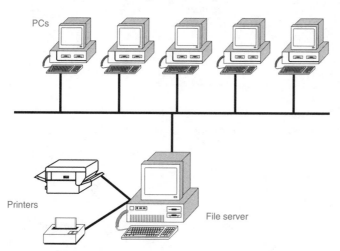

Networked PCs can share files, applications, and peripherals such as printers. Also, users can communicate with each other by electronic mail.

31

1

Because more than one user might be running programs or accessing files at the same time, networks require software that can support multiple users. Instead of using a single-user operating system, networks must use a network operating system, such as Novell's Netware. Even applications programs must be designed for multiple users.

Users on a network can communicate with each other on-line. They can use electronic mail (*e-mail*) to send and receive messages. They can share the same data files and directories. In some cases, they can communicate in *real time*, which means that the information entered at one user's keyboard appears on another user's display.

Lessons Learned

- The PC revolution is no more difficult to understand than the home video revolution. MS-DOS and your personal computer are about to unlock a new dimension in entertainment and productivity.

- If you feel comfortable with a computer, you can accept and enjoy all that goes with it, just like your VCR.

- Your PC is a product of years of development and more than one company's efforts.

- Computer terminology is simple. The words are basic, and the definitions are easy to understand.

- Hardware, software, screen displays, keyboards, disks, drives, mice, modems, and memory are the tools of microcomputer technology.

- Some PCs are linked into networks, allowing users to share data, software, and peripherals.

The next chapter teaches you the computing ABCs.

Learning Your DOS ABCs

One of the greatest fears is the fear of the unknown. On your first day at kindergarten, you may have walked down those unfamiliar corridors with a stomach that churned like a mass of oatmeal.

Perhaps thoughts of what your first teacher would be like caused you to conjure up an image of the Wicked Witch of the West from *The Wizard Of Oz*. Children often see new authority figures as frightening, all-powerful people. Being small and vulnerable in strange surroundings, you probably were already insecure. With a little time, however, the unknown became familiar, and kindergarten was not so frightening after all.

You cannot escape the unknown. You face it whenever you reach out to gain knowledge or to experience new events. So, as you stare at your new personal computer and flip through your DOS manual, you need not fear that the computer screen will dissolve into a churning fog and then clear to reveal the Wicked Witch of the West.

Computers can add a new and pleasurable dimension to your life. Believe it or not, the classic "hero" and friend who helps you through this fear of the unknown is the *disk operating system*, or *DOS*. DOS is a product of ingenuity. At first, it may feel distant and overpowering, but many heroes present that image. Soon DOS will feel familiar and you will lose your fear of this unknown.

Chapter 1 discussed software, mechanics, computer systems, and component parts. This chapter introduces

What is an operating system?

Files and what they do

The three parts of DOS

What DOS does

DOS, the most important link between hardware, other software, and you. It brings DOS closer to you by defining the disk operating system, its uses, and its interesting history. After all, even heroes have a past.

2

Key Terms Used in This Chapter	
Program	Instructions that tell a computer what to do and how to do it.
BIOS	Basic input/output system. The program that performs basic communications between the computer and its peripherals.
Applications program	Instructions that tell the computer to perform a program-specific task, such as word processing. It's a "how to" for the computer.
Interface	A connection between parts of the computer, particularly between hardware devices. Also, the interaction between you and an applications program.
Command	An instruction that you give to DOS to perform a task.
Batch file	A series of DOS commands placed in a disk file. DOS executes batch-file commands one at a time.

What Is an Operating System?

An *operating system* is a collection of computer programs that provides special services to other programs and to the user of a computer. DOS unleashes the potential of your computer by translating into action, through commands, your desire to manipulate data. You, or a program, tell DOS what action you want to take, and DOS directs the hardware to carry out your wishes.

If you think of the computer hardware as a theater's empty stage, and an applications program as an ongoing play, you can see the void between them. Behind the scenes are many supporting characters.

2

Operating system software does the computer-equivalent job of the set-preparation crews, the lighting crews, the stage hands, the makeup artist, and even the janitor. All the services that must bridge the gap between the hardware and the program are performed by the operating system software. The program is not burdened with routine details. Can you imagine the lead actress having to push her own backdrop onto the stage just before the curtain goes up?

Imagine yourself as the producer/director. You have full control over the stage (hardware) and stage crew (operating system), and which plays (application programs) you will produce. You now have a good idea where you fit into the equation.

If a computer's operating system did not supply these services, you would have to deal directly with the details of controlling the hardware. Without the disk operating system, for example, every computer program would have to hold *instructions* telling the hardware each step to take to do its job.

Because operating systems already contain instructions, you or a program can call on DOS to control your computer. Disk operating systems get their name from the attention given to the disks in the computer system.

IBM PC-compatible personal computers use MS-DOS, the disk operating system developed (though not invented) by Microsoft Corporation. Manufacturers of some personal computers—manufacturers such as Zenith, IBM, and COMPAQ—modify MS-DOS for their computers. These firms place their own names on the disks and include different manuals with the DOS packages they provide. Some firms add one or two modified utility programs as an improvement, but all DOS versions are similar after you load them into a personal computer.

When you read about DOS in this book, you can assume that the information is generalized to cover your manufacturer's version of DOS. In special cases, differences are noted. As in Chapter 1, the terminology in this book is simple. DOS is not mystical; it is designed to simplify your relationship with your personal computer.

Understanding DOS Files

The files on your disks can be divided into a variety of categories. The *file name* can help you determine what type of file it is. A file name can be as long as eight characters or as short as one character. You also can add a period and a three-character *extension* to the file name: SADIE.LET, for example. In many cases, you specify the file name and the program adds the file extension. Over the years, a kind of universal shorthand has evolved to simplify identification of computer files. This identification appears as the extension at the end of the file name, as shown in table 2.1.

Programs are files that contain computer instructions. Most of the DOS files represent programs. When you buy an *applications program*, you are buying computer instructions to perform certain tasks, such as word processing or spreadsheet manipulation. A program file is called an *executable file* because in computer lingo, to run a program is to execute it. Executable files usually have an EXE file extension.

A *command file* is an executable file in a special format. A command file has a COM file extension. Some of the DOS program files have EXE file extensions and others have COM file extensions. Ignore the different extensions, and treat both types of files as programs.

A *text file* is created by a word processing or text editing program. Text files usually have a TXT or DOC file extension. A text file might be a letter written to your Aunt Sadie in Podunk. Another kind of text file is the one that comes with most software. This file, often titled README.DOC, usually supplies additional instructions for the program that were not included in the printed manual.

Many other types of files and file formats exist. Applications programs might have their own special formats and file extensions. The types of files and file extensions used by DOS are listed in the following tables.

Table 2.1
Examples of the Files That Make Up DOS

File Name	Description
COMMAND.COM, FORMAT.COM, EDIT.COM	The COM file extension identifies a command file.
EGA.CPI, LCD.CPI	Files with CPI extensions operate the display screen.
CATAPULT.BAS	A program written in the BASIC language ends in BAS. Many games are written in BASIC.

File Name	Description
AUTOEXEC.BAT	A batch file has the file extension BAT. DOS looks for this batch file and runs it automatically when you start your computer.
BACKUP.EXE, MEM.EXE, CHKDSK.EXE	Executable program files end with EXE.
DOSSHELL.HLP, EDIT.HLP	HLP files display on-screen assistance.
DOSSHELL.INI	INI files are initiation files that contain program default information.
KEYBOARD.SYS, CONFIG.SYS, ANSI.SYS	SYS files are system files. They are also called *device drivers*.

If you ask DOS for a listing of the files contained on a disk, the dot for the extension does not appear. DOS manuals don't explain, but certainly the roots of this curious behavior are sunk deep in the antiquity of DOS folklore. Table 2.2 shows the way file names appear in an on-screen listing and the way they look when you type them.

Table 2.2
How File Names Appear

What a file listing looks like on-screen	*What file names look like when typed*
COMMAND COM	COMMAND.COM
EGA CPI	EGA.CPI
AUTOEXEC BAT	AUTOEXEC.BAT
FIND EXE	FIND.EXE
SELECT HLP	SELECT.HLP
DOSSHELL INI	DOSSHELL.INI
KEYBOARD SYS	KEYBOARD.SYS

The Three Parts of DOS

DOS has three main functional components:

- The command interpreter
- The file and input/output system
- The utilities

These components are contained in files that come with your DOS package. In the following sections, you are introduced to these components and their duties.

The Command Interpreter

The *command interpreter* is DOS's "electronic butler" because it interacts with you through the keyboard and screen when you operate your computer. The command interpreter also is known as the *command processor* and is often referred to as, simply, COMMAND.COM.

When you give COMMAND.COM an instruction, it determines what you want to do and starts the program you request. COMMAND.COM also contains the most commonly used commands, such as commands to list the files on a disk or to copy a file.

You can give commands to COMMAND.COM in two ways. You can type a command at the *DOS prompt* or you can use the *DOS Shell*. Both techniques are demonstrated in the next chapter and explained in detail in later chapters.

When COMMAND.COM displays the DOS prompt, it is ready to receive a command. When you enter a command, you are really telling COMMAND.COM to interpret what you type and to process your input so that DOS can take the appropriate action.

When you use the DOS Shell, you use the keyboard or a mouse to select files, commands, and programs from lists and menus. You do not have to remember the names of commands or how to spell them. The DOS Shell is much easier to use than the DOS prompt, but you cannot execute all commands from the Shell. In some cases, you must use the DOS prompt.

The File and Input/Output System

The file and input/output system is made up of so-called "hidden" files and programs that are actually part of your computer's hardware. Your computer cannot run without these special files. Hidden files do not appear on a normal directory listing or other lists of files, and you cannot delete or copy them. These files are not hidden to trick you into thinking that they don't exist, but to protect you from accidentally deleting or changing them.

The two or three hidden files (the number depends on your computer) define the hardware to the software. When you start a computer, these DOS system files are loaded into RAM. Combined, the files provide a unified set of routines for controlling and directing the operation of the computer's hardware. These files are known as the *input/output system*.

The hidden files interact with programs stored in special read-only memory (ROM) that is part of your computer's hardware. The special ROM is called the ROM *basic input/output system*, or *BIOS*. Responding to a program's request for service, the system files translate the request and pass it to the ROM BIOS. The BIOS provides a further translation of the request that links the request to the hardware.

The Utility Programs

The DOS *utilities* are command programs that are not built into COMMAND.COM. DOS utilities carry out useful housekeeping tasks, such as preparing disks, comparing files, finding the free space on a disk, and printing in the background. Several utilities supply statistics on disk size and memory, whereas others compare disks and files.

The utility programs are files that reside on disk and are loaded into memory by COMMAND.COM when you type a command. These commands are often called *external commands* because they are not built into COMMAND.COM. Those commands that are built into COMMAND.COM are called *internal commands*. You do not have to be concerned with which commands are internal and which are external.

By now you may suspect that DOS makes technical moves that are difficult to understand. True, much of DOS's activity falls into a technical category, but the features you need to master to make DOS work for you are easy to understand. This section briefly describes the DOS functions you will use repeatedly as your expertise grows. Later chapters treat these topics in detail.

2

Disk operating systems insulate you and your programs from the need to know exactly how to make the hardware work. You don't need to know the capacity or recording format of the disk or how to tell the computer to direct the output to the screen; DOS does it all for you. Software (applications programs) that stores data on a disk does not have to reserve space on the disk, keep track of where on the disk the data is stored, or know how the data is encoded. DOS takes care of all these tasks.

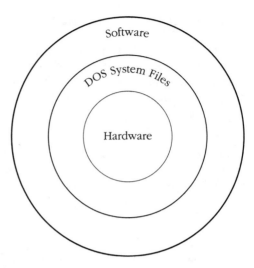

DOS provides a uniform service to the hardware by getting support from the permanent ROM BIOS in the computer. The ROM BIOS can vary among computer makers, but your computer will work best if the design of the ROM BIOS is integrated with DOS.

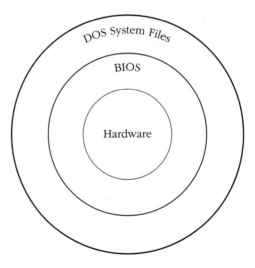

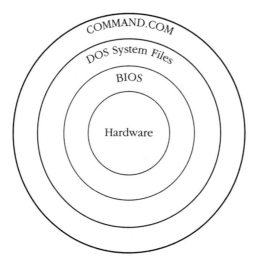

Your communications with DOS are actually instructions to COMMAND.COM, a special type of software that permits you to address the file and input/output systems of the computer through the keyboard. Rather than instructing the hardware directly, you instruct COMMAND.COM. You never need to know the details of how the hardware operates.

2

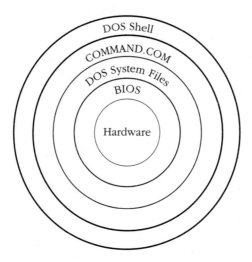

The DOS Shell is an easy-to-use program interface between your need for DOS services and the details of DOS commands. The Shell is a final layer that insulates you from learning how to control details of the computer's hardware.

What DOS Does

DOS's many activities can be organized into several general categories. The following sections describe the most frequently performed services of DOS.

Managing Files

One of DOS's main functions is to help you organize the files that you store on your disks. Organized files are a sign of good computer housekeeping. Good housekeeping becomes crucial when you begin to take advantage of the storage capacity available on today's disks.

The smallest-capacity floppy disk can hold the equivalent of 100 letter-sized pages of information. Suppose that each sheet of information makes up one file; you have 100 files to track! If you use disks that can hold more information than a standard floppy (such as a hard disk), file organization becomes even more crucial.

Fortunately, DOS gives you the tools to be a good computer housekeeper. DOS lists files, tells their names and sizes, and gives the dates when they were created or last modified. You can use this information for many organizational purposes. In addition to organizing files, DOS provides commands to duplicate files, discard outdated files, and replace files whose file names match.

Managing Directories

When you work with a hard disk, you can have thousands of files. To help you keep track of all these files, you can group them into *directories*. Think of the hard disk as a file cabinet and the directories as folders. You can look into one folder at a time. Each folder can contain any number of programs and data files.

When you ask DOS to list the files on your disk, you really are asking DOS to list the files in only one directory. The manner in which you set up directories on your disk is the most important method you have to help you keep track of all the files on your disk.

DOS provides commands you can issue to create and name directories. DOS also gives you commands you can use to change from one directory to another when you want to work with a different set of files. The directory that you are working in is called the *current directory*. The particular disk you are using is called the *current disk*.

2

The first directory on a disk is called the *root directory*. You can think of the root directory as an entire file cabinet. The root directory can contain both files and other directories. These other directories, called *subdirectories*, can be compared to the folders inside the file cabinet. You can have further subdirectories under each directory, which is like having smaller folders inside a larger folder. Unlike a real folder, a directory expands automatically. You can put as many files and subdirectories into a directory as will physically fit on the disk. You learn the details of using directories in Chapter 5.

When you install DOS on your hard disk, the Install program creates a directory with the name DOS and copies all the DOS files that you need from the floppy disks into this directory. When you install other programs, the installation program may create a directory to hold the program files, or it may tell you to create a new directory before you run the installation program.

Disk drives have drive letters, such as A, B, or C. Directories have names, like DOS, WORD, or DATA. A complete listing of a drive and directory is called a *directory path*. After you install DOS on a hard disk, the complete directory path to the DOS files is C:\DOS.

Using directories enables you to deal with a few or a few dozen files at one time, instead of hundreds or thousands. Directories are one of the basic concepts that you need to know if you have a hard disk. Don't worry about this concept just yet. This book covers directories in detail later. After you understand how directories work, you will find them easy to use.

Managing Disks

Certain DOS functions are essential to all computer users. For example, you must prepare all disks before you can use them in your computer. This preparation is called *formatting*. You learn about formatting in Chapter 6. Other functions in DOS's disk-management category are

- Labeling disks electronically (Chapters 6 and 11)
- Making reconstructable backup copies of files for security purposes (Chapter 10)
- Restoring damaged files on disk (Chapter 13)
- Copying disks (Chapter 7)
- Checking a disk for errors (Chapter 11)

2

Running Applications Programs

Computers require complex and exact instructions (programs) to provide useful output. Computing would be totally impractical if you had to write a program for each job you needed to complete. Happily, this extra work is not necessary. Programmers spend months writing the specialized code that permits computers to function as many different tools: word processor, database manipulator, spreadsheet, and graphics generator. Through these programs, the computer's capabilities are applied to a task. These programs are called *applications programs*.

Applications programs are distributed on disks. DOS is the go-between that permits you access to these programs through the computer. By simply inserting a disk into a computer's disk drive and pressing a few keys on the keyboard, you have at hand a wide variety of applications. Applications programs are discussed in Chapter 8.

Applications programs constantly read data from disk files to see what you have typed and to send information to the screen or printer. These input and output operations are common, repetitive computer tasks. DOS furnishes applications with a simple connection, or program *interface*, that attends to the details of these repetitive activities. As you use your computer, you may want to view information about disk files, memory size, and computer configuration. DOS provides these services. You learn about these services later in the book, starting with Chapter 4.

Running Batch Files

Most of your interaction with DOS takes place through the keyboard. You type commands for COMMAND.COM to carry out. You also can place these commands in a disk file, called a *batch file*, which you can "play back" to COMMAND.COM. COMMAND.COM responds to these batches of commands from the file exactly as if you typed the commands. Batch files automate often-used command sequences, making keyboard operation simpler. Hard-to-remember command sequences make ideal candidates for batch-file treatment. Chapter 12 teaches you how to create and use batch files.

Handling Miscellaneous Tasks

Some DOS functions fall into the category of miscellaneous tasks. One example is maintaining the computer's clock and calendar so that files and applications programs can have access to dates and times. You might need to use DOS's text editor to create text files, such as memos or notes. You can even see the amount of computer memory available for applications programs.

Knowing the Uses of DOS

When you consider that a computer will not start without DOS, you should clearly see that anyone using a personal computer benefits from a working knowledge of DOS. Sure, someone may be willing to do the DOS-related work for you so that you can avoid learning about the operating system, but if you learn DOS basics, you will become much more skilled at computing. The reward—gaining the computer's use as a productivity tool—far exceeds the effort you spend learning DOS.

In the following chapters, you will see that DOS is useful in a variety of ways. DOS contains about 100 commands and functions. This book emphasizes only those features needed to use a personal computer to run off-the-shelf programs. You can quickly become familiar with the essentials of DOS through this easy, step-by-step approach.

Development of DOS

Table 2.3 lists some of the important improvements and changes among the different versions of DOS, beginning in 1981.

Table 2.3
Quick Reference to Versions of DOS

MS-DOS Version	Significant Change
1.0	Original version of DOS.
1.1	Accommodates double-sided disks.
2.0	Includes multiple directories needed to organize hard disks.

continues

Table 2.3 *(Continued)*

MS-DOS Version	Significant Change
3.0	Supports the IBM AT and high-capacity floppy disks.
3.1	Supports networking.
3.2	Accommodates 3 1/2-inch drives.
3.3	Accommodates high-capacity 3 1/2-inch drives; includes new commands.
4.0	Introduces the DOS Shell and the MEM command; accommodates larger files and disk capacities.
5.0	Provides an enhanced DOS Shell with a graphical interface, on-line help, access to extended memory, full-screen editor, enhanced directory listings, and automatic installation.
6.0	Provides advanced file, disk, and memory management to optimize system performance.

Experts estimate that a typical computer user spends about 20 percent of his or her time using DOS functions, which facilitate disk and file management.

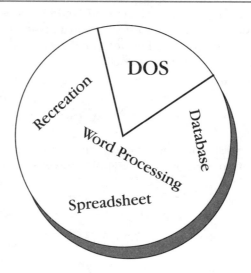

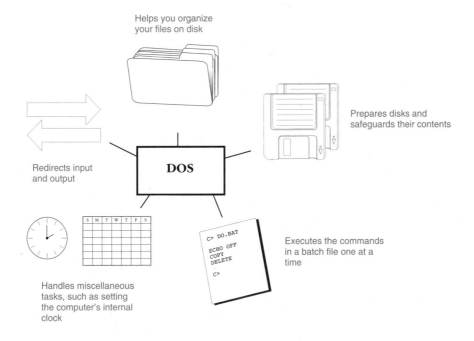

Helps you organize
your files on disk

Prepares disks and
safeguards their contents

Redirects input
and output

DOS

Handles miscellaneous
tasks, such as setting
the computer's internal
clock

Executes the commands
in a batch file one at a
time

Lessons Learned

■ Learning DOS is a task you shouldn't fear.

■ Software can be divided into basic categories, which can be defined by a three-letter file-name extension.

■ Files contain information stored on the magnetic surface of a disk.

■ Some files hold instructions; others contain data. Some DOS files are hidden, but all are helpful.

■ Batch files and the DOS Shell make using DOS easier.

■ DOS provides your computer with "behind the scenes" assistance.

■ DOS is designed to put you in full control of your PC.

■ COMMAND.COM is the most efficient assistant you will ever have.

Now that you understand what a loyal servant DOS is, read Chapter 3 to learn how to start DOS and to see what the Shell looks like.

2

Starting DOS

Put on your goggles and prepare for takeoff. Don't worry; you will not fly solo. Before leaving the ground, however, you should first taxi around the runway a bit, which is what you will do for the next few pages as you learn the methods of operation and basic controls of your computer and DOS.

The first two chapters showed you the inside of the computer, how it and DOS evolved, and how peripherals enhance your system. This chapter explains how to get your PC up and running and covers related topics such as setting the computer's internal clock and looking at a list of files. You will find just enough definitions to keep you from being confused by DOS.

At times, you might wonder whether the time you spend learning the basics of DOS is necessary. After all, it's not as gratifying as flipping a switch or turning a key and seeing an instant physical response. Rest assured; you will find the time well invested when you gain enough computer mastery to make intelligent decisions. When you finish this book, no quick-talking salesperson or self-proclaimed DOS wizard will intimidate you.

Through Chapters 1 and 2 your computer has remained sleeping on your desk. Now you are going to bring your PC to life.

Creating a
good physical
environment

Booting
your PC

Looking at DOS

Stopping the
computer

3

Key Terms Used in This Chapter	
Cold boot	Starting your PC by turning on the power switch.
Warm boot	Restarting, or resetting, your PC by pressing Ctrl-Alt-Del instead of turning off the power.
Cursor	The blinking line or solid block that indicates where the next keyboard entry will appear.
Logged drive	The default disk drive and directory that DOS uses to carry out commands that involve disk services. Unless you change the prompt with a command, the letter of the default drive is the DOS prompt.
Prompt	A symbol or character(s) that appears on-screen to indicate that you must enter information before anything else can happen.
Directory	A portion of a disk. A directory is like a file folder in a file cabinet. You keep files in directories so that you can isolate a set of files to work with at one time.
Command	An instruction you give to DOS to perform a task.
DOS Shell	A graphical, menu-driven interface that enables you to execute DOS commands easily without having to learn the names of commands.

Definitions Made Simple

Most computer terms have simple origins and meanings. For example, to *boot* your PC means either turning on the computer (*cold boot*) or instructing the computer to reset itself without your turning it off (*warm boot*). The derivation comes from the expression, "pulling yourself up by your bootstraps."

Much of this chapter emphasizes DOS Version 6.XX, rather than earlier versions. Many experienced users, however, may still use DOS 3.3. (Incidentally, there is no DOS 6.XX. The Xs represent any refinement of DOS 6, such as 6.01 or 6.10. A reference to DOS 6 also means any version between 6.00 and a possible future version 7.00.)

Software developers love the decimal-number concept. By definition, the smaller the decimal increment of a new version, the fewer refinements you will find. A jump to the next higher whole number implies a quantum leap in technology. The improvement is usually there, but occasionally the new number is simply a sales-boosting technique.

One of the most important features of DOS 6 is its Shell. The Shell was introduced in DOS 4, but it was not well received until it was improved in DOS 5. You will use the Shell for most of your DOS commands.

3

The Shell is a program that acts as an interface between you and DOS. Often, shells make using your PC easier, and many experienced PC owners use them. On the other hand, you cannot do everything in DOS with its Shell. At times you must use the command line. This book concentrates on the Shell in the beginning and uses the command line only when absolutely necessary. Toward the end of the book, when you are more comfortable with using DOS, you are introduced to the command line in more detail. You then will learn some of the more advanced commands that you cannot execute from the DOS Shell.

The term *shell* can be confusing because the command processor part of an operating system is also referred to as a shell. In this book, the term refers to the graphical user interface, not the command processor.

If you learn a few computer terms and the basic start-up process before you turn on the computer, you will feel more confident. Just remember, don't get nervous about the operations mentioned here. More than likely, you will understand these operations with further reading or by glancing at help screens.

With early computers, operators started by entering a binary program—called a *bootstrap loader*—and instructing the computer to run the program. The term *booting* stuck; even now, booting still refers to the start-up procedure. With today's DOS, the booting process is easy.

The material in this chapter assumes that you neither know how to boot your computer nor know the process that occurs during booting. Actually, booting is as simple as turning on your stereo. Right now, you might feel more comfortable turning on your stereo, but this situation will change.

Creating a Good Physical Environment

3

Before leaving the ground, a pilot runs through a checklist to affirm that the aircraft is airworthy. As a pilot's preliminary check is important, so too is a check of your computer equipment. Preliminary checks prevent future crashes.

Computers like a clean, steady current. Select a good electrical outlet that does not serve devices such as copy machines, hair dryers, or other electrical gadgets. Ask your computer dealer about a line conditioner if you must share an outlet. Unless you use your computer in a modern office building, a surge protector is cheap insurance against electrical spikes and surges. In fact, you should use a surge protector to protect all your electronic equipment, not just your computer.

Make sure that the power switch is off before you plug in your computer. Some computers have power switches marked with 0 and |. The position marked 0 is off.

Your PC needs room to breathe. A computer must dissipate the heat generated by its electronic components. Keep paper, books, beverages, and other clutter away from the system unit's case and keyboard. More importantly, make sure that the cooling fan in back of your PC works properly. Electronic components and excessive heat do not mix well, especially in humid environments.

Have your DOS manual and PC system documentation nearby for reference. Most personal computers today have a built-in hard disk that contains the DOS files needed to boot. If you do not have a hard disk, you need working DOS disks to boot your computer and execute DOS commands. Refer to Appendix A for instructions on installing DOS on floppy disks or hard disks. Most likely, if you have a hard disk, your computer dealer installed DOS on the hard disk, and you can skip the installation instructions in the appendix.

Following good work habits in an unfamiliar environment can save you a lot of grief. It is comparable to wearing a seat belt, even though the belt may feel uncomfortable initially.

Booting Your PC

If your computer supplier installed DOS on your hard disk, you can boot automatically from the hard disk simply by turning on the computer; however, you still should learn to boot from a floppy disk. If you have problems with your hard disk or make an error when you try to customize DOS on your hard disk, you might lose the ability to boot from the hard disk. You should have a floppy disk available that you can use to boot.

If you are using DOS 6, the disk that boots your computer is labeled *Startup*. If you are using another version of DOS, the boot disk might be called *System*, *Main*, or *DOS*. Check your manual if you are uncertain which disk is bootable, or ask your computer specialist for a bootable DOS system disk. From here on, the bootable DOS disk is called the *DOS Master* disk.

The Cold Boot

The cold boot consists of two steps: inserting the floppy disk into drive A and turning on the computer's switch. In addition, if you have a lock on the front of the system unit, you need to unlock the unit. Very few people ever use this lock.

Insert the DOS Master disk into drive A. Check your PC's system manual for the location of drive A and for disk-insertion instructions. Drives are mounted either horizontally or vertically. Depending on your system unit's configuration, drive A is the left slot (for vertically positioned drives) or top slot (for horizontally positioned drives) in the system unit's cabinet.

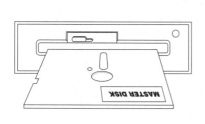 

A properly inserted disk usually has its label facing left on vertical drives and up on horizontal units.

You insert disks into horizontal and vertical drives in the same way. After inserting a 5 1/4-inch disk, close the drive door or turn the latch clockwise.

Insert 3 1/2-inch disks gently, pushing until you hear a click. The drive closes by itself.

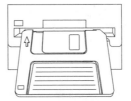

3

If the disk does not go in, make sure that the drive doesn't already hold another disk. Never force a disk into the drive door because you could damage the disk, the drive, or both.

If your display has a power switch, turn on the display. Some displays are powered from the system unit and do not have a switch. Locate the computer's power switch. On older computers, the power switch usually is on the right side and toward the rear of the system unit. The IBM PS/2 power switch is conveniently located in the front. Turn on the switch. At this point, the cold boot begins.

What Booting Looks Like

The instant you flip the switch, the computer performs a Power-On Reset (POR), which means that the RAM, the microprocessor, and other electronics are "zeroed out," like a chalkboard cleaned with an eraser.

The system then begins a Power-On Self-Test (POST). POST ensures that your PC's electronics are working properly. Some computers permit you to watch the action of the POST. The test verifies that the computer is working correctly. The POST takes from a few seconds to several minutes to complete. During the POST, you may see a description of the test or a blinking cursor on the display. When the POST ends, the computer beeps and drive A spins. Finally, a bootstrap loader loads DOS from the Master DOS disk into RAM.

If drive A does not contain a disk and you have a hard disk, the bootstrap loader loads DOS from the hard disk. If drive A does contain a disk, the bootstrap loader tries to load DOS from the disk in drive A, even if you have a hard disk. *If you have a hard disk, do not try to boot the computer with a disk in drive A.*

When DOS completes loading, the DOS prompt, or command prompt, appears. The DOS prompt is a letter followed by the greater-than symbol (>), which together represent the current, or active, drive. You can enter DOS commands when the command prompt appears.

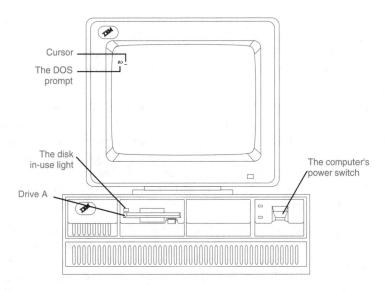

The Warm Boot

The warm boot differs little from the cold boot. For the cold boot, you insert the DOS system disk, if necessary, and switch on the computer. For the warm boot, your PC is already running. Make sure that your DOS system disk is in drive A or that the operating system is installed on your designated start-up drive, which is usually the hard disk drive C. You then press three keys simultaneously.

Look at the keyboard and locate the Ctrl, Alt, and Del keys. The warm boot requires pressing and holding Ctrl and Alt and then pressing Del. The PC skips the preliminary tests and immediately loads DOS. Don't worry if nothing happens on the first try. With some systems that have been running programs, you may have to press Ctrl-Alt-Del twice.

Looking at DOS

You have two ways to view DOS and enter commands.

- The DOS Shell view
- The prompt view

The DOS Shell view is a graphical user interface (GUI). The Shell first appeared in DOS 4 and was greatly improved in DOS 5. In DOS 6, the Shell remains unchanged in appearance although some functions have been improved. It is described in greater detail later in this chapter and in Chapter 4.

The *prompt* view is the traditional, simple look of DOS. The prompt view appears on a plain screen with the DOS prompt. The DOS prompt indicates that DOS is waiting for you to give it a command. If you do not have a hard disk, the standard prompt is one letter of the alphabet that represents the current, or active, or logged, drive. The letter is followed by a greater-than symbol (>). If you boot your system with the DOS disk in drive A, the prompt appears as A> on-screen.

If your computer has a hard disk drive, the standard DOS prompt is the drive letter, followed by a colon (:), followed by the *directory path*, followed by the greater-than symbol. After you boot from the hard disk, the prompt appears as C:\> on-screen. (The directory path is a complete listing of the drive and the directory. Directories and the directory path were introduced in Chapter 2.)

Why is the letter B missing? The first floppy drive is always called drive A. The second floppy drive, if present, is always called drive B. The first hard drive, if present, is almost always called drive C. If you have only one floppy drive and a hard drive, the hard drive is called drive C, and DOS treats the floppy drive as both A and B.

The Current Logged Drive

After the boot is complete, the command prompt appears, indicating the *current*, or *logged*, drive. The logged drive is the active drive, or the drive that responds to commands. For example, A> tells you that DOS is logged onto drive A, and B> means that DOS is logged onto drive B.

To switch drives, type the letter of the drive to which you want to switch, followed by a colon, and then press Enter. DOS reads the drive letter and colon as the disk drive's name. For example, if you have a computer with two floppy drives, you can change the logged drive from A to B by typing **B:** at the A> prompt and pressing Enter.

Before you press Enter, your prompt looks like this:

    A>B:

After you press Enter, the following prompt appears:

    B>

What does this command mean? It means that you have instructed your PC that you want to work with any information accessible through drive B. It also means that you have begun to take charge!

DOS remembers the logged drive as its current drive. Many commands automatically use the current drive and other current information; you don't have to specify them in the command. You will learn about this phenomenon later as the *rule of currents*.

Remember that you need not specify the drive if you request information from the logged drive. You will learn later how to include the drive name when you request information from a drive other than the current drive.

Looking at Directories

When you work with a hard disk, you usually work with one directory at a time. This directory is called the *current directory*. The standard DOS prompt with a hard disk displays the current directory path. If you booted your computer from the hard drive, the current prompt is C:\>.

A directory can have subdirectories under it. The complete subdirectory path shows the drive letter and all the directories to the current directory. The complete list of all the directories on a disk is called the *directory tree*.

To make a different directory current, you use the CD (change directory) command. For example, to make DOS the current directory, type **CD DOS** at the C:\> prompt, and then press Enter. The current prompt is now C:\DOS>.

The DOS files are copied to the C:\DOS directory during installation. After you type **DIR /W** at the C:\DOS> prompt and press Enter, DOS displays all the files and any subdirectories in the DOS directory in wide format and then displays the DOS prompt to indicate that it is ready for the next command.

This display
shows the files in
the DOS direc-
tory. The files are
displayed by
using the DIR /W
(directory)
command. The
current prompt is
C:\DOS>.

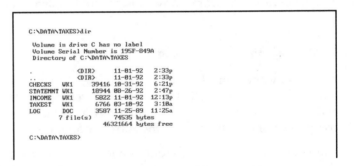

```
   Volume in drive C has no label
   Volume Serial Number is 195F-849A
   Directory of C:\DOS

[.]            [..]           DOSSHELL.INI   MOUSE.COM      FORMAT.COM
PKUNZIP.EXE    NLSFUNC.EXE    KEYB.COM       ANSI.SYS       DEBUG.EXE
EXPAND.EXE     BACKUP.EXE     FDISK.EXE      SYS.COM        UNFORMAT.COM
ATTRIB.EXE     CHOICE.COM     DEFRAG.EXE     INTERLNK.EXE   INTERSVR.EXE
MSD.EXE        EDLIN.EXE      POWER.EXE      MIRROR.COM     [TEMP]
DOSSHELL.COM   DOSSWAP.EXE    MODE.COM       SETVER.EXE     SMARTMON.EXE
FASTOPEN.EXE   SHARE.EXE      PRINT.EXE      MEM.EXE        XCOPY.EXE
RECOVER.EXE    DOSHELP.EXE    MSHERC.COM     ASSIGN.COM     QBASIC.EXE
COMP.EXE       HELP.COM       EDIT.COM       APPEND.EXE     CHKDSK.EXE
GRAFTABL.COM   DISKCOMP.COM   DISKCOPY.COM   FC.EXE         FIND.EXE
LABEL.EXE      EXE2BIN.EXE    MORE.COM       JOIN.EXE       RESTORE.EXE
SORT.EXE       GRAPHICS.COM   DOSSHELL.EXE   REPLACE.EXE    TREE.COM
DOSKEY.COM     SUBST.EXE      LOADFIX.COM    UNDELETE.EXE   MWUNDEL.EXE
MWAV.EXE       MWAVTSR.EXE    VSAFE.COM      MSAV.EXE       MEMMAKER.EXE
MWBACKUP.EXE   SIZER.EXE      MSBACKUP.EXE   DBLSPACE.EXE   DELOLDOS.EXE
EMM386.EXE     SMARTDRV.EXE   COMMAND.COM
        78 file(s)      3239145 bytes
                       46635008 bytes free

C:\DOS>
```

A DATA directory is commonly used to contain data files for applications
programs. Subdirectories of \DATA contain the files for each application.

This directory
listing displays
the data files
in the
C:\DATA\TAXES
directory and is
displayed by
using the DIR
command.

```
C:\DATA\TAXES>dir

   Volume in drive C has no label
   Volume Serial Number is 195F-849A
   Directory of C:\DATA\TAXES

.            <DIR>      11-01-92   2:33p
..           <DIR>      11-01-92   2:33p
CHECKS   WK1     39416  10-31-92   6:21p
STATEMNT WK1     18944  08-26-92   2:47p
INCOME   WK1      5822  11-01-92  12:13p
TAXEST   WK1      6766  03-10-92   3:10a
LOG      DOC      3587  11-25-89  11:25a
        7 file(s)      74535 bytes
                    46321664 bytes free

C:\DATA\TAXES>
```

The First Look at Commands

You just saw the results of using the CD and DIR commands. DOS 6 has about
100 commands. You will use some of these commands quite often. Many of
them you may never use. To execute a command from the DOS prompt, you
type the command and press Enter. COMMAND.COM, the command processor, determines whether you typed the name of a command that is built-in to
COMMAND.COM. DIR is an example of a built-in, or *internal*, command.
Internal commands are already in the computer's memory; they execute as
soon as you type the command and press Enter.

When you type a command that is not built-in, COMMAND.COM looks for a
program file with the name you typed. These commands are called *external
commands*. FORMAT is an example of an external command.

3

Most commands require more information than just the command name. For example, to copy a file, you must specify the file or files you want to copy and the destination where you want the files copied. Commands also may have options, called *switches*, or parameters. The /W you used with the DIR command in a previous example is a switch. It told DOS to switch the directory listing to a wide format display. Parameters also tell DOS where and how to execute the command. For example, if you type **DIR A:**, you are using a parameter (A:) that specifies that DOS should display a directory list of the files on drive A.

If you correctly type the command at the DOS prompt and then press Enter, the command executes. If you make an error, you receive an error message.

Using the command line, or prompt view, is very fast and easy once you know the commands and their options. When you first start out using DOS, however, the DOS Shell view eliminates the need to know the names of commands and the options.

Looking at the DOS Shell

The Shell view is a full-screen graphical window display. You can issue the same DOS commands that you type at the DOS prompt by using a mouse or the keyboard to point to and select pull-down menus and dialog boxes. You do not have to remember the names of commands to use the Shell. You just select actions from menus, type answers to questions, and check off options in dialog boxes.

Many shells, desktop publishing programs, and the latest generation of "window style" software were designed for use with a mouse. If, on the other hand, you know your way around a typewriter keyboard, you can perform some functions more quickly in the DOS Shell with cursor keys.

The Shell view is the friendliest way to use DOS. For example, a directory listing is automatic when you are in the Shell. You always see a listing of the subdirectories and files in the current directory.

For many users, the Shell is easier to master than DOS, but you still can profit from knowing the DOS commands and terminology. DOS 6 commands remain substantially unchanged from previous versions. The Shell is a shortcut for those who already understand the basics of DOS.

3

The First Look at the DOS Shell

The DOS Shell has changed very little in DOS 6. The Shell view is a full-screen window with menus and pop-up help screens. The Shell interacts with you in a manner similar to Microsoft's other mouse-and-menu products. For example, if you have ever used Excel, Windows, or Works, the DOS Shell will be very familiar to you. If you have never used these products, you still will find the Shell very easy to learn and to use. Then, in the future, if you ever use any of these other Microsoft products, or any Windows applications, you will have a head start.

The Shell provides a visual presentation of DOS, with options from which you make selections. You can manage your computer from the Shell by using graphical alternatives to the DOS prompt commands.

The next chapter discusses the Shell in greater detail. Right now you simply are taking a "first look."

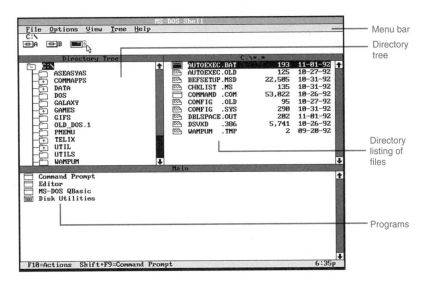

The DOS Shell automatically displays information about a disk, a directory, and programs. You use a mouse or the keyboard to move around the display, to select menu items, and to execute programs.

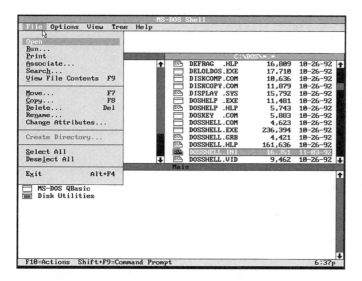

When you make a
selection from a
menu, the menu
commands for
that selection pop
down.

3

To move, copy, or rename files or to execute other commands, you don't have
to remember command names; you just select items from command menus.

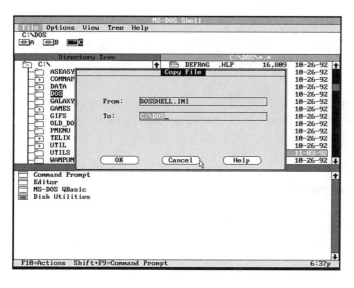

When DOS needs
you to supply
more information
to complete a
command, DOS
displays a *dialog
box.* You type the
answers to the
prompts, and
DOS completes
the command.

Stopping the Computer

Occasionally you will want to stop the computer from carrying out a command. Besides switching off the power (the last resort), you have three key combinations you can use to stop a command in DOS. Remember that you press and hold the Ctrl key and then press the other key(s) in the sequence.

Ctrl-Break   The Ctrl-Break combination cancels the current process.

Ctrl-C   This key combination stops commands in which DOS pauses for you to type more information. Be aware that DOS carries out many commands too quickly for you to intervene with Ctrl-C.

Ctrl-Alt-Del This combination is the warm boot key sequence. Ctrl-Alt-Del should not be your first choice for stopping a command, but sometimes Ctrl-C or Ctrl-Break doesn't work. If the Ctrl-Alt-Del approach fails, turn off the power as a last resort. Some newer computers come with a Reset switch that performs the same function as Ctrl-Alt-Del.

Esc   In DOS and in many applications, pressing the Esc key stops the current process, often reverting to the previous process.

These key sequences are "panic buttons" you can use to stop DOS. Don't worry if you have to use them to prevent disasters. Practice using them with a nondestructive command, such as DIR. You may perspire a little, but soon you will have everything well in hand.

Lessons Learned

■ Computer terminology is basic, and it is simple to understand.

■ You shouldn't be intimidated by the numbers and decimals often added to software names. These numbers identify different versions of products. The higher the number, the newer the version or release.

■ The booting process is automatic if the DOS system files are on a disk in the computer.

■ Providing a good environment for your computer and its software may prevent hardware failure and data loss.

■ Placing Xs at the end of a product version is computer shorthand for indicating that your statements work for all refinements of that version.

■ Changing the drive you want to use is as easy as typing a letter and colon.

■ When you work with a hard disk, you divide the disk into directories that are like file folders in a file cabinet.

■ You can tell DOS to execute commands from either the DOS prompt or the Shell. The Shell provides an easy way for beginners to execute DOS commands. Navigating the Shell is simple, and pull-down menus list all options.

Now firmly at the helm, you are ready to use the DOS Shell to command DOS.

3

3

Understanding and Using the DOS Shell

4

Now that you have the basics of DOS under your belt, you're ready to start taking control. With some earlier versions of DOS, all you had was the manual, perhaps a book such as this one, and the "dreaded" DOS prompt. If you wanted your computer to do any task, you had to know which words to type and what keys to press; otherwise, nothing happened. If you made a mistake, all you got was an error message. DOS provided no help to guide you. No wonder so many people were afraid of DOS.

That changed with the development of the DOS Shell. Once you enter the DOS Shell, you will find the power of DOS displayed in front of you: no commands to memorize or forget, no file names to remember, and help at the touch of a key.

The Shell makes DOS much easier to use. You will see the Shell in action in this chapter, and you will be at the controls.

4

Key Terms Used in This Chapter	
Graphical user interface (GUI)	A graphical way to present information on-screen and to accept information from the user. This type of interface is used in the DOS Shell and Microsoft Windows.
Shell	The interface used to operate DOS.
Icon	A small picture that graphically represents an object such as a file or a program.
Mouse pointer	A symbol, usually an arrow, that shows you the position of the mouse.
Click	The action of pressing the mouse button.
Double-click	The action of quickly pressing the mouse button twice.
Drag	To press and hold down the mouse button as you move the mouse.
Selection cursor	The highlighted band or area that indicates that an item is selected.
Pull-down menu	A secondary menu displayed below the menu bar when you select a menu option.
Dialog box	A window containing options that appears when a command needs additional information.
Shortcut key	A key or key combination you can use in place of a menu selection to execute a command.

Understanding the DOS Shell

When you install and set up DOS 6, you can tell DOS to load the DOS Shell automatically. To load the Shell manually from the DOS prompt, type **DOSSHELL** and press Enter.

The Shell displays information about your files and programs. You can choose from a number of different ways to display this data. These different views are called *display modes*.

When you start the DOS Shell, you see a full-screen display. This display contains much information that is displayed automatically. The display shows you the list of disk drives in your computer, the files in the root directory, and a list of some of the DOS programs available.

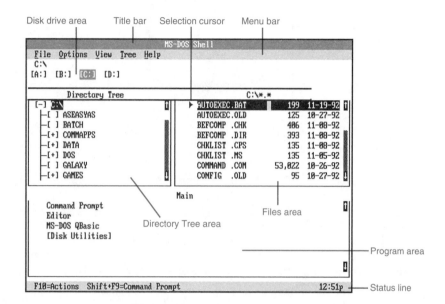

The initial Shell view can contain up to 25 lines of text. Use this display mode if your monitor can display only text or if you have a low-resolution CGA monitor. This Shell view has three *areas*: The directory tree at the left, the list of files at the right, and a list of programs at the bottom.

Some of the items in the Shell display appear highlighted. The highlighted items are *selected*. One of the disk drive letters is highlighted. That drive is the selected drive, and the displayed list of directories (in the Directory Tree area) is for the selected drive. One of the directories in the displayed list is highlighted. This directory is the selected directory, and the displayed list of files (in the Files area) is for the selected directory. When you use the Shell, it is important to know which items are selected. This concept will become quite clear throughout this chapter.

If you have an EGA or VGA display, you can display the Shell in *graphics mode*. Changing the display options for this mode is discussed later in this chapter.

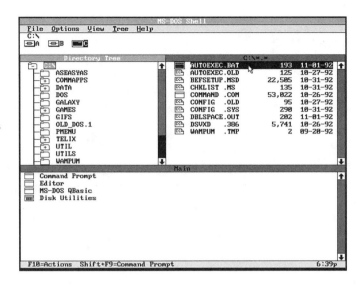

This Shell view is in 34-line graphics mode. Use this mode if your monitor has EGA or better resolution.

In graphics mode, the Shell uses *icons*—small pictures—to represent disk drives, directories, programs, and text files. Other parts of the display, such as the scroll bars and the mouse pointer, are easier to read in graphics mode. See table 4.1 for a description of the basic parts of the Shell display.

Table 4.1
DOS Shell Parts

Part	Description
Title bar	Identifies the name of the current window or dialog box.
Menu bar	Provides a list of pull-down menu options. The menu bar is below the title bar of the main window.
Disk drive area	Lists the disk drives that your computer recognizes. The selected drive is highlighted. Drives A and B are floppy drives. The first hard disk drive is C. If your hard disk drive or drives are partitioned into separate logical drives, each drive letter is treated as a separate physical drive.

Part	Description
Directory Tree area title	Identifies the Directory Tree area. The title is highlighted when this area is selected.
Directory Tree area	Shows the directories for the selected drive. The selected directory is highlighted.
Files area title	Identifies the Files area. The title is highlighted when this area is selected.
Files area	Shows the files for the selected directory. The selected file is highlighted.
Program area title	Identifies the program area. The title is highlighted when this area is selected.
Program area	Lists the programs available from the current program group, and lists other program groups. Program groups are discussed in Chapter 9.
Selection cursor	In text mode, the selection cursor is a small triangular arrow. In graphics mode, it indicates the selected drive, directory, file, or program with a highlighted area or band.
Status line	Shows function key commands, messages, and the current time at the bottom line of the Shell display.
Mouse pointer	Indicates the current position of the mouse on the display. You use the mouse pointer to select items.
Scroll bars	Scrolls any list of directories, files, or programs that is too long to fit in the display area.

4

From the Shell you can execute DOS commands, run programs, view the contents of files, and change the way that the Shell display appears. All these actions are performed by selecting menu options. You do not have to remember command names or the format and parameters of the commands. Just browse through the Shell to see the available commands.

Selecting Items

The concept of selecting an *item* and then performing some action with that item is one of the main concepts behind the Shell graphical user interface. An item can be a disk, a directory, a file, or a program. You select an item by using either the mouse or the keyboard, as you will learn in this section. You select an action from a menu or you use a *shortcut key*, as explained in the section "Making Menu Selections," later in this chapter.

Using the Mouse

Although you can use the Shell with the keyboard or the mouse, you will find that using the mouse is much easier. The graphical user interface was designed to be used with a mouse. In fact, the mouse was designed and developed specifically to control a graphical interface.

With the mouse, you can select items and menu options. As you move the mouse, the mouse pointer moves in the same direction on-screen. The mouse pointer takes on different shapes in the various modes of DOS 6. In graphics mode, for example, the mouse pointer is an arrow. In text mode, the mouse pointer is a gray rectangle. The mouse pointer changes shape to indicate the action taking place.

To select an item with the mouse, make sure that the tip of the mouse pointer is over the item you want to select and *click* the left mouse button. Your mouse may have two or three buttons, but in most cases you use only the left button.

When you click a mouse button, you press and release the button once without moving the mouse. Don't press too hard. Gentle pressure with one finger is all that is needed to click the mouse. If you press too hard, you may move the mouse as you click, thereby making the wrong selection.

You should be familiar with mouse terminology. To *click on* an item means to move the mouse pointer until it is over the item and then click the mouse. At times, you *double-click* the mouse, which means to click the mouse twice in rapid succession. To *drag* the mouse, move the mouse pointer over an object and then press and hold down the mouse button as you move the object with the mouse pointer. Unlike the keyboard cursor keys, you can move the mouse in any direction: up, down, left, right, or at any angle.

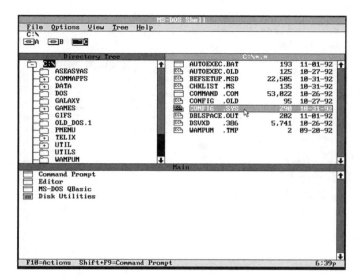

Move the mouse pointer to the item you want to select, and click the left mouse button. The selection cursor highlights the selected item. In this example, CONFIG.SYS is selected.

Using the Keyboard

Although slower than using a mouse, the keyboard works just as well. To use the keyboard to select an item, use any of the following procedures:

- Press the Tab key to select the area you want. Pressing Tab highlights the selected area title. If no title bar is highlighted, the selected area is the disk drive area near the top of the display.

- Press Shift-Tab to move back to the previously selected area.

- Use the up- and down-arrow keys to move the selection cursor to the directory, file, or program you want to select.

- In the disk drives area, use the left- and right-arrow keys to select a different disk drive.

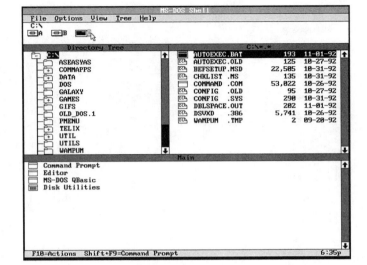

If no title bar is
highlighted, the
selection cursor
is in the disk
drives area.

Making Menu Selections

After you select an item, you choose an action. Most often you choose an
action from a menu. The initial menu options are listed in the menu bar. The
possible menu selections are File, Options, View, Tree, and Help. When the
program area is highlighted, the Tree menu is not available.

When you select a menu option, you activate a *pull-down menu*. From the
pull-down menu, you select the specific action you want to use, such as a DOS
command. Menu options that appear dimmer than others are unavailable for
selection. Sometimes, depending on the color scheme you select, they do not
appear at all.

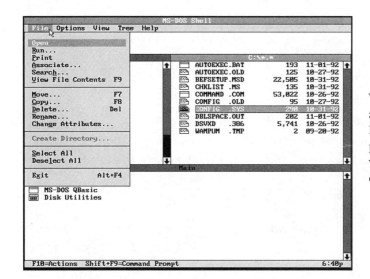

When you choose a menu option, DOS displays a pull-down menu with a list of commands.

4

Using the Mouse with Menus

Selecting a menu option and a command from the pull-down menu with a mouse is easy. Follow these steps:

1. Move the mouse pointer to the menu option and click the mouse button.

2. Move the mouse pointer to the menu command you want to execute and click the mouse button again.

Using the Keyboard with Menus

To select a menu option and a command from the pull-down menu with the keyboard, follow these steps:

1. Press Alt or F10 to activate the menu bar.

   This action highlights the File menu option.

2. Press ← or → to highlight the menu option you want.

3. Press ↓ to activate the pull-down menu for that menu option.

4. Press ↓ or ↑ to select the command you want.

5. Press ↵Enter.

You also can use another keyboard method to make selections from a menu. This second method is faster, but may feel awkward if you are a beginner. For the quick keyboard method, follow these steps:

1. Press (Alt) or (F10) to activate the menu bar.

   This action highlights the File menu option.

2. Type the underlined letter of the menu option you want.

   This step activates the pull-down menu for that menu option.

3. Type the underlined letter of the command you want to execute.

You can press Alt or F10 to activate the menu bar without using the mouse. You can use the arrow keys to select a menu option, or you can type the option's underlined letter.

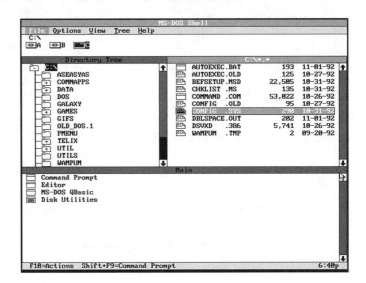

Cancelling Menus

If you select a menu in error, you can cancel the selection and make a different menu selection. To cancel a menu with the mouse, just click anywhere outside the menu area, or click the right mouse button. To cancel a menu with the keyboard, press Esc.

If you make the wrong menu selection with the mouse, just click on the correct menu option in the menu bar. The incorrect pull-down menu disappears, and the new menu opens. If you make the wrong menu selection with the keyboard, just press the left-arrow or right-arrow key to select the menu choice you want.

Using Dialog Boxes

Some commands need additional information before DOS can carry out the command you selected. When DOS needs additional information, it opens a dialog box. When a command has a dialog box, the command name in the pull-down menu is followed by an ellipsis (...). A dialog box may request one piece of information or many separate pieces of information, depending on the command.

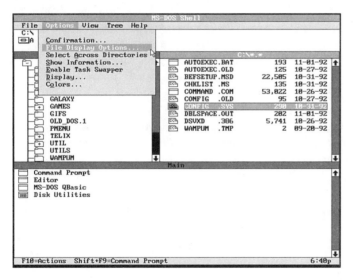

If you choose File Display Options from the Options menu, for example, DOS opens a dialog box that enables you to change the way data is displayed in the files area.

75

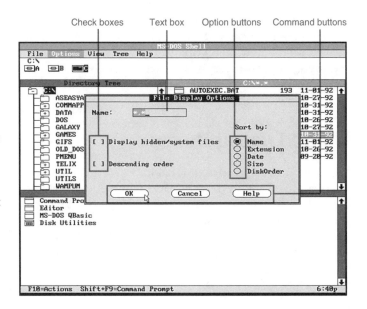

The File Display Options dialog box requests that you enter the files you want to see, how you want them sorted, and whether you want the hidden, or system, files displayed.

The dialog box is one of the most powerful features of a graphical user interface. With some menu systems, you must choose many different levels of menus to get to the one you want. Often, you must make more than ten selections to execute one command. With pull-down menus and dialog boxes, however, you select a menu and a command; then, if additional information is needed, DOS prompts you for that information in a dialog box, which can be as large as a full screen if necessary.

Dialog boxes can contain the following elements:

- A *text box* is a box in which you type text, such as a file name.

- A *check box* is an on-and-off or yes-or-no question and is enclosed in square brackets. If the option is selected, an X appears in the square brackets.

- An *option button* is a circle next to a specific option. The selected option has a black dot in the circle. Related option buttons are grouped together. You can choose only one option button at a time from a group.

- A *list box* is like a list of option buttons in a different format. You can choose only one option from the list.

- A *command button* represents a possible action you can take from the dialog box. The OK button processes the command. The Cancel button cancels the command. The Help button displays on-line help for the dialog box.

Entering Text in Dialog Boxes

To use the mouse to select a text box in a dialog box, move the mouse pointer to the text box and click the left mouse button. If you are using the keyboard, press Tab or Shift-Tab to move to the text box.

To type over an existing entry, just type the new entry. To change an existing entry, press the left-arrow or right-arrow key to position the cursor. Press Backspace to delete a character to the left of the cursor and Del to delete the character at the cursor; then type any new text.

4

Selecting Options in Dialog Boxes

To select or deselect a check box with a mouse, move the mouse pointer between the square brackets and click. To use the keyboard, press Tab or Shift-Tab to move to the check box, and then press the space bar.

To use the mouse to select an option from a list of option buttons, move the mouse pointer to the option button and click. A black dot appears in the selected option button and disappears from any other button in the list. If you click on the black dot, nothing happens. With a keyboard, use the up-arrow and down-arrow keys to move the black dot to the option you want to select.

In some dialog boxes, a list of possible options is displayed in a box. You select from this list. To select an option from a list box with the mouse, move the mouse pointer to the option you want and click. With the keyboard, use the down-arrow and up-arrow keys to highlight the option you want.

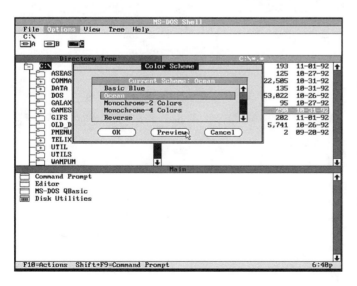

This list box enables you to select from a number of different color schemes, depending on the type of monitor you have.

4

Using Command Buttons

After you supply the requested information in a dialog box, you select the OK command button to execute the command with your choices. Select the Cancel button to ignore all information entered in the dialog box and cancel the command. Other command buttons may be available, such as Help.

To select a command button with the mouse, move the mouse pointer to the button and click the left mouse button. If you are using the keyboard, press Tab or Shift-Tab until an underline appears in the command button you want; then press Enter or the space bar. You can press Esc to cancel a command at any time.

Using Scroll Bars

Sometimes a list is too long to fit within a display area or dialog box. If you use a mouse, you can use *scroll bars* to view text that is not visible. The scroll bar runs the length of a list. The *scroll box* is a gray, rectangular box inside the scroll bar. The scroll box represents the position and the fraction of the data in the currently displayed list. In the Directory Tree area, the scroll box starts at the top of the scroll bar, which means that the list of directories displayed starts at the top (at the root directory).

To scroll down a list, click the black area of the scroll bar, below the scroll box. The scroll box moves down and the list scrolls down to display another part of the list.

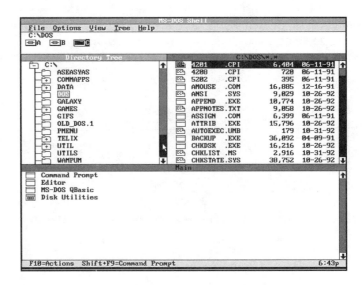

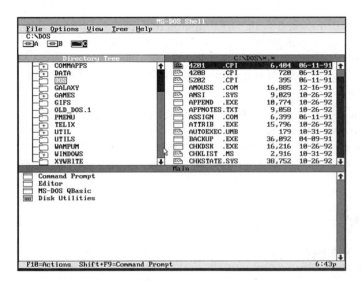

After you click below the scroll box, the display scrolls down, revealing the bottom of the list of directories.

4

At the top and bottom of the scroll bar is a *scroll arrow*—an arrow you can click to scroll the screen in the direction of the arrow. To scroll up or down by one line, move the mouse pointer to the up scroll arrow or the down scroll arrow and click. For every click, the display scrolls one line and the scroll box moves accordingly.

The size of the scroll box tells you how much of the list is visible. If the scroll box is small compared to the total length of the scroll bar, the list is long and you can see only a small part of the list at any one time.

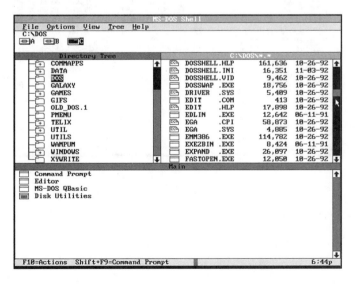

The DOS directory contains about 150 files. The scroll box indicates that only about one-twelfth of the files in the list is visible.

When a list is long, you can scroll swiftly by dragging the scroll box. To drag a scroll box, move the mouse pointer to the scroll box, hold down the mouse button, and move the pointer up or down. As long as you keep the mouse button pressed as you move the mouse, the scroll box moves with the mouse pointer and the list scrolls as well.

You also can scroll with the keyboard. Press Tab to select the area you want; then press the up-arrow or down-arrow key to move the selection cursor one item at a time in the direction of the arrow. Press PgUp or PgDn to scroll up or down, respectively, one full screen at a time.

Getting On-Line Help

The DOS Shell has extensive on-line help available to you at all times. To get help for a specific menu option, command, or dialog box, select the item for which you want help and press F1. For general help with using the Shell, commands, procedures, or the keyboard, select the Help option from the menu bar.

General on-line help is always available with the Help menu option. Select any of the Help options for additional help choices.

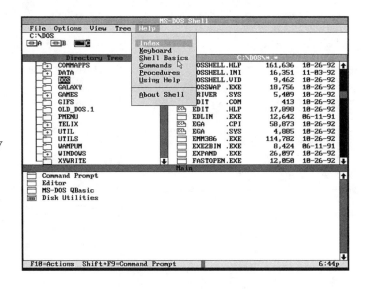

Shell Basics help topics are high-lighted on the Help screen.

4

To use the mouse to get help on any of the general help topics, double-click on a topic. If you are using the keyboard, press Tab to underline a topic, and then press Enter.

Each Help screen contains the following command buttons:

Command Button	Description
Close	Cancels help
Back	Displays previous Help screen
Keys	Displays help on keyboard keys
Index	Displays the Help index
Help	Displays help on how to use the Help system

Running Programs from the Shell

Although you learn how to run applications programs in Chapter 9, this chapter introduces the idea of executing programs from the Shell. Programs are files that have an EXE or COM file extension. Batch files with a BAT file extension contain DOS commands and execute programs.

You can execute a program or batch file in a number of ways. You can select **Run** from the File menu, type the name of the program, and press Enter. You also can select the program or batch file in the file area and press Enter. If the program is listed in the program area, you can select the program from this area and press Enter to execute it. You learn how to add programs to this area in Chapter 9.

After the program completes its processing or you exit from the program, you see the message Press any key to return to MS-DOS Shell. After you press a key, you return to the Shell.

4

Using the Task Swapper

A powerful feature of the DOS Shell is the *Task Swapper*. With the Swapper enabled, you can run more than one program at the same time and swap between them. This feature can be handy if you regularly use more than one program, such as a word processor and a spreadsheet.

To enable the Task Swapper, select the Options menu, and then select **Enable Task Swapper**. A black diamond appears to the left of the command on the menu to indicate that the Swapper is enabled.

When the Task Swapper is enabled, the program area at the bottom of the screen is split into two areas. The Active Task List area lists all programs that have been started.

With the Swapper enabled, you can start a program, such as Lotus 1-2-3 or Microsoft Works, and then suspend the program and return to the Shell. To return to the Shell from a program, press Alt-Esc. Once back in the Shell, you can start one or more other programs, which also can be suspended by pressing Alt-Esc.

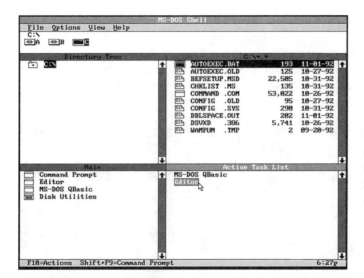

In this example,
MS-DOS QBasic
and the DOS
Editor are loaded
as active tasks,
and then action is
returned to the
Shell.

When you start one or more programs and return to the Shell, the programs
are listed in the Active Task List area. To resume an active task, double-click
the task name, or select the task and press Enter.

When you return to an active task, you return to the exact environment you
left. The same file or files are in memory, the cursor is in the same spot, and
any options are unchanged. Because the Task Swapper is so handy, you may
want to leave it enabled.

Changing the Shell Display

As you can see, a great deal of information is available to you in the Shell
display. You are in control of this display. You can change the way the Shell
looks in a number of ways.

83

Changing the Shell View

The Shell display used so far has three or four areas: a directory area, a files
area, a program area, and if the Swapper is enabled, an active task list area.
You can change this display with the View menu options. Each display choice
is called a *view*. Five possible view choices are available.

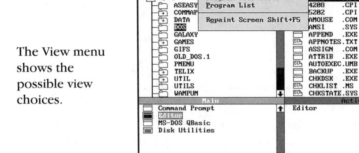

The View menu
shows the
possible view
choices.

The default view is Program/File Lists. This view lists directories and files at the
top of the screen and programs at the bottom of the screen. The current view
choice is gray because you cannot change the view to the current view.
Program/File Lists is the most common view because it permits you to work
with both files and programs at the same time.

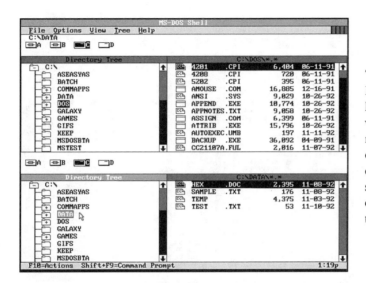

The Dual File Lists view is handy when you want to copy or move files. You can display two directories on the same disk or on different disks at the same time.

4

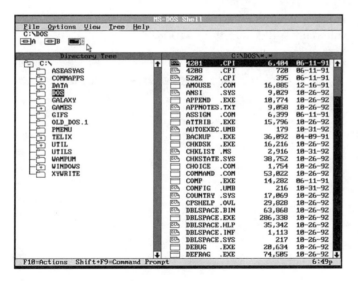

The Single File List view is handy when you want to look at a large group of files. With this view, you can see the entire directory tree and many more files in the DOS directory.

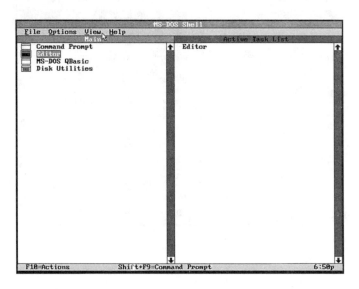

The All Files view
lists every file
on the disk,
regardless of
the directory.

The All Files view is handy when you are trying to locate a specific file or
looking for duplicate file names in different directories.

The Program List
view is useful
only if you have a
long list of
programs you are
using and they do
not all fit in the
program area
with the Program/
File Lists view.

You will learn how to add programs to the program area in Chapter 9.

Changing the Shell Display Mode

The way information appears on-screen is controlled by the display/screen mode. In figures at the beginning of this chapter, you saw the Shell in 25-line text mode and then in 34-line graphics mode. You have a number of display mode options. The best display mode for your system depends on the type of display adapter you have and the size of your monitor. You can try different options and select the one you like best.

The options described here are available if you have a VGA display. If you have a different display adapter, you may see different options.

To change the display mode, choose **D**isplay from the Options menu. DOS displays the Screen Display Mode dialog box.

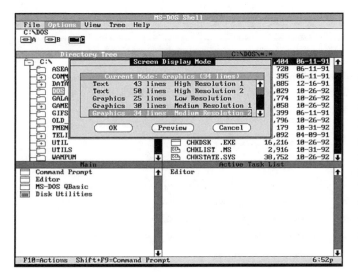

Scroll through the screen modes available for your computer system. Choose the Preview button to see what a screen mode looks like on your display. When you find the screen mode you like, choose OK.

Changing the Shell Colors

If you have a color monitor, you can view the Shell in color. You have a choice of available color schemes. Ocean is the color scheme selected for the screens used to illustrate this book; the screens are printed, of course, in shades of gray.

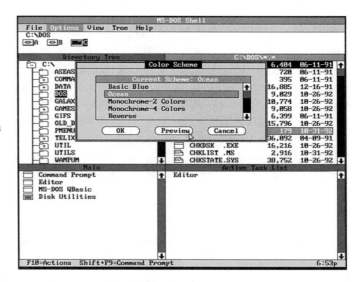

To change the
color scheme,
select Colors from
the Options
menu. The Color
Scheme dialog
box opens.

Scroll through the color schemes available for your computer system. You can
choose the Preview button to see what a color scheme looks like on your
display. When you find the color scheme you like, choose OK.

Using Shortcut Keys

A shortcut key enables you to press a key or combination of keys instead of
making a menu selection to execute a command. Some of the most common
commands have shortcut keys. Although you don't have to use shortcut keys,
these keys do save time when you execute a command frequently.

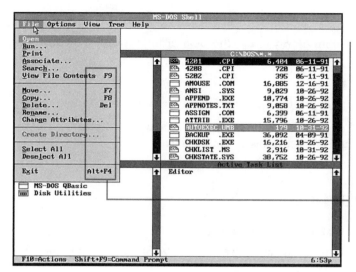

Shortcut keys are listed next to the command name in the pull-down menus. If no key is listed, that command has no shortcut key. If two keys are listed together, press both keys at the same time.

Leaving the DOS Shell

Although you will find that you can do almost all computer work from the Shell, you will sometimes want to work from the command prompt. You can exit the Shell in two ways. You can quit the Shell and remove it from memory, or you can suspend it temporarily.

If the Task Swapper is enabled, you must first exit all active tasks before you can quit the Shell. To quit the Shell, you can do any of the following:

- Press F3.
- Press Alt-F4.
- Choose Exit from the File menu.

To return to the Shell, type **DOSSHELL** at the prompt and press Enter.

To suspend the Shell temporarily to use the DOS prompt, you can do any of the following:

- Press Shift-F9.
- Select Command Prompt from the program area and press Enter.

To resume the Shell, type **EXIT** at the DOS prompt and press Enter. You return to the Shell, and any active tasks remain active.

4

Lessons Learned

■ The DOS Shell is an easy-to-use graphical interface.

■ A mouse is the fastest and easiest way to use the Shell, but using the keyboard is also easy.

■ You can use the Shell to perform many DOS commands and execute programs without knowing the names of commands.

■ To use the Shell, you first select an item and then select an action. An item can be a disk, a directory, a file, or a program.

■ You select items from lists and actions from menus. You don't have to memorize names of items or actions.

■ On-line help is always just a keystroke away.

The Shell is an easy way to see a disk's directory structure. In the next chapter, you learn how to build and use a directory structure for your disks.

Understanding and Using Directories

5

Before the oil crisis of the 1970s, you could stop at any service station and pick up a free map. In fact, one oil company even provided travel routes. All you did was write to a special address and tell the oil company where you planned to go. Within a few weeks, a map arrived showing both the quickest and the most scenic routes. DOS's directory structure provides something resembling that kind of personal touch.

Understanding the DOS directory concept

Navigating a hard disk's directories

Finding paths in the tree structure

Viewing directories

Exploring sample subdirectories

Managing a hard disk drive

Viewing directories and file information

Key Terms Used in This Chapter	
Hierarchical directory	An organizational structure used by DOS to segregate files into levels of subdirectories.
Tree structure	A term applied to hierarchical directories to describe the concept in which directories "belong" to higher directories and "own" lower directories. Viewed graphically, the ownership relationships resemble an inverted tree.
Directory	An area of the DOS file system that holds information about files and directories. The root directory is the highest directory of DOS's tree structure. All DOS disks have a root directory, which DOS creates automatically.
Subdirectory	A directory created within another directory and subordinate to that directory. Also called, simply, a directory.
Directory specifier	A DOS command parameter that tells DOS where to find a file or where to carry out a command.
Path name	Another name for the directory specifier. The path name gives DOS the necessary directions to trace the directory tree to the directory that contains the desired commands or files.
Backslash (\)	The character used in commands to separate directory names. Used alone as a parameter, the backslash signifies the root directory.

Understanding the DOS Directory Concept

DOS doesn't strand you on the road without a map. Understandably, people beginning to use a PC don't know the "proper address" to write for the scenic or direct routes. This chapter is designed to be your map to DOS.

In Chapters 3 and 4, you saw file lists of the contents of a disk directory. A directory is more than a file list displayed on-screen. It also is part of an internal software listing that DOS stores in a magnetic index on the disk. A poorly structured disk directory turns any hard drive into a bewildering tangle of misplaced files.

This chapter explains DOS's hierarchical directory structure. You discover how to use DOS to group and organize files. You also learn how DOS commands can help you organize your disk directories logically.

Navigating a Hard Disk's Directories

5

DOS uses directories to organize files on a disk. A directory listing contains file information—the name, size, and creation or revision date for each file. Computer operators use the directory of a disk to find specific files. DOS also uses some or all of this directory information to service requests for data stored in the files on disks.

All DOS-based disks have at least one directory. One directory usually is adequate for a floppy disk. Because floppy disks have relatively limited capacities, the number of files that fit on a floppy is limited. Hard disks, on the other hand, have very large storage capacities. A hard disk can contain hundreds or even thousands of files. Without some form of organization, you will waste time sifting and sorting through your disk's directories to find a specific file.

Although floppy disks can use DOS's multiple directory structure, this feature is more important for extending order to the storage capacity of hard disks. DOS incorporates the hierarchical directory system. This term means that one directory leads to another, which can lead to another, and so on. This multi-level file structure enables you to create a filing system. With a bit of foresight, you can store your files in logically grouped directories so that you (and DOS) can locate your files more easily.

Computer people use the term *tree structure* to describe the organization of files into hierarchical levels of directories. Try picturing the tree structure as an inverted tree. You can visualize the file system with the first-level directory as the root or trunk of the tree. The trunk branches into major limbs to the next level of directories under the root. These directories branch into other directories. Directories have files, like leaves, attached to them.

5

In DOS's directory structure, viewed as a tree-structure hierarchy, the root directory is the topmost directory.

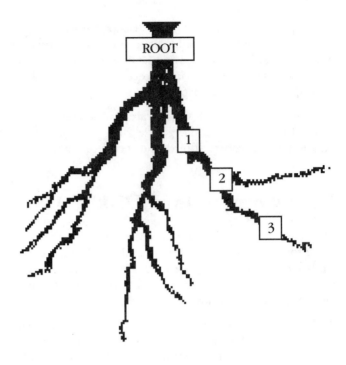

The numbered boxes represent directories on branches of the tree-structured hierarchy.

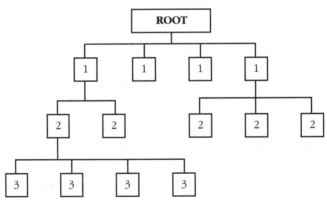

When you format a disk, DOS creates a main directory for that disk. This directory is called the *root directory*. The root directory is the default directory until you change to another directory. DOS designates the root directory with the backslash (\) character. You cannot delete the root directory.

A *subdirectory* is any directory, excluding the root directory. A subdirectory can contain data files as well as other subdirectories. Subdirectory names must conform to the rules for naming DOS files, but subdirectory names normally do not have extensions. You should name subdirectories for the type of files they contain so that you will remember what type of files each subdirectory contains.

The terms *directory* and *subdirectory* frequently are used interchangeably. A subdirectory of the root can have its own subdirectories. By naming the branches, you can describe where you are working in the tree structure. You simply start at the root and name each branch that leads to your current branch. Directories also are frequently called "parent" and "child" directories. Each child of the parent can have "children" of its own. In the directory hierarchy, each directory's parent is the directory just above it.

Any directory, except the root, can have as many subdirectories as space on the disk permits. Depending on the disk drive, the root directory can handle a preset number of subdirectories. In the 5 1/4-inch size, 360K floppies hold 112 entries and 1.2M floppies handle 224 entries in the root directory. In the 3 1/2-inch size, 720K and 1.4M floppies can hold, respectively, 112 and 224 entries. Hard disks have a typical root directory capacity of 512 entries.

Directories do not share information about their contents with other directories. In a way, each subdirectory acts as a disk within a bigger disk. This idea of privacy extends to the DOS commands you issue. The directory structure permits DOS commands to act on the contents of the current directory and leave other directories undisturbed.

When you issue a command that specifies a file but not a directory, DOS looks for that file in the default, or current, directory. You can access any point in the tree structure and remain at your current directory.

Any squirrel knows that you cannot reach the farthest branch of a limb without starting from the limb nearest the base. From there, the limb branches off to several others. The important thing to note is that you cannot use more than one limb to reach any of the limb's potentially numerous branches. Consider a directory path as a series of stopping points (limbs) on the way to a destination (branch).

Finding Paths in the Tree Structure

Before DOS can locate a file in the tree structure, it must know where to find the file. The *directory specifier* simply tells DOS the directory in which a certain file resides. DOS must know the drive that you want to use, the directory name, and the name of the file. In the command line, you type the disk drive, the directory name, and finally, the file name. DOS uses this information to find and act on the file.

Path Names

You can compare DOS to a corporate empire that has an extremely strict order of command. All communications must "go through channels." If a subsidiary at level 3 wants to communicate with the parent corporation, for example, the message must go through subsidiaries 2 and 1. In DOS, this routing is called a *path*.

5

The parent corporation is analogous to the root directory, and the subsidiaries are analogous to subdirectories.

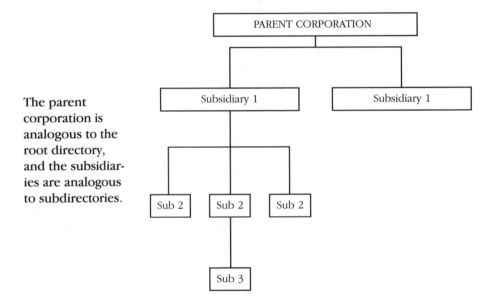

A *path name* is a chain of directory names that tells DOS how to find the file that you want. You must build complete path names when you use the DOS prompt. When you use the Shell, the paths are supplied visually in the Directory Tree area. If you understand paths now, you can easily use the command line later.

To create a path name chain, you type the drive name, a subdirectory name (or sequence of subdirectory names), and the file name. Make sure that you separate subdirectory names from each other with a *backslash* (\) character. Using symbolic notation, the path name looks like the following:

d:\directory\directory...\filename.ext

In this notation, *d:* is the drive letter. If you fail to specify the drive, DOS uses the logged drive as the default drive. *directory\directory...* names the directories you want to search. The ellipsis (...) simply means that you can add other directories to the specifier list. If you omit the directory specifier from the path name, DOS assumes that you want to use the current directory.

filename.ext is the name of the file. Notice that you use a backslash (\) to separate directory names and the file name. The path name fully describes to DOS where to direct its search for the file.

Use the following simple directory setup to understand directory paths in DOS. Each subdirectory in this sample is a subdirectory of the root directory.

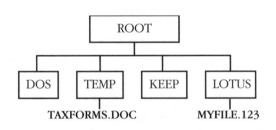

The subdirectory TEMP has a file called TAXFORMS.DOC, and the subdirectory LOTUS has a file called MYFILE.123.

5

The complete path name for the MYFILE.123 file is the chain of directories that tells DOS how to find MYFILE.123. In this case, the chain consists of just two directories: the root (\) and LOTUS. The path name is

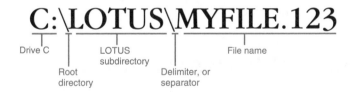

The path name for the TAXFORMS.DOC file is

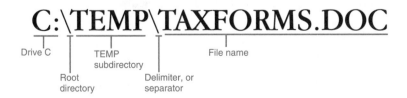

97

The Search's Starting Point

When you type a path name, DOS searches in the first specified directory. It then passes through the other specified directory branches to the file. The root directory is represented by the backslash (\) instead of a directory name. If you want the search path to start at the root directory, from which all directories grow, begin the directory specification with a \. DOS then begins its search for the file in the root and follows the subdirectory chain you included in the command.

Suppose that you want to see the directory listing for a budget file you created with your Lotus 1-2-3 program. You might use the DIR command to give DOS a path similar to the following:

        DIR C:\LOTUS\DATA\BUDGET.WK1

DOS searches on drive C, beginning with the root directory, proceeds to the LOTUS subdirectory, and then arrives at the DATA subdirectory, where it finds the BUDGET.WK1 file.

If you omit the \ root name designator, the search starts in your current directory, not the root directory. DOS uses the path to your current directory as its default. If the current directory doesn't lead to the subdirectory that contains the file, the error message File not found appears on-screen. If the current directory contains the subdirectory, however, you do not have to type all the directory names in the path. Using the preceding example, if the current directory is C:\LOTUS, you can see the listing for the budget file by typing the following command at the DOS prompt:

        DIR DATA\BUDGET.WK1

Viewing the Directory Structure

In the last chapter, you saw some rather complex hard disk directory structures. This section starts with some simple directory structures using drive A. Although floppy drive A is used here as a sample, these directory structures really are more applicable to hard disks, not floppy disks.

A variety of arrangements for the directory structure is possible. This sample structure has four subdirectories under the root, or A:\, directory.

Many times, a second level of directories is useful. For example, you might want to group a series of related program directories under one directory, or group a number of data directories under one directory. Many people find that two levels of subdirectories are sufficient.

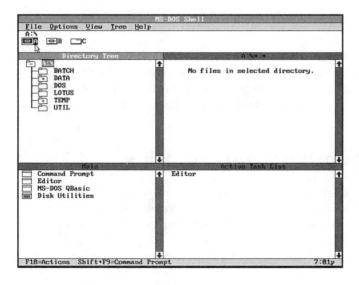

This sample directory structure has two levels of directories under the root. Only the first level appears. If a directory has additional levels of subdirectories under it, a plus sign (+) appears in the file folder icon.

When you see a plus sign in a file folder icon for a directory, you can expand the directory listing to see the subdirectories for that directory. To use the mouse to expand a single directory, click on the plus sign. To use the keyboard to expand a single directory, select that directory and press the plus (+) key. To expand all the directories in the directory tree, choose Expand **All** from the Tree menu, or press Ctrl-* (asterisk).

5

In this sample directory struc- ture, the DATA directory has three subdirec- tories and TEMP has one.

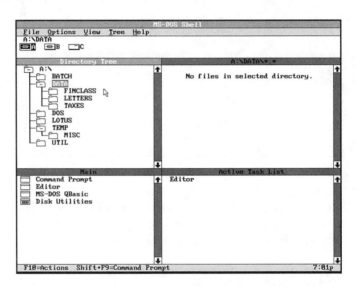

When you see a minus sign (–) in a file folder icon for a directory, you can collapse that directory's listing to hide the subdirectories. To use the mouse to collapse a single directory, click on the minus sign. To use the keyboard to collapse a single directory, select that directory and press the minus (–) key.

Exploring Sample Subdirectories

Although you may not know exactly what kind of directory organization you need, now is a good time to give some thought to establishing your directory tree. Use the following sample directories to help you decide what directories you want to build on your hard disk. If your computer is part of a network, check with the network administrator before you make any changes.

The Root Directory

DOS creates the root directory for you, but you control which files to include in the root. As a general rule, you should avoid cluttering the root directory of a hard disk with files.

Because the root is the default directory for DOS when you boot your system, you must include COMMAND.COM in the root directory of your first hard disk and any floppy disk that you use to boot your computer. DOS expects to find COMMAND.COM in the current directory when you boot. If DOS cannot load COMMAND.COM, it cannot communicate with you. DOS only manages to warn you that it cannot find the command interpreter.

In addition to COMMAND.COM, the root directory probably contains AUTOEXEC.BAT and CONFIG.SYS files. DOS uses these files when you boot the computer. Chapter 12 discusses these files. Almost all other files should find a home in an appropriate subdirectory.

5

The \DOS Directory

When you install DOS on your hard disk, the installation procedure creates the \DOS directory and copies the DOS files into this directory. Never place any files in the \DOS directory except DOS files.

The \BATCH Directory

Batch files are text files that contain DOS commands and execute programs. You can place many commands in one batch file. Even if you use the Shell to execute commands and programs, you still will use batch files. Most users keep their batch files in a separate \BATCH directory. Chapter 12 discusses batch files in more detail.

The \UTIL or \UTILITY Directory

Just as you keep all your DOS files in the \DOS directory, you may want to keep utility programs in their own directory. Most people accumulate a variety of small utility programs such as print spoolers, mouse drivers, file compression utilities, disk utilities, and so on, and keep them in the \UTIL or \UTILITY directory. Do not place these utility programs in the \DOS directory. If you upgrade your version of DOS later, these programs may no longer be available to you.

The \DATA Directory

You probably use your personal computer for many different purposes. Therefore, you create many different data files. Some people create a data subdirectory under each program directory. If they have a \LOTUS directory with the 1-2-3 program files, for example, they create a \LOTUS\DATA or \LOTUS\FILES directory for worksheet files.

This structure works, but there is a better one. Create a directory called \DATA, and then create subdirectories for each project or application. For example, you would put all the files related to your taxes in the \DATA\TAXES directory. If you take a class in finance, you could put all the homework assignments in the \DATA\FINCLASS directory. The \DATA\FINCLASS directory might contain both worksheet files and word processing files, but they are all related to one activity.

With a \DATA directory, you can back up your data easily without making a backup copy of your programs. Creating backups is covered in Chapter 10.

The \TEMP Directory

Many users find that they need a directory to store temporary files. You might find a directory named \TEMP useful. You can copy files to \TEMP as a temporary storage place until you copy the files to a more appropriate directory. A \TEMP directory also is useful for making copies of floppies in a single floppy, low-memory system.

You can copy files from the source disk to the \TEMP directory and then copy them back to the destination disk. If you have a single floppy drive, this copy method keeps you from swapping disks in and out of the single floppy drive.

Do not use the \TEMP directory as a permanent home for a file, however. You should be able to erase all the files in this directory periodically so that you can keep the \TEMP directory empty for later use.

If you are using Microsoft Windows, be careful when using a \TEMP directory. Windows creates a directory to store temporary files when you install the program. The default for this directory is C:\WINDOWS\TEMP. Because Windows uses these files, you should never delete any files from the Windows temporary directory while Windows is running. If the Windows temporary directory is C:\WINDOWS\TEMP, you can use C:\TEMP without causing any problems. Although the directories both have the name \TEMP, DOS knows that the two directories are different and unrelated because their complete paths are different.

The \MISC or \KEEP Directory

You may have files in different directories that are no longer active, but that you may still need. Inactive files in a directory tend to increase clutter and make sorting through the directory confusing. With a \MISC or a \KEEP directory, you have an easily remembered home for those inactive files.

Applications Software Directories

Many applications packages create directories when you install them on your hard disk. If a program doesn't create a directory, you should create one with a name that suggests the software name. For example, you might name your spreadsheet directory LOTUS. You can then copy the 1-2-3 package's files to that directory.

If you work with multiple versions of the same program, you might name a subdirectory 123R24 for the 1-2-3 Release 2.4 program files and 123R31 for the 1-2-3 Release 3.1 program files. If you have enough disk space, you should keep both the old version and the new version of a program available for a while in case you have problems with the new version.

Managing a Hard Disk Drive

The examples presented so far in this chapter provide information on the structure of hierarchical directories. The following commands relate to your directory system's maintenance and use. With directory commands, you can customize your file system and navigate through it.

Creating a New Directory

To make a new directory, follow these steps:

1. Select the parent directory where you want to add a subdirectory. For example, if you want to add a subdirectory to the root, select the root directory.

2. Select Create Directory from the File menu to create a new directory under the selected directory. The Create Directory dialog box appears.

Making a new
directory with the
Create Directory
command.

3. Type the name of the new directory in the text box. A directory name
   must be a valid file name of one to eight characters.

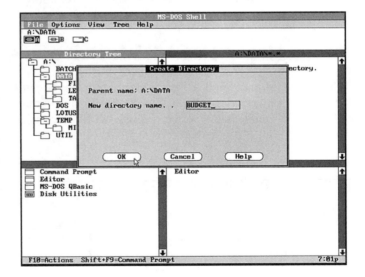

In this example,
the new directory
name is BUDGET.

4. Choose OK.

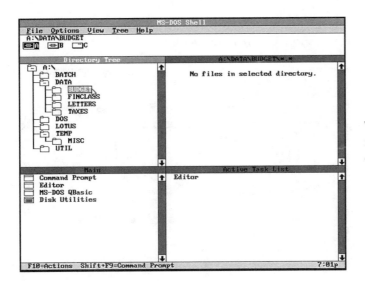

\DATA\BUDGET
is added to the
directory tree.

As soon as you create a new directory, it appears in the Directory Tree area.

Changing the Current Directory

The directory selected in the Directory Tree is the *current directory*. The
files for the current directory are listed in the Files area to the right of
the Directory Tree. Generally, the term "current" is used when you use
the command line instead of the Shell.

To use the mouse to change the current directory, click on another directory
name. To use the keyboard to change the current directory, press the Tab key
until you select the Directory Tree area, and then use the down-arrow and
up-arrow keys to select the directory you want.

If the directory you want to select is a subdirectory of another directory and
does not appear on the Directory Tree, expand the Directory Tree and then
select the subdirectory.

Removing a Directory

Before you remove a directory, you must first delete all the files from the
unwanted directory. To delete a file, you select it in the Files area and then
choose **Delete** from the File menu or press the Del key. Choose Yes in the
Delete File Confirmation dialog box. You learn the details of how to delete
files in Chapter 7.

105

To remove an empty directory, first select the directory. Then choose **Delete** from the File menu or, as a shortcut, press the Del key.

When you delete a directory, a confirmation dialog box appears. Choose Yes to remove the directory, or choose No or Cancel if you do not want to remove it.

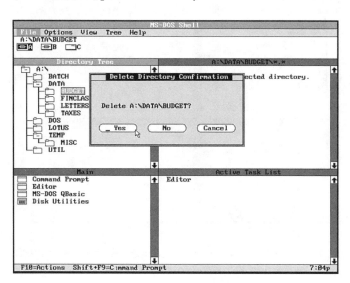

If you try to delete a directory that has one or more subdirectories or contains files, an error dialog box appears.

Because the selected directory, TEMP, has a subdirectory, MISC, you cannot delete TEMP until you first delete MISC. Click Close to clear the error dialog box and cancel the command.

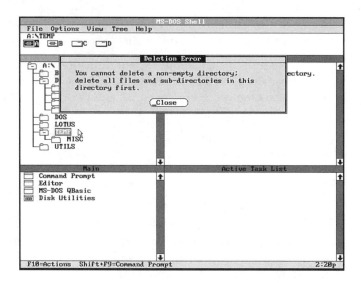

5

Viewing Directories

The standard file list displays all the files in the selected directory in file name order. The Files area title bar indicates the selected directory and the file specification.

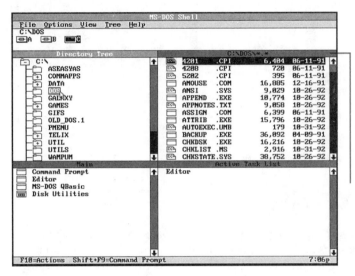

The Files area title bar indicates the selected directory and the file specification.

5

You can change this file list display in two ways. First, you can change the order in which DOS displays the files; or, if you want to see only specific files from a directory with many files, you can change the type of files DOS displays. You use the File Display Options dialog box to accomplish both of these tasks.

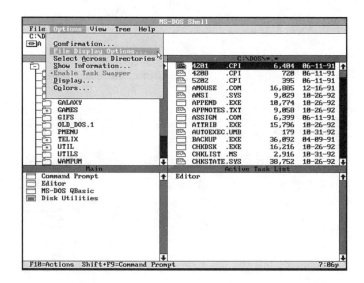

To access this dialog box and change the display of the file lists, choose File Display Options from the Options menu.

Changing the Sort Order

You can sort files according to five sort options. *Name* sorts alphabetically by name. *Extension* sorts alphabetically by file name extension. *Date* sorts numerically by the date the file was created or altered. *Size* sorts numerically by file size. *DiskOrder* sorts according to where the files are stored on the disk.

You also have two additional options. You can select the Descending order box to reverse the sort order; for instance, you select this box to list files that begin with the letter *Z* before those that begin with *A*. And you can select the Display hidden/system files box to display those files.

Note: If you are updating many files in a large directory, you may want to list the files by date instead of by name, or by date in descending order so that you can easily tell which files are new.

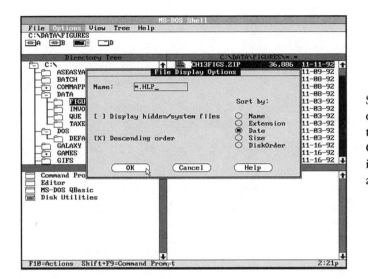

Select the sort order you want in the Sort by: area. Choose Descending order if applicable.

After you choose the appropriate sort order in the File Display Options dialog box, choose OK to complete the command.

Changing the File Specification

The *file specification* tells DOS what files to display. The default *.* file specification displays files with any file name and any file extension. The asterisk is a *wild card* that matches any number of characters in the file name or extension.

To change a file specification, simply type a file specification in the Name text box in the File Display Options dialog box. When you enter a file specification, you must enter a file name, a period to separate the name from the extension, and an extension.

109

The following table shows some sample file specifications that contain the asterisk wild card:

File Specification	Files Displayed
.	All files
*.BAS	All files with a BAS extension
*.DOC	All files with a DOC extension
.WK	All files with an extension that begins with WK, such as WKS or WK1
BUDGET.*	All files with the name BUDGET and any extension
TAX199*.*	All files with a name that starts with TAX199 and any extension, such as TAX1990.DOC, TAX1991.WK1, or TAX199.TXT

In most cases, you will want to display all files with a certain file extension.

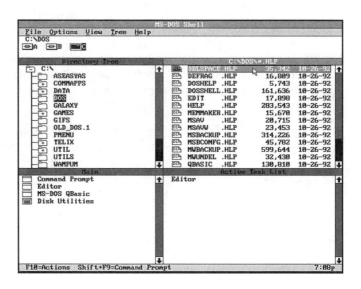

This Files area title bar shows that only files with a HLP file extension are displayed.

The selective file display can be even more powerful when you want to look at all the files on a disk in one display. You can display files with a certain file extension, regardless of where they are located on the disk. This option can help you find misplaced files or the names of files you have forgotten.

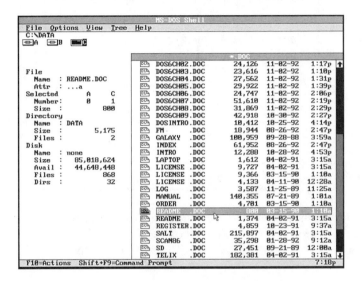

In this example, all files with the file extension DOC are displayed.

5

This display is the result of using File Display Options to display files with the file specification *.DOC and changing the View option to All Files. Detailed file information on the selected file appears on the left. The disk contains two files with the name README.DOC. The selected file is in the \DATA directory. To find the location of the other README.DOC file, select it and read the file information for that file.

Displaying File Information

When you set the View option to All Files, detailed file information for the selected file appears to the left of the file list. To display this information in the other views, select the file and choose Show Information from the Options menu.

111

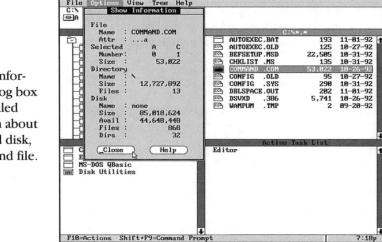

The Show Information dialog box shows detailed information about the selected disk, directory, and file.

You see the selected file, the selected directory, the total size of the directory, the number of files in the directory, the disk label of the selected disk, total size of the disk, number of bytes available on the disk, and the number of files on the disk.

Lessons Learned

■ You can use DOS's hierarchical directory system to organize your files so that they are easy to find.

■ The path concept is essentially the mapping out of a course for DOS to search.

■ The root directory is the beginning, or default, directory.

■ You can create and remove directories easily with the Shell.

■ You can view a directory listing many different ways.

■ Detailed information about the current file, directory, and disk are only a menu choice away.

In the next chapter, you will learn how to prepare floppy disks.

5

The DOS Format

When you were in grade school, your favorite day was probably the last day before summer recess. Your second favorite day might have been the first day of the new school year, when you bought loose-leaf binders, section sheets, tabs, and paper. There was something special about prying open those big chrome rings and arranging all the items necessary for organized note taking. The paper was lined and pristine, everything was sectioned off, and labels identifying subjects were written as neatly as small fingers allowed. These notebooks would never be this neat again.

Preparing your computer to hold and organize information also can be a pleasing experience. Reading this chapter teaches you how to format any DOS disk, hard or floppy. Topics range from formatting different types of floppy disks, assigning volume labels, transferring system files, and understanding FORMAT error messages.

Learning how to format disks is easy if you accept the role of the patient student. The agreeable part of formatting disks is that DOS does it all. You don't even have to worry about poor penmanship.

Key Terms Used in This Chapter	
Format	Initial preparation of a disk for data storage.
Volume label	A disk-level name that identifies a particular disk.
Track	A circular section of a disk's surface that holds data.
Sector	A section of a track that acts as the disk's smallest storage unit.
Allocation unit	A group of sectors that DOS uses to keep track of files on the disk.
Unformat	To recover the files on a disk after it has been formatted.

6

Understanding Floppy Disks

A floppy disk is a Mylar pancake in a plastic dust cover. The Mylar disk is covered with magnetic material similar to the metallic coating on recording tape. Out of the box, disks usually aren't ready for you to use. You must *format* them first. Some stores carry preformatted disks that are ready for use.

DOS's FORMAT command performs the preparation process for disks. You simply enter the command, and FORMAT analyzes for disk defects, generates a root directory, sets up a storage table (called a *file allocation table*), and alters other parts of the disk.

The magnetic disk is like unlined paper—hardly a good medium for proper magnetic penmanship. If you use blank pages, you could wind up with wandering, uneven script. Lines on the paper serve as guides to help keep you on track. Although you can write on unlined paper, DOS is not that flexible. Your computer cannot use a disk at all until it is formatted.

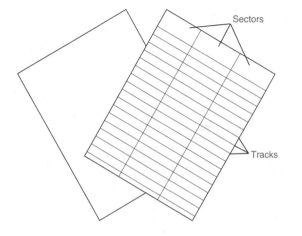

Formatted disks can be compared to lined paper, with horizontal lines subdivided by vertical lines.

Just as lines on paper are guides for the writer, tracks and sectors on a disk are guides for the computer. Because the storage medium of a spinning disk is circular, the "premarked lines," or magnetic divisions called *tracks*, are placed in concentric circles. These tracks are further subdivided into areas called *sectors*.

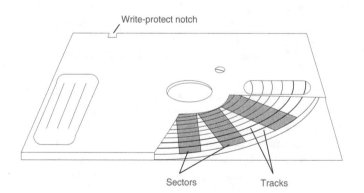

When you format a blank disk, DOS magnetically *encodes* (marks) tracks and sectors onto the disk's surface.

DOS decides what type of drive you have and then positions the tracks and sectors accordingly. DOS stores data in these sectors and uses both the track and sector numbers to find and retrieve information.

Understanding Different Floppy Disks

Before you can buy the right disks for your computer, you must understand the different types of floppy disks available. Unfortunately, disks are described in many different ways. If you walk into a computer store to buy 1.44 megabyte disks, for example, the boxes of disks might reveal everything about the disks, except the capacity. The following information helps you understand how to buy the different types of disks you may need.

Floppy disks differ in capacity, size, and number of tracks and sectors. Over the years, the maximum capacity of floppy disks has increased steadily. In 1981, a floppy disk could hold 160K (kilobytes). Today, the maximum capacity is 1.44M (megabytes), and 2.88M floppy disks are starting to appear.

Determining the disk size is the easy part of understanding floppy disks. Two sizes of floppy disks are available: 5 1/4-inch and 3 1/2-inch. The larger disks were available first and are more common. The smaller disks have a higher capacity, have rigid cases that protect the disk from damage, and are more reliable. The size of the disks is clearly marked on the box and is easy to determine from the size of the box itself.

Floppy disks can be either *single-sided* or *double-sided*. Double-sided disks have tracks on both sides of the disk and, therefore, twice the capacity of single-sided disks. Only double-sided disks are used in today's PCs. Some computer stores may still sell single-sided disks for very old PCs and other computers. Boxes of floppy disks should be labeled *two-sided, 2S, double-sided,* or *DS*. So far so good.

Floppy disks come in different *densities*. The density is a measure of how closely the bytes of information are placed on the disk. Today, floppy disks are either double-density or high-density. High-density is sometimes called *quad-density*. Single-density disks have never been used in PCs, but they have been used in older types of computers. Double-density disks usually are labeled *DD* or *2DD* (the *2* means double-sided), and high-density disks are labeled *HD* or *2HD*.

Sectors on all types of disks hold 512 bytes (.5K). Disks have different capacities because they have more sectors per track or more tracks per side.

The standard floppy disks generally used are summarized in the following list:

Disk Type	Sectors per Track	Tracks per Side	Capacity
5 1/4-inch			
Double-density	9	40	360K
High-density	15	80	1.2M
3 1/2-inch			
Double-density	9	80	720K
High-density	18	80	1.44M

720K disks are often labeled *1M*, and 1.44M disks are often labeled *2M*. These numbers refer to the unformatted capacity of the disk and, unfortunately, add to the confusion.

You don't need to remember all this information about floppy disks because the computer and DOS handle this information for you. When you buy disks and when you format them, however, you should understand that different types of disks are available.

Matching Floppy Disks and the Disk Drive

Just as there are different types of floppy disks, there are different types of disk drives. The most obvious difference is the disk drive size. Drives can be either 5 1/4-inch or 3 1/2-inch. If you have one or two 5 1/4-inch drives, you cannot use 3 1/2-inch floppy disks, and vice versa. If you are lucky enough to have one drive of each size, you can read both sizes of disks.

Size is not the only consideration, however. Disk drives also have a maximum capacity. A 5 1/4-inch drive might be a standard (360K) drive or a high-capacity (1.2M) drive. A 1.2M drive can read and write 360K disks, but a 360K drive cannot read or write 1.2M disks. The 1.2M floppy disks fit in the drive, but you cannot use them.

Although you can use 360K floppy disks in 1.2M drives, the results can be unreliable at times. If you write to a 360K disk in a 1.2M drive, you should have no trouble reading that disk in the same drive. You may, however, have

6

trouble reading the disk in a 360K drive. This problem is intermittent and occurs more often with older drives. Keep this in mind if you copy files onto a floppy disk to be read by another computer. If you run into this problem, try using another floppy disk or format the disk again.

The same situation exists with 3 1/2-inch drives. If you have a 720K drive, you cannot use 1.44M disks. If you have 1.44M drives, you can use both types of 3 1/2-inch floppy disks.

Formatting Floppy Disks

As formatting your disks becomes a routine task, remember to use care. Formatting clears all information that a disk contains. If you format a disk you have used earlier, everything stored on that disk disappears. Be careful not to format disks that contain files you want to keep. Labeling your disks helps you avoid such a mishap. You also should use the DIR command to check the list of files on a disk before you try to format a used floppy. Another precaution is to write-protect disks that hold important information. You write-protect a disk by adding tape tabs on 5 1/4-inch disks or setting the write-protect switch on 3 1/2-inch disks. On a 5 1/4-inch disk, put the tape tab over the notch on the upper-right side of the disk. The write-protect switch on a 3 1/2-inch disk is behind the disk's upper-right corner. To set the switch, slide it up so that the window is open. When the window is closed, write-protection is off.

Place some type of indicator on each disk you format to avoid mistaking formatted disks for unformatted disks. The indicator may be as simple as a dot, a check mark, or the letter *F* for *formatted*. When you buy floppy disks, adhesive labels are included. A simple method to keep track of formatted disks is to put a label on each disk that you format. Then you know that a disk without a label has never been formatted.

If you have two floppy drives, you can format disks in either drive A or B. When you use the Shell to format a disk, the default drive is A. By default, the program area at the bottom half of the Shell is labeled *Main*. This label refers to the Main *program group* that DOS sets up when you install DOS on your hard disk. Program groups are like file folders that contain related programs. Program groups are discussed in Chapter 9.

In the program area, program groups and programs are listed in the Main group. DOS sets up the Main and Disk Utilities program groups automatically. To format a disk from the Shell, you must access the Format program, located in the Disk Utilities program group.

6

118

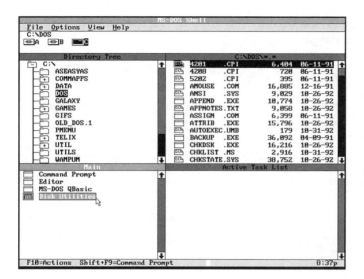

You can tell that Disk Utilities is a program group and not a program because its icon is different.

To execute a program from the Shell, first you open the program group, and then you select the program in that group.

To use the Shell to format a floppy disk, follow these steps:

1. Open the Disk Utilities group by double-clicking on it, or select it and press ⏎Enter.

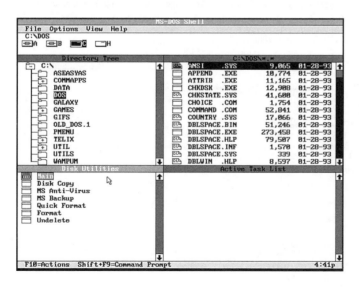

The Disk Utilities program group contains DOS commands that help you manage disks. Most of these commands are covered in Chapters 7 and 10.

119

2. Execute the FORMAT command by double-clicking Format or by selecting Format and pressing ⏎Enter.

The Format
dialog box
opens.

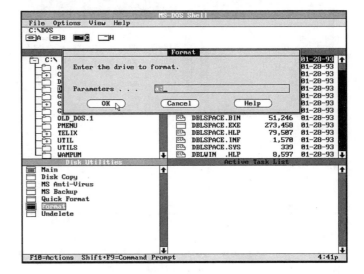

DOS assumes that you want to format a disk in drive A. If you want to format the floppy disk with no special options, you can accept the default and choose OK. To format a floppy disk in drive B, type **b:**. When you type anything in the text box, the highlighted default text disappears.

3. Choose OK from the Format dialog box.

Even if you have already put a floppy disk in the drive before you started the format, DOS prompts you to insert a disk into the drive.

```
Insert new diskette for drive A:
and press ENTER when ready...

Checking existing disk format.
Saving UNFORMAT information.
Verifying 1.2M
Format complete.

Volume label (11 characters, ENTER for none)?
```

6

4. Insert a floppy disk into the drive if you have not already done so, close the disk drive door on 5 1/4-inch drives, and press `⏎Enter`.

   The Format program checks the existing disk format. If the disk has never been formatted, nothing needs to be checked, and the program formats the disk. If it has been formatted, DOS saves the existing format information, which you can use to unformat the disk later. (You learn about unformatting in Chapter 10.) As the disk is formatted, the percentage of the disk that has been formatted is displayed. When the formatting process is complete, you see the following message:

   ```
   Format complete.

   Volume label (11 characters, ENTER for none)?
   ```

5. Type a volume label and press `⏎Enter`, or just press `⏎Enter` for no label.

   DOS reserves a few bytes of space on disks so that you can place an electronic identifier, called a *volume label*, on each disk. Think of a volume label for a disk in the same context as the title of a book. When you assign a volume label, you can use the following characters, in any order:

   - Letters A to Z and a to z
   - Numerals 0 to 9
   - Special characters and punctuation symbols:

     ~ ! @ # $ ^ & ( ) – _ { } '

   If you try to enter too many characters, you hear a beep after the 11th character. If you enter an illegal character, you see an error message and a prompt to enter the volume label again. If you do not want to name the disk, press `⏎Enter` without typing a name.

6. DOS displays detailed information about the formatted disk and then asks whether you want to format another disk. Press `N` and `⏎Enter` if you do not want to format any more disks. Press `Y` and `⏎Enter` if you want to format another disk while the Format program is still loaded in the computer's memory.

7. When you are done formatting, press any key to return to the Shell.

6

Understanding Safe Formatting

When you format a disk that has been formatted previously, DOS saves some information that allows you to *unformat* the disk. Remember, when you format a disk, you tell DOS to completely clear the disk so that you can use it again; however, DOS saves the information that was on the disk. If you format a floppy disk in error and do not put any other files on the disk, you can unformat the disk and recover these files. This process is called *safe formatting*.

When a disk has been formatted before, DOS saves the information on the disk so that you can unformat the disk and recover the data.

```
Insert new diskette for drive A:
and press ENTER when ready...

Checking existing disk format.
Saving UNFORMAT information.
Verifying 1.2M
Format complete.

Volume label (11 characters, ENTER for none)?
```

You learn about unformatting in Chapter 10.

In some cases, DOS cannot save the unformat information and warns you that the disk cannot be unformatted.

```
Insert new diskette for drive B:
and press ENTER when ready...

Checking existing disk format.
Existing format differs from that specified.
This disk cannot be unformatted.
Proceed with Format (Y/N)?
```

You can proceed with the format with no hope of recovering the data, or you can cancel the FORMAT command.

Formatting Different Types of Disks

At times, DOS may not know what type of disk you want to format. If you have a 5 1/4-inch, 360K drive or a 3 1/2-inch, 720K drive, you have no problems. These drives can use only one type of disk, so DOS always knows what type of disk is in the drive.

6

High-capacity disk drives can format more than one type of disk. If you have a 1.2M drive, you can use either 360K or 1.2M floppy disks. If you have a 1.44M drive, you can use either 720K or 1.44M floppy disks. In some cases, you must specify the disk type in the Format dialog box. The default type of disk is always the highest-capacity disk that can work in the drive.

When you format a new disk in a 1.2M drive, DOS assumes that it is a 1.2M disk, unless you tell it otherwise. So if you want to format a 1.2M disk in a 1.2M drive, you do not have to do anything special. If you want to format a 360K disk in a 1.2M drive, however, you must tell DOS the disk type. You specify the disk type in the Parameters text box in the Format dialog box.

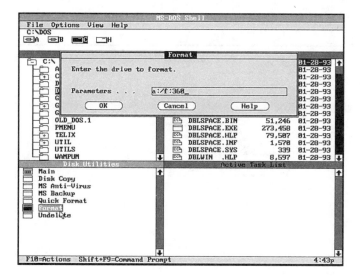

The information in this Parameters text box says to format a 360K disk in drive A. The /F: parameter is known as a size switch; however, it specifies the capacity of the disk, not its size.

Before you type the size parameter, you must clear the highlight in the text box. If you begin typing without clearing the highlight, the current parameter (a:) disappears. Press the End key or click the mouse pointer at the end of the parameter to cancel the highlight.

To specify the size, first type a slash (/) to let DOS know that a command switch follows. A *switch* is special information that gives instructions to a command. The size switch is /F: followed by the capacity of the disk. In this case, you would type **/F:360**.

To format a 720K disk in a 1.44M drive, use the switch **/F:720**. To format a disk in drive B, do not press End to clear the highlight, just type **b:** followed by the switch.

123

Looking at the FORMAT Command's Output

After the format is complete and you type a volume label and press Enter, you
see a report of the status of the disk. The report shows the total disk space and
total bytes available on the disk. If FORMAT detects *bad sectors* on the disk, it
marks them as unusable. FORMAT also reports how many bytes are unavailable because of bad sectors. Other information includes how many bytes each
allocation unit contains, how many allocation units are available on the disk
for storage, and the volume serial number that DOS automatically assigns to
every disk. An allocation unit is a group of sectors that DOS uses to keep track
of where files are on a disk.

The numbers for various sizes of disks vary, as shown in the following figures.

This report
shows disk
information for a
1.2M disk with
bad sectors.

```
Insert new diskette for drive A:
and press ENTER when ready...

Checking existing disk format.
Saving UNFORMAT information.
Verifying 1.2M
Format complete.

Volume label (11 characters, ENTER for none)?

    1213952 bytes total disk space
      15360 bytes in bad sectors
    1198592 bytes available on disk

        512 bytes in each allocation unit.
       2341 allocation units available on disk.

Volume Serial Number is 1B47-1CD3

Format another (Y/N)?
```

This report shows
disk information
for a 720K disk.

```
Insert new diskette for drive B:
and press ENTER when ready...

Checking existing disk format.
Saving UNFORMAT information.
Verifying 720K
Format complete.

Volume label (11 characters, ENTER for none)?

    730112 bytes total disk space
    730112 bytes available on disk

      1024 bytes in each allocation unit.
       713 allocation units available on disk.

Volume Serial Number is 2A65-1CD9

Format another (Y/N)?
```

Quick Formatting

If a floppy disk has been formatted before, you can clear the entire disk quickly by using the *quick format*. When you format a disk, DOS lays out the sectors, checks every track for bad sectors, and builds the directory and file allocation table. If the disk has been formatted before, you can skip most of this work and just clear the directory and file allocation table in a few seconds. You do not have to specify which type of disk is in the drive because DOS can determine the disk type from the previous format. To perform a quick format, choose Quick Format from the Disk Utilities program group.

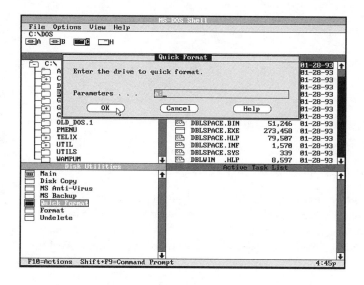

The Quick Format dialog box opens. A Quick Format proceeds just like a regular format except that it takes only a few seconds.

Learning FORMAT's Switch Options

You can add switches to modify the FORMAT command. You can add more than one switch if you separate each one with a slash. For example, the parameter **A:/F:360/S** in the Format dialog box uses two switches, /F and /S, as explained in the following sections.

The /S (Transfer System Files) Switch

The /S switch places the DOS system files on the formatted disk. Use this switch if you want to be able to boot your PC with that disk. You cannot see these hidden files in the disk directory list, but the files are there, along with COMMAND.COM.

Always keep at least one A drive–size floppy disk handy that contains the system files, in case you have trouble booting from your hard disk. You can then boot from the floppy disk to get to the hard disk and fix the problem.

This report is
for a 360K disk
formatted with
system files.

```
Insert new diskette for drive A:
and press ENTER when ready...

Checking existing disk format.
Saving UNFORMAT information.
Verifying 360K
Format complete.
System transferred

Volume label (11 characters, ENTER for none)? BOOT DISK

     362496 bytes total disk space
     131072 bytes used by system
     231424 bytes available on disk

       1024 bytes in each allocation unit.
        226 allocation units available on disk.

Volume Serial Number is 1A87-1CD0

Format another (Y/N)?
```

6

The /U (Unconditional Format) Switch

Normally, DOS tries to perform a safe format and save the information needed to unformat the disk. You can use the /U switch to override the safe format and tell DOS not to save the unformat information. You might use this switch to clear a disk of confidential data before you give the disk to someone else.

The /F (Size) Switch

The /F switch specifies the capacity of the formatted disk. Several /F size switch options enable you to format disks with less than the maximum capacity of the disk drive. For example, you can format disks for early-model computers or for computers that use the first versions of DOS, as follows:

Parameter	Disk
/F:160	Single-sided disk with DOS 1.x
/F:180	Single-sided disk
/F:320	Double-sided disk with DOS 1.x
/F:360	Double-sided, double-density 5 1/4-inch disk
/F:720	Double-sided, double-density 3 1/2-inch disk

126

You can specify the current default disk types as well. If you get a 2.88M drive or a future higher-capacity 5 1/4-inch drive, you may need these parameters:

Parameter	Disk
/F:1.2	1.2M high-density disk
/F:1.44	1.44M high-density disk

Versions older than DOS 5 did not use the /F switch. They used a variety of different switches (/1, /8, /B, /N, and /T) to accomplish the same thing.

Understanding FORMAT's Error Messages

6

The most common DOS error messages that occur during floppy disk formatting are rarely catastrophes. They are little more than statements suggesting that you did something wrong or that DOS had trouble carrying out the command. For example, if you reformat a completely full disk, there is no room to save the information that would allow the disk to be unformatted. You see a warning message that the disk cannot be unformatted. If you try to format a write-protected disk, for example, you see a message that the format cannot be completed.

The following sections describe three common formatting error messages.

Not Ready

If you respond to the Press any key when ready prompt without placing a disk in the disk drive, or if the drive door is open, DOS displays the message:

```
Not ready
Format another (Y/N)?
```

Just insert the disk, close the door if necessary, press Y and Enter to start the format. If you specified the wrong disk drive, press N and Enter. Then execute the command again with the correct drive letter.

```
Insert new diskette for drive B:
and press ENTER when ready...

Checking existing disk format.
Not ready
Format another (Y/N)?
```

This message means that DOS cannot read from the disk drive.

127

If the disk is in the drive and the drive door is closed and you get this error, the disk is probably write-protected. Take the disk out and check the write-protect tab.

To format a write-protected disk, remove the write-protect tape from a 5 1/4-inch disk or slide the tab on a 3 1/2-inch disk, reinsert the disk, and press Y and Enter at the prompt.

Bad Sectors

Although not a true error message, a bad-sectors report points out a possible problem with the disk.

If the FORMAT command detects unusable areas on the disk, you see a line describing the problem in the report.

```
Insert new diskette for drive A:
and press ENTER when ready...

Checking existing disk format.
Saving UNFORMAT information.
Verifying 1.2M
Format complete.

Volume label (11 characters, ENTER for none)?

    1213952 bytes total disk space
      15360 bytes in bad sectors
    1198592 bytes available on disk

        512 bytes in each allocation unit.
       2341 allocation units available on disk.

Volume Serial Number is 1B47-1CD3

Format another (Y/N)?
```

The bytes in bad sectors message means that MS-DOS found bad sectors on the disk. These sectors cannot be used to hold information. The total amount of free space on the disk is reduced by the number of bytes in the bad sectors.

Try reformatting the disk. If it still has bad sectors and is a new disk, you can have your dealer replace the disk, or you can use the disk as is. Before you do either, though, try formatting the disk again.

If you get a very large number of bad sectors, you may have tried to format a 360K disk as a 1.2M disk. DOS tries to format the disk, but after the computer grinds and chugs, you end up with mostly bad sectors. Format the disk again with the /F:360 switch.

Disk Unusable

The worst disk-error message you can get is the following:

```
Invalid media or Track 0 bad - disk unusable
```

```
Insert new diskette for drive B:
and press ENTER when ready...

Checking existing disk format.
Existing format differs from that specified.
This disk cannot be unformatted.
Proceed with Format (Y/N)?y
Formatting 1.44M
Invalid media or Track 0 bad - disk unusable.
Format terminated.
Format another (Y/N)?
```

This disk may have a scratched surface; DOS couldn't read disk-level information on the first track.

You may receive this error message for two possible reasons. If you try to format a 720K disk as a 1.44M disk, you will get this message. Format the disk again with the /F:720 switch.

This message also can mean that the areas on the disk that hold important DOS system data are bad. If you get the disk unusable error message on a new disk, take it back to your dealer. If the disk is old, throw it away. Disks are inexpensive and, in this case, should be discarded. Trying to use a bad disk is being penny-wise and pound-foolish.

Cautions about Formatting a Hard Disk

Hard disks are a desirable part of a computer system because of their speed and storage capacity. Just like floppy disks, you must format them before you use them. Unless you are familiar with the procedure, however, *do not attempt to format your hard disk.*

Many computer dealers install the operating system on a computer's hard disk before you receive it. If your dealer has installed an applications program, such as a word processor, *do not* format the hard disk. If you reformat your hard disk, you will erase all programs and data.

Should you ever attempt to reformat your hard disk, first perform a complete backup. You also should have a bootable floppy disk ready that contains a copy of the DOS Backup program. Que's *Using MS-DOS 6*, Special Edition, devotes several pages to preparing and formatting a hard disk. If you must format your hard disk, consult that book or your computer's manual.

6

Remember that the FORMAT command erases all the data a disk contains. Always check the directory of the disk you want to format; it may hold data you need. Check the command line thoroughly when you use the FORMAT command.

Lessons Learned

- Different types of floppy disks and disk drives are available.
- You have to match the disks you buy to the disk drive in your computer.
- You can give your disks electronic labels.
- You can "quick format" a previously formatted disk in a few seconds.
- You can format a floppy disk to include the DOS system files and use this disk to boot your computer.
- Error messages can be helpful. Most of them do not indicate an impending catastrophe.
- Hard disks demand special treatment and care when you use the FORMAT command.

In the next chapter, you learn the most important DOS commands to manage your data.

6

Maintaining Files

Disk files are the primary storage place for data and programs. You must know how to manage these files if you want to be in control of your work. In this chapter, you learn how to complete the following tasks: copy the contents of one disk to another disk and compare them for accuracy, copy single or groups of files between disks, copy files with the same or different file names, erase or rename files in groups, and use the COPY command to enhance disk organization. You also learn how to erase unneeded files and rename existing files.

When you work with floppy disks, keep the following ideas in mind:

- Always keep the labels on your disks current. Use a felt-tipped pen and indicate the contents on the disk label as you work. Disks not labeled or labeled incorrectly are an invitation to lost data. If you do not label disks, you might mistake them for blank, unformatted disks.

- Never use a ball point pen to write on a label that has been placed on a 5 1/4-inch floppy disk. The jacket doesn't keep the pen point from possibly damaging the magnetic media and harming the disk.

Copying and moving files with the Shell

Deleting files

Renaming files

Using Disk Copy to copy disks

Key Terms Used in This Chapter	
Point-and-shoot	To use a mouse to select files and copy or move the files visually by dragging the mouse pointer to the destination.
Drag	To move the mouse pointer while holding down the left mouse button.
Source	The disk or file from which you are copying or moving files.
Destination	The disk or file to which you are copying or moving files.
Target	Synonymous with *destination*.
Current directory	The directory that DOS uses as the default directory. The current directory is highlighted in the Directory Tree area in the DOS Shell.
Overwrite	To write new information over old information in a disk file.

Copying and Moving Files with the Shell

Copying and moving are probably two of the most frequently used tasks in the DOS Shell. Copy, Move, and their shortcut equivalents are powerful commands. You should not, however, use Copy or Move—or Rename or Delete, for that matter—if your mind is occupied with matters unrelated to your PC. Take a nap, watch TV, or drink coffee first. These commands are DOS power tools, and you should use them only when you are alert and careful.

In the DOS Shell, you can copy and move files by using the keyboard and the DOS Shell File menu. You also can copy and move files by using a mouse. Using a mouse greatly simplifies copying and moving files. A mouse gives you a point-and-shoot method of copying and moving files. When you use the point-and-shoot method, you select the files, hold the mouse button down, and drag the mouse pointer to the destination disk or directory. You do not need to type commands or use menus.

The capability to select the files to copy and move is one advantage of the DOS Shell. You can select a single file, a contiguous group of files, or even a noncontiguous group of files.

Understanding the Principles of Copy and Move

Copying or moving a file or group of files is a relatively straightforward process. You have a *source* file you select to copy or move, and you have a *destination* where the file will finally reside.

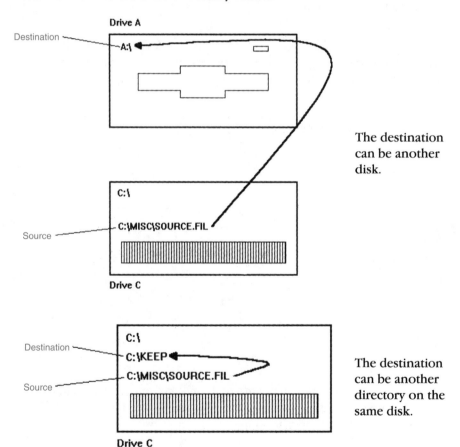

The destination can be another disk.

The destination can be another directory on the same disk.

133

Selecting to copy a file is different from selecting to move a file. Copying a file gives you two identical files, each stored in a different place. While the source file remains in its original location, an exact duplicate of the file now resides in a second location. If you copy the file more than once, the file can reside in many locations.

You should avoid having multiple copies of the same file in many locations without a reason. If you have copies of a data file in multiple directories on your hard disk, you can update one copy and leave several out-of-date copies on the disk. Because they all have the same name, you easily could use an old copy instead of an updated one.

Generally speaking, when you copy a file, you do so for one of two reasons: you want to make a backup copy to protect the original file, or you want to modify the copy, saving you the time of creating a brand new file. In Chapter 10, you learn other techniques to make backup copies of files.

To copy a file means to place an exact duplicate of it in another location without affecting the source file.

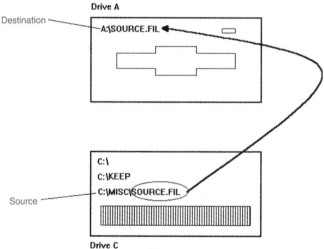

Periodically, you may decide that a file no longer belongs on a certain disk or in a certain directory, so you will want to place a copy of the source file at a new destination and remove the source file from its original location. You may want to move a file for one of two reasons: you have restructured your hard disk and the file no longer belongs in the directory it is in, or you no longer use the file and therefore decide to move it to a floppy disk for storage.

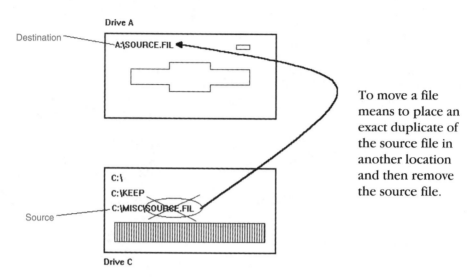

To move a file means to place an exact duplicate of the source file in another location and then remove the source file.

Selecting the Correct View

You learned in Chapter 4 that the DOS Shell has multiple views. The view you usually use is the Program/File Lists view. This view displays the contents of the current disk drive and the programs you can start from the Shell.

For copying or moving files using the same disk, the Program/File Lists view is just fine. You can display the files you need to copy or move and the directory tree of the drive, enabling you to determine the source and destination of the copy or move.

If you are copying files from one disk to another, the capability to view the contents of both disks is quite helpful. Selecting the Dual File Lists view displays the contents of both disks, enabling you to ensure the correct source and destination.

135

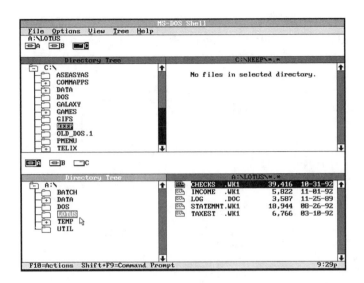

In this example, the Dual File Lists view enables you to see both the source files you plan to copy from drive A and the destination directory, C:\KEEP.

Follow these steps to use the keyboard to select Dual File Lists view:

1. Press [Alt] and then press **V** to activate the View menu.
2. Select **D**ual File Lists and press [↵Enter].
3. Press [Tab⇄] to switch between the two file lists.

Follow these steps to use the mouse to select Dual File Lists view:

1. Point to the View menu and click the left mouse button.
2. Point to the **D**ual File Lists option and click the left mouse button.
3. Point to one of the file lists and click the left mouse button to switch between the two file lists.

You can use the preceding steps to switch among the different views, but instead of selecting **D**ual File Lists, you select the view you want.

Selecting Source Files

Before you can copy or move a file or group of files, you must select the files you want to copy or move. When you select a file, DOS highlights that file name. When you execute a command, DOS performs the command on the selected files.

You select files in many different ways. You can, for example, select a single file, or you can select multiple files. If you select multiple files, you can select files that are listed together. Or, you can select files that are not listed together. You also can select groups of files that are not together. The combinations are nearly endless.

This section outlines a few of the most common ways to select files. Although selecting files is easier with a mouse, selecting files with the keyboard is not a difficult task.

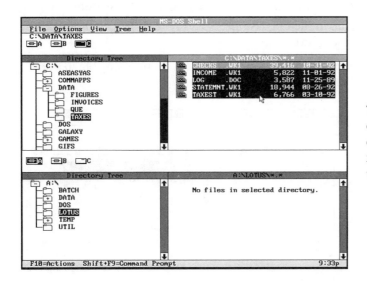

To manipulate all of the files in a directory, you first must select them all.

Follow these steps to select all files in a directory by using the keyboard:

1. Press [Ctrl] and the drive letter to activate the correct drive. Press [Ctrl]-C, for example, to activate drive C.
2. Press [Tab ⇵] to activate the Directory Tree area.
3. Using [↑] and [↓], select the correct directory.
4. Press [Tab ⇵] to activate the File List.
5. Press [Alt]-F to select the File menu.
6. Choose Select All from the File menu.

As a shortcut to select all files in the File List, perform steps 1 through 4 and then press Ctrl-/, the Select All shortcut key combination.

To deselect all files in the File List by using the keyboard, follow these steps:

1. Press [Alt]-F to select the File menu.
2. Choose Deselect All from the File menu.

As a shortcut to deselect all files in the File List, press Ctrl-\.

Follow these steps to select all files in a directory by using the mouse:

1. Point to the correct drive letter and click the left mouse button.

2. Point to the correct directory in the Directory Tree and click the left mouse button.

3. Point to the first file in the File List and click the left mouse button.

4. Point to the last file in the File List, press and hold ⇧Shift, and then click the left mouse button.

To deselect all files in the File List by using a mouse, point to any file in the File List and click the left mouse button.

You can easily select a contiguous group of files for processing.

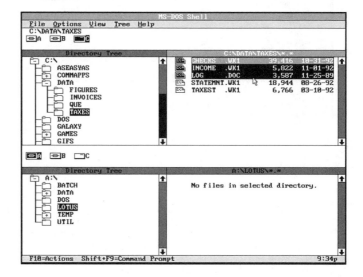

Follow these steps to select a contiguous group of files in a File List by using the keyboard:

1. Press Ctrl and the drive letter to activate the correct drive. Press Ctrl-C, for example, to activate drive C.

2. Press Tab⇆ to activate the Directory Tree.

3. Using ↑ and ↓, select the correct directory.

4. Press Tab⇆ to activate the File List.

5. Using ↑ and ↓, select the first file in the group.

6. Press and hold ⇧Shift and then use ↓ to select the last file in the group.

To deselect the contiguous group of files in the File List by using the keyboard, press the up- and down-arrow keys.

Follow these steps to select a contiguous group of files in a directory by using the mouse:

1. Point to the correct drive letter and click the left mouse button.

2. Point to the correct directory in the Directory Tree and click the left mouse button.

3. Point to the first file in the File List of the group you want to select, and click the left mouse button.

4. Point to the last file in the File List of the group you want to select. Press and hold ⇧Shift and then click the left mouse button.

To deselect the contiguous group of files in the File List by using the mouse, point to any file in the File List and click the left mouse button.

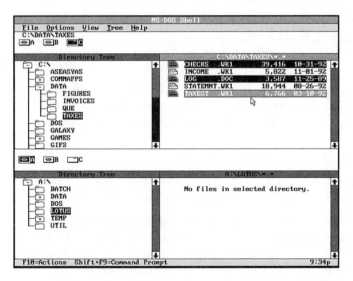

You can select non-contiguous files for copying, moving, or deleting.

Follow these steps to select a noncontiguous group of files in a File List by using the keyboard:

1. Press Ctrl and the drive letter to activate the correct drive. Press Ctrl-C, for example, to activate drive C.

2. Press Tab⁚ to activate the Directory Tree.

3. Using ↑ and ↓, select the correct directory.

4. Press Tab⁚ to activate the File List.

5. Using ⬆ and ⬇, select the first file in the group.

6. Turn on Add mode by pressing ⇧Shift-F8. The word *Add* appears in the status line at the bottom of the display.

7. Press ⬇ to move to the next file you want to select.

8. Press the space bar to select the file. If you select a file in error, press the space bar again to deselect the file.

9. Repeat steps 7 and 8 until all files are selected.

10. Press ⇧Shift-F8 to turn off Add mode.

To deselect the noncontiguous group of files in the File List by using the keyboard, press the up- and down-arrow keys with Add mode off.

Follow these steps to select a noncontiguous group of files in a File List by using the mouse:

1. Point to the correct drive letter and click the left mouse button.

2. Point to the correct directory in the Directory Tree and click the left mouse button.

3. Point to the first file you want to select in the File List and click the left mouse button.

4. Point to the next file you want to select in the File List, press and hold Ctrl, and then click the left mouse button. If you select a file in error, press and hold Ctrl and click the left mouse button again to deselect the file.

5. Repeat step 4 until all files have been selected.

To deselect the noncontiguous group of files in the File List by using the mouse, point to any file in the File List and click the left mouse button.

Using the steps outlined, you can select any combination of files. Sometimes you can make selecting multiple files easier by changing the order of the files in the File List. You can do so by using **File Display Options** from the Options menu. If you want to copy the files you created today to another disk, for example, you view the File List by date in descending order. All the files created today appear at the beginning of the list.

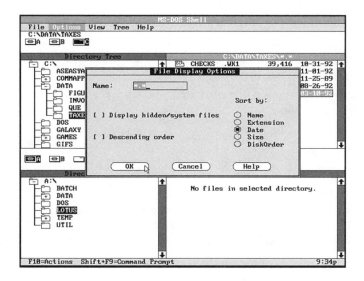

You can change
the sort order of
the files in the
File List to make
file selection
easier.

Copying Files between Disks

You can copy one file or many files from one disk to another. Although you
usually copy files to another disk to preserve a copy of the file, copying also
is useful when you need to transfer files from one computer to another.

Follow these steps to copy files from one disk to another by using the keyboard (if you are copying to or from a floppy disk, be sure that the disk is in
the correct drive):

1. Press Alt-V to open the View menu.

2. Press D to choose Dual File Lists.

3. Press Tab until you activate the lower Directory Tree (the destination directory tree).

4. Press Ctrl and the drive letter to activate the destination drive.
   Press Ctrl-A, for example, to activate drive A.

5. Press Tab to activate the destination directory tree and select the
   destination directory if the destination disk contains directories.

6. Using ⌞Tab↹⌟, activate the upper Directory Tree (the source directory tree).

7. Press ⌞Ctrl⌟ and the drive letter to activate the source drive. Press ⌞Ctrl⌟-C, for example, to activate drive C.

8. Press ⌞Tab↹⌟ to activate the source directory tree, and use ⌞↑⌟ and ⌞↓⌟ to select the correct directory.

9. Press ⌞Tab↹⌟ to activate the File List.

10. Select the files you want to copy.

11. Press ⌞Alt⌟-F to open the File menu.

12. Press ⌞C⌟ to choose Copy from the File menu.

    The Copy File dialog box appears on-screen. Two text boxes appear in the dialog box: the From text box displays the files you have selected; the To text box is where you type the name of the destination disk.

13. In the To text box, type the destination drive name and directory, such as A:\, and press ⌞↵Enter⌟.

You can use the shortcut key F8 rather than perform steps 11 and 12.

Using the mouse, follow these steps to copy files to another disk:

1. Open the View menu and select Dual File Lists.

2. In the lower Directory Tree (the destination directory tree), point to the drive letter to which you want to copy the files and click the left mouse button.

3. Select the destination directory if the destination disk contains directories.

4. In the upper Directory Tree (the source directory tree), point to the drive letter from which you are copying the files and click the left mouse button.

5. Point to the correct directory in the source directory tree and click the left mouse button.

6. Select the files you want to copy from the File List.

7. Point to one of the selected files, and press and hold the left mouse button.

8. Drag the selected files to the destination directory tree.

7

9. Release the left mouse button to complete the copy.

10. If mouse confirmation is selected, the Confirm Mouse Operation dialog box appears. You must choose Yes to complete the copy. This confirmation safeguards you in case you selected the wrong disk. If you did select the wrong disk, choose No in the Confirm Mouse Operations dialog box.

This set of steps illustrates the point-and-shoot method of copying files with a mouse. This method is very accurate because you select by sight both the files you want to copy and the destination drive.

As you drag the files, the mouse pointer changes from an arrow to one of three other pointers. The first type of pointer is a circle with a line through it, which indicates that you are dragging the files to an invalid area of the screen. If you release the mouse button in an invalid area, nothing happens; no files are copied.

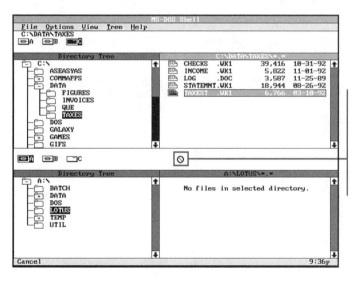

When you drag files through an invalid area of the screen, the mouse pointer looks like a circle with a line through it.

When dragging one file through a valid area, the pointer looks like a file icon. As the pointer crosses each directory, the directory becomes selected. At the lower left corner of the screen, the status line indicates the selected directory as well.

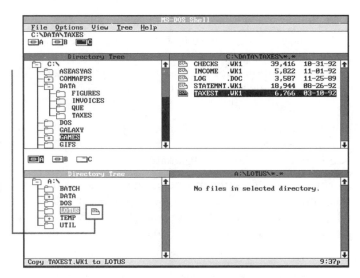

The pointer appears as a file icon when you have dragged a file to a valid area for copying. The status line confirms the selected directory.

7

The pointer appears as three stacked boxes when you drag more than one file.

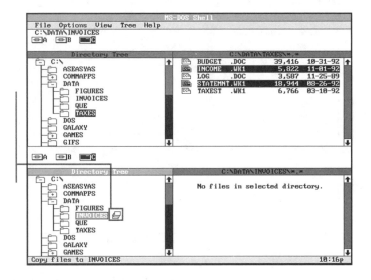

When the correct directory is selected, release the mouse button. DOS copies the files to this directory.

Copying a File to the Same Disk Directory

One rule of DOS is that no two files in a single directory can have the same name. Why doesn't DOS allow this?

Think of a directory on a disk as a house on a block. Suppose that two people named Fred Smith live in the same house. When you want one of them and call, "Hey, Fred Smith!" both of them come running to you. To avoid confusion, you might call one Freddy Smith and the other Fred Smith.

The same dilemma faces DOS. You cannot have two files named MEMO1229.DOC, for example, in the same directory. You can have, however, one file named MEMO1229.DOC and another named MEMO1229.TXT. Although the root name—MEMO1229—is the same, the file extensions are different—DOC and TXT. DOS can differentiate between the two files based on the extension.

When you copy a file to the same directory, you must give it a different name. Perhaps you have a file called EXPJAN93.WK1 that contains your expenses for January. Now it is time to begin creating a file with your expenses for February. Suppose that your expenses for each month are quite similar. Rather than create a brand new file, you copy the file EXPJAN93.WK1, naming the new file EXPFEB93.WK1. You then can edit EXPFEB93.WK1 for the correct February expenses. When you use the Shell, you can copy only one file to the same directory at a time.

Follow these steps to copy a file to the same directory by using the keyboard (if you are copying using a floppy disk, be sure that the disk is in the correct drive):

1. Press `Ctrl` and the drive letter to activate the correct drive. Press `Ctrl`-C, for example, to activate drive C.
2. Using `Tab⇆`, activate the upper Directory Tree.
3. Using `↑` and `↓`, select the correct directory.
4. Press `Tab⇆` to activate the File List and select the file you want to copy.
5. Press `Alt`-F to select the File menu.
6. Choose Copy from the File menu.

   The Copy File dialog box appears on-screen. Two text boxes appear in the dialog box: the From text box contains the file you selected; the To text box is for the destination file. The box already displays the directory path.
7. In the To text box, type the new file name and press `↵Enter`.

   The new file appears in the file list.

7

145

You can use the shortcut key F8 rather than perform steps 5 and 6.

Using the mouse, follow these steps to copy files to the same directory:

1. Point to the correct drive letter you want to activate and click the left mouse button.

2. Point to the correct directory in the Directory Tree and click the left mouse button.

3. From the File List, select the file you want to copy.

4. Click the File menu.

5. Click Copy in the File menu.

   The Copy File dialog box appears on-screen. Two text boxes appear in the dialog box: the From text box contains the file you have selected; the To text box is for the destination file. The box already displays the directory path.

6. In the To text box, type the new file name and click OK with the mouse.

   The new file appears in the File List.

Copying Files across Directories

Copying a file or a group of files from one directory to another on a disk is just like copying a file or a group of files from one disk to another. The only difference is that the destination is another directory on the same disk instead of just another disk.

Even though the source and destination are on the same disk, you do not have to worry about file names being the same. Remember the dilemma that occurred when two people named Fred Smith lived in the same house? When you called for Fred Smith, both came running. Suppose that Fred Smith #1 moved to the house next door. Now there is no confusion. When you want Fred Smith #1, you go to his house. To get Fred Smith #2, you go to his house.

Different directories on a disk are similar to different houses on the same block. Although each directory is on the same disk, each directory is a separate entity, much as each house has its own address.

In many cases, using Dual File Lists is easier than using a Single File List when you copy files between directories, but using Dual File Lists isn't required.

Many times, you will use a Single File List to copy files between directories because both the source directory and the destination directory are visible in the same Directory List. The following examples use Dual File Lists.

To copy files from one directory to another by using the keyboard, follow these steps:

1. Press [Ctrl] and the drive letter to activate the source drive. Press [Ctrl]-C, for example, to activate drive C.
2. Press [Alt]-V to open the View menu.
3. Choose Dual File Lists from the View menu.
4. Press [Tab⇄] to activate the lower Directory Tree (the destination directory tree).
5. Using [↑] and [↓], select the destination directory.
6. Using [Tab⇄], activate the upper Directory Tree (the source directory tree).
7. Using [↑] and [↓], select the source directory.
8. Press [Tab⇄] to activate the Files List and then select the files you want to copy.
9. Press [Alt]-F to open the File menu.
10. Choose Copy from the File menu.

    The Copy File dialog box appears on-screen. Two text boxes appear in the dialog box: the From text box contains the files you selected; the To text box is where you specify the destination directory.
11. In the To text box, type the directory name to which you want to copy the files (for example, type \MISC) and press [⏎Enter]. Because the source and destination directories are on the same disk, you do not have to type the disk letter.

You can use the shortcut key F8 rather than perform steps 9 and 10.

With a mouse, you use the point-and-shoot method to copy files to a different directory on the same disk. Follow these steps:

1. In the Directory Tree, point to the source drive letter and click the left mouse button.
2. Open the View menu and choose Dual File Lists. You do not have to use the Dual File Lists display when the source and destination directories are on the same disk, but the display enables you to see the files in both directories at the same time.

7

3. Use the scroll bar if necessary to select the destination directory.

4. Point to the source directory in the Directory Tree and click the left mouse button.

5. Select the files you want to copy.

6. Point to one of the files selected with the mouse, and press and hold the left mouse button.

   The DOS Shell defaults to a Move function when you drag files on the same disk. Press and hold Ctrl to change the function to Copy.

7. Drag the selected files to the destination directory.

8. Release the left mouse button and Ctrl to complete the copy.

9. If mouse confirmation is selected, the Confirm Mouse Operation dialog box appears. You must select Yes to complete the copy. This confirmation safeguards you in case you selected the wrong directory. If you did select the wrong directory, select No in the Confirm Mouse Operation dialog box.

7

Copying Safety versus Speed

In its default configuration, the DOS Shell prompts you for confirmation before completing an action that might change or delete an existing file. When you copy files over files with the same name, for example, the Replace File Confirmation box appears on-screen. This safety feature helps you to avoid possible disasters.

The Shell uses three types of confirmation prompts:

- Confirm on Delete prompts you before DOS deletes a file or directory.
- Confirm on Replace prompts you before DOS replaces a file by moving or copying.
- Confirm on Mouse Operation prompts you before DOS completes any mouse action that involves moving or copying files.

The Confirm Mouse Operation dialog box requires that you accept a mouse operation before it is performed.

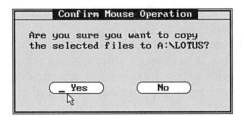

148

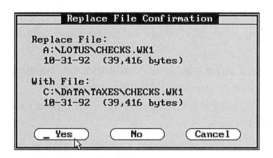

The Replace File Confirmation dialog box displays the file being replaced, the replacement file, and the size and creation date of each file.

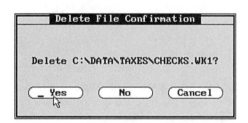

The Delete File Confirmation dialog box requires you to accept a deletion before it is performed.

You can disable these confirmation prompts to speed up the copy process. You can disable one or more of the three prompts. Working without confirmation prompts, however, can be risky.

Follow these steps to change confirmation by using the keyboard:

1. Press [Alt]-O to open the Options menu.
2. Select Confirmation from the Options menu.
3. Press [Tab ↹] to select Confirm on Delete, Confirm on Replace, or Confirm on Mouse Operation.

   Beside each confirmation option is a selection box. If an X is in the box, confirmation is enabled. A blank box means that confirmation is disabled.
4. Press the **space bar** to toggle between disabling and enabling the confirmation option.
5. When finished, press [↵Enter] to save the changes to the dialog box, or press [Esc] to abandon the changes.

Follow these steps to change confirmation by using the mouse:

1. Click the Options menu.
2. Click Confirmation from the Options menu.

149

3. Click Confirm on Delete, Confirm on Replace, or Confirm on Mouse Operation with the mouse to toggle between disabling and enabling the confirmation option.

   Beside each option is a selection box. If an X is in the box, confirmation is enabled. A blank box means that confirmation is disabled.

4. When finished, click OK to save the changes to the dialog box, or click Cancel to abandon the changes.

Any changes that you make to these confirmation options become permanent until you change them again. Unless you are sure that you will not erase or copy over files in error, you should leave all confirmations enabled.

Moving Files between Disks

While you are working on a file, you can copy that file regularly to a disk for safekeeping. While working on the 1993 budget, for example, you can copy the budget file daily so that you have a current backup of the file, just in case something happens to the original. When you complete the 1993 budget and print the necessary reports and graphs, you most likely will copy the file to a disk for backup storage and delete the file from your active disk. In other words, you will move the file from your current disk to another disk.

Moving files from one disk to another is very similar to copying files from one disk to another. In fact, the process is identical, except for one menu choice. Follow these steps to move files from one disk to another by using the keyboard (be sure that the disk is in the correct drive):

1. Press Alt-V to open the View menu.

2. Choose Dual File Lists from the View menu.

3. Press Tab until you activate the lower Directory Tree (the destination directory tree).

4. Press Ctrl and the drive letter to activate the destination drive. Press Ctrl-A, for example, to activate drive A.

5. Press Tab to activate the destination directory tree and select the destination directory if the destination disk contains directories.

6. Using Tab, activate the upper Directory Tree (the source directory tree).

7. Press Ctrl and the drive letter to activate the source drive. Press Ctrl-C, for example, to activate drive C.

8. Press Tab to activate the source directory tree and use ↑ and ↓ to select the correct directory.

150

9. Press [Tab⁻] to activate the File List, and then select the files you want to move.

10. Press [Alt]-**F** to open the File menu.

11. Choose **M**ove from the File menu.

   The Move File dialog box appears on-screen. Two text boxes appear in the dialog box: the From text box contains the files you have selected; the To text box is where you specify the destination drive and directory.

12. In the To text box, type the destination drive and directory (for example, type **A:**) and press [↵Enter].

You can use the shortcut key F7 rather than perform steps 10 and 11.

Use the point-and-shoot method for moving files between disks with a mouse. Follow these steps:

1. Open the View menu and select **D**ual File Lists.

2. In the lower Directory Tree (the destination directory tree), point to the drive letter to which you want to move the files, and then click the left mouse button.

3. Select the destination directory if the destination disk contains directories.

4. In the upper Directory Tree (the source directory tree), point to the correct drive letter from which you want to move the files, and then click the left mouse button.

5. Point to the correct directory in the source directory tree and click the left mouse button.

6. Select the files you want to move.

7. Point to one of the files selected with the mouse, and press and hold the left mouse button.

   The DOS Shell defaults to a Copy function when you drag files between disks. Press and hold [Alt] to change the function to Move.

8. Drag the selected files to the destination directory tree.

9. Release the left mouse button and [Alt] to complete the move.

10. If mouse confirmation is selected, the Confirm Mouse Operation dialog box appears. You must select Yes to complete the move. This confirmation safeguards you in case you selected the wrong disk. If you selected the wrong disk, select No in the Confirm Mouse Operation dialog box.

7

The mouse pointer changes when you drag files for moving, just as it does during copying. It indicates an invalid area with a circle with a line through it and a valid area with three stacked boxes or a file icon.

Notice the message line when you are dragging files with the mouse. If you forget to press the Alt key, the message line tells you that you are copying files rather than moving them. When you use the dragging method to move files, you must hold down the Alt key before you press and hold the left mouse button.

The status line indicates that the files are being moved.

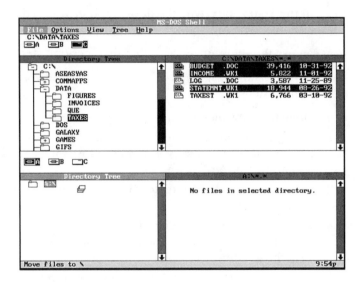

Moving Files to Another Directory

Moving files from one directory to another is similar to copying files from one directory to another.

In many cases, using Dual File Lists is easier than using only a Single File List when you move files between directories, but isn't required. Many times, you will use only a Single File List to move files between directories because both the source directory and the destination directory are visible in the same Directory List. The following examples use Dual File Lists.

To move files from one directory to another by using the keyboard, follow these steps:

1. Press Ctrl and the drive letter to activate the source drive. Press Ctrl-C, for example, to activate drive C.

2. Press Alt-V to open the View menu.

3. Choose Dual File Lists from the View menu.

4. Press Tab↹ to activate the lower Directory Tree (the destination directory tree).

5. Using ↑ and ↓, select the destination directory.

6. Using Tab↹, activate the upper Directory Tree (the source directory tree).

7. Using ↑ and ↓, select the source directory.

8. Press Tab↹ to activate the File List and select the files you want to move.

9. Press Alt-F to open the File menu.

10. Choose Move from the File menu.

    The Move File dialog box appears on-screen. Two text boxes appear in the dialog box: the From text box contains the files you selected; the To text box is where you specify the destination disk and directory name.

11. In the To text box, type the destination directory name (for example, type \MISC) and press ↵Enter. Because the source and destination directories are on the same disk, you do not have to type the disk letter.

You can use the shortcut key F7 rather than perform steps 9 and 10.

Using the mouse, follow these steps to move files to another directory:

1. In the Directory Tree point to the source drive letter and click the left mouse button.

2. Open the View menu and select Dual File Lists to see exactly where you are moving the files.

3. Use the scroll bar if necessary to select the destination directory.

4. Point to the correct directory in the source directory tree and click the left mouse button.

5. Select the files you want to move.

6. Point to one of the files selected with the mouse, and press and hold the left mouse button.

7. Drag the selected files to the destination directory.

8. Release the left mouse button to complete the move.

9. If mouse confirmation is selected, the Confirm Mouse Operation dialog box appears. You must select Yes to complete the move. This confirmation safeguards you in case you selected the wrong directory. If you selected the wrong directory, select No in the Confirm Mouse Operation dialog box.

Deleting Files

When you no longer need a file, you can remove the file from the disk. Erasing old files you no longer use is good computer housekeeping. Free space on disks, especially hard disks, gets scarce if you do not erase unneeded files.

As with other tasks you perform with the DOS Shell, you can use the keyboard or mouse to select the file or files you want to delete. You also can use a command from the menu or a shortcut key to remove the files. This section explains how to delete files.

Deleting files is not a difficult task. The steps for deleting files with a keyboard and those for using a mouse are nearly identical to each other. Follow these steps to delete a file by using the keyboard:

1. If you need to make another disk drive active, press Ctrl and the drive letter to activate the drive. Press Ctrl-C, for example, to activate drive C.

2. Press Tab↹ to activate the Directory Tree. Use ↑ and ↓ to select the correct directory.

3. Press Tab↹ to activate the File List for the current directory.

4. Select the file or files you want to delete.

5. Press Alt-F to select the File menu.

6. Choose Delete from the File menu.

154

7. Follow the dialog boxes that appear on-screen. (If you are deleting a single file and Delete Confirmation is disabled, DOS simply deletes the file(s). No dialog boxes appear.)

   The Delete File dialog box appears on-screen if you selected more than one file in step 4. The text box contained in the dialog box displays all the files you selected. You can press Tab↹ to select this text box and then use the arrow keys to review the file selections if all the files do not fit on-screen at one time.

8. Choose OK to continue with the deletion process, or Cancel to discontinue the process.

   If Delete Confirmation is enabled, the Delete File Confirmation dialog box appears on-screen. You must press ↵Enter to delete each file as its name is displayed. The file or files are deleted from the disk.

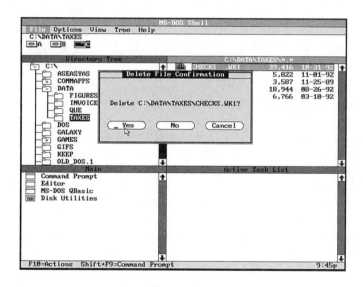

The DOS Shell default of confirming a file deletion can keep you from accidentally deleting the wrong file.

To use the mouse to delete files, follow these steps:

1. If you need to make another disk drive active, click the correct drive icon.

2. Click the directory from which you want to delete files. Use the scroll bar to view directories not displayed on-screen.

3. Select the file or files you want to delete.

4. Select the File menu.

5. Select Delete from the File menu.

   If Delete Confirmation is enabled, you must click OK in the Delete File Confirmation dialog box to delete the file. If you have selected more than one file to delete, the Delete File dialog box appears first. You can review the selected file names in the text box before clicking OK or Cancel.

Whether you use the keyboard or the mouse, after you select the file or files you want to delete, you can press the Del key to delete the files instead of selecting Delete from the File menu.

Renaming Files

From time to time, you may want to rename a file. If you created a file with the wrong name—such as TAXAS.WK1 instead of TAXES.WK1—you would want to rename it.

Suppose that you have a file called BUDGET.DOC that contains information about your current household budget. At the end of 1992, you want to start a new budget called BUDGET.DOC for 1993. You cannot have two files with the same name in the same directory, so you rename BUDGET.DOC to BUDGET92.DOC.

Follow these steps to rename a file by using the keyboard:

1. Press Ctrl and a drive letter to activate the correct drive. Press Ctrl-C, for example, to activate drive C.

2. Press Tab↹ to activate the Directory Tree, and then use ↑ and ↓ to select the correct directory.

3. Select the file you want to rename.

4. Press Alt-F to open the File menu.

5. Choose Rename from the File menu.

   The Rename File dialog box appears on-screen, with the current file name displayed.

6. In the New name text box, type the new file name and press ↵Enter.

Follow these steps to rename a file by using the mouse:

1. Point to the correct drive letter and click the left mouse button.

2. Point to the correct directory in the Directory Tree and click the left mouse button.

3. Select the file you want to rename.

4. Point to the File menu and click the left mouse button.

5. Point to the Rename option and click the left mouse button.

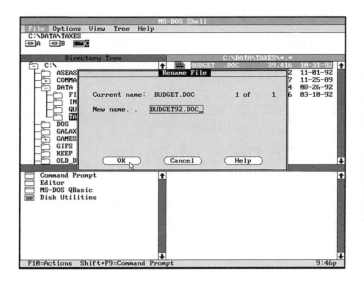

The Rename File dialog box appears on-screen. The current file name is listed above the text box in which you enter the new name.

6. In the New name text box, type the new file name and then click OK.

To rename more than one file in a directory, select the files you want to rename and choose Rename from the File menu. DOS presents you with a separate Rename File dialog box for every selected file. When you complete one dialog box, DOS renames that file and shows you the dialog box for the next file. The Rename command does not have a shortcut key.

You can use the same technique to rename a directory. Just select a directory name with the keyboard or mouse, and then choose Rename from the File menu.

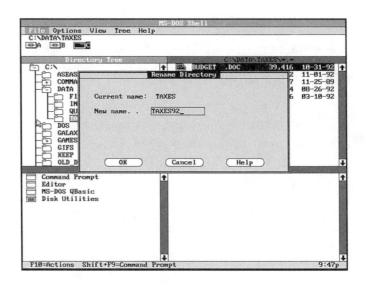

To rename a directory, select the directory and then choose **Rename** from the File menu. Enter the new directory name in the Rename Directory dialog box.

7 Using Disk Copy To Copy Disks

You learned how to copy one or more files on a disk. You also can duplicate all the files and directories from one floppy disk to another with the Disk Copy command. This chapter has taught you to execute commands from menus. You do not execute Disk Copy from menus, but from a program group at the bottom of the DOS Shell display. Disk Copy is in the Disk Utilities program group.

When you use Disk Copy, DOS executes the DISKCOPY command to make an exact copy of another disk. DOS reads the input, or source, disk and then writes the data to another disk—the destination, or target, disk. Any files on the destination disk are lost.

Disk Copy is good to use when you want to make backup copies of program disks. You then can store the original disks in a safe place. Disk Copy also copies the system files from a bootable source disk to make a copy that is bootable.

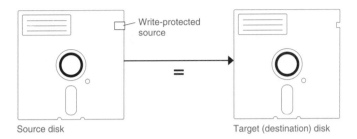

Source disk   Target (destination) disk

Disk Copy creates a duplicate of an entire disk. Both the source disk and the destination disk must be the same size and capacity. You cannot use Disk Copy to duplicate a 5 1/4-inch disk onto a 3 1/2-inch disk or vice versa. Que's *Using MS-DOS 6*, Special Edition, provides even more information on Disk Copy.

If you have two disk drives, both the same size, using Disk Copy is a breeze. Simply place your source disk into drive A, the source drive. Place the destination disk into drive B, the destination drive.

If you have only one disk drive to use for disk duplication, you must use the same disk drive as both the source and the destination. DOS tells you when to insert the source disk and when to insert the destination disk as it makes the duplicate. You may have to switch disks a number of times before the Disk Copy is complete.

To run Disk Copy, first open the Disk Utilities program group, and then select the Disk Copy program. The Disk Copy dialog box appears.

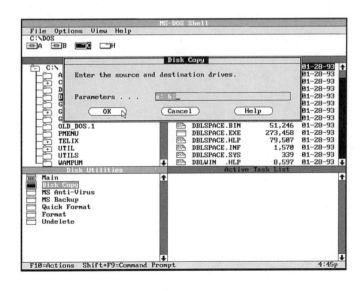

The parameters in the Disk Copy dialog box specify the source and target disk drives.

159

Follow these steps to duplicate a disk by using the keyboard:

1. Press Tab↹ until you select the Program Group area.

2. Press ↑ or ↓ until you select Disk Utilities.

3. Press ↵Enter to open the Disk Utilities program group.

4. Press ↓ to select Disk Copy and then press ↵Enter.

   The Disk Copy dialog box appears on-screen.

   The default parameters are a: b:, meaning that drive A is the source and drive B is the destination drive. If you have only one disk drive, DOS assigns it to both the source and the destination.

5. If necessary, enter different parameters. For instance, if you want drive B to be the source and drive A to be the destination, type **B: A:** in the Parameters text box.

   If you have two disk drives of different sizes, you need to designate one drive as both the source and the destination. Specify the correct drive for the size disk you want to copy. For example, to copy a 5 1/4-inch disk on a computer with a 5 1/4-inch drive A, specify **A: A:**.

6. Press ↵Enter to begin copying.

   You are prompted to insert the required disks in the selected drives. If you have two, compatible disk drives, you are prompted to place the source and destination disks into the appropriate drives. If you have only one disk drive, you are prompted to place the source disk into drive A. If you have disk drives of different sizes, you receive a prompt to place the source disk in the drive that you specified in step 5.

During the copy process, DOS prompts you when it is time to insert the destination, or target, disk. Be careful not to confuse the two disks.

```
Insert SOURCE diskette in drive A:

Press any key to continue . . .

Copying 80 tracks
15 sectors per track, 2 side(s)

Insert TARGET diskette in drive A:

Press any key to continue . . .

Insert SOURCE diskette in drive A:

Press any key to continue . . .

Insert TARGET diskette in drive A:

Press any key to continue . . .
```

7. When the disk copy is complete, you are asked whether you want to copy another disk. Type Y and press ⏎Enter if you want to copy another. Type N and press ⏎Enter if you are done copying. Press any key to return to the DOS Shell.

Follow these steps to duplicate a disk by using the mouse:

1. Point to Disk Utilities in the Main program group and double-click the left mouse button to open the Disk Utilities program group.

2. Point to Disk Copy and double-click the left mouse button.

   The Disk Copy dialog box appears on-screen.

   The default parameters are a: b:, meaning that drives A and B are the source and destination drives, respectively. If you have only one disk drive, DOS assigns it to both the source and the destination.

3. If necessary, enter different parameters. For instance, if you want drive B to be the source and drive A to be the destination, type B: A: in the Parameters text box.

   To make drive A both source and destination, type A: A:.

4. Click the OK button in the dialog box to begin copying.

   If you have two, compatible disk drives, you are prompted to place the source and destination disks into the proper drives. If you have only one disk drive, you are prompted to place the source disk into drive A. If you have two differently sized disk drives, the prompt indicates the drive that you specified in step 3. DOS then prompts you again when it is time to replace the source disk with the destination disk.

5. When the copy is complete, press N and ⏎Enter, and then press any key to return to the DOS Shell.

Remember, you can use two disk drives to duplicate disks only if the drives are compatible. If your system contains two 360K floppy drives, for example, Disk Copy works fine.

If you have one or two 1.2M drives, you can use Disk Copy with 360K disks, but the disks may not be readable on some 360K drives on other computers. If you have one or two 1.44M drives, you can use Disk Copy with 720K disks with no trouble.

7

Using Disk Copy with Different Types of Drives

When you have two different types of drives, the Disk Copy procedure is more complicated. You may have to specify the same drive letter as both the source and target drive in the Disk Copy dialog box. If drives or disks are incompatible, an error message appears and the copy operation stops.

Four types of floppy disk drives are commonly used:

- High capacity 5 1/4-inch drives (1.2M)
- Low capacity 5 1/4-inch drives (360K)
- High capacity 3 1/2-inch drives (1.44M)
- Low capacity 3 1/2-inch drives (720K)

You can use both drives in either of the following situations:

- Both drives are the same size.
- You want to use Disk Copy with a low capacity disk. With 5 1/4-inch drives, you use the low capacity drive as the target drive. (This procedure is not a DOS requirement, but if you use the high capacity drive as the target drive, the disk may not be readable on some low capacity drives of other computers.)

You must use a single drive letter in the following situations:

- Your two drives are different sizes (one 5 1/4-inch drive and one 3 1/2-inch drive).
- You have a high capacity drive and a low capacity drive, and you want to use Disk Copy with a high capacity disk.

In each of the following examples, the steps for using Disk Copy are exactly the same as the steps in the previous section except for the parameters in the Disk Copy dialog box.

If you have a 1.2M drive A and a 360K drive B:

- To use Disk Copy with a 360K disk, use the 1.2M drive A as the source drive and the 360K drive B as the target drive. The parameters are **a: b:**.
- To use Disk Copy with a 1.2M disk, use the 1.2M drive A as both the source and the target drive. The parameters are **a: a:**. Follow the prompts to switch disks.

If you have a 1.44M drive A and a 720K drive B:

- To use Disk Copy with a 720K disk, use the 1.44M drive A as the source drive and the 720K drive B as the target drive. The parameters are **a: b:**.
- To use Disk Copy with a 1.44M disk, use the 1.44M drive A as both the source drive and the target drive. The parameters are **a: a:**. Follow the prompts to switch disks.

If you have a 5 1/4-inch drive A and a 3 1/2-inch drive B:

- To use Disk Copy with a 5 1/4-inch disk, use the 5 1/4-inch drive A as both the source drive and the target drive. The parameters are **a: a:**. Follow the prompts to switch disks.
- To use Disk Copy with a 3 1/2-inch disk, use the 3 1/2-inch drive B as both the source drive and the target drive. The parameters are **b: b:**. Follow the prompts to switch disks.

Verifying with Disk Copy

Many times the disks you copy contain very important information. Your disk might contain documents concerning the incorporation of your business. When copying this disk, you want to be sure that the copy is as accurate as possible.

Before you leave your house, you no doubt lock your door. And when you close your door, you probably wiggle the door knob to verify that the door really is locked. You do this to protect the contents of your house. Just as you wiggle the door knob, you can instruct Disk Copy to "wiggle its knob," or verify the copy, ensuring that the contents of the disk are protected.

You verify Disk Copy by using the /V (Verify) switch. This switch instructs Disk Copy to reread the destination disk after it has transferred information. You enter the /V switch in the same Parameters text box where you give the drive parameters.

Follow these steps to enter the /V switch:

1. Start Disk Copy with either the keyboard or mouse.
2. When the Disk Copy dialog box appears on-screen, enter the correct drive parameters, followed by a space and /V.

163

To use only drive A as the source and destination, type the following parameters:

a: a: /V

To use drive A as the source and drive B as the destination, type the following parameters:

a: b: /V

3. Press ⏎Enter or click the OK button to begin Disk Copy.

Disk Copy prompts you to place the correct disks in the correct drives. When the disk has been copied, you are prompted to press **Y** to copy another disk.

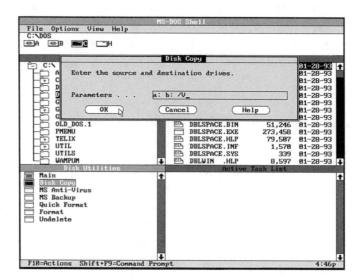

When using Disk Copy, use the /V switch to verify that data is duplicated correctly.

All the work the /V switch performs is "behind the scenes." The only difference you will notice when using the verify switch is that DOS needs a little more time to complete the copy process. There is no visible evidence that the disk is being verified.

Lessons Learned

■ The computer revolution enables you to copy text more quickly and accurately than ever before.

■ The Copy command copies single or multiple files on one disk or from one disk to another.

- The Copy command places a copy of a file into any directory you want.
- The Move command enables you to move files from one disk or directory to another.
- The Delete command deletes one or more files.
- The Rename command renames one or more files or directories.
- Disk Copy makes an exact copy of a disk.

Now that you know the basics of using DOS, it's time to learn how to use your computer for the reason you bought one in the first place: to run applications programs. Chapter 8 covers that topic.

7

7

Running Applications

Although you can play with your personal computer, you probably bought the computer because it is useful. DOS is necessary to help you with the main reason you have the computer: to run applications programs.

Most people use a personal computer primarily for word processing. The next most common use is working with spreadsheets. Both types of programs are applications programs. Your computer isn't limited to this kind of work, though. Games and graphics programs—also applications programs—are becoming increasingly popular.

The DOS Shell can make starting applications programs easier. In this chapter you learn how to use the Shell to set up and organize your applications programs. You also learn how to put programs into program groups, how to enter program properties, and the different ways to execute programs from the Shell.

Understanding programs and program groups

Creating a new program group

Adding a program to a program group

Maintaining program and group information

Changing program properties

Running programs

Advanced techniques for running applications

Key Terms Used in This Chapter	
Program group	A set of programs that you group together.
Properties	Information about a program or a program group that tells DOS how to display information and how to execute the program(s).
Association	A relationship that you establish between a program and a file extension.
Parameter	Additional information that you provide to DOS when you execute a command or a program. When you use the DOS Shell, you can save parameters, and DOS uses those parameters when you execute the application.
Replaceable parameter	A parameter that you specify each time you execute a program.

8

Understanding Programs and Program Groups

Throughout this book, you have learned how to execute (run) various DOS commands. Some of these commands, such as FORMAT and DISKCOPY, are programs in the DOS directory. You execute these programs in the Shell by opening the Disk Utilities *program group* in the Program area and then selecting the appropriate program. This section describes program groups in more detail and shows you how to build your own program groups and add programs to them.

168

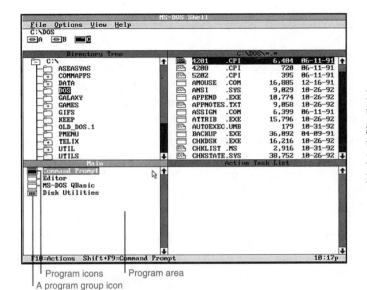

In this example, the Main program group is open in the Program area. Main is the root program group.

Program icons | Program area
A program group icon

Disk Utilities is also a group, which is evident because group icons are different from program icons. Program groups are like file folders for programs. You also can have program groups inside other program groups.

The Original DOS Groups

When you install DOS, it creates the Main program group and the Disk Utilities program group. The Main group is similar to the root directory on a disk. All programs in the Program area are in the Main group or in program groups inside the Main group. When you install DOS, the only program group in the Main group is Disk Utilities. The Main group is the *parent* of the Disk Utilities group. The Disk Utilities group is the *child* of the Main group. This relationship is similar to the subdirectory tree you learned about in Chapter 5.

The Main group contains the following programs:

Program	Description
Command Prompt	Pauses the Shell and enables you to use the DOS command line.
Editor	Starts the text editor.
MS-DOS QBasic	Starts the Quick Basic interpreter, which you can use to write and execute Basic programs.

8

169

Opening Groups and Running Programs

To run a program in a program group, you first must *open* the group. An open group is similar to the current directory: you can access the files in the current directory and you can run the programs in the open group. The name of the currently open group is shown in the Program area title bar. When you first start the Shell after installing DOS, the Main group is open.

To open a group with the mouse, double-click the group name or the group icon. To open a group with the keyboard, select the group and press Enter. (To select a group, press Tab repeatedly until the Program area is selected, and then use the up- and down-arrow keys to select the program group. For more information on selecting, refer to Chapter 4.)

When you open a program group, DOS displays a list of the programs in that group. When the open group is not the Main group, the first icon in the program list is for the parent of the open group— Main in this case.

8

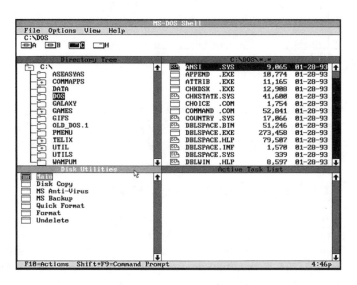

The Shell remembers which group is open when you exit the Shell. The next time you enter the Shell, the same group is open.

To run a program from the open group with the mouse, double-click the program name or the program icon. To run a program with the keyboard, select the program and press Enter.

Creating a New Program Group

The easiest way to run a program is from a program group. Before you can run an application from a program group, however, you must add the program to a group. You can create any number of program groups, but if you use just a few programs, you might want to create just one group named *Applications* (or any other name).

To create a new program group, follow these steps:

1. Open the group in which you want to add the new group. Initially, you probably will add groups to Main. Make sure that the open group name is selected in the Program area title bar. Within the open group, it does not matter which program or program group is highlighted.

2. Select the File menu.

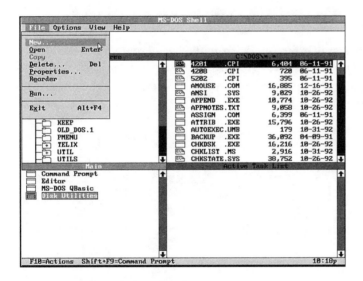

When a program group is selected, the File menu contains options different from those that appear when the Directory Tree or Files area is selected. If the File menu does not appear as shown here, the Program area is not the selected area.

3. Select New from the File menu.

8

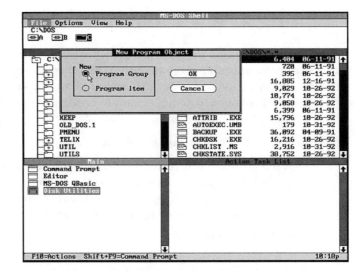

The New Program
Object dialog box
appears.

4. Choose the Program Group option from the New Program Object
   dialog box and choose OK. The Add Group dialog box appears.

5. Complete the Add Group dialog box and choose OK. Only the group
   title (the name of the group) is required.

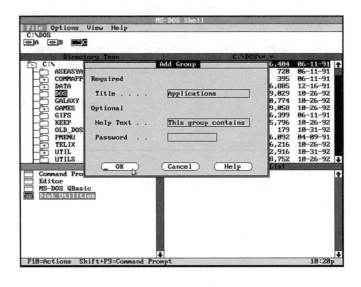

The name you
enter in the Title
box will appear in
the Program area
with a program
group icon.

The group title can be up to 74 characters long. The optional Help Text can display information about the group when you highlight the group title and press F1. If you password-protect the group, you must enter the password to open the group.

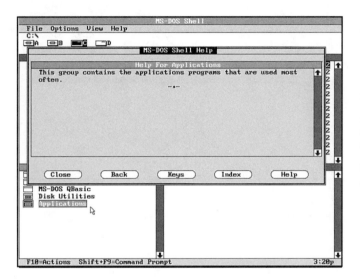

This screen shows an example of optional Help Text for a program group called Applications.

Adding a Program to a Program Group

Now that you have created an Applications program group, you can add your applications programs to that group.

To add a program to a program group, follow these steps:

1. In the Program area, open the program group to which you want to add a program.

2. Pull down the File menu and choose New.

   DOS displays the New Program Object dialog box.

173

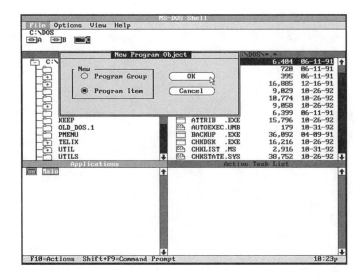

Program Item
is the default
selection and is
the option you
want, because
you are adding a
new item to a
program group.

3. Choose OK from the New Program Object dialog box. The Add Program dialog box appears.

8

In the Program
Title box, enter
the name that you
want to appear in
the Program area
with a program
icon. In the
Commands box,
enter the name of
the program you
want to execute.
In the Startup
Directory box,
enter the direc-
tory you want
DOS to make
current before
it executes the
program.

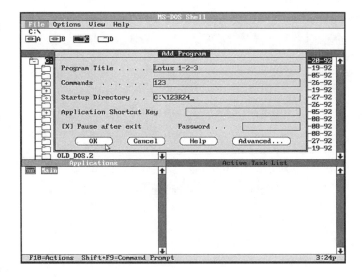

174

4. Complete the Add Program dialog box and choose OK.

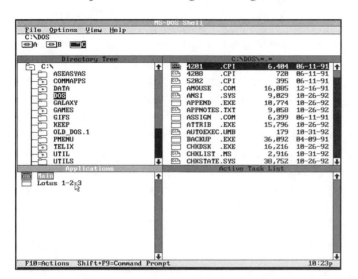

The new program title appears with an icon in the Applications program group.

Completing the Add Program Dialog Box

The information entered in the Add Program dialog box is called the *program properties*. The program properties tell DOS details such as where to find the program and data files and how to execute the program.

The Commands box in the Add Program dialog box can be confusing if you have never run the program from the DOS prompt. When you install an applications program, the installation instructions tell you what you must type to execute the program. Usually, you type the name of the program; for example, you type **123** to run Lotus 1-2-3, you type **word** to run Microsoft Word, and you type **fb** to run Fastback.

What you enter in the Startup Directory box depends on how the program works. The start-up directory is the directory that must be current when the program starts. With some programs, such as Lotus 1-2-3, the current directory when you start the program must be the directory that contains the program files. With other programs, such as Word and other Microsoft programs, the directory where the document or data files are located must be current.

When you enter a program name in the Commands box, DOS checks the current directory (entered in the Startup Directory box) for the program. For 1-2-3, if the current directory contains the program files, DOS executes the program with no problem. It finds the directory in which the 1-2-3 worksheet

8

175

files are located by reading a configuration file that is part of the program files. Therefore, if your 1-2-3 files are in the C:\LOTUS directory, you must make C:\LOTUS the start-up directory. If your 1-2-3 files are in the C:\123R24 directory (for 1-2-3, Release 2.4), you must make C:\123R24 the startup directory.

For Word, however, which you can start from any directory, DOS checks the current directory (entered in the Startup Directory box) for the directory where the Word document files are located. In this case, you must enter the directory you use for Word data files in the Startup Directory box.

For applications programs such as Word that do not require the start-up directory to contain the program files, the Commands box must contain the complete path to those files. For example, if the Word program files are in the C:\WORD directory, the Commands box must contain C:\WORD\WORD. The C:\WORD\ is the directory that contains the program files and the final WORD is the name that executes the program.

If your Word document files are in the C:\DATA\DOCS directory, you must enter C:\DATA\DOCS in the Startup Directory box. The Commands box must contain the complete path to the applications program.

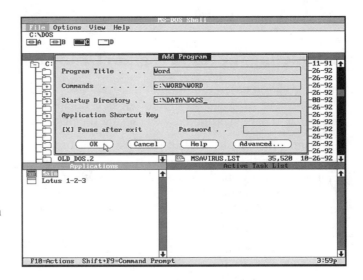

If you leave the Startup Directory box blank, the directory selected in the Directory Tree area becomes the current directory for the program when you start that program.

If you enter a password in the Password box, you must enter that password each time you execute the program. Note that if you forget your password, you cannot execute the program, change the program properties, or delete the program from its programming group.

176

Copying a Program to a Program Group

After you define a program, you can copy the program definition to other groups. By copying the program, you can run it from more than one group.

Suppose that you work on two types of projects. Most of the time, you develop financial reports using 1-2-3 and Word. For your other project, you write a newsletter using Word, CorelDRAW, and Ventura Publisher. You can set up a program group for each project. After you add Word to the Applications group, which you use for your financial reports, you can copy its program definition to the Newsletter group. Then Word is available when either group is open.

To copy an existing program to another group, follow these steps:

1. Open the group that contains the program you want to copy.

2. Select the program you want to copy.

3. Select Copy from the File menu.

4. Open the group to which you want to copy the program. This group must already be created.

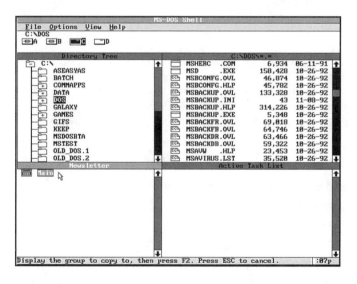

In this example, the Newsletter group is selected as the group to which DOS will copy the program.

5. Press F2.

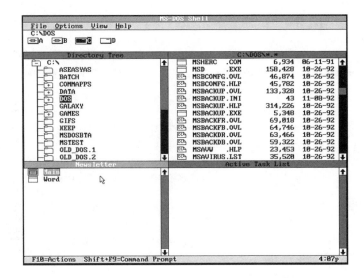

The copied program—Word in this example—is added to the program list.

When you copy a program to another group, you are not copying the program files; instead, you are copying the information in the Add Program dialog box that tells DOS how to execute the program.

Organizing Programs and Groups

After you create program groups and add programs to those groups, you can organize them within the Shell. For example, you may want to reorganize the way your programs and groups are displayed. You can put them in any order you want.

To move a program or group title within a group, follow these steps:

1. Select the title of the program or group you want to move.

2. Choose Reorder from the File menu.

3. With the mouse, double-click the new location. With the keyboard, select the new location and press ⏎Enter.

To delete a program from a group, select the program, press Del, and then choose OK in the confirmation dialog box. The program files remain on the disk.

To delete a program group, you must first delete all of the programs in that group. When the group is empty, open its parent group, select the group you want to delete, press Del, and then choose OK in the confirmation dialog box.

178

To add a program similar to a program already in the group, copy that program to the same group and then, as explained in the next section, change the program properties of the copy. For example, you can have two Word programs in the same group: one might use the data files in the /DATA/DOCS directory and one might use the data files in the /DATA/MEMOS directory.

Changing Program Properties

After you add a program to a group, you can change the program properties you entered in the Add Program dialog box. For example, if you want two Word programs in one group, you can change the properties to indicate the correct start-up directory.

To change program properties, follow these steps:

1. Open the group that contains the program you want to change.
2. Select the program you want to change.
3. Select Properties from the File menu. The Program Item Properties dialog box appears.
4. Complete the Program Item Properties dialog box and choose OK.

8

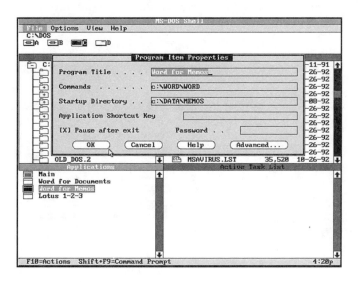

You can change the title and change the start-up directory to the appropriate data directory. You can create many program items that run Word, each with a different title (so you can tell them apart) and a different start-up directory.

179

Running Programs

You can run programs from the Shell in many ways, but the easiest way is to run programs from program groups.

After you build program groups and add programs to those groups, you can execute applications programs the same way you execute DOS utilities in the Main and Disk Utilities groups:

1. Open the group that contains the program you want to execute.
2. With the mouse, double-click the program or, with the keyboard, select the program and press ⏎Enter.

After you run the program and quit or exit the program, you return to the Shell.

If you did not specify a start-up directory for the program, highlight the disk and directory that you want the program to use as the current directory before you execute the program.

Using the Task Swapper

In Chapter 4, you had a glimpse of the Task Swapper. Remember that to enable the Task Swapper, you choose Enable Task Swapper from the Options menu.

When the Task Swapper is enabled, the Active Task List shows any programs that are started and available.

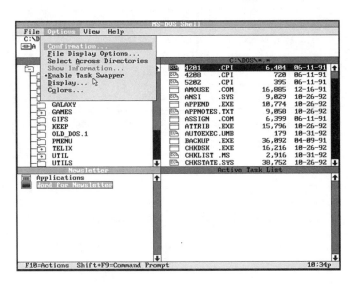

The Task Swapper enables you to load multiple programs at one time and "swap" among them with a keystroke. Swapping programs can be very handy if you regularly use more than one program at a time. If you use both 1-2-3 and Word to develop financial reports, for example, you can start both programs and swap between them in a few seconds. When you return to a program, the program is exactly the way you left it: the same files are loaded, the cursor is in the same position, and the same options are set.

You can use three key combinations to swap programs:

Ctrl-Esc	Returns to the Shell. If you are in the Shell, this key combination is ignored.
Alt-Tab⇆	Switches to the preceding program, including the Shell. If you hold down Alt and press Tab repeatedly, the top line of the display shows the name of each active task in reverse order of use. When the name of the program to which you want to switch appears, release Alt.
Alt-Esc	Switches to the next application in the Active Task List.

When you are in the Shell, the Active Task List shows the tasks in reverse order of use. The most recently used program (the program from which you switched to get to the Shell) is always at the top of the list.

8

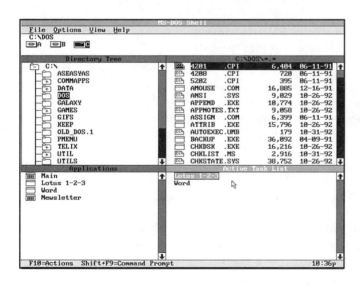

In this example, Lotus 1-2-3 is the most recently used program and therefore is at the top of the Active Task List.

181

When you are in the Shell, you can switch to an active task the same way you start a program. With the mouse, double-click the program name in the Active Task List. With the keyboard, select the program in the Active Task List and press Enter.

To remove a program from the Active Task List, switch to the program, save any files, and quit the program. You return to the Shell, and the program no longer appears in the Active Task List.

If a program "hangs," or freezes, and you cannot quit the program, try to switch to the Shell by using any of the three key combinations for swapping programs. If you can return to the Shell, follow these steps to cancel the program:

1. In the Active Task List, select the program you want to cancel.
2. Press Del.
3. Select OK in the confirmation dialog box.

Deleting the program from the Active Task List is not the normal way to quit a program and you might lose some data. Use this method to quit a program only if the program hangs and booting your computer is the only alternative.

When you switch out of a program, the program is *suspended*. If you start a long recalculation in 1-2-3, for example, and then swap to another program, the recalculation does not resume until you return to 1-2-3. 1-2-3 does not do any recalculation while suspended. In this sense, perhaps the name *Active Task List* is deceiving—only one task is really active at a time.

Because you suspend a program when you switch to another program, do not switch out of a communications program or a terminal emulation program while such programs are connected to another computer. When your computer is connected to another computer, the program that manages the connection must be active at all times, or the other computer may break the connection.

Running Programs from the Files List

Although you should run programs you use regularly from program groups (because this method is easiest), you also can run programs from the Files list by following these steps:

1. Select the disk that contains the program you want to run.
2. Select the directory that contains the program.

3. With the mouse, double-click the program file name or, with the keyboard, select the program file name and press ⏎Enter.

The program file name can have an EXE or COM file extension.

When you execute a program from the Files list, the directory that contains the program is the current directory.

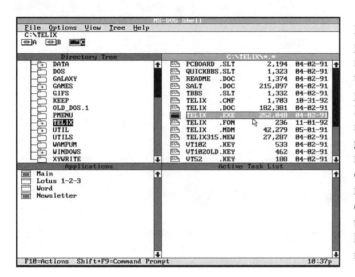

Double-click the program file name or select the program and press Enter. Notice that the icon for a program is different from the icon for other types of files. You can execute only those files that have program icons.

Running Programs with the Run Command

Because the most difficult way to execute a program in the Shell is with the Run command, use the Run command only with programs you rarely use. To execute a program with the Run command, follow these steps:

1. Select the disk and directory that you want to be current when the program executes.

2. Select **R**un from the File menu.

3. Type the path and the command to start the program.

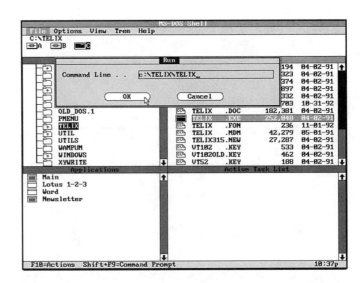

You can execute any program by using the **R**un command from the File menu. In most cases, you must provide the complete path to the program. For example, the TELIX program is in the C:\TELIX directory.

Running Programs from Associations

8

So far, you have learned how to make the correct data directory the current directory when you execute a program. You can then use the program's commands to load or read the data file you want to use. You can go one step further and not only execute a program, but also load a data file.

First, you must form an *association* between a file extension and a program. Then, when you open an associated data file, DOS runs its associated program and loads the data file you opened.

To form an association between a file extension and a program, follow these steps:

1. Select the directory that contains the file with the extension you want to associate with a program.

2. Select the file.

3. Choose **A**ssociate from the File menu. The Associate File dialog box appears.

4. In the Associate File dialog box, enter the path and the file name of the program you want associated with the file extension, and then choose OK.

184

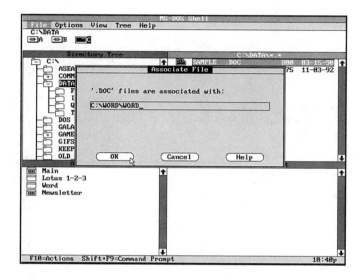

In this example, the file extension DOC is associated with the Word program in the C:\WORD directory.

You can associate one program with up to 20 file extensions, but you can associate a file extension with only one program.

After you associate a file extension with a program, follow these steps to start the program and load the data file:

1. Select the directory that contains the data file you want to load with a program.

2. Select the data file you want to load with a program.

3. Choose Open from the File menu and press ⏎Enter, or point to the data file with the mouse pointer and double-click.

   DOS starts the program associated with the file and loads the selected data file.

185

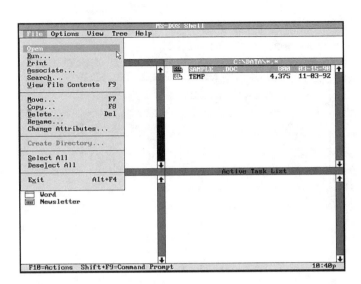

The SAMPLE.DOC
file in the
C:\DATA direc-
tory is selected.
Because the DOC
extension is
associated with
Microsoft Word,
DOS starts Word
when you choose
Open from the
File menu.

Loading a data file with this technique works only with certain programs. You
must be able to run the program from any directory and you must be able to
specify a data file name when you run the program. The technique does not
work with a program such as Lotus 1-2-3, Release 3.x because you cannot load
a named data file when you start this program.

To load a data file when you open Lotus 1-2-3 Release 2.4, you must use a
special *batch file*. The problem with a program such as 1-2-3 Release 2.4 is
that you must start the program from the program directory. To start a program from an association, you start the program from the directory that
contains the data file. The other problem with this technique is that you
cannot just add a data file name when you start 1-2-3; you need to use a
special switch. You will learn how to use batch files in Chapter 12.

Advanced Techniques
for Running Applications

The purpose of *MS-DOS 6 QuickStart* is to give you the knowledge and skills
to use DOS effectively and run your applications. Each application is different,
however, and many applications require special considerations before you can
run them by using the techniques in this chapter. Some of these considerations are mentioned in this book. For more information, consult Que's *Using
MS-DOS 6*, Special Edition, your DOS manuals, and the manuals for your
applications programs.

Installing Applications

Before you buy a program, investigate its hardware requirements. The program may require a certain type of monitor, such as an EGA or VGA monitor. You may need a certain amount of memory in your computer. Some programs are difficult to use without a mouse. Many applications require more than a megabyte of disk space and require a hard disk. Make sure that you have the appropriate hardware to run the program.

Some programs also have software requirements. Many programs, such as Microsoft Excel, require Windows. Some programs require certain versions of DOS or run only with a certain network operating system, such as Novell Netware. Make sure that you have the appropriate software to run the program.

Most applications have an *install* or *setup* procedure you must execute before you can use the program. Read the entire installation procedure before you do anything. In some cases, you must create a directory before you start the installation; in others, the installation procedure creates the directory for you. In some cases, you have a choice of the directory name; in others, you must install the program in a specific directory.

The installation procedure for most programs tells you the DOS commands to run to prepare for the installation. These instructions probably use the DOS command line, discussed in the next chapter. You also can use the Shell instead of the command line to create directories and copy files.

Some installation programs run incorrectly if executed from the Shell. If the installation does not run correctly, press F3 to cancel the Shell; then run the installation program from the command line.

Completing the Commands Box
in the Program Properties Dialog Box

After telling you how to install the program on your hard disk, the program's manual tells you how to execute the program. If the manual states that you must make the program directory the current directory, then you must use the program directory as the Startup Directory when you add the program to a program group. You must use this technique when you add Lotus 1-2-3 to a program group.

Often you can enter just the program name to start the program. If so, enter the program name in the Commands box when you create the program item in a program group. For Microsoft Word, you enter **WORD**. For 1-2-3, you enter **123**.

In some cases, you can or must enter additional *parameters* when you start the program. A parameter is any additional information that tells the program what to do when it runs. To start some versions of WordPerfect and load the entire program into memory, you type the command **WP/R**. With 1-2-3, you can use alternate screen settings with most monitors; if you have a settings file named VGA43 to display 43 lines, you can tell 1-2-3 to use this settings file by typing the command **123 VGA43**.

If you want to include a parameter when you start a program, add the parameter to the Commands box when you create the program item in a program group. For WordPerfect, enter **WP/R**. For 1-2-3 with a 43-line settings file, enter **123 VGA43**.

Within a program group, you can have several similar program items that have different parameters in their Commands boxes. For example, you can have a 1-2-3 program item that starts 1-2-3 with a 25-line display and another 1-2-3 program item that starts 1-2-3 with a 43-line display.

8

You can include a program several times in one group with different parameters. The optional parameter in this Commands box is for the 43-line display.

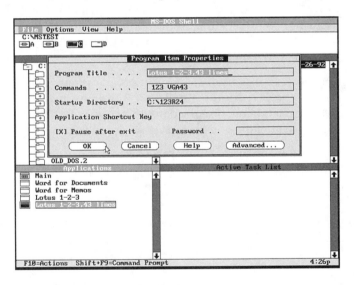

Using Replaceable Parameters in the Commands Box

Some programs enable you to use many different parameters when you start the program. You can set up a separate program item for each combination of parameters that you might use, or you can use *replaceable parameters*. A replaceable parameter is a parameter you specify when you run the program, rather than when you fill in the Commands box.

For example, you can run 1-2-3 with a Super VGA display using many different display settings. First you must use the 1-2-3 install program to create each settings file; then you can set up a program item for 1-2-3 with a replaceable parameter for the settings file name. You enter the appropriate settings file name each time you run 1-2-3.

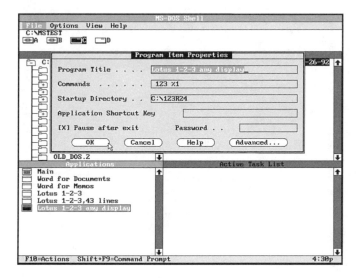

To specify a replaceable parameter, enter a percent sign (%) followed by a single-digit number (1–9) in the Commands box. A single replaceable parameter is usually specified as %1.

When you enter a replaceable parameter and choose OK, DOS displays another Program Item Properties dialog box. The data in this dialog box will be displayed in an information dialog box whenever you start the application.

8

189

When DOS
displays the
information
dialog box before
executing the
program, you
can enter data in
the text box to
change the start-
up parameters, or
you can accept
the default.

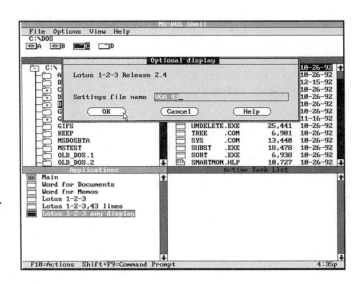

When you choose OK in the information dialog box, DOS replaces the parameter with the contents of the text box and executes the program.

8

If the data file is
not in the current
directory, you
must include the
path. In this
example, no
default data file
name was speci-
fied in the Default
Parameters text
box of the Pro-
gram Item
Properties dialog
box, so the text
box is blank.

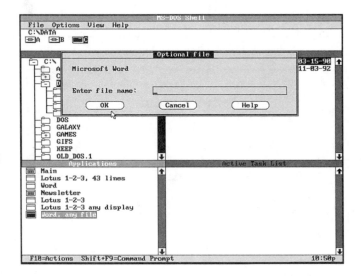

If you use more than one replaceable parameter, call the parameters %1, %2,
and so on. Complete a separate dialog box for each replaceable parameter.

When you use replaceable parameters, you often want to have another version of the program without replaceable parameters in the same program group. Select the program without replaceable parameters if the parameters are not needed. You then bypass the information dialog box and go directly to the program.

Starting a Program with a Batch File

Some programs create a batch file during installation and tell you to execute the batch file to start the program. DOS executes a batch file the same way it executes a program file. The difference is that the batch file can execute any number of separate commands and programs, whereas a program file executes just the program. You will learn the secrets of batch files in Chapter 12. For now, treat the batch file as if it were the name of the program, and put the batch file name in the Commands box when you create the program item in a program group.

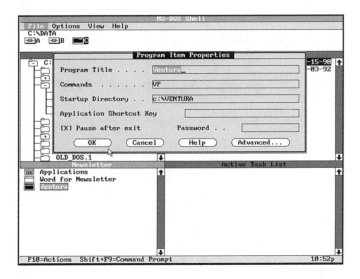

Ventura Publisher is a program you must execute from the directory that contains the program files. The installation process creates a batch file named VP.BAT. The batch file then executes the Ventura Publisher program.

Other Program Properties

You also can specify other parameters for a program in a program group. When you exit a program, DOS displays a blank screen with the message Press any key to return to MS-DOS Shell at the bottom of the screen.

You can eliminate the display of this message and return directly to the Shell when you exit a program: turn off the Pause After Exit option in the Program Item Properties dialog box.

Click on the Pause After Exit option, or select it and press the space bar, to remove the *X* from the check box; then choose the Advanced button for additional parameters you can enter for the program.

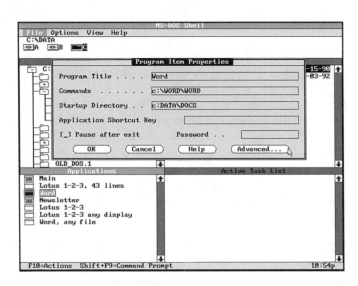

8

DOS displays the Advanced dialog box.

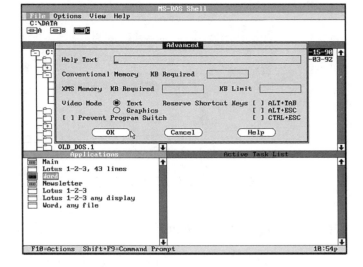

The Advanced dialog box offers several options:

- DOS displays any information you type in the Help Text box when you press F1 while the program is highlighted.

- The memory options tell DOS how much memory the program needs to run. DOS does not start a program if less than 384K of memory is available. If the program is very small, you can specify a smaller amount of memory in kilobytes.

- If the program displays in graphics mode, such as 1-2-3 Release 3.1 and Ventura Publisher do, choose the graphics options to ensure that DOS has enough memory available to save the screen display.

- If your application program uses any of the Task Swapper shortcut keys, you can tell DOS not to use those keys, so that they remain available to the program. If you reserve all three keys for use by the program, you cannot switch out of the program without quitting.

  You should not switch out of a connected communications program. To prevent such a switch, choose the Prevent Program Switch option.

After you finish setting options in the Advanced dialog box, choose OK to return to the Program Item Properties dialog box. Choose OK again to return to the DOS Shell.

8

Lessons Learned

- You easily can run programs in a number of ways by using the Shell.
- You can organize programs into groups.
- You can specify properties that tell DOS how to execute each program.
- You can run multiple programs at the same time and switch among them easily by using Task Swapper.
- You can associate a file extension with a program. When you open that data file, DOS runs the program associated with that data file.
- You can run a program with replaceable parameters that the user specifies when running the program.

So far, you have worked only in the DOS Shell. In the next chapter, you will venture beyond the Shell and learn how to operate your computer from the command line.

8

Using the DOS Command Line

Have you ever met someone who intimidated you? Maybe the person was taller, spoke in an authoritative voice, or projected an unusually strong image. This feeling happens to everyone. Often, though, your initial impressions of someone have little to do with the true nature of that person. The same is true of initial impressions of DOS. Despite what you may hear, DOS is designed to be well-mannered. So far we have avoided the "dreaded DOS prompt," as it is sometimes called, but soon you will find that executing commands from the command line is not so hard.

Before DOS 5, you first had to learn the command line to do any useful work. Now, because the Shell is so easy to use, you can learn the command line after you become familiar with using DOS and running programs. With eight chapters of DOS experience under your belt, using the command line will be easy to master.

Understanding commands and the command line

Issuing commands

Using DIR to view file lists

Using the COPY command

Using other commands

Getting on-line help

Executing programs

Key Terms Used in This Chapter	
Command	A collection of characters that tells the computer what you want it to do. Most commands are mnemonics of English words, with single numbers or letters often added as optional instructions.
Command line	The line at the DOS prompt on which you type DOS commands rather than using the Shell.
Syntax	The specific set of rules you follow when you issue commands.
Parameter	Any additional information you type after the command name in the command syntax to refine what you want the DOS command to do.
Switch	A part of the command that turns on an optional instruction or function.
Delimiter	A character that separates the parts of a command. Common delimiters are the space and the slash (/).
Path	A DOS command parameter that tells DOS where to find a file or where to carry out a command.
Wild card	A character you substitute for another character or characters.

Moving from the Shell to the Command Line

This book has covered a lot of territory already. You have learned about the structure of DOS, about disks and directories, and how to use the DOS Shell to perform the most important commands and to run programs. You now know how to be fully productive with your personal computer, DOS, and your applications programs—all accomplished without using the DOS command line.

So why bother with the command line now? There are a number of reasons:

- You cannot execute all DOS commands from the Shell. Sometimes you must use the command line.

- You must know the command line to create batch files to customize your system, as explained in Chapter 12.

- You sometimes used the command line from within the Shell without knowing it. When you complete the parameters in the dialog box for the Format command, for example, you are really using the command line. When you complete the Commands box in a Program Properties dialog box, you are completing a command for the command line. After you know more about using the command line, you will find that using the Shell is even easier.

Most of what you can do in the Shell you can do at the command line. Usually the Shell is much easier to use. At times, however, you will find that certain commands or command sequences run faster from the command line. When you know how to use both methods, you have more control over your personal computer.

When you use the *command line*, you use the *DOS prompt*, or the *command prompt*. All three terms mean exactly the same thing. The *prompt* on the command line is how DOS tells you that it is ready for your next command. You can alter this prompt, as explained in Chapter 12. The standard prompt that most people use with a hard disk displays the current drive and path. With this prompt, you always know the current directory. For example, when you first boot your computer, the prompt is C:\>.

9

Understanding Commands and the Command Line

To tell DOS what you want it to do, you enter DOS *commands*. Commands are letters, numbers, and acronyms separated—or *delimited*—by certain other characters. Stripped of jargon, using a DOS command is like telling your dog to "sit," "heel," or "stay." Additionally, you can tell your computer to "sit and bark" concurrently. DOS commands frequently, though not exclusively, use slash marks (/) to indicate such additional instructions.

A command you give to DOS is similar to a written instruction you might give to a work associate, but with DOS you must be precise. People use interconnecting words and inferences that the human brain can grasp easily. DOS knows only what its developers programmed it to understand.

When you type a command in its proper form—or *syntax*—at the DOS prompt, both the DOS command and any additional parameters communicate your intent. Both relay the action you want to perform and the object of that action. Remember, your main tool for communication with your PC is the keyboard. Your PC is ready to work for you, but it doesn't respond to humor, anger, frustration, or imprecise syntax.

Assume that you have an assistant with a limited vocabulary. If you want a sign on a bulletin board duplicated for posting on another bulletin board, you might instruct, "Copy sign A to sign B. Make sure that the copy is free from errors."

Similarly, if you want DOS to duplicate all the data from a disk in drive A to a disk you have placed in drive B, you give DOS the following instruction:

DISKCOPY A: B:

To have DOS, the efficient helper, compare the copy and the original, type the following command:

DISKCOMP A: B:

DISKCOPY and DISKCOMP are good examples of DOS commands that are clearly named to explain the activity they execute. A: and B: indicate the disk drives you want DOS to use.

Although you will rarely use more than ten commands, DOS recognizes and responds to dozens of them. The most common of these commands are built into the command processor (COMMAND.COM) and are instantly available at the system prompt. Because these commands are always ready for use, they are called *internal* commands. When you execute commands by using the Shell menus, you are really executing internal commands.

Other commands are stored as individual programs in the DOS directory of your hard disk. These commands, called *external* commands, are located, loaded, and executed when you type them at the system prompt and press Enter. External commands can execute from the system prompt in the same way as internal commands. The commands in the Main and Disk Utilities program groups in the Shell are examples of external commands.

Learning the ins and outs of issuing DOS commands takes practice. DOS commands follow a logical structure, but that structure is far more rigid than a casual conversation with a neighbor. Some of this rigidity is masked when you use the Shell.

The strength of DOS is that after you understand its rules, everything flows easily. Commands conform to standard rules in their command-line structure. DOS is easier to use when you understand the concepts behind the commands. You can then generalize rules to different commands.To feel comfortable with DOS commands, remember these rules:

9

- DOS requires you to use a specific set of rules, or syntax, when you issue commands.

- Parameters, part of a command's syntax, change the way DOS executes a command.

You can think of the command name as the action part of a DOS command. In addition to the name, many commands require or allow further directions. Any such additions are called *parameters*. Parameters tell DOS what to apply the action to or how to apply the action. Using DOS commands is quite easy if you follow the rules of order and use the correct parameters.

The worst part about many DOS manuals is that they present you with something that may resemble a French menu if you speak no French. And like the waiter standing over you with a casual, smug attitude, these other DOS books make little effort to help you navigate through the menu. In fact, most DOS manuals are agony for the new user. Even the experienced user can be driven to hair-pulling in fruitless quests for information.

MS-DOS 6 QuickStart is designed to be pleasurably read from cover to cover. The book introduces DOS to new users, but much of it can serve as a review for the more experienced user. This book makes a gourmet presentation, but the menu is in English.

Syntax

9

Syntax is the structure, order, and vocabulary in which you type the elements of the DOS command. Using proper syntax when you enter a DOS command is comparable to using proper English when you speak. To carry out your command, DOS must clearly understand what you are typing.

When you use the Shell, you do not have to know some of the syntax, because the information is built into the menus and program items. You do run into the rules of syntax, however, when you need to complete the Program Properties dialog box. With the Shell, you must know the syntax when you complete the Program Properties dialog box. With the command line, you must know the syntax every time you execute the program.

Unfortunately, many DOS manuals use *symbolic form* to describe command syntax. Simply stated, symbolic form is the use of a letter or name for illustrative purposes. DOS manuals, however, rarely reveal what each letter or name means. A file used to illustrate a command might be called EXAMPLE.COM. Actually, EXAMPLE.COM exists only in the mind of the writer. It is an example. When you enter the real command, you are supposed to substitute a real name for the symbolic one.

Such books frequently list every command switch (option), as though multiple switches are a normal part of the command. Many DOS commands, however, cannot be issued to accept every possible option. Using all the options is like ordering a sandwich with white, rye, whole wheat, *and* cinnamon-raisin bread. The choice is usually either/or, rather than all. A command should contain nothing more than what you want to instruct DOS to do.

Symbolic form is used to describe not only files, but also the entire command line. A DIR command shown in symbolic form might look like this:

DIR *d:path\ filename.ext* /W /P /A:*attributes* /O:*order* /S /B /L

On the other hand, a command that you might use in the real world might look like the following example:

DIR C: /W /P

As you can see, symbolic notation can confuse, rather than enlighten, until you understand the concept behind the form.

Switches

A *switch* is a parameter that turns on an optional function of a command. In the preceding DIR example, /W and /P are switches. Note that each switch is a character preceded by a slash. Not all DOS commands use switches. In addition, switches may have different meanings for different commands.

You can use the /W switch with the DIR command to display a wide directory of files. Normally, DIR displays a directory with one file listing per line. The date and time the file was created are displayed next to the file name. As the screen fills, the first files scroll off the top of the display. The /W switch displays a directory listing that shows only file names and extensions and displays them in multiple columns across the screen.

Sometimes a directory contains too many files to display on one screen. When you use the /P switch with the directory command, 23 lines of file names— approximately one full screen—are displayed. The display pauses when the screen fills. At the bottom of a paused directory listing, DOS prompts you to Press any key to continue to move to the next screen of files. The /P switch thus enables you to see all the files in the directory, one screen at a time.

When DOS says Press any key to continue, you can press *almost* any key. If you press the Shift, Alt, Caps Lock, Num Lock, or Scroll Lock keys, DOS ignores you. The easiest keys to press are the space bar and the Enter key.

Many DOS commands can be typed in several forms and still be correct. Although the simple versions of DOS syntax work effectively, most DOS manuals show the complete syntax for a command, which (again) can be confusing. For example, the complete syntax for the DIR command looks like this:

Parameters

DIR *d:path\filename.ext* /W /P /A:*attributes* /O:*order* /S /B /L

Command — Delimiter (space)

Now break down the sample command, piece by piece. You see that, rather than being an actual command, it is the symbolic form of all the alternatives.

Syntax	Description
DIR	A command that runs a directory listing. If you don't use any switches (options) with this command, the directory listing appears in vertical form. The listing shows not only file names, but also the file size and the time and date of each file's last modification. To get this listing, type **DIR**. Do not type a space between the prompt > symbol and the command name.
d:	The drive containing the directory listing. If the current drive is the drive you want, you don't need to specify a drive. If you want a directory listing of a different drive, type the appropriate drive letter.
path	The route DOS follows to find the directory that contains the files for which you want a directory listing. If you want a listing of the files in the current directory, you don't need a path. In fact, you rarely use the path in the DIR command. Using a path is more common with other commands, such as the COPY command.
filename.ext	The file name parameter, including its extension. You substitute your own file name in its place. DOS never allows more than one file with the same name in any one directory. Other than to display that file's size and the amount of space free on that disk, this syntax has little meaning when you use the DIR command.

continues

9

201

Syntax	Description
	The following example includes the command (DIR), the drive (C:), and the file name parameter (MYFILE.TXT):
	DIR C:MYFILE.TXT
/W	A switch that requests a horizontal directory listing (wide), instead of a single vertical listing. The wide listing provides no information other than the file name. The command DIR /W displays a wide directory listing. The / is a delimiter that tells DOS that a switch is about to follow.
/P	A switch that pauses the directory listing. Normally DOS scrolls down a directory from beginning to end without stopping. The /P switch causes DOS to pause when the screen is filled. Pressing a key displays another screen of files.
	Typing **DIR** at the DOS prompt produces a directory of the disk that is on the current drive. Long listings may scroll off the screen. To halt scrolling temporarily, press Ctrl-S or Pause. Press any key to continue.
/A:*attributes*	A switch that lists only files with certain file attributes. You can list or exclude the following items from the list: hidden files (*H*), system files (*S*), directories, archived files (*A*), and read-only files (*R*). A minus sign before the attribute tells DOS not to list a file with that attribute. The colon (:) after /A is optional, but makes the command easier to understand. You do not include parentheses when you specify attributes.
/O:*order*	A switch that specifies the sort order of the listing. The order may be alphabetical by name (*N*) or extension (*E*), by date and time (*D*), by size (*S*), or with directories grouped before files (*G*). A minus sign before the sort order means to reverse the order. The colon (:) after /O

9

202

Syntax	Description
	is optional but makes the command easier to understand. You do not include parentheses when you specify attributes.
/S	A switch that lists the files in all subdirectories.
/B	A switch that lists only the file names, with no spaces between the name and the extension.
/L	A switch that displays the information in lowercase letters instead of uppercase.

At this point, you probably think that the DIR command is much too complicated for anyone except the most advanced DOS experts. Actually, DIR is the easiest command to use because you can ignore most of this information. In the Shell, the Directory Tree area and the Files area display the same information as the DIR command, in a slightly different format. Most of these DIR options are available by choosing Display from the Options menu.

Among the many thousands of possible DIR command possibilities, you can type the DIR command in the following ways:

```
DIR
DIR /P
DIR /W
DIR /W /P
DIR A:
DIR A: /P
DIR /P /A:D
DIR /W /O:D
DIR /B
DIR /A:E /S
DIR /L
```

9

The command
DIR /P displays
the directory
listing page by
page, and displays
the message
Press any key
to continue at
the bottom of the
screen. The
command itself
scrolls off the
screen after you
type the com-
mand and press
Enter.

```
 Volume in drive C has no label
 Volume Serial Number is 195F-849A
 Directory of C:\DOS

 .            <DIR>      10-30-92   3:59p
 ..           <DIR>      10-30-92   3:59p
 MOUSE    COM    28898   11-25-91   4:05p
 FORMAT   COM    33087   10-26-92   6:00a
 PKUNZIP  EXE    23528   03-15-90   1:10a
 NLSFUNC  EXE     7052   10-26-92   6:00a
 4201     CPI     6404   06-11-91   5:00a
 4208     CPI      720   06-11-91   5:00a
 5202     CPI      395   06-11-91   5:00a
 KEYB     COM    14986   10-26-92   6:00a
 AMOUSE   COM    16885   12-16-91  10:01a
 ANSI     SYS     9029   10-26-92   6:00a
 DEBUG    EXE    20634   10-26-92   6:00a
 EXPAND   EXE    26097   10-26-92   6:00a
 BACKUP   EXE    36892   04-09-91   5:00a
 APPNOTES TXT     9058   10-26-92   6:00a
 FDISK    EXE    57224   10-26-92   6:00a
 SYS      COM    13440   10-26-92   6:00a
 UNFORMAT COM    18560   10-26-92   6:00a
 Press any key to continue . . .
```

The command
DIR /W displays
the directory
listing in a wide
arrangement, but
does not display
information about
individual files.

```
 Volume in drive C has no label
 Volume Serial Number is 195F-849A
 Directory of C:\DOS

 [.]            [..]           DOSSHELL.INI   MOUSE.COM      FORMAT.COM
 PKUNZIP.EXE    NLSFUNC.EXE    KEYB.COM       ANSI.SYS       DEBUG.EXE
 EXPAND.EXE     BACKUP.EXE     FDISK.EXE      SYS.COM        UNFORMAT.COM
 ATTRIB.EXE     CHOICE.COM     DEFRAG.EXE     INTERLNK.EXE   INTERSVR.EXE
 MSD.EXE        EDLIN.EXE      POWER.EXE      MIRROR.COM     [TEMP]
 DOSSHELL.COM   DOSSWAP.EXE    MODE.COM       SETVER.EXE     SMARTMON.EXE
 FASTOPEN.EXE   SHARE.EXE      PRINT.EXE      MEM.EXE        XCOPY.EXE
 RECOVER.EXE    DOSHELP.EXE    MSHERC.COM     ASSIGN.COM     QBASIC.EXE
 COMP.EXE       HELP.COM       EDIT.COM       APPEND.EXE     CHKDSK.EXE
 GRAFTABL.COM   DISKCOMP.COM   DISKCOPY.COM   FC.EXE         FIND.EXE
 LABEL.EXE      EXE2BIN.EXE    MORE.COM       JOIN.EXE       RESTORE.EXE
 SORT.EXE       GRAPHICS.COM   DOSSHELL.EXE   REPLACE.EXE    TREE.COM
 DOSKEY.COM     SUBST.EXE      LOADFIX.COM    UNDELETE.EXE   MWUNDEL.EXE
 MWAV.EXE       MWAVTSR.EXE    VSAFE.COM      MSAV.EXE       MEMMAKER.EXE
 MWBACKUP.EXE   SIZER.EXE      MSBACKUP.EXE   DBLSPACE.EXE   DELOLDOS.EXE
 EMM386.EXE     SMARTDRV.EXE   COMMAND.COM
        78 file(s)      3239145 bytes
                       46635008 bytes free

 C:\DOS>
```

The command
DIR /A:D lists only
the directories.

```
 C:\DATA>DIR /A:D

 Volume in drive C has no label
 Volume Serial Number is 195F-849A
 Directory of C:\DATA

 .            <DIR>      10-31-92   6:22p
 ..           <DIR>      10-31-92   6:22p
 QUE          <DIR>      10-31-92   6:23p
 INVOICES     <DIR>      11-01-92   1:15p
 TAXES        <DIR>      11-01-92   2:33p
 FIGURES      <DIR>      11-01-92   6:55p
         6 file(s)            0 bytes
                       41152512 bytes free

 C:\DATA>
```

9

```
C:\DATA>DIR /A:D/O:N

 Volume in drive C has no label
 Volume Serial Number is 195F-849A
 Directory of C:\DATA

.              <DIR>      10-31-92    6:22p
..             <DIR>      10-31-92    6:22p
FIGURES        <DIR>      11-01-92    6:55p
INVOICES       <DIR>      11-01-92    1:15p
QUE            <DIR>      10-31-92    6:23p
TAXES          <DIR>      11-01-92    2:33p
        6 file(s)             0 bytes
                      41136128 bytes free

C:\DATA>
```

The command DIR /A:D /O:N lists only the directories, sorted by name.

```
A:\>DIR /A:S

 Volume in drive A is BOOT DISK
 Volume Serial Number is 1A07-1CD0
 Directory of A:\

IO          SYS       39590 10-26-92    6:00a
MSDOS       SYS       37416 10-26-92    6:00a
        2 file(s)         77006 bytes
                        231424 bytes free

A:\>
```

In the root directory of a bootable disk, DIR /A:S lists the DOS system files. These files normally do not appear on a directory listing.

```
[.]            [..]            [XTALK]          [PCTALK]
        4 file(s)          0 bytes

Directory of C:\COMMAPPS\PCTALK

[.]            [..]            PC-TALK.BAS      COPYTALK.BAT    PRINTDOC.BAT
TALK128.BAT    TALK64.BAT      PC-TALK.DEF      PC-TALK.EXE     PC-TALK.KEY
PCTKREM.MRG
        11 file(s)        151436 bytes

Directory of C:\COMMAPPS\XTALK

[.]            [..]            HWCLEAR          PRODS1D         COMMAND.COM
XTHELP.DIR     XTALK.EXE       XTALK.HLP        ATEX1.XTK       ATEX2.XTK
NEWUSER.XTK    SETUP.XTK       STD.XTK          CSERV.XTS       DELPHI.XTS
DOWJONES.XTS   MCIMAIL.XTS     NEWSNET.XTS      NEWUSER.XTS     OAG.XTS
SETUP.XTS      SOURCE.XTS
        22 file(s)        153631 bytes

Total files listed:
        37 file(s)        305067 bytes
                        41107456 bytes free

C:\COMMAPPS>
```

9

The command DIR /W /O:E /S lists, in wide format, the files in subdirectories, sorted by file extension. In this example, the command line and the first directory have scrolled off the screen.

Don't worry about your PC pulling something sneaky when you type a command. No command you type is executed until you press the Enter key. Operating DOS is simpler than you might expect. Just remember that as you gain experience, you might begin to use even potentially dangerous commands in a routine manner.

Issuing Commands

The command name is a key to DOS. The command processor, COMMAND.COM, reads the command you type. COMMAND.COM can carry out several "built in" commands. It also knows how to load and run the external utility programs you enter at the DOS prompt. In the Shell, you choose a command from a menu or a list of programs in a group. At the command line, you type the command name.

Typing the Command Name

When you type a command, do not leave a space after the DOS prompt's greater-than sign (>). Enter the command name directly after the prompt. If the command has no parameters or switches, press the Enter key after the last letter of the command name. For example, you type the directory command as **DIR** at the prompt and then press Enter.

Adding Parameters

Parameters that are not switches appear in this book in two ways: lowercase and uppercase. You must supply the value for the lowercase text. The lowercase letters are shorthand for the full names of the parts of a command. For example, remember earlier in this chapter you learned that when you read *filename.ext*, you are supposed to type the name of the actual file. Uppercase means that you enter letter-for-letter what you see.

Remember that you delimit, or separate, parameters from the rest of the command. Most of the time the delimiter is a space, but other delimiters exist, such as the comma (,) and the backslash (\ ) and the colon (:). Just look at the examples in this book to learn the correct delimiter.

If the example command has switches, you can recognize them by the preceding slash (/). Always enter the switch letter as shown. Remember to type the slash. These rules also apply when you complete the Commands text box in the Program Properties dialog box or a replaceable parameter dialog box in the Shell. In Chapter 8, you were really learning rules for using the command line.

Ignoring a Command (Esc)

Don't worry if you mistype a command. Until you press Enter, DOS does not act on the command. You can correct a mistake by using the arrow keys or the Backspace key to reposition the cursor. Press Esc if you want to start again from the beginning. The Esc key withdraws the entry and gives you a new line. Just remember that these line-editing and canceling tips work only before you press the Enter key. Some commands can be successfully stopped with the Ctrl-C or Ctrl-Break sequence, but checking that the command is typed correctly before you press Enter is always a good practice.

Executing a Command

The Enter key is the action key for DOS commands. Make it a habit to pause and read what you have typed before you press Enter. After you press Enter, the computer carries out your command. During the processing of the command, DOS does not display any keystrokes you might type, but it does remember them. Be aware that the characters you type can end up in your next command.

Using DOS Editing Keys

When you type a command and press the Enter key, DOS copies the command into an input *buffer*, a storage area for commands. You can recall the last command from the buffer and use it again. This feature is helpful when you want to issue a command that is similar to your last command. Table 9.1 lists the keys you use to edit the input buffer.

9

Table 9.1
DOS Command Line Editing Keys

Key	Action
Tab⇄	Moves cursor to the next tab stop.
Esc	Cancels the current line and does not change the buffer.
Ins	Enables you to insert characters in the line.
Del	Deletes a character from the line.
F1 or →	Copies one character from the preceding command line.

continues

207

Table 9.1 *(Continued)*

Key	Action
F2	Copies all characters from the preceding command line up to the next character you type.
F3	Copies all remaining characters from the preceding command line.
F4	Deletes all characters from the preceding command line up to, but not including, the next character typed (opposite of F2).
F5	Moves the current line into the buffer, but does not allow MS-DOS to execute the line.
F6	Produces an end-of-file marker when you copy from the console to a disk file.

Controlling Scrolling

Scrolling describes the way in which a screen fills with information; the lines of the display "scroll off" the top of the screen as the screen fills with information. To stop a scrolling screen, press the key combination Ctrl-S. Press any key to restart the scrolling. On enhanced keyboards, you can press the Pause key to stop the scrolling.

Using DIR To View File Lists

The DIR command displays more than a list of file names. As your computing expertise grows, you will find many uses for the information provided by the full directory listing.

9

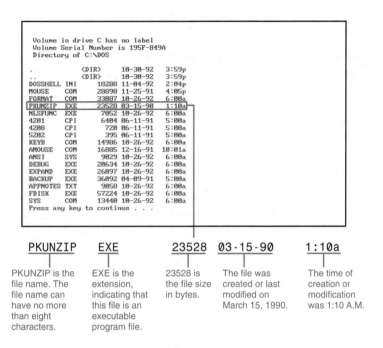

```
Volume in drive C has no label
Volume Serial Number is 195F-849A
Directory of C:\DOS

.              <DIR>      10-30-92   3:59p
..             <DIR>      10-30-92   3:59p
DOSSHELL INI      18288   11-04-92   2:04p
MOUSE    COM      28098   11-25-91   4:05p
FORMAT   COM      33087   10-26-92   6:00a
PKUNZIP  EXE      23528   03-15-90   1:10a
NLSFUNC  EXE       7052   10-26-92   6:00a
4201     CPI       6404   06-11-91   5:00a
4208     CPI        720   06-11-91   5:00a
5202     CPI        395   06-11-91   5:00a
KEYB     COM      14986   10-26-92   6:00a
AMOUSE   COM      16885   12-16-91  10:01a
ANSI     SYS       9029   10-26-92   6:00a
DEBUG    EXE      20634   10-26-92   6:00a
EXPAND   EXE      26097   10-26-92   6:00a
BACKUP   EXE      36092   04-09-91   5:00a
APPNOTES TXT       9058   10-26-92   6:00a
FDISK    EXE      57224   10-26-92   6:00a
SYS      COM      13440   10-26-92   6:00a
Press any key to continue . . .
```

PKUNZIP	EXE	23528	03-15-90	1:10a
PKUNZIP is the file name. The file name can have no more than eight characters.	EXE is the extension, indicating that this file is an executable program file.	23528 is the file size in bytes.	The file was created or last modified on March 15, 1990.	The time of creation or modification was 1:10 A.M.

Defining the DIR Command

A *directory* is a list of files. With the DIR command, you get the following information:

- The drive letter
- The volume label
- The volume serial number assigned by DOS
- The name of the directory
- Five columns of information about the files
- The number of files listed
- The total number of bytes in the files listed
- The amount of unused space on the disk

Try the DIR command now. Type **DIR** and press Enter. You just told DOS to list the files on the logged drive. You also can type **DIR A:** to list the files on drive A, or **DIR C:** to specify drive C. The A and C are the drive parameters. If you don't specify a drive, DOS uses the current drive by default.

In the Shell, you changed the current drive by choosing a drive from the list of disk drive icons. At the command line, you can change the current drive by typing a drive letter and a colon and pressing Enter. For example, by typing **A:** at the DOS prompt and pressing Enter, you change the current drive to drive A. (Note that you must have a disk in a drive before DOS can make it the current drive.) By changing the current drive, you can switch between a hard disk and a floppy disk.

Specifying Other Directories

Most DOS commands use one or more files. When you issue a command that involves files, DOS uses the files in the current directory as the default. To tell DOS to look at files in another directory, you must specify the path to the other directory. The path was defined in Chapter 5. Because paths can be very important when you use the command line, this section reviews paths.

Path Names

A *path name* is a chain of directory names that tells DOS where to find the files you want. You must build complete path names when you use the prompt. When you use the Shell, the paths are visually supplied in the Directory Tree area.

To create a path name chain, you type the drive name, a directory name (or sequence of directory names), and the file name. Make sure that you separate directory names from each other with a backslash (\ ) character. Using symbolic notation, the path name looks like this:

> *d:\directory\directory...\filename.ext*

In this notation, *d* is the drive letter. If you do not specify a drive, DOS uses the current drive by default. The first \ after the drive letter is the root directory.

directory\directory... names the directories you want to search. The ellipsis (...) simply means that you can add other directories to the specifier list. If you omit the directory specifier from the path name, DOS assumes that you want to use the current directory.

filename.ext is the name of the file. Notice that you use a backslash to separate directory names and the file name. The path name fully describes to DOS where to direct its search for the file. When you use the DIR command, if you do not specify a file name, DOS will list all files in the directory. With other

210

commands, such as COPY, you must specify a file name. The following examples show only the paths to specific directories.

To specify files in the DATA directory on drive C, the complete path is

C:\DATA

For files in the TAXES subdirectory of the DATA directory on drive C, the complete path is

C:\DATA\TAXES

If drive C is the current drive, you do not have to include the drive letter. The path therefore can be

\DATA\TAXES

Where the Search Starts

When you type a path name, DOS starts in the first specified directory. Then it passes through the other specified directory branches. The root directory has no name and is represented by a backslash (\ ). All directories grow from the root directory. If you want the search path to start at the root directory, begin the directory specification with a \ . DOS begins its search for the file in the root and follows the subdirectory chain you include in the command.

To list all the files in the C:\DATA\TAXES directory, use the following command:

DIR C:\DATA\TAXES

If drive C is the current drive, you can use the following command:

DIR \DATA\TAXES

If the current directory is C:\DATA, you can tell DOS to start the search at the current directory and simplify the command to the following:

DIR TAXES

Notice that the path above does not start with a backslash. This means that the path starts in the current directory, which in this case is C:\DATA.

When you change directories, the rules for directory paths are the same as those rules are for the DIR command. If you start the path with a backslash, the path starts at the root directory. If you omit the initial backslash, the path starts at the current directory. To change to the \DATA\TAXES directory, use the following command:

CD \DATA\TAXES

9

211

If the \DATA directory is the current directory, you can simplify the command to

> CD TAXES

When the root directory is the current directory, it does not matter whether you use the initial backslash. From the root directory

> CD \DATA\TAXES

has the same effect as

> CD DATA\TAXES

If you specify an invalid path name—one that is incomplete or incorrect—you get an error message. The error message depends on the command you are using. For example, if you type the command

> DIR TAXES

from the root directory, you get a File not found error message. No files named TAXES are in the root directory. If you issue the same command from the DATA directory, however, you get a listing of all the files in the C:\DATA\TAXES directory.

Changing Directories

In the Shell, you changed the current directory by selecting a directory from the Directory Tree area. At the command line, you use the change directory command: CD or CHDIR. Both commands are identical. Most people just use CD to change directories because it is shorter than CHDIR.

The CD command changes your position in the tree structure of directories. Decide which subdirectory you want as a working directory. Issue the command at the DOS prompt in the following form:

> CD *path*

To change to the DOS directory, enter the command

> CD \DOS

With the standard prompt, you can see that you have changed directories because the prompt changes to C:\DOS>. You can use CD to change to a directory from which you want information. Whenever you are positioned in the directory that holds the commands or data you need to use, you can omit the directory name from the command line. When you issue the CD command, the directory you change to becomes the current, or default, directory.

Understanding File Names and Extensions

The complete file name contains two parts: the name and the extension. A period separates the file name from its extension. In the directory listing, however, spaces separate the file names and extensions.

In any single directory, each file must have a unique name. DOS treats the file name and the extension as two separate parts. The file names MYFILE.WK1 and MYFILE.ABC are unique because each file has a different extension. The file names MYFILE.WK1 and YOURFILE.WK1 are also unique. Many DOS commands make use of the two parts of the file name separately. For this reason, giving each file a name and an extension is a good idea.

File names should help you identify the contents of a file. DOS file names can contain only eight alphanumeric characters, plus a three-character extension. With this built-in limit, meeting the demand of uniqueness and meaningfulness needed for some file names can require ingenuity.

DOS is also specific about which characters you use in a file name or an extension. To be safe, use only letters of the alphabet and numbers, not spaces or a period. DOS truncates excess characters in a file name.

9

Considering File Size and Date/Time Stamps

In the directory listing, the third column shows the size of the file in bytes. This measurement is an approximation of the size of your file. Your file can actually contain somewhat fewer bytes than shown. Because computers reserve blocks of data storage for files, files with slightly different data amounts may have identical file-size listings. This disk-space allocation method also explains why your word processing memo with only five words can occupy 2K of file space.

The last two columns in the directory listing display a date and a time. These entries represent the time you created the file or, with an established file, the time you last altered the file. Your computer's internal date and time are the basis for the date and time stamp in the directory. As you create more files, the date and time stamps become invaluable tools in determining the most recent version of a file.

Defining Wild Cards

Technically, a *wild card* is a character in a file specification that depicts one or more characters. In DOS, the question mark (?) character represents any single character. The * represents all characters in a file name.

For example, although the command COPY A:*.BAT C: /V looks like hieroglyphics from an Egyptian tomb, all it says is this:

- This is a copy function.
- From the disk in drive A, copy everything (designated by the asterisk) that ends with the three-letter extension BAT.
- Place a copy of these files in drive C.
- And verify (represented by the /V) that the copy is the same as the original.

Using Wild Cards in the DIR Command

You can use wild cards with the DIR command. The following text provides examples of the use of wild-card characters.

One form of the DIR command looks like this:

    DIR *d:filename.ext*

When you use DIR alone, DOS lists all files in the current directory. When you use DIR with a file name and extension parameter, DOS lists files that match the parameter. In place of *filename.ext*, you might use the file name MYFILE.WK1, as follows:

    DIR MYFILE.WK1

This DIR command tells DOS to list all files in the current directory matching MYFILE.WK1. The directory lists only one matching file: MYFILE.WK1.

If you want a listing of all files in the current directory that have an extension of WK1, the correct command is

    DIR *.WK1

DOS lists all files (designated by the * character) in the current directory that have the extension WK1. For example, the file names MYFILE.WK1 and YOURFILE.WK1 both display.

9

214

If you issue the command

DIR MYFILE.*

you might get a listing of MYFILE.WK1 and MYFILE.MEM.

You can use extensions of file names to specify what the file contains. Files containing correspondence can have the extension LET, and memo files the extension MEM. This practice enables you to use the DIR command with a wild card to get separate listings of the two types of files.

The ? wild card differs from the * wild card. Any character in the precise position as the ? is a match. For example, the command DIR MYFILE?.WK1 lists files such as MYFILE1.WK1 and MYFILE2.WK1, but not MYFILE.WK1. These same rules apply to other commands that allow wild cards.

Using the COPY Command from the Command Line

In Chapter 7 you learned how to use the COPY command from the Shell: you select the file you want to copy, choose the Copy command from the File menu, and specify a destination in a dialog box. Using the COPY command from the command line is similar to the procedure you follow in the Shell; however, from the command line, you specify all information at one time, before you press Enter to tell DOS to execute the command.

The syntax for the COPY command is as follows:

COPY *source destination*

The *source* is the path and file specification of the file or files you want to copy. The *destination* is the path and file specification for each copied file. Paths follow the rules discussed in preceding sections for DIR and CD.

Because of the use of wild cards, you may find that copying groups of files from the command line is more convenient than copying them from the Shell. The best way to learn how to use the COPY command is to look at a few examples.

To copy MYFILE.WK1 from the current directory to drive A, type

COPY MYFILE.WK1 A:

Because no destination file name is specified, the file name is not changed and MYFILE.WK1 now exists in two places.

9

To make a duplicate of MYFILE.WK1 in the current directory with the name MYFILE.BAK, type

> **COPY MYFILE.WK1 MYFILE.BAK**

To copy MYFILE.WK1 from the current directory to drive A and change its name to MYFILE.BAK, type

> **COPY MYFILE.WK1 A:MYFILE.BAK**

To copy all files with the WK1 extension from the current directory to drive A, type

> **COPY *.WK1 A:**

To copy all files with a file name that starts with BUDGET from the current directory to drive A, type

> **COPY BUDGET*.* A:**

The preceding command copies files with names such as BUDGET.WK1, BUDGET1.WK1, BUDGET93.WK1, BUDGET.DOC, and BUDGET93.ZIP.

To copy all files from the current directory to drive A, type

> **COPY *.* A:**

To copy all files with the WK1 extension from the \DATA\TAXES directory to the \BACKUP directory, type

> **COPY \DATA\TAXES*.WK1 \BACKUP**

9

Getting On-Line Help from the Command Line

In Chapter 4 you learned how to get on-line help from within the Shell. You also have access to a complete on-line help system from the command line. *MS-DOS Help* provides information about each DOS command. To start the on-line help system from the command line, use the HELP command. Simply type **HELP** at the DOS prompt and press Enter.

If you know the specific command you need help with, you can specify that command name as a parameter. The syntax for the HELP command is

> **HELP** *command*

If you want to display help information about the COPY command, type **HELP COPY**.

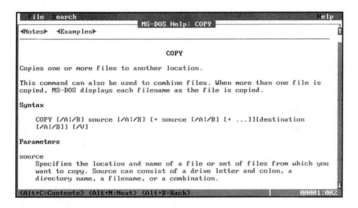

When you press Enter, MS-DOS Help displays syntax information about the COPY command.

MS-DOS Help not only displays syntax information, but also provides notes and examples for each command. The Notes screens provide suggestions on how to use the command, and the Examples screens show you examples for using the command. To access these screens, move the cursor to the word *Notes* or *Examples* (or *Syntax*) at the top of the screen and press Enter, or you can click on the word. To page forward through the Help screens, press Alt-N. To page backward, press Alt-B. To return to the command reference, press Alt-C.

MS-DOS Help is actually a program within DOS that has its own shell that works almost the same way as the DOS Shell. When you start Help without specifying a command, it displays a command reference that lists all DOS commands. A menu line extends across the top of the display, a status line across the bottom, and a scroll bar along the right side. You can use the keyboard or the mouse to choose items.

9

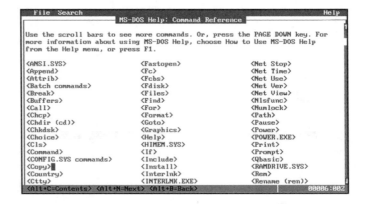

MS-DOS Help's
Command
Reference lists all
DOS commands.

To use the mouse to display help for a command, point to the command and double-click. With the keyboard, use the up- and down-arrow keys to highlight the command, and then press Enter. If you type the first letter of the command, Help will take you to that part of the alphabet in the list.

You also can get help with MS-DOS Help itself.

9

To display
information about
how to use Help,
press F1 or
choose How To
Use MS-DOS Help
from the Help
pull-down menu.

The File pull-down menu enables you to print the displayed information or exit to the command line. The Search pull-down menu enables you to search for any topic within the Help program. To search for help on a specific topic, choose Find from the Search pull-down menu.

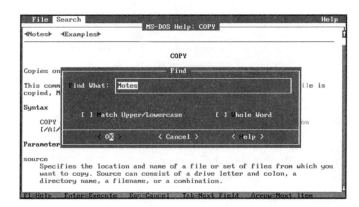

MS-DOS Help opens the the Find dialog box. Type the word you want Help to search for, and then choose OK.

To display information about an item on Help's menu line, highlight the item and press F1. To display information about a Help dialog box, press F1 while the dialog box is open on-screen.

When you are finished using Help, choose Exit from the File menu, just as you do in the DOS Shell.

Using Other Commands from the Command Line

This chapter has discussed the DIR, CD, COPY, and HELP commands to demonstrate how to use the command line. All the commands you can execute from the Shell can be executed from the command line if you know the command name. All commands follow the same rules for specifying paths and files.

You can find more detailed information about these commands in Chapter 14, a command reference of common DOS commands.

Some of the more common command names follow:

Command	Shell Command and Comments
DIR	Displays automatically in the Files area. Use File Display Options from the Options menu to change which files display and in what order.
CD or CHDIR	Change the highlighted directory in the Directory Tree area.

continues

219

Command	Shell Command and Comments
TREE	Displays automatically in the Directory Tree area.
COPY	Copy from the File menu, or the F8 key.
DEL or **ERASE**	Delete from the File menu, or the Del key.
MOVE	Move from the File menu, or the F7 key.
TYPE	View File Contents from the File menu, or the F9 key. In the Shell, you get a full-screen display. With TYPE, the file text just scrolls down the screen.
REN or **RENAME**	Rename from the File menu.
MD or **MKDIR**	Create Directory from the File menu. On the command line, MD means *make directory*.
RD or **RMDIR**	Delete from the File menu, or the Del key with an empty directory highlighted. On the command line, RD means *remove directory*.
ATTRIB	Change Attributes from the File menu.
EDIT	Editor in the Main group.
DISKCOPY	Disk Copy in the Disk Utilities group.
MSBACKUP	Backup Fixed Disk in the Disk Utilities group.
FORMAT	Format or Quick Format in the Disk Utilities group. The same command is used for both formats. To quick format, use the /Q switch.
UNDELETE	Undelete in the Disk Utilities group.

Executing Programs from the Command Line

You execute programs from the command line by using the same commands you enter into the Commands text box in the Program Properties dialog box when you are using the Shell. For example, to add Microsoft Word to a program group in the Shell, you type the following command in the Commands text box:

C:\WORD\WORD

You type the same command at the command line to start Word.

For some programs, such as 1-2-3, you must also specify a start-up directory in the Program Properties dialog box because the directory that contains the program files must be current before you can start the program. To start such a program from the command line, you must first make the correct directory current. If the \123R24 directory contains the program files, for instance, you type **CD\123R24** at the DOS prompt. Then type **123** to start the program.

You can use the PATH command and batch files to make executing programs easier. This topic is covered in Chapter 12.

Lessons Learned

- The commands you execute from the Shell can also be executed from the command line.

- DOS requires accuracy in issuing commands—not because it is unfriendly, but because its syntax is limited. Don't be intimidated by the DOS command line.

- Although DOS has dozens of commands, you use fewer than ten with any frequency.

- Fancy terms can have simple descriptions. For example, a *delimiter* is a character used as a separator.

- DOS uses the current path as the default when you execute commands. You can specify a different path, or you can change the current directory before you execute the command.

- Wild cards are the shorthand of DOS commands. The asterisk (*) can stand for any number of characters, and the question mark (?) substitutes for one letter in a command.

- The DIR command lists files in a directory.

- A directory listing tells you the file name, the file's size (in bytes), and the time and date of the last update.

- Using wild-card characters to copy groups of files can be easier then using the Shell.

9

■ The on-line MS-DOS Help program contains information about every DOS command you can execute from the command line.

■ You execute programs from the command line by using the commands you enter in the program's Program Properties dialog box.

Now that you know the command line, you can explore additional commands.

9

Protecting Your PC's Data

The time to plan for possible data loss is before it happens. If you wait until you actually lose data, it may be too late. Remember Murphy's Law: Anything that can go wrong will go wrong. When you least expect (or can afford) it, disaster strikes.

The most common cause of data loss is simple human error. A disaster also can sneak up on you as a computer malfunction, disk aging, or inconsistent electrical current. Sooner or later, you will lose important data.

The information presented in this chapter might save your invaluable data. You learn how to prevent hardware and software failures and how to protect your PC from viruses. You learn how to use the Undelete program and the UNFORMAT command to recover lost data, and you learn how to use MS Backup to safeguard your data and restore that data if it cannot be recovered.

Avoiding data loss

Recovering from data loss

Using MS Backup to protect your data

Avoiding DOS version conflicts

Key Terms Used in This Chapter	
Surge suppressor	A protective device inserted between a power outlet and a computer's power plug. Surge suppressors help block power surges that often damage computer circuits.
Static electricity	An electrical charge that builds on an object and can discharge when another object is touched. Electronic circuits are easily damaged by static electricity discharges.
Self-parking heads	Heads on most newer disk drives that move to a position on the disk in which there is no data. These heads protect the disk from data loss when it is moved.
Head-parking program	A program that parks heads on a disk that does not have self-parking heads.
Delete tracking file	A special file created by the Undelete program and used by DOS to make undeleting files easier and more reliable.
Back up	To copy files from the hard disk to floppy disks or other DOS-compatible devices, such as tape drives.
Restore	To copy backup copies of files from floppy disks or other DOS-compatible devices, such as tape drives, to a hard disk.
Virus	A set of instructions hidden inside a computer program designed to wreak havoc on your computer system.

10

Avoiding Data Loss

As you use your computer, you create files that contain valuable information. Because you are very careful and today's computers are very reliable, you may be tempted to trust that these files will be there when you need them. However, as an old computer saying goes, "There are two kinds of computer users: those who have lost files, and those who are going to lose files."

You learn three techniques to avoid data loss in this chapter. The techniques are as follows:

- Minimize the chances of loss by taking preventative measures.
- Learn and use DOS commands that enable you to recover from some cases of accidental loss.
- Maintain backup copies on other disks.

When you take preventative measures, you save yourself the aggravation of losing data and the time to recover it. When you recover data, you save yourself the time to find and restore the data from a backup. The first two techniques are not foolproof, however. The only way to ensure that data loss is not permanent is to have another copy available.

Taking Preventative Measures To Avoid Data Loss

The first way to avoid data loss is to prevent it before it happens. Unfortunately, no matter what you do, it is impossible to guarantee that you will never lose data. You can minimize the risk, however, with preventative measures.

Preventing Your Mistakes

As you gain experience with your computer, you use it more. You create, copy, and erase more files. You also become a little less careful when you copy and erase files. One difference between a novice and an expert is that the expert makes many more mistakes.

Commands such as COPY, ERASE, and FORMAT perform their jobs without regard to your intentions. DOS does not know when a technically correct command will produce an unwanted effect. For this reason, always study the commands you enter before you execute them.

10

With the Shell, DOS displays a confirmation dialog box each time you erase, copy, or move a file into a directory that already contains a file with the same file name.

If you use the Confirmation choice in the Options menu to disable these confirmation dialog boxes, you increase your risk of making an error.

Whether you use the command line or the Shell, it is too easy to develop a rhythm that speeds you through confirmation prompts and into ruin. Pressing Ctrl-C, Ctrl-Break, or Ctrl-Alt-Del may cancel a command before it does any harm, but it may be too late.

The most common errors that cause data loss do not occur in DOS, however. Most people spend much more time using applications programs than they spend using DOS. You can lose data in your spreadsheet, word processor, or database management system in many ways. You can, for example, issue a command that erases a large part of your forecasting spreadsheet. Then the next time you retrieve your spreadsheet, you may find that some of your data is gone.

Just as you must exercise care when you use DOS commands, you must be just as careful when you use commands in your applications. Each application has different commands; therefore, make sure that you have copies of all your important files before you change them.

Preventing Software Failures

Each software program you buy is a set of instructions for the microprocessor. Some software packages have mistakes called *bugs*. Software bugs are usually minor and rarely cause more than keyboard lockups or jumbled displays.

226

Utility programs, such as disk caches and partition utilities, however, can interfere with complex programs, such as Windows. A faulty utility program can wipe out an entire hard disk. This occurrence is rare, but that is of little consolation when it happens to you.

Bugs usually occur in the first releases of programs. Most software contains version numbers. Version 1 or 1.0 is the first version of a program. Version 1.1 is a minor upgrade, and Version 2.0 is a major upgrade. Many people try to avoid Version 1 of any program. Some people avoid Version x.0 of any program (such as 2.0 or 3.0), because a major upgrade is also likely to have bugs.

Perhaps the best way to avoid software errors is to talk to other people about a program before you buy or use it. Talk to friends and coworkers. You can meet people at computer user group meetings and find out about their experience with the program. If the program gets good reviews, the chances of serious software errors are minimal.

Preventing Hardware Failures

Today's personal computers are reliable and economical data-processing machines. The latest generation of PCs does the work of mainframe computers that only a fortunate few could access a decade ago. As is true of any machine, however, computer components can break down.

Computers contain thousands of integrated circuits. Under ideal conditions, most of these circuits can last a century or more. Disk drives incorporate precise moving parts with critical alignments. Although disk drives are very reliable, most common hardware failures occur on disk drives.

10

Computer hardware is vulnerable to a number of physical threats. These threats include humidity, static discharge, excessive heat, and erratic electrical power. By following the precautions presented in this section, you reduce the odds of losing time and information because of hardware failure.

Be vigilant about your computer's environment. A power strip with a built-in surge protector is a good start. If your power flutters and lights flicker, you probably need a line voltage regulator. Make sure that no electrical appliances near your computer pollute your power source. Connect your computer equipment to power sources not shared by copiers, TVs, fans, or any other electrical equipment that contains a motor or uses a surge of power when it is turned on.

Power strips keep your cables neat and rid your work area of strings of extension cords. Power surge suppressors are built into many power strips.

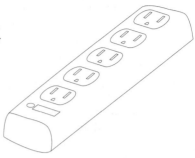

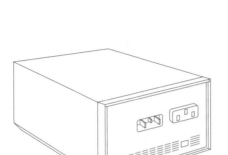

Line voltage regulators remove "dips" and "spikes" in electric power lines caused either by motors turning on or by other power reducers.

Is the fan on the back of your computer choked with dust? Clean the air vents and check to make sure that your computer has room to breathe. If the outside of your computer is dusty, the inside may be full of dust, too. Remove the cover and vacuum the inside occasionally, especially the air-intake vents to the power supply.

Use a soft blind-cleaner attachment on your vacuum cleaner to remove the dust build-up from your computer's breathing system.

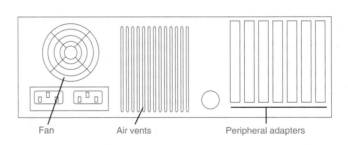

Fan   Air vents   Peripheral adapters

Your computer can become erratic when the temperature climbs. Circuits are not reliable when they overheat and can cause jumbled data. To ensure that your computer can function properly, keep it cool.

Your body generates static electricity when humidity is low, when you wear synthetic fabrics, or when you walk across carpet. Static electricity appears harmless, but electronics are very sensitive to it. Just touching the keyboard

10

while carrying a static charge can send an electrical shudder through your computer, causing data loss or circuit failure. Fortunately, you can avoid static problems by touching your grounded system unit's cabinet before touching the keyboard. If static electricity is a serious problem for you, ask your dealer about antistatic products.

Moving or shaking your computer can damage the disk drives. Never move your computer while the power is on and the hard disk is spinning. While a hard disk is on, the heads float a fraction of an inch above the disks. When you turn off your computer the hard disk stops spinning and the heads settle onto the disks. Even if you move your computer with the power off, the heads can move or bounce on the disks and damage the surface of the disk.

To prevent data loss, most hard disks have *self-parking heads*. When you turn off your computer, the heads move to a part of the disk that is not used for data. Even if the heads damage the disk surface, no data is lost. If your hard disk does not have self-parking heads, a *head-parking program* came with your hard disk to park the heads manually. Always run the park program before you move your computer.

The heads on floppy disks also can be damaged when you move your computer. To protect them, insert a floppy disk that does not contain any data, and close the drive door before you move your computer.

Stopping small hardware problems before they become big ones takes a little planning and forethought. Table 10.1 lists a few simple, yet successful, preventive solutions.

10

Table 10.1
Hardware Problems and Remedies

Problem	*Remedy*
Static electricity	Antistatic liquid.
	Antistatic floor mat.
	"Touch Pad" on desk.
Overheating	Clean clogged air vents.
	Remove objects blocking vents.
	Use air-conditioned room in summer.
Damaged hard disks	Don't move the computer while the disk is running.
	Park the heads before you move the computer.

continues

Table 10.1 (Continued)

Problem	Remedy
Damaged floppy disks	Don't leave disks to be warped by sun. Use protective covers.
	Avoid spilling liquids on disks. Store disks in a safe place.
	Don't move the computer while the disk is running.
	Avoid magnetic fields from appliances such as TVs and microwave ovens. Even the PC on your desk has a magnetic field from its hard drive.

Protecting Your Computer from Viruses

One type of software problem that can cause serious data loss is a software *virus*. A computer virus is a set of computer instructions, hidden inside a program, that can take over your computer and destroy all your programs and data files. Viruses are the work of computer vandals who destroy the property of others for "fun."

A virus rarely infects commercial software. Viruses usually are found in free software distributed through electronic bulletin board systems (BBSs) and passed around on floppy disk. Operators of bulletin board systems work very hard to avoid viruses, but the risk is not completely eliminated.

To practice "safe computing," never use a program from someone you do not know. Before you use any program, talk with others who have used the program and make sure that they have had no problems. Also make sure that the date and file size of both versions of the program are identical. Two "copies" of what should be the same program with different sizes is a clue that the larger one is infected with a virus.

Unfortunately, viruses are becoming all too common. Fortunately, there are anti-virus protection programs you can use to detect and remove viruses from your computer. MS-DOS 6 includes two such anti-virus programs: MS Anti-Virus and VSafe. MS Anti-Virus scans your PC's memory and disk drives to detect and clean viruses. It comes in two versions—one for DOS and one for Windows. MS Anti-Virus for DOS is discussed in the next section, and MS Anti-Virus for Windows is explained in Appendix B.

10

VSafe is a terminate-and-stay-resident (TSR) program that continuously monitors your PC for viruses. If it suspects that a virus exists, it displays a warning message. To install VSafe, type **VSAFE** at the command line. It will remain in memory until you shut off your computer. To load it each time you start your computer, add the command to your AUTOEXEC.BAT file. Editing your AUTOEXEC.BAT file is discussed in Chapter 12.

Using MS Anti-Virus for DOS

You can run MS Anti-Virus for DOS from the command line or add it to your AUTOEXEC.BAT file so that it starts each time you start your PC. It is an optional program you install during setup. If it is not already installed, consult Appendix A. To run MS Anti-Virus from Windows, consult Appendix B.

To start MS Anti-Virus for DOS from the command line, type **MSAV** and press Enter. MS Anti-Virus' Main Menu opens on-screen.

MS Anti-Virus uses a shell similar to the DOS Shell. You can use the keyboard or the mouse to make selections from the Main Menu. In addition, the program displays a list of shortcut keys along the bottom of your screen. With a mouse, you can click on the word. Press F1 to display context-sensitive help screens.

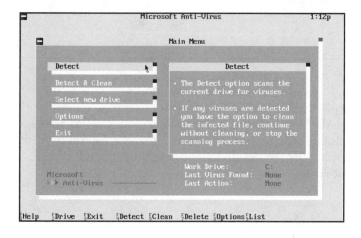

From the MS Anti-Virus Main Menu, you can choose to detect viruses or to detect and clean at the same time. You can specify the drive you want scanned, and you can specify configuration options.

To scan the current drive for viruses, choose **D**etect from the Main Menu. To scan and clean the current drive, choose Detect & Clean. If you want to check a different drive, choose **S**elect New Drive. Drive icons appear at the top of your screen. Choose the one you want to scan.

MS Anti-Virus comes preset to scan your disks and memory for certain known viruses. You can see a list of the viruses and display or print out information about each one. To see the list, press F9 or click the word *List* at the bottom of your screen. To display information about a particular virus, either click on it or select it and press Enter.

The configuration options for MS Anti-Virus are preset so that, in addition to scanning for the known viruses, the program scans for changes in executable files that may indicate an unknown virus. If the program detects a change, it displays a warning prompt. A change in an executable file is not proof that a virus is present. For example, updating an applications program can change an executable file.

If an executable file has changed, MS Anti-Virus displays the Verify Error dialog box, in which you must specify whether to update the file, delete the file, continue with the scan, or stop the scan.

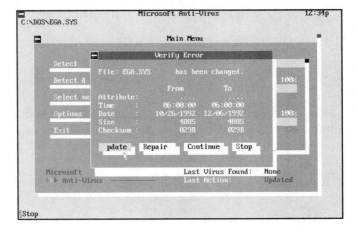

10

You can change the configuration options for MS Anti-Virus by turning the options settings on or off. To change the default options settings, choose **O**ptions from the Main Menu. The selected settings have check marks beside them. To select an option, highlight it and click the left mouse button or, with a keyboard, press the space bar. To deselect an option, press the left mouse button or the space bar again.

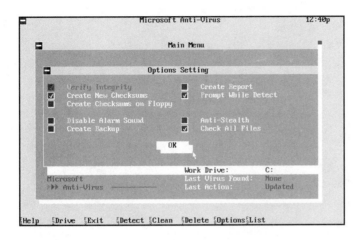

The options settings enable you to specify levels of performance for MS Anti-Virus.

The following list contains brief descriptions of each option. A check mark indicates a default setting.

✓	Verify Integrity	Scans for changes in executable files.
✓	Create New Checksums	Creates a checklist file for each directory scanned. If changes are detected in executable files, a warning message is displayed.
	Create Checksums on Floppy	Creates the checklist files on floppy disks.
	Disable Alarm Sound	Turns off the audible alarm.
	Create Backup	Creates a backup file of any file containing a virus before the file is cleaned.
	Create Report	Creates an ASCII text file of action taken during a scan.
✓	Prompt While Detect	Displays a dialog box when a virus is detected, giving you the option of cleaning the file, continuing the scan, or stopping the scan.
	Anti-Stealth	Activates a deeper level of virus detection.
✓	Check All Files	When on, scans all files. When off, scans only executable files.

10

233

As MS Anti-Virus scans a disk, it displays a status window showing you how much memory is being scanned, then how many directories and files are being scanned.

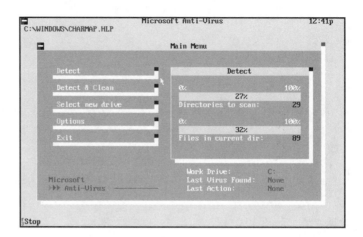

To interrupt the scan, press F3 or Esc, or point at the word *Stop* at the bottom of your screen and press the left mouse button.

When the scan is complete, MS Anti-Virus displays the Viruses Detected and Cleaned report, telling you how many disks and files were scanned and whether they were infected and cleaned. Choose OK to return to the Main Menu.

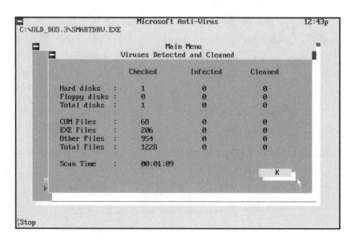

10

When you have finished using MS Anti-Virus for DOS, choose Exit and OK to return to the command line.

Recovering from Data Loss

Despite all of your precautions, chances are you will experience data loss at some time. With earlier versions of DOS, you cannot recover lost data. When you erase a file or format a disk, all the data is gone forever. In many cases, however, the data still exists on the disk, but you cannot access it.

Many utility programs were written to recover this lost data. Some of the most well-known programs were part of Norton Utilities, Mace Utilities, and PC Tools Deluxe. Microsoft incorporated some of the utilities from PC Tools Deluxe, Version 6, into DOS 5 to provide recovery for lost data. With DOS 6, Microsoft improves the utilities to make data recovery even easier and more reliable.

With these utilities, you can *undelete* a file you erased and *unformat* a disk you formatted in error.

These programs are possible because the ERASE and FORMAT commands do not really remove the files from the disk. Instead, these commands clear the information from the file allocation table and the directory. The file allocation table is present on every disk. It tells DOS which areas of the disk contain data and which are available for storing new data. The directory tells DOS information about the file, such as the file name and size.

After you erase a file or format a disk, all the files are still on the disk, but the space is freed by DOS so that the next time you create a file, DOS can write over the deleted files. Therefore, if you want to recover a file, you should do it immediately, before DOS uses the disk space to write another file.

Some lost data cannot be recovered. If you copy a file to a disk or subdirectory that already contains a file with that name, the old file is overwritten and is lost. If you save a file in an applications program and save it under the same name as an existing file, the program may give you a warning message. If you override the warning and save the file, the old file is overwritten and is lost. Your only recourse is to restore a backup copy.

10

Using Undelete To Recover a Deleted File

If you delete a file or group of files in error, you might be able to recover the files by using the Undelete utility. Undelete is an optional program you install during setup. It comes in two versions—one for DOS and one for Windows. If Undelete is not installed, see Appendix A. If you want to use Undelete for Windows, see Appendix B.

Undelete offers three levels of file protection—Delete Sentry, Delete Tracker, and MS-DOS. It can only use one level at a time and it defaults to the highest level available.

Delete Sentry is the highest level of protection. It is a TSR program you must install from the command line. Once in memory, it creates a hidden directory called SENTRY, where deleted files are stored. In addition, the file allocation table is left unchanged, and DOS therefore acts as if the deleted file is still in place on the disk. It will not store a new file in its place. If you undelete the file, it is returned to its original location on the disk. (Note that Undelete automatically purges the SENTRY directory after seven days.)

Delete Sentry can give you peace of mind when it comes to recovering deleted files. One minor drawback to consider is that Delete Sentry, as a TSR program, occupies memory space and the SENTRY directory occupies disk space. To load Delete Sentry into memory, type **UNDELETE** /S at the command line. DOS adds it to your AUTOEXEC.BAT file so that it loads each time you start your PC.

Delete Tracker is the middle level of protection. It is also a TSR program you must install from the command line. Delete Tracker records the location of deleted files in a hidden file called PCTRACKER.DEL, making it easier for Undelete to locate the file. However, even with Delete Tracker installed, the file allocation table is changed when you delete a file, enabling DOS to use the space on the disk to store a new file. If that is the case, you will not be able to recover the deleted file, or you might be able to recover only part of it.

To load Delete Tracker into memory, type **UNDELETE** /T at the command line. DOS adds it to your AUTOEXEC.BAT file so that it loads each time you start your PC.

You can remove Delete Sentry or Delete Tracker from memory by typing **UNDELETE** /U at the command line.

MS-DOS offers the standard level of protection. Once Undelete is installed, the standard MS-DOS protection is active whenever you turn on your computer. If you use the Undelete command immediately after deleting the file, MS-DOS ensures that you will be able to recover the file. However, if you do not use Undelete immediately, it is possible that DOS already used that part of the disk for a new file, which means that you will not be able to recover the deleted file or that you might be able to recover only part of it.

No matter which level of Undelete you install, the procedure for recovering a file is the same. You can use Undelete from the Shell or from the command line.

10

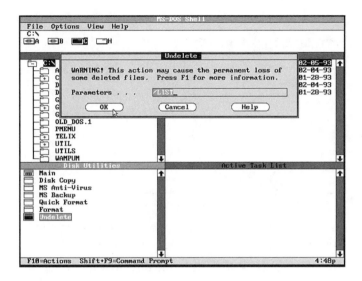

When you choose Undelete from the Disk Utilities program group, DOS displays the Undelete dialog box.

The default parameter is /LIST, which lists the files that have been deleted but does not undelete any files. The list tells you which method of delete protection is being used, and whether the deleted files have been retained in the Delete Sentry control file, the deletion tracking file, or the MS-DOS directory.

To undelete one or more files, ignore the default and enter the name of the file you want to undelete. You can use wild cards in the file name; for example, you can type ***.BAT** to undelete all deleted batch files in the current directory.

You also can include a command switch to specify where Undelete should look for the deleted files. For example, /DOS recovers files in the DOS directory, /DT recovers deletion tracking files, and /DS recovers delete sentry files. To recover all files in the Delete Sentry file, for instance, type *.* **/DS** in the Undelete dialog box. If Delete Sentry is the current level of protection, but you want to recover all files from the MS-DOS directory, type *.* **/DOS**.

10

Whether you execute Undelete from the Shell or the command line, DOS displays an analysis of the files available to undelete and a prompt to undelete each file.

```
UNDELETE - A delete protection facility
Copyright (C) 1987-1993 Central Point Software, Inc.
All rights reserved.

Directory: C:\DATA\FIGURES
File Specifications: *.*
                                     ....
    Delete Sentry control file contains    0 deleted files.

    Deletion-tracking file contains    5 deleted files.
    Of those,    5 files have all clusters available,
                 0 files have some clusters available,
                 0 files have no clusters available.

    MS-DOS directory contains    0 deleted files.
    Of those,    0 files may be recovered.

Using the Deletion-tracking method.

    10FIG07  PCX    25696 11-07-92 10:47a  ...A  Deleted: 11-07-92 10:48a
All of the clusters for this file are available. Undelete (Y/N)?
```

Press **Y** to undelete the file, **N** to skip the file, and Esc to cancel the command and return to the Shell or the DOS prompt.

When a file is deleted, the information still exists in the directory, but the first letter of the file name is changed to an asterisk (*). If you try to undelete a file with only the MS-DOS level of protection, DOS lists the deleted files in the current directory with a question mark (?) in place of the first character and asks whether you want to undelete each one. If you press **Y**, DOS prompts you for the first character of the file name.

10

To undelete a file with the basic MS-DOS level of protection, you must supply the first character of the file name.

```
Copyright (C) 1987-1993 Central Point Software, Inc.
All rights reserved.

Directory: C:\DATA\TAXES
File Specifications: *.*
                                     ....
    Delete Sentry control file contains    0 deleted files.

    Deletion-tracking file contains    2 deleted files.
    Of those,    2 files have all clusters available,
                 0 files have some clusters available,
                 0 files have no clusters available.

    MS-DOS directory contains    2 deleted files.
    Of those,    2 files may be recovered.

Using the MS-DOS directory method.

    ?AXEST   WK1     6766  3-10-92  3:10a  ...A  Undelete (Y/N)?y
    Please type the first character for ?AXEST   .WK1: t

File successfully undeleted.

    ?UDGET   DOC    39416 10-31-92  6:21p  ...A  Undelete (Y/N)?y
    Please type the first character for ?UDGET   .DOC:
```

If the deleted file is fragmented or on the disk in sections, DOS can recover only the first section.

When you return to the Shell after undeleting one or more files, the undeleted files are not included in the file list display. Press F5 to refresh the display.

At the DOS prompt, enter the UNDELETE command followed by the file or files to undelete, as follows:

> UNDELETE SAMPLE.TXT

or

> UNDELETE *.BAT

Remember that you can use switches to specify which files to recover. The command reference in Chapter 14 lists additional UNDELETE options.

Using UNFORMAT To Recover a Formatted Disk

If you format a disk in error and do not write any new files to the disk, you can use UNFORMAT to recover the files of the disk. When you format a disk that contains data, DOS saves the UNFORMAT information about the files on the disk before it clears the file allocation table and directory.

```
Insert new diskette for drive A:
and press ENTER when ready...

Checking existing disk format.
Saving UNFORMAT information.
Verifying 1.2M
Format complete.

Volume label (11 characters, ENTER for none)?

    1213952 bytes total disk space
    1213952 bytes available on disk

       512 bytes in each allocation unit.
      2371 allocation units available on disk.

Volume Serial Number is 300D-12CC

Format another (Y/N)?
```

When you format a disk, DOS saves the information needed to unformat the disk later, provided that you do not put any files on the disk.

10

DOS uses a program called MIRROR to save the UNFORMAT information. This process is called *safe formatting*. UNFORMAT then uses the MIRROR information to unformat the disk.

UNFORMAT is not available in the Shell. You can use it only from the command line. The syntax for the UNFORMAT command follows:

> UNFORMAT *drive:*

The command reference in Chapter 14 lists additional UNFORMAT options.

After you initiate
the UNFORMAT
command, you
must confirm that
you want to
proceed; DOS
then recovers the
files on the
formatted disk.

```
C:\DOS>unformat a:

Insert disk to rebuild in drive A:
and press ENTER when ready.

Restores the system area of your disk by using the image file created
by the MIRROR command.

    WARNING !!          WARNING !!

This command should be used only to recover from the inadvertent use of
the FORMAT command or the RECOVER command.  Any other use of the UNFORMAT
command may cause you to lose data!  Files modified since the MIRROR image
file was created may be lost.

Searching disk for MIRROR image.

The last time the MIRROR or FORMAT command was used was at 11:03 on 11-07-92.

The MIRROR image file has been validated.

Are you sure you want to update the system area of your drive A (Y/N)?
```

Make sure that you unformat a disk immediately after you format the disk in
error and before you write any files on the disk. After you write files on a disk,
the information that used to be on the disk is lost.

Restoring Backup Copies

Remember that you can take measures to prevent data loss, and in some cases
you can recover from data loss, but these measures are not foolproof. The
only way to avoid data loss is to make sure that you always have a backup copy
of every file.

The most important data-protection measure you can take is learning to
make backup copies of all your disk files. It is a good idea to use DISKCOPY to
copy every disk that comes with any new software you buy, even before you
install it on your hard disk. Whenever you create or change a very important
data file, immediately copy it to a floppy disk. If something happens to the
original file or disk, you can use the copies. Of course, you should immediately make copies of the copies. You learned how to use COPY and DISKCOPY
in Chapter 7.

Using MS Backup To Protect Your Data

COPY and DISKCOPY are effective for backing up individual floppies and files.
To back up all your data for safekeeping, use the new MS Backup program
included in DOS 6. Earlier versions of DOS had a BACKUP command. The MS
Backup program in DOS 6 is a utility program that also includes restoration
and comparison capabilities.

10

MS Backup has several advantages over COPY and DISKCOPY for backing up all your data:

- You can back up an entire disk or directory structure with one command.
- You can back up files that are larger than the capacity of your floppy disks.
- You can back up only those files created or changed since the last time you ran MS Backup.
- You need fewer floppy disks.

MS Backup simplifies the routine of backing up disks and directories. The rest of this chapter covers backup techniques, including how to restore the data from backup disks. With the examples in this chapter, you learn to back up and restore your entire hard disk or selective directories and files. You also learn the various options available for adapting MS Backup to your particular needs.

MS Backup can copy files from your hard disk to the destination floppy disk or to another MS-DOS compatible backup device, including network drives. The internal format of the backed-up file is different from that of normal files; therefore, you cannot use COPY to retrieve files stored on a backup disk. Your computer can use the files produced by MS Backup only after you run them through the Restore portion of the MS Backup program.

MS Backup and its Restore feature are effective insurance against file loss. You can protect against the loss of hours or weeks of work through methodical use of MS Backup to make backup disks of your files. Of course, you also should master the Restore feature, which uses your backup disks to replace files lost from your hard disk.

10

If you have not yet tried to back up disk files, or if you are learning your way around DOS, the rest of this chapter is important. If you apply this information, you can avoid losing data.

Understanding MS Backup

MS Backup is an optional DOS 6 program you install during setup. It is available for both Windows and DOS. If MS Backup is not installed on your PC, see Appendix A. If you want to use MS Backup for Windows, see Appendix B.

MS Backup lets you back up your hard disk files to floppy disks or to other Microsoft-compatible backup media such as network drives. Your computer may have several different methods available to back up your files. For example, your computer may have a tape backup unit as part of its peripheral hardware. The methods for backing up files to tape vary. You should know how to create and manipulate disk-based backups, however, in case you need to restore files to a computer that is not equipped with a tape backup.

When you use MS Backup, you create a backup set of disks that contains the files you selected to back up. You can use MS Backup to compare the backup sets to the original files or other files on the hard disk, and you can restore the backup sets to their original location on the disk or to a different location. You can even restore them to a different computer.

Using simple menu commands, you can back up an entire fixed disk. You also can set up options for backups such as partial backups of the disk, selected files for backup, and for data verification. The same menu commands enable you to compare and restore the backed up files.

Types of Backup

Three types of backup are available with MS Backup:

- A *full* backup makes backup copies of all the files you select before running MS Backup.
- An *incremental* backup automatically makes backup copies of all files that have changed since the last time you ran a full or incremental backup.
- A *differential* backup automatically makes backup copies of all files that have changed since the last time you ran a full backup.

You can determine which backup type or which combination is most effective for your needs.

Performing a full backup about once a week is a good habit. A daily incremental backup keeps your backup data thoroughly up-to-date. If you do not regularly schedule partial backups to copy your most important files, do a complete backup more often.

On any day, ask yourself, "If my hard drive failed today, how much data would I lose?" Performing a backup is easier than trying to reconstruct lost data. DOS does not prompt you to make backups. The decision is yours; it's your data.

10

242

The BACKUP command used in earlier versions of DOS could get very confusing. You had to know which command switches to set and which parameters to use to back up the files you wanted in the way that you wanted. In DOS 6, MS Backup is a flexible, menu-driven program. You can select on-screen options and then save them in setup files you can use again and again.

Starting MS Backup

You can start MS Backup from the Shell or from the command line. From the Shell, choose MS Backup from the Disk Utilities program group. To start MS Backup from the command line, type **MSBACKUP**. MS Backup's main program dialog box opens. Like Anti-Virus, MS Backup has its own shell, which makes it easier to use. You choose items from dialog boxes and menus by using either the keyboard or the mouse. You can display Help screens at any time by pressing F1.

The first time you run MS Backup, you should configure it for your hardware system, a procedure you will learn in the following section. You can check the configuration by running a compatibility test. If you do not run a compatibility test, the first screen you see when you start MS Backup is a warning, reminding you that without the compatibility test, reliable disk backups cannot be guaranteed. Choose OK to remove the warning and display MS Backup's main program dialog box.

From this main dialog box, you can perform a backup, restore backup files, compare files that have been backed up to the originals, or configure MS Backup.

10

Configuring MS Backup

To configure MS Backup and perform the compatibility test, choose Configure from the main program dialog box.

The MS Backup configuration is semi-automatic, meaning that the program checks your system and adjusts the configuration itself. To set the configuration, MS Backup runs through a series of tests on your video display, your mouse, and your MS Backup devices. It tests your floppy drive configurations, your processor's speed, your hard disk's reading capability, and certain other performance indexes, and it displays the results on-screen.

MS Backup
displays your
system configu-
ration in the
Configure dialog
box. To change
the configuration
or see more
details about a
specific option,
choose the option
you want.

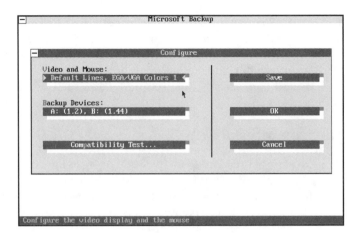

The compatibility test verifies whether MS Backup is correctly installed and
configured to perform reliable file backups and restorations on your PC. The
test consists of performing a small backup. You can skip the test, but then you
cannot be sure whether MS Backup is working correctly. Also, each time you
start MS Backup, it will display the warning screen.

Before you start the compatibility test, make sure that you have two blank
disks available. They should be the correct size and density for the drive you
are going to use. The program displays a dialog box when it is time for you to
choose the drive where the backup disk will be placed, and again when it is
time to insert the backup disk.

To start the compatibility test, choose Compatibility Test from the Configure
dialog box, and then choose Start Test.

MS Backup first tests the compatibility of the backup. When the test is complete, a report screen is displayed. Choose OK to continue. MS Backup uses
the Compare function to verify the backed up files (see "Comparing Files,"
later in this chapter). When the comparison is complete, another report
screen is displayed. Choose OK to complete the compatibility test. Choose OK
again to return to the Configure dialog box. Choose Save to save the configuration settings and return to MS Backup's main program dialog box.

If you ever change your hardware, you should reconfigure MS Backup by
choosing Configure from the main program dialog box and running a compatibility test again.

Backing Up Files

The MS Backup program consists of a series of menu screens and dialog boxes. You can use the mouse or the keyboard to make selections. Every item also has a shortcut key, highlighted in a different color.

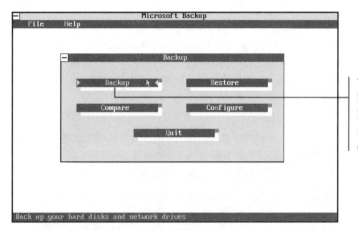

To perform a backup, choose **B**ackup from the main program dialog box.

A Full Backup

To perform the default backup, follow these steps:

1. Choose **B**ackup from MS Backup's main program dialog box. The Backup dialog box appears. The Backup dialog box enables you to choose the type of backup you want to perform, the source drive, the destination drive, and the files you want to include or exclude.

10

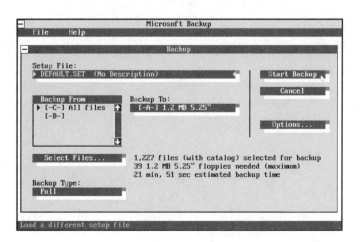

If you accept the default settings, all the files on drive C will be backed up to floppies in drive A.

245

Notice that the Backup dialog box also displays the number of files selected for backup, how many disks the backup requires, and how long the backup will take.

2. Choose the source drive in the Backup From box. To back up all files on drive C, highlight drive C and press the space bar, or click on drive C with the right mouse button.

3. Choose the Backup Type box, choose Full, and choose OK.

4. Verify that the destination drive in the Backup To box is drive A. If necessary choose the Backup To box, choose drive A, and choose OK.

5. To verify the disk backup options, choose the Options button. The Disk Backup Options dialog box appears.

Options include verifying data, compressing data, password protecting data, using error correction, and pausing to issue prompts. When options are the way you want them, choose OK.

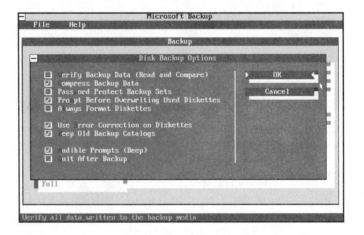

10

6. Choose the Start Backup button to back up the selected files. MS Backup prompts you to insert a disk into the correct drive.

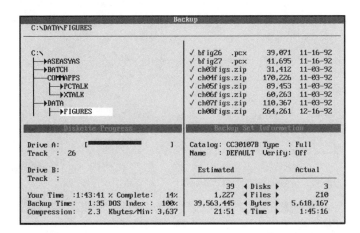

During the backup procedure, MS Backup displays a status screen.

Always label your backup disks clearly, including the disk number, the files backed up, and the date you performed the backup. Put the backup disks in the proper sequence and store them in a safe place.

A full backup can take a long time, depending on the number of files and directories on your hard disk. When the backup is complete, MS Backup displays a status report. Choose OK to return to the main program dialog box.

Backing Up Selected Files

You do not have to back up every file each time you perform a backup. MS Backup is very flexible—you can select only one file, you can select files from different directories, or you can select entire directories.

To back up selected files, follow these steps:

1. Choose Backup from MS Backup's main program dialog box. The Backup dialog box appears.

2. Select the source drive (drive C) in the Backup From box.

3. Choose the Select Files button. The Select Backup Files screen opens.

10

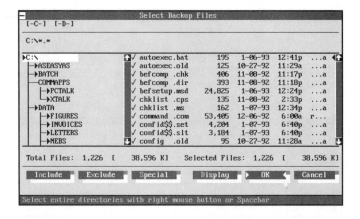

The Select
Backup Files
screen displays
the files located
on the source
disk.

4. Select a directory or file by highlighting it and then pressing the space
bar or by clicking on it with the right mouse button. Notice the check
marks that appear beside the selected files.

To deselect a directory or file, highlight it and press the space bar, or
click on it with the right mouse button.

To change the sort order of the listed files, choose the Display button
at the bottom of the screen. The buttons at the bottom of the Select
Backup Files screen enable you to specify by name the files you want
to include or exclude from the backup. You can use the Include and
Exclude buttons to specify the path to individual files. Enter the path
and file name and choose OK.

10

If you select the
Special button,
the Special
Selections dialog
box appears,
enabling you to
exclude files
based on their
attributes or
according to
the date they
were created or
modified.

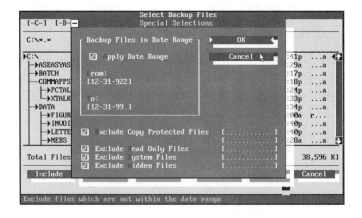

5. After you select the files you want to back up, choose OK to return to the Backup dialog box.

6. Choose the Backup Type box, choose the backup type you want (such as Incremental), and then choose OK.

7. Select the destination drive (drive A) in the Backup To box.

8. Choose the Options button. The Disk Backup Options screen appears. Select the options you want and deselect the options you do not want. Choose OK to return to the Backup dialog box.

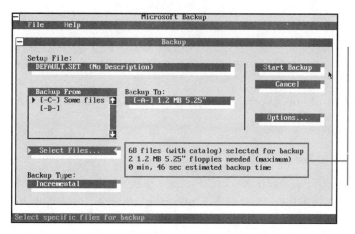

MS Backup displays the number of selected files, the number of disks you need, and how much time the backup will take.

9. Choose the Start Backup button.

10

During the backup process, MS Backup displays status information.

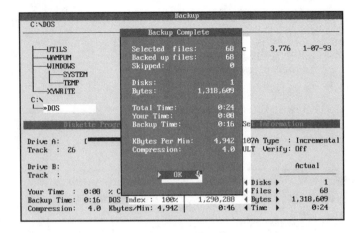

When the backup is complete, MS Backup displays a Backup Complete report. Choose OK to return to the main program dialog box.

To return to the command line, choose Quit from MS Backup's main program dialog box.

Setup Files

The MS Backup menus and dialog boxes make it easy to set up for any kind of backup, but DOS has included an even easier way. You can save your backup settings in a *setup file* you can use for future backups. That way, whenever you want to perform a backup, you can select a setup file instead of specifying all the backup settings. The default setup file that MS Backup uses is called DEFAULT.SET. You can save up to 50 different setup files for the different types of backups you commonly perform.

To save the current backup settings in a setup file, follow these steps:

1. In the Backup dialog box, choose Save Setup As from the File pull-down menu. The Save Setup File dialog box opens.

2. In the File Name box, enter an eight character file name, such as DATAFILE. MS Backup automatically enters the extension SET.

3. In the Description box, enter a description of the backup settings. For example, enter \DATA files, verify, correct. MS Backup displays this information beside the file name in the Backup dialog box. If you have many setup files, the description helps you differentiate one from another.

4. Choose the Save button.

10

To select the setup file you want to use, follow these steps:

1. Choose the Setup File box from the Backup dialog box. A list of setup files appears.

2. Select the setup file you want to use and press the space bar, or click the setup file with the right mouse button. Notice the check mark beside the selected file name.

3. Choose the Open button. MS Backup displays the setup file information in the Backup dialog box.

4. Choose the Start Backup button to begin the backup procedure.

Catalog Files

Each time you perform a backup, MS Backup creates a *Backup Set Catalog* file and stores it on your hard disk and on the backup disk. (If the program uses more than one floppy disk for the backup, it stores the catalog file on the last disk.) The catalog contains information about the files and directories you backed up and the setup file you used. You use the catalog to compare backed up files to the originals and to select files you want to restore.

MS Backup uses a naming scheme for catalog files that helps you know what the file contains. Each name includes the first and last drives backed up in the set, the last digit of the year when the backup was performed, the month and day of the backup, the position of the backup in sequence if more than one backup was performed on the same day, and the backup type. For example, the catalog file for the first incremental backup from drive C on November 7, 1992 would be named CC21107A.INC. The catalog file name for a second full backup would be CC21107B.FUL.

MS Backup also creates a *master catalog* file each time you back up. The master catalog contains a list of each Backup Set Catalog file created using a particular setup file. A master catalog file has the same name as the setup file, with the extension CAT. For example, DATAFILE.CAT is the master catalog file for the DATAFILE.SET setup file.

If you delete a catalog from your hard disk, you can retrieve it from the backup set. If you cannot use the catalog on your hard disk, you can rebuild it.

Catalog files are not necessary for comparing and restoring files, but they do make it easier, as explained in the next two sections.

10

251

Comparing Files

You can use Compare to verify that a backup set is identical to the original files and that you can restore it. You also can use Compare to find out whether changes have been made to files on the hard disk since the last backup. You can compare one file, selected files, or all files in the backup set.

Follow these steps to compare a backup set of files to the files on your hard disk:

1. Choose Compare from MS Backup's main program dialog box.

The Compare dialog box opens. The catalog file for the most recently completed backup is loaded, but you can load the catalog file for the backup set you want to compare.

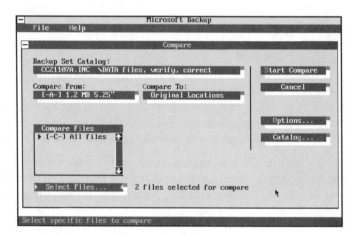

2. From the Backup Set Catalog box, select the catalog file you want and press the space bar, or click on the catalog file with the right mouse button. Then choose the Load button.

3. In the Compare From box, select the drive or device that contains the backup set.

4. In the Compare Files box, select the drives or files you want to compare. To select all files on a drive, press the space bar or click the right mouse button. To select individual files, choose the Select Files button.

5. To compare files to a drive or directory other than the original location, select that drive or directory in the Compare To box.

6. Choose the Options button to turn audible prompts off or on and to set MS Backup to exit after the comparison is complete.

10

The Catalog button enables you to load, retrieve, or rebuild a master catalog file.

7. Choose the Start Compare button. The program prompts you to insert the disk containing the backup set into the correct drive.

When the comparison is complete, the program displays a status report. Choose OK to return to MS Backup's main program dialog box. Choose Quit to return to the command line.

Restoring Files

MS Backup makes it easy to restore files to a hard disk or to a different computer. Like Compare, Restore uses the Backup Set Catalog files. The procedure for restoring files is similar to the procedure for comparing files.

Follow these steps to restore a backup set of files to your hard disk:

1. Choose Restore from MS Backup's main program dialog box. The Restore dialog box opens.

2. Load the catalog file for the backup set you want to restore. The catalog file for the most recently completed backup is loaded. To load a different catalog file, select the file from the Backup Set Catalog box and press the space bar, or click on the catalog file with the right mouse button. Then choose the Load button.

3. In the Restore From box, select the drive or device that contains the backup set.

4. To restore files to a drive or directory other than the original location, select the drive or directory in the Restore To box.

5. In the Restore Files box, select the drives or files you want to restore.

6. Choose the Options button to set restore options such as verification of data and whether you want the program to use prompts.

   The Catalog button enables you to load, retrieve, or rebuild master catalog files.

7. Choose the Start Restore button. The program prompts you to insert into the correct drive the disk containing the backup set.

When the restoration is complete, the program displays a status report. Choose OK to return to MS Backup's main program dialog box. Choose Quit to return to the command line.

10

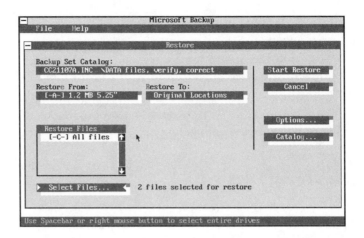

Press the space
bar or click the
right mouse
button in the
Restore Files box
to select all files
on a drive. To
select individual
files, choose the
Select Files
button.

Avoiding DOS Version Conflicts

Different versions of DOS use different methods for producing the contents
of a backup disk. Versions 3.3 and later can restore files you backed up with
previous versions of DOS. Versions earlier than 3.3, however, cannot restore
backups made with versions 3.3, 4.x, or 5.x. No earlier versions can restore
backups made with DOS 6.

Although you cannot restore backup files from newer versions of DOS on
computers running early versions of DOS, you can use COPY to move the files.
Be careful when you use RESTORE or COPY to copy files to a computer
running another version of DOS. Make sure that you do not copy any of the
files in the /DOS directory. Each version of DOS has its own set of DOS files,
and you cannot execute a command from one version of DOS on a computer
running another version of DOS. If you have a computer running DOS 3.3, for
example, and you copy the files from the /DOS directory of a computer that
runs DOS 6, you get an error message every time you run an external command, such as CHKDSK.

This problem occurs most often when you do a full backup on one computer
and restore on another computer that runs a different version of DOS. This
process results in a mismatch of DOS files, and you get errors when you try to
run external DOS commands. To avoid this problem, restore copies of all files
except the hidden system files that make up the part of DOS you load into
memory when you boot.

10

If you have files that were backed up using the BACKUP command from a version of DOS earlier than DOS 6, you can restore those files by using the DOS 6 RESTORE command. The syntax for the RESTORE command is as follows:

RESTORE *d: d:* /S

For example, to restore the files from a floppy disk in drive A to your hard drive C, type **RESTORE A: C:*.* /S**. The /S switch causes DOS to restore all subdirectories.

DOS will prompt you to insert the backup disks into the correct drive.

Lessons Learned

- You can make mistakes that result in the loss of valuable data.
- At times, your computer hardware can fail, resulting in the loss of valuable data.
- You can avoid some hardware and software failures.
- You can detect software viruses by using MS Anti-Virus or VSafe.
- You can undelete files you delete in error.
- DOS 6 offers three levels of deletion protection.
- You can unformat disks you formatted in error.
- The only sure way to avoid data loss is to have a backup copy of all your files.
- MS Backup enables you to make an exact backup of your hard disk drive.
- MS Backup makes it easy to compare and restore backed up files.
- The RESTORE command enables you to restore files backed up with earlier versions of DOS.

DOS provides utilities that perform valuable services with just a few simple keystrokes. The next chapter covers some more commands that let you access the power of DOS.

10

10

Other Commands

One of the most intimidating areas of DOS is handling the hundreds of files contained on a hard disk. When you first sat at a keyboard, you probably felt that manipulating this hodgepodge of DOS programs was beyond the grasp of all but the most fanatical enthusiast.

Although DOS contains dozens of commands, some are more useful than others. Many long-time DOS users rarely exploit more than a fraction of DOS's commands. The preceding chapters covered the DOS commands that are most critical to using your computer. This chapter looks at some of the more common other DOS commands that can make your life a little easier.

You can "get by" without using these commands, but once you feel comfortable with the basics, you will find these commands to be handy helpers.

11

Key Terms Used in This Chapter	
ASCII file	A file whose contents are alphanumeric and control characters, which can be text or other information that can be read by you. Control characters include characters generated by keys such as Ctrl, Alt, and Esc.
Hexadecimal	A way to display binary codes used by computers. Except for computer programmers, humans do not use hexadecimal displays.
Lost clusters	Information on the disk that is lost to you because DOS has lost its directory entries.
Fragmentation	One or more files physically spread over two or more separate parts of the disk. Fragmentation slows down disk operations.
Noncontiguous	Not together. If a file is fragmented, it contains one or more noncontiguous blocks.
Defragment	To remove disk fragmentation so that every file on the disk is on one contiguous block.

Viewing File Contents

The DOS Shell contains a handy command to view the contents of files. You can view batch files, explained in Chapter 12, and other text files.

To view the contents of a file, first select the disk and then the directory that contains the file you want to view. You then select the file from the Files List area.

11

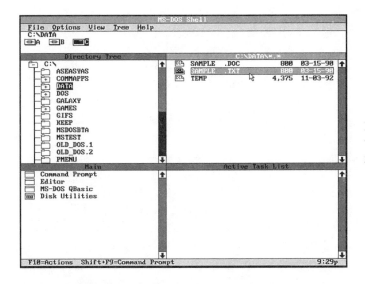

In this example, the SAMPLE.TXT file is selected.

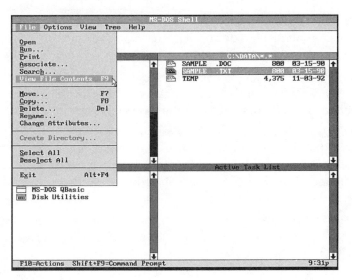

From the File menu, select View File Contents. As a shortcut, you can press the F9 key.

11

DOS displays the
contents of the
selected file. To
clear the display
and return to the
DOS Shell, press
the Esc key.

The SAMPLE.TXT file is an example of a *text file*, or *ASCII file*. ASCII files
contain only text characters and a few control characters you can enter on
your keyboard, such as tabs and hard returns.

You also can view files that are not simple ASCII files, such as a word processing file. A word processing file is mostly text, but it also contains special
format and control information used by your word processing program.

When you view a file that is not a pure text file, DOS displays the file in
hexadecimal format—a format the computer uses to store information
internally. Because you just want to look at the text part, press F9 to convert
the display to ASCII. Some of the display will be gibberish, but you can read
the text.

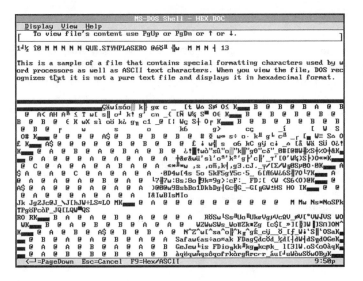

When you view a file that is not a pure ASCII file, DOS displays the file in hexadecimal format with the ASCII display along the right side. Press F9 to convert the hexadecimal display to ASCII.

Because the display does not break lines between words, a word processing file is harder to read than a text file with a hard return at the end of each line.

Some files, such as program files with EXE or COM file extensions and other binary files, contain very little text and display only gibberish when you view them.

261

11

To view the contents of a text file from the command line, use the TYPE command. First, switch to the disk and directory that contains the file you want to view. At the DOS prompt, type the following command, replacing *filename* with the name of the file you want to view:

   TYPE *filename*

If you type **TYPE
SAMPLE.TXT**,
DOS displays the
SAMPLE.TXT file.

```
C:\DATA>TYPE SAMPLE.TXT


This is a sample of a plain text file.
The file contains only characters that you can enter on the keyboard.
When you view this file, it is displayed in text format.

C:\DATA>
```

The TYPE command works on text files. Using the TYPE command on a binary file shows nothing but gibberish.

Locating a File

A hard disk usually contains hundreds of files. You begin by organizing these files so that you can remember where every file is located. There will be times, however, when you can't remember which subdirectory a file is in. When this happens, you can use the Search command from the DOS Shell to locate the file. You also can use Search to locate a group of files with similar names if you are unsure of the file name.

Make the Direc-
tory Tree or the
Files List area
active. Then
choose Search
from the File
menu to find the
location of a file
or group of files.

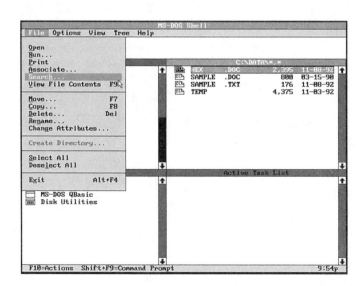

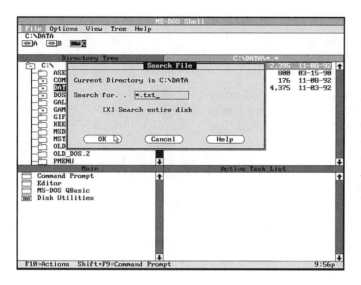

DOS displays the
Search File dialog
box. In the text
box, type the
name of the file
you want to
locate.

The default is *.*, which lists all files. To locate all files with a TXT file extension, enter *.**TXT**. You can search just the current directory or the entire disk. In almost all cases, you will want to search the entire disk, so leave the default X in the Search entire disk check box. Press Enter to start the search.

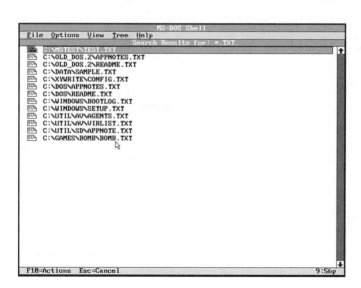

A list of all files on
the disk that have
the extension
TXT is displayed.

11

DOS displays a full-screen list of all the files that match the file specification you indicated in the dialog box. If you are unsure about what a text file contains, use the up- and down-arrow keys or the mouse to highlight the file name, and then press F9 to view the file. Press Esc to return to the DOS Shell.

To search for a file from the command line, use the DIR command. For example, type **DIR *.TXT /S** and press Enter. DOS displays a directory listing of all files with the extension TXT in the current directory, including any TXT files located in subdirectories.

Using MEM (Memory Report)

The MEM command reports the amount of system memory available for programs to load and run. To execute MEM from the DOS Shell, choose **R**un from the File menu, type **MEM** in the dialog box, and press Enter.

The MEM command tells you about the types of memory available on your computer and the size of the largest program you can execute.

```
Memory Type       Total =  Used  +  Free

Conventional       640K     183K     457K
Upper              131K      40K      92K
Adapter RAM/ROM    253K     253K       0K
Extended (XMS)    3072K    3072K       0K
Expanded (EMS)       0K       0K       0K

Total memory      4096K    3548K     548K

Total under 1 MB   771K     223K     548K

Largest executable program size    457K  (467696 bytes)
Largest free upper memory block     91K   (93680 bytes)
MS-DOS is resident in the high memory area.




                            Press any key to return to MS-DOS Shell
```

To execute MEM from the command line, type **MEM** at the DOS prompt and press Enter.

Using CHKDSK (Check Disk)

CHKDSK is the DOS command that checks disk space and provides a detailed report of disk and memory status. CHKDSK also can repair certain errors on the disk.

264

To execute CHKDSK from the command line, type **CHKDSK** at the DOS prompt.

The most common syntax for CHKDSK is

CHKDSK *d:* /F

d: is the drive letter of the disk you want to check. The optional /F switch tells DOS to fix problems on the disk if it finds errors. If you omit the name of the disk, the command checks the current disk.

CHKDSK displays a status report of the disk and available memory. Before it displays its status report, CHKDSK checks every file on the disk and makes sure that the information in the file allocation table agrees with the information in the disk directory. Any errors represent *lost clusters*, or files that have been lost. You can lose files if a program freezes as it updates a file, or if you turn off or boot the computer as a program updates a file.

```
Volume Serial Number is 1968-6C4F
Errors found, F parameter not specified
Corrections will not be written to disk

C:\WINDOWS\WINHELP.EXE
    Allocation error, size adjusted

  85018624 bytes total disk space
  12648448 bytes in 3 hidden files
     88064 bytes in 37 directories
  30552064 bytes in 974 user files
  41730048 bytes available on disk

      2048 bytes in each allocation unit
     41513 total allocation units on disk
     20376 available allocation units on disk

    655360 total bytes memory
    467536 bytes free

Press any key to return to MS-DOS Shell
```

If it finds any errors, CHKDSK displays a warning message. You must use the /F switch to fix these errors.

Fixing Disk Errors

Proper use of the /F switch is a common "fix" to convert lost clusters on disks into files. The /F switch sometimes can recover important data you may have lost.

11

The /F switch
causes DOS to fix
errors it finds on
the disk.

```
C:\>CHKDSK /F
Volume Serial Number is 1968-6C4F
C:\WINDOWS\WINHELP.EXE
    Allocation error, size adjusted

   85018624 bytes total disk space
   12648448 bytes in 3 hidden files
      88064 bytes in 37 directories
   30556160 bytes in 974 user files
   41725952 bytes available on disk

       2048 bytes in each allocation unit
      41513 total allocation units on disk
      20374 available allocation units on disk

     655360 total bytes memory
     510592 bytes free

C:\>
```

Avoid using /F until you know the implications of the fix action. Que's *Using
MS-DOS 6*, Special Edition, explains the /F switch actions in detail.

You should be careful running CHKDSK /F from the DOS Shell or when any
other program is running. If another program is using a file, CHKDSK might
consider that file a lost cluster, and you could lose part of a good file.

Checking for Fragmentation

As you add and delete files on a disk, the free space for new files becomes
spread around the surface of the disk.

When you create or change a file and your applications program or a DOS
command writes a file to disk, DOS allocates data storage space by finding the
next available disk space. If the first available space is too small to hold the
entire file, DOS fills that space and puts the rest of the file into the next
available space(s).

This phenomenon is called *fragmentation*. Even technological marvels can be
sloppy housekeepers; fragmented files lower disk performance.

You can use the CHKDSK command to check for fragmentation. The syntax is

>   CHKDSK *d:filespec*

d: is the drive letter of the disk you want to check, and *filespec* is the file
specification for the file or files you want to check for fragmentation.

When a file is fragmented, CHKDSK reports the number of noncontiguous
blocks used to contain the file. Each block is a separate area of the disk used
to hold part of the file.

```
     655360 total bytes memory
     510592 bytes free

All specified file(s) are contiguous

C:\>CHKDSK *.*
Volume Serial Number is 1968-6C4F

  85018624 bytes total disk space
  12648448 bytes in 3 hidden files
     88064 bytes in 37 directories
  30574592 bytes in 975 user files
  41707520 bytes available on disk

      2048 bytes in each allocation unit
     41513 total allocation units on disk
     20365 available allocation units on disk

    655360 total bytes memory
    510592 bytes free

All specified file(s) are contiguous

C:\>
```

CHKDSK reports whether a file is fragmented—that is, *not* stored in a contiguous block. In this example, all the files in the current directory are checked and all of them are contiguous.

Fragmentation is not serious. It happens to all active disks. But fragmentation does slow down disk operations. DOS 6 includes a disk defragmentation program that lets you quickly and easily *defragment* a disk. See the section "Using DEFRAG (Defragmenter)," below.

Another way to defragment a disk is to back up all the files to another disk, delete the files from the hard disk, and then restore the files to the hard disk. The procedures for backing up and restoring files are covered in Chapter 10.

Using CLS (Clear Screen)

The CLS command erases or clears the display and positions the cursor at the top of the screen, after the DOS prompt. Use CLS when the screen becomes too "busy" with the output of previous commands. CLS has no parameters. You simply type **CLS** at the DOS prompt and press Enter to clear the screen.

The main use for CLS is with batch files, which are covered in Chapter 12.

Using DEFRAG (Defragmenter)

The DEFRAG command starts a utility program called Microsoft Defrag. Like Anti-Virus and MS Backup, it has a shell that lets you use menus and dialog boxes to perform simple commands. You can use the mouse or the keyboard to make your selections. You also can press F1 to display context-sensitive help about the program.

267

11

Defrag offers two methods of defragmentation. If a disk is very fragmented, you can perform a Full optimization. If it is not very fragmented, you can perform an Unfragment optimization. Defrag analyzes your disk and recommends one of the two methods. You can ignore the recommendation and select your own configuration, or you can accept the recommendation.

To defragment a disk, follow these steps:

1. Type **DEFRAG** at the command line and press ⏎Enter.

Defrag displays a dialog box in which you can select the drive you want to optimize.

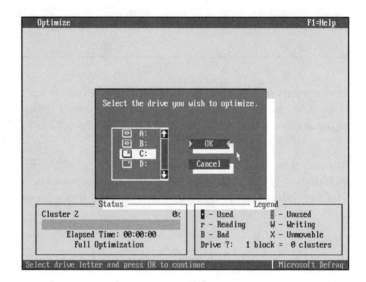

2. Select the drive you want to defragment and choose OK.

Drive C is selected by default. Defrag analyzes the disk and makes a recommendation.

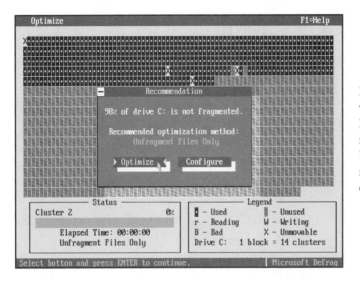

If the disk is not very fragmented, Defrag recommends using the Unfragment method of optimization.

3. To proceed with the recommended optimization, choose Optimize. To select a different optimization, choose Configure.

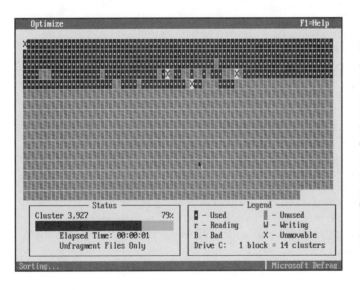

During the optimization, Defrag displays a status screen. X indicates an unmovable block. • indicates a used block. r indicates that Defrag is reading a block. W indicates that Defrag is writing a block.

4. When the optimization is complete, select OK from the Finished Condensing dialog box.

5. Select to optimize another drive, configure optimization, or exit to the command line.

269

11

Using VER (DOS Version)

You may find it useful to know the exact version of DOS your computer is using.

VER reports the
manufacturer's
name and the
version number
of DOS. Your
particular VER
report may look
slightly different
than the one
shown here.

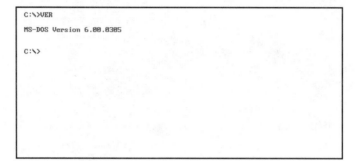

```
C:\>VER

MS-DOS Version 6.00.0305

C:\>
```

VER is useful if you must work on another person's computer. You can issue this command before you start work to see which DOS version the computer is using. As a result, you will know which commands or switches the computer accepts.

VER also is useful when you boot your system from a disk you did not prepare. The floppy may contain system files from a version of DOS you normally do not use. The VER command has no parameters, and you issue it at the DOS prompt.

Using VERIFY (File-Writing Verification)

The VERIFY command checks the accuracy of data written to disks. VERIFY can use only one of two parameters: ON or OFF. If you type **VERIFY ON** at the prompt, DOS rereads all data to ensure that it is being recorded to the disk correctly. When VERIFY is set to ON, DOS operations are slower; therefore, you might want to use the command with only important data. Type **VERIFY OFF** to turn verification off.

```
C:\>VERIFY
VERIFY is on

C:\>
```

To display the
status of VERIFY,
type **VERIFY** and
press Enter.

11

Using VOL (Display Volume Name)

When you format a disk, you can enter a volume label for the disk. Labeling a
volume is useful for keeping track of your disks (labeling disks is discussed in
the next section). You can use the VOL command to find out what your disk's
volume name is.

```
C:\>VOL

 Volume in drive C has no label
 Volume Serial Number is 1968-6C4F

C:\>VOL a:

 Volume in drive A is DISK     6
 Volume Serial Number is 4504-3814

C:\>
```

When you type
VOL at the DOS
prompt, DOS
displays the
volume name of
the current disk,
if you entered a
name when you
formatted the
disk.

The VOL command also displays the volume serial number automatically
assigned by DOS when you formatted the disk. If you add a drive letter after
the command, DOS displays volume information for that drive.

Viewing volume names is much easier than wading through directory listings
when you sort through floppy disks.

Using LABEL (Change a Volume Name)

After you format a disk, you can add or change the volume label with the
LABEL command. You should change a disk's volume label when you change
the use for the disk. When you first formatted the disk, you might have labeled
it *TAX92*, for example. Later, you want to use the disk to keep a backup copy
of your 1993 business files, so you change the label to *BUSINESS93*.

The syntax for the LABEL command is

    LABEL *d: label*

271

where *d:* is the drive letter and *label* is the new label. If you omit the drive letter, DOS uses the current drive. If you do not specify a label, DOS displays the current volume label and prompts you to enter a new label. If you want to remove the existing label, just press Enter at this prompt.

In this example, the LABEL command is used to change the label of the volume in drive A from TAX92 to BUSINESS93. Then the VOL command is used to display the new volume name.

```
C:\>LABEL a:
Volume in drive A is TAX92
Volume label (11 characters, ENTER for none)? BUSINESS93

C:\>VOL a:

 Volume in drive A is BUSINESS93

C:\>
```

You can use Quick Format to change the volume label and erase all files and subdirectories on a disk with one command. You learned about Quick Format in Chapter 6.

Lessons Learned

- You are likely to use only a fraction of DOS's commands.
- You can view file contents easily from the DOS Shell or the command line.
- If you misplace a file, you can use DOS Shell's Search command to locate it.
- DOS commands such as MEM, VER, CHKDSK, VOL, and LABEL are quick commands for controlling and monitoring your hardware and software.
- Defragmenting your disk can increase the speed of your computer's performance.
- When you copy critical files, you can use the VERIFY command to double-check that the file was copied successfully.

Next, you learn to customize and add some personality to your PC with batch, CONFIG.SYS, and AUTOEXEC.BAT files.

Customizing
DOS

Up to now everything you have done with your
personal computer has been based on how DOS does
things, especially at the command line. In this chapter
you take control. You learn how to construct your own
commands so that DOS works the way you want.

In this chapter, you learn how to customize your DOS
environment to meet your specific needs. You can make
working with your computer lively or dull, somber or
splashy. Your most useful tool is the batch file.

This chapter is not designed to make you a batch file
expert, although you may be surprised to find how
much you can learn in a few pages.

If you have read this far, you are a reasonably skilled
DOS user. The following sections teach you how to
create and modify batch, AUTOEXEC.BAT, and
CONFIG.SYS files. Also included here are some useful
sample batch files.

12

Key Terms Used in This Chapter	
PATH command	The command that instructs DOS to search through a specified set of directories for programs or batch files. If you try to execute a program or batch file that is not in the current directory, DOS searches through the directories in the search path. If the program or batch file is found in one of the search path's directories, DOS executes it.
Batch file	A text file that contains DOS commands that DOS executes as though the commands were entered at the DOS prompt. Batch files always have the extension BAT.
Meta-string	A series of characters that takes on a different meaning to DOS than the literal meaning. DOS displays substitute text when it finds meta-strings in the PROMPT command.
AUTOEXEC.BAT file	A batch file that executes automatically each time you boot your computer. AUTOEXEC.BAT is an ideal place to include commands that initialize and personalize the control of a PC.
CONFIG.SYS file	A file whose contents DOS uses to tailor hardware devices and to assign the computer's resources.
Buffer	The area of RAM allocated by DOS as a temporary storage area for data that is moving between the disks and an executing program.

Understanding the PATH Command

You have seen the effects of using the PATH command throughout this book without knowing it. When you installed DOS, part of the automated installation procedure added a PATH command to your AUTOEXEC.BAT file or made sure that the C:\DOS directory was included in the PATH.

Using the PATH command is one of the most important techniques you can employ to make your computer a little easier to use. So far, PATH has been kept under wraps. Now you will learn its power.

When you tell DOS to execute an *internal* command that is built into COMMAND.COM, such as DIR, DOS has that command in memory, ready to execute. When you execute an *external* command, such as FORMAT, DOS must find the FORMAT program on your disk. First DOS looks in the current directory. If it cannot find the program, DOS then looks in the directories specified in the PATH command.

By setting up a PATH command that included C:\DOS, your DOS installation made sure that you could use FORMAT and all the other external DOS commands from any current directory. You can add other directories to the PATH command so that you can execute batch files and other programs from any disk or directory on your computer.

Actually, DOS can find programs and batch files in these three situations:

- The file is in the directory in which you are working, the current directory. An example of this situation is when you execute Lotus 1-2-3 from the directory that contains the 1-2-3 program files, such as 123R24, as explained in Chapter 8.

- The file is not in the current directory, but you include the full path on the command line. An example of this situation was when you included the path to the Microsoft Word directory in the Program Properties Commands box for Word in Chapter 8. The command to execute Microsoft Word was C:\WORD\WORD.

- The directory in which the file is located is on the *search path* established by the PATH command. This situation is the case when you execute external DOS commands and, as you will see, when you execute batch files.

The search path is the list of directories specified in the PATH command. The following PATH command instructs DOS to search each directory shown:

    PATH=C:\DOS;C:\BATCH;C:\UTIL

275

If you do not specify a path on the command line, and the program or batch file is not found in the current directory, DOS uses the path in the PATH command. In this example, DOS first looks for the file in the C:\DOS directory. If the file still is not found, DOS checks the C:\BATCH directory and then the C:\UTIL directory.

If you include more than one directory in the PATH command, you must separate the directories with a semicolon (;). To issue the PATH command at the DOS prompt, type the following:

PATH *d:path specifier;d:path specifier...*

The drive specifier *d:* names the drive on which DOS is to search. The first *path specifier* is the first directory on the search path. The semicolon (;) separates the first directory from the optional second directory. The ellipsis (...) shows that you can have other path specifiers in your command line.

DOS needs some time to search the directories in a search path for a program or batch file. Because DOS searches the directories in the order listed in the PATH command, you should list the directories in the order of most use. If you mostly use DOS commands, place the C:\DOS directory first in the path. As you become more experienced with batch files, you may find that you use batch files more than DOS commands. In that case, place the C:\BATCH directory first in the path.

DOS retains the PATH until you change the command or reboot the computer. Because you must specify a search path every time you boot your computer, the PATH command is usually added to the AUTOEXEC.BAT file of every computer with a hard disk. You will learn more about the AUTOEXEC.BAT file later in this chapter.

Using the PROMPT Command

The DOS prompt is another visible part of your computer system that you can customize. In fact, if you have a hard disk, you almost have to customize the DOS prompt.

The default prompt displays the current drive followed by the greater-than sign:

A>

This prompt is useful if you have only floppy disk drives. If you have a hard disk, however, the default prompt is inadequate. You want the prompt to show the current disk and the current directory. If you have a hard disk, the

276

standard prompt, used by almost everyone, is the current path and the greater-than sign:

    C:\DOS>

This prompt has been the standard throughout the book. Now you will learn how to use the PROMPT command to customize the prompt. The symbolic syntax for the PROMPT command is

> PROMPT *text*

You replace *text* with any combination of words or special characters. The term used to describe the special characters is *meta-string*.

Understanding Meta-strings

A meta-string consists of two characters—the first is the dollar sign ($) and the second a keyboard character. DOS interprets meta-strings to mean something other than the literal character definition. For instance, the meta-string $t in the PROMPT command specifies that you want DOS to display the current time in the format HH:MM:SS.XX in the DOS prompt. $t displays the current system time as part or all of the command prompt.

DOS recognizes the symbols > and < and the vertical bar (¦) as special characters. These characters have meta-string equivalents, which enable you to use them in PROMPT text. You must substitute an appropriate meta-string to cause these special characters to appear in the prompt. Otherwise, DOS tries to act on the characters in its usual way. Table 12.1 summarizes meta-string characters and their meanings to the PROMPT command.

Table 12.1
Meta-string Characters

Character	Produces
$	The dollar sign ($)
_ (underscore)	Moves the cursor to the next line
b	The pipe symbol (¦)
d	The current date
e	The Esc character
g	The greater-than character (>)

continues

12

277

Character	Produces
h	The Backspace character; erases the preceding character
l	The less-than character (<)
n	The current disk drive letter
p	The current drive and path
q	The = character
t	The current time
v	The DOS version
Any other character	Ignores the character

Table 12.1 (*Continued*)

Customizing Your Prompt

The standard prompt results from the following command:

    PROMPT pg

$p displays the current path, including the drive, and $g displays the greater-than sign.

You can use the meta-string characters with the PROMPT command to produce your own DOS prompt. PROMPT permits words or phrases in addition to meta-strings. You can experiment with different combinations of meta-strings and phrases.

When you find a combination you like, add the PROMPT command and the meta-string and phrase to your AUTOEXEC.BAT file. Then, each time you boot your computer, your custom prompt appears. Issuing the PROMPT command alone with no parameters restores the prompt to its default—the drive name and the greater-than sign (C>).

If you want your prompt to tell you the current DOS path with words, not just symbols, you can use this command:

    PROMPT THE CURRENT PATH IS $p

When your current location is on drive C in the DOS directory, the preceding PROMPT command produces the following prompt:

```
THE CURRENT PATH IS C:\DOS
```

By adding the > character (using the meta-string $g), the command becomes

PROMPT THE CURRENT PATH IS pg

Now your DOS prompt appears as

```
THE CURRENT PATH IS C:\DOS>
```

Defining the Batch File

A *batch file* is a text file that contains DOS statements. These statements execute DOS commands, execute programs, change the computer environment, or even provide special processing that is possible only in a batch file. DOS executes these statements one line at a time, treating them as though you had entered each statement individually.

Batch files always have the extension BAT in their full file names. When you type a batch file's name at the DOS prompt, COMMAND.COM searches in the current directory and then through the search path for a program or batch file with that file name. COMMAND.COM then reads the batch file and executes the statements in that file. The whole process is almost automatic. You simply enter the batch file name, and DOS does the work.

You can name a batch file anything you want as long as it has a BAT extension. When you type a name at the DOS prompt, however, DOS first looks for that name as an internal command built into COMMAND.COM. For example, if you name a batch file COPY.BAT, you can never execute that batch file because DOS will execute the COPY command instead. If DOS does not find the name in its list of internal commands, it looks for a program file with a COM or EXE file extension before looking for a file with a BAT extension. For this reason, never use a batch file name that is the same as a DOS command name. If the \DOS directory is before the \BATCH directory in the PATH command, the DOS command executes. If the \BATCH directory is first, the batch file executes. You can avoid this conflict and confusion by using unique names.

Nobody says that batch files can accomplish everything because they cannot. But batch files can make using your computer easier and more pleasant. The batch file varies from being the most ignored to being the most abused of all programs. Many books are devoted to the batch file's capabilities, some to a point where readers walk away scratching their heads in confusion. In truth, you can consider the batch file to be a nonprogrammer's programming language. A batch file constitutes a limited yet powerful language: each word can have the power of several lines of DOS commands.

12

In the Shell, you can review the contents of a batch file by highlighting the file and pressing F9 or by choosing **V**iew File Contents from the File menu. At the command line, you can use the TYPE command to review the contents of a batch file. In seconds, you can alter a file that changes your PC's personality.

You will find the most uses for batch files when you use the command line. Batch files are less useful with the Shell. In fact, a number of techniques enable you to eliminate the need for many batch files by putting the information in the Program Properties Commands box when you create program groups. Even if you use the Shell most of the time, however, you will find batch files useful.

If you use the command line, batch files are useful for issuing multiple commands that are complex, potentially destructive, or easy to mistype at the command line. For example, if you commonly use the COPY command to copy the files from directories on your hard disk to floppy disks, or to copy them from one directory to another, you may want to use a batch file.

COPY is not a difficult command to use, but if you mistype a drive letter or leave off a directory specifier, you may end up copying the files to the wrong place. A batch file enables you to enter the command once, make sure that it is correct, and then save it for future use. You never have to enter the command again.

Because batch files can display text that you enter, you can compose screens that enable you to execute commands, along with syntax examples, reminders, and explanatory notes about the commands. You also can simply display a message of the day.

In their advanced form, batch files resemble programs. This chapter teaches you the basic forms of batch files. If advanced techniques in batch processing interest you, be sure to read about batch files in Que's *Using MS-DOS 6*, Special Edition.

Creating a Batch File

Batch files contain ASCII text characters. Many word processing programs enable you to save a file as unformatted text. Word processors save documents in a special format with special codes for margins, indents, formats (such as boldface, type style, and size), and other information. Most programs, however, give you the option of saving the file without these special codes. The word processing program may call this format *unformatted*, *text*, or *ASCII*. If you save a formatted file as a batch file, the results may be unpredictable.

DOS has a handy, easy-to-use, full-screen text editor called Editor. If you have heard about the DOS line editor, EDLIN, from earlier versions of DOS, forget that EDLIN ever existed. EDLIN was not only difficult to use, but also allowed you to change only one line at a time.

Storing Batch Files

The best place to store batch files is in a directory named \BATCH. Do not put your batch files in the root directory or the DOS directory.

In a way, the root directory is the most important directory on your hard disk because it contains the files needed to boot your computer, and it contains the first level of subdirectories, such as \DOS and your applications directories. When you view the files in the root directory, you do not want the file list to be complicated by any other files.

Do not put the batch files in the DOS directory, because this directory should contain only files that are part of DOS. When you upgrade to another version of DOS, you do not want to sort through a directory that contains DOS files and other files to determine the files you want to keep and those you want to upgrade.

To create a \BATCH directory in the Shell, follow these steps:

1. Make the root directory current.
2. From the File menu, choose Create Directory.
3. Name the directory **BATCH** and click on OK.

To create a \BATCH directory at the command line, simply type **MD \BATCH** and press Enter.

Creating a Batch File with COPY CON

You are familiar with the COPY command. An easy way to create a very short and simple batch file from the command line is to use the COPY CON command, discussed later in this section. CON is a *reserved device name* in DOS, which means that DOS has reserved the device name CON to refer to the monitor and keyboard. To copy a file from CON means to copy from whatever you type at the keyboard. To copy a file to CON means to display it on-screen.

Using COPY CON, you can create a batch file that clears the screen and presents a wide directory. This batch file automates the CLS screen clearing command and the DIR command with the /W (wide display) switch. The name of the batch file is WDIR.BAT, and you create it by following these steps:

12

1. Make the \BATCH directory current.

2. Type **COPY CON WDIR.BAT** and press ⏎Enter. The cursor moves to the next line, and DOS waits for your keyboard input.

   Make sure that you type each line correctly. Use ⬅Backspace to correct mistakes, and press ⏎Enter at the end of each line. If you do make a mistake and press ⏎Enter, press Ctrl-C to abort the procedure and return to the DOS prompt; then resume the process from this step.

3. Type **CLS** and press ⏎Enter.

4. Type **DIR /W** and press ⏎Enter.

5. Press Ctrl-Z or press F6 to save the information you have typed.

6. Press ⏎Enter.

DOS displays
the message 1
file(s) copied.

```
C:\>CD BATCH

C:\BATCH> COPY CON WDIR.BAT
CLS
DIR /W
^Z
          1 file(s) copied

C:\BATCH>
```

To see that the directory contains the new batch file, type **DIR WDIR.BAT** and press Enter. You have just created a new DOS batch file, using COPY CON. To try the new batch file, type **WDIR** and press Enter.

The WDIR batch
file clears the
screen and
then displays
the current
directory's files
in wide format.

```
C:\BATCH>DIR /W

   Volume in drive C has no label
   Directory of C:\BATCH

[.]            [..]           WDIR.BAT       4EFADOSC.BAT   ASEASY.BAT
AUTOEXEC.BAT   BANANOID.BAT   BOMB.BAT       C241DOSC.BAT   COPYTALK.BAT
GALAXY.BAT     GTX.BAT        JUNK.BAT       MW.BAT         PRINTDOC.BAT
README.BAT     SD.BAT         SETUP.BAT      TALK128.BAT    TALK64.BAT
TELIX.BAT      TMP$.BAT       WAMPUM.BAT     WOLF3D.BAT
        24 file(s)        6512 bytes
                      100810752 bytes free

C:\BATCH>
C:\BATCH>
```

At best, use COPY CON to create very short batch files. After you press Enter to complete a line, you cannot go back and change that line. Most of the time, you should use the DOS Editor to create and modify batch files.

Creating a Batch File with the DOS Editor

The full-screen editor that comes with DOS 6 is the best way to create and change batch files, and it is very easy to use. The interface is much like the DOS Shell that you are used to using. The DOS Editor looks and feels like a simplified version of Microsoft Works.

To start the Editor from the Shell, follow these steps:

1. Select the C:\BATCH directory.
2. Open the Main program group if necessary.
3. Double-click Editor, or select Editor and press ⏎Enter.
4. Type the name of the file you want to create or change in the File to Edit dialog box and choose OK.

To start the Editor from the command line, follow these steps:

1. Make the C:\BATCH directory current.
2. Type **EDIT** and a space.
3. Type the name of the file you want to create or change, and press ⏎Enter.

Whether you start the DOS Editor from the Shell or the command line, you do not have to include a data file name. If you include the name of an existing file, that file loads into the Editor. If you do not include a data file name, the Editor starts with no data file. If you include the name of a new file that does not exist, the Editor starts with no file loaded but shows the name of the new file.

This PDIR.BAT file, created with the DOS Editor, clears the screen and lists the files in the current directory, pausing at each full screen.

12

You type the batch file commands with the DOS Editor just as you type them at the DOS prompt. Press Enter at the end of each command. Use the arrow keys to move the cursor to make corrections.

The menus in the Editor work just like the menus in the Shell. The File menu in the Editor contains most of the commands you use to create and change batch files:

- The **New** command clears the current file from memory. The file name changes to *Untitled*. Use this command after you save the current file and want to create a new file from scratch.

- The **O**pen command reads a file into memory. Use this command after you save the current file and want to change another file.

- The **S**ave command saves the current file. Use this command after you change or create a file. If the file has never been saved and the file name is still *Untitled*, the Save command acts like Save **As**.

- The Save **As** command saves the file but first asks you to supply a file name. Use this command to save the file with a different name.

- The **P**rint command prints the file. Use this command to keep a printed copy of the file.

- The **Exit** command leaves the Editor.

Before you edit a file, you must first use the **O**pen command to read it into memory. When you choose **O**pen from the File menu, the Open dialog box opens. The default file name in the File Name box is always *.TXT.

To see the list of batch files in the current directory, type *.**BAT** in the File Name box and press Enter. Then double-click the name of the file you want to read, or select the file name and press Enter.

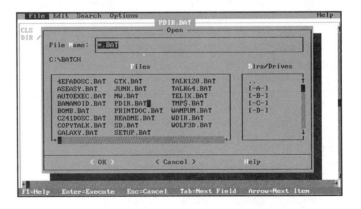

If the file name you want is not visible, use the scroll bar at the bottom of the Files list. The scroll bar is similar to the scroll bars in the Shell, but is horizontal rather than vertical.

Observing Rules for Batch Files

When you create batch files, you must follow certain rules. The following list is a summary of those rules:

- Batch files must be ASCII text files. If you use a word processing program, make sure that you save the file as a text or ASCII file.
- The name of the batch file can be from one to eight characters long. The name must conform to the rules for naming files. Using alphabetical characters is preferable.
- The file name must end with a period (.) followed by the BAT extension.
- The batch file name should not be the same as a program file name (a file with an EXE or COM extension).
- The batch file name should not be the same as an internal DOS command (such as COPY or DATE).
- The batch file can contain any DOS commands that you enter at the DOS prompt.
- You can include program names in the batch file that you usually type at the DOS prompt.
- Use only one command or program name per line in the batch file.

Observing Rules for Running Batch Files

You start batch files by typing the batch file name (excluding the extension) at the DOS prompt. The following list summarizes the rules DOS follows when it loads and executes batch files:

- If you do not specify the disk drive name before the batch file name, DOS uses the current drive.
- If you do not specify a directory path, DOS searches the current directory for the batch file.
- If the batch file isn't in the current directory and you didn't precede the batch file name with a directory path, DOS searches the directories in the search path.

12

- If a batch file has the same name as a program and both are in the same directory, DOS executes the program instead of the batch file. If the program and the batch file are in different directories, DOS executes the item it finds first in the search path.

- If DOS finds a syntax error in a batch file command line, DOS displays an error message, skips the errant command, and then executes the remaining commands found in the batch file. Depending on the error, DOS may not pause at the error, but flash an error message too fast to read, and then continue. Do not assume that a batch file is correct because it seemed to end normally. Check to make sure that every command actually worked correctly.

- You can stop a batch command by pressing Ctrl-C or Ctrl-Break. DOS prompts you to confirm that you want to terminate the batch file. If you answer no, DOS skips the current command (the one being carried out) and resumes execution with the next command in the batch file.

If you try to run a batch file and DOS displays an error message, you probably made a mistake when you typed the name.

Understanding the AUTOEXEC.BAT File

One batch file has special significance to DOS. The full name of this batch file is *AUTOEXEC.BAT*. DOS automatically searches for this file in the root directory when you boot your computer. If an AUTOEXEC.BAT file is present, DOS executes the commands contained in that file.

Technically, having an AUTOEXEC.BAT file is optional; however, every computer with a hard disk should have one. If for no other reason, you need an AUTOEXEC.BAT file so that you can specify a path and prompt every time you boot your computer.

Most users and system managers put an AUTOEXEC.BAT file of their own design on their boot disk. Using a custom AUTOEXEC.BAT file enables you to benefit from commands that automatically launch operating parameters.

You can omit AUTOEXEC.BAT and manually enter the commands you might include in an AUTOEXEC.BAT file, thereby accomplishing the same result as an AUTOEXEC.BAT file. DOS, however, executes the file if it is there, so why not take advantage?

During the automated installation, DOS creates, verifies, or changes your AUTOEXEC.BAT file to include a PATH to the \DOS directory plus any other commands it needs to run on your computer. Some applications programs come with installation programs that create or modify AUTOEXEC.BAT as an installation step of the package's main program.

If you have doubts about which commands to include in your AUTOEXEC.BAT file, the following sections may give you some ideas. You can include any commands you want in the AUTOEXEC.BAT file. Decide what you want the AUTOEXEC.BAT file to do, and follow certain rules. The following list is a summary of these rules:

- The full file name must be AUTOEXEC.BAT, and the file must reside in the root directory of the boot disk.

- The contents of the AUTOEXEC.BAT file must conform to the rules for creating any batch file.

- When DOS executes AUTOEXEC.BAT after a boot, you are not prompted for the date and time automatically. You must include the DATE and TIME commands in your AUTOEXEC.BAT file if your computer does not have a built-in clock with a battery backup (only the oldest PCs lack a clock).

Using AUTOEXEC.BAT is an excellent way to set up system defaults. That is, AUTOEXEC.BAT is the place to put commands you want to enter every time you start your system. You can use AUTOEXEC.BAT, for example, to tell your computer to change to the directory that holds your most commonly used program and then to start it. Used this way, AUTOEXEC.BAT runs your program as soon as you boot your computer.

This screen is an example of an AUTOEXEC.BAT file—a batch file whose commands DOS executes each time you boot the computer.

Table 12.2 lists some commands frequently included in simple
AUTOEXEC.BAT files, plus a few other commands, to give you an idea
of what you can add to your file.

12

Table 12.2
AUTOEXEC.BAT File Commands

Command	Function in the AUTOEXEC.BAT file
DATE	Sets the computer's clock to set up the correct date so that DOS can accurately "date stamp" new and modified files. Most computers have a built-in clock and do not need this command.
TIME	Sets the computer's clock to establish the correct time so that DOS can accurately "time stamp" new and modified files. The DATE and TIME commands also provide the actual date and time to programs that use the computer's internal clock. Most computers have a built-in clock and do not need this command.
PROMPT	Customizes the system prompt. The DOS prompt configuration can include information that makes navigating in directories easier. If you use the PROMPT command in the AUTOEXEC.BAT file, you don't need to enter the optional parameters each time you boot.
PATH	Tells DOS to search the named subdirectories for files that have EXE, COM, or BAT extensions.
VCONFIG	Turns on a screen saver, which automatically blanks the screen after five minutes of inactivity. VCONFIG is not a typical command found in an AUTOEXEC.BAT file, but rather is a program that comes with a certain brand of video adapter card. This command is included here to demonstrate that each AUTOEXEC.BAT file can contain special commands that fit each computer's environment. The more complicated your computer environment, the more of these special commands you are likely to have.

Command	Function in the AUTOEXEC.BAT file
SET TEMP	Stores temporary files. DOS, Windows, and other programs need a place on the hard disk to store temporary files. If you do not have a SET TEMP command in your AUTOEXEC.BAT file, DOS adds it during installation.
CHKDSK /F	Verifies that no errors are in the directory or file allocation table on your boot disk. Many people like this verification each time they boot.
PAUSE	Pauses until you press a key so that you have a chance to see the result of the preceding command before the next command executes.
CD *path*	Changes the current path. For example, CD \DATA\DOCS changes to the /DATA/DOCS directory. If you have a data directory you use often, you might want to change to that directory each time you boot.
ECHO	Enables you to include a message as part of your startup. On a floppy disk system, this message can remind you to insert a program disk in drive A.
DIR /O:D	Lists all files in the current directory in date order.
d:	Changes to another disk drive.
UNDELETE /S	Loads the Delete Sentry level of file deletion protection.
DOSSHELL	Starts the Shell automatically when you boot.

Creating an AUTOEXEC.BAT File

The AUTOEXEC.BAT file is a privileged batch file because DOS executes this file's batch of commands each time you boot your computer. In every other sense, however, AUTOEXEC.BAT is like any other batch file. The best way to create and modify an AUTOEXEC.BAT file is with the DOS Editor, as discussed in "Creating a Batch File with the DOS Editor," a previous section in this chapter.

Viewing the AUTOEXEC.BAT File

You can see whether AUTOEXEC.BAT exists in your root directory or on your logged floppy disk. If your hard disk is the logged drive, change to the root directory by entering

CD

To look at the directory listing of all the files with BAT extensions, enter

DIR *.BAT

To view the contents of AUTOEXEC.BAT, enter

TYPE AUTOEXEC.BAT

To view the contents of AUTOEXEC.BAT from the Shell, select the AUTOEXEC.BAT file and press F9. You also can use the DOS Editor to read the contents of the AUTOEXEC.BAT file. You can use the Editor to print a copy of the AUTOEXEC.BAT file, as well.

If you choose not to print a copy of your AUTOEXEC.BAT file, make sure that you write down the contents before you make any changes. Copy the syntax correctly. This copy serves as your worksheet. You can use your copy of AUTOEXEC.BAT to find out whether the file contains a PROMPT or PATH command. If you want to add or alter PROMPT or PATH commands, jot the additions or changes on your worksheet. Use your paper copy of the AUTOEXEC.BAT file to check for proper syntax in the lines you change or add before you commit the changes to disk.

Backing Up the Existing File

Always make a backup copy of your existing AUTOEXEC.BAT file before you make any changes to the file or install any programs. Remember that some program-installation procedures automatically change your AUTOEXEC.BAT file. Save the current version by renaming it with a different extension.

Use the following procedure to make an archive copy of your AUTOEXEC.BAT file for future use:

1. Make the root directory current.
2. Copy AUTOEXEC.BAT to another name, such as AUTOEXEC.ARC for archive. Do not use BAK or OLD as a file extension.

Now you can change your AUTOEXEC.BAT file, and if something goes wrong, you still have a copy of the original file. If the new file has an error, restore the original by copying AUTOEXEC.ARC to AUTOEXEC.BAT. You can use the Shell or the command line to make these copies.

Do not use BAK as a file extension. With some text editor programs, such as EDLIN, every time you save a file, the program saves the old file with a BAK extension. This action would write over your archive copy of AUTOEXEC.BAT. Do not use OLD as a file extension because some automated installation procedures that change the AUTOEXEC.BAT file rename the existing file AUTOEXEC.OLD. This action would write over your archive copy of AUTOEXEC.BAT. As an extra precaution, keep an extra copy of your AUTOEXEC.BAT file on a floppy disk.

In fact, before you start making changes to the AUTOEXEC.BAT file, use FORMAT A: /S to make a bootable floppy disk. Keep this disk handy in case you cannot boot from your hard disk. You might make an error in your AUTOEXEC.BAT file that causes your computer to *hang*, or *freeze*, as soon as you boot it. If you press Ctrl-Break repeatedly, you may be able to stop the AUTOEXEC.BAT file execution. If this action does not work, boot from the floppy disk. Put the disk in drive A and boot your computer. Switch to drive C and correct your AUTOEXEC.BAT file. Then take the disk out of drive A and try to boot from your hard disk again.

Modifying an AUTOEXEC.BAT File

After you make an archive copy of your AUTOEXEC.BAT file and create a separate boot floppy disk, you can safely modify the file. Follow these steps:

1. From the Shell, open the DOS Editor and type AUTOEXEC.BAT in the File to Edit dialog box; then choose OK.

   Or, from the command line, change to the root directory, type EDIT AUTOEXEC.BAT, and then press ⏎Enter).

2. Use the Editor to add, delete, and change commands.

3. Save the file, exit the Editor, and boot the computer to test the new file.

Keeping Several Versions of AUTOEXEC

Technically speaking, you have only one AUTOEXEC.BAT file. You can benefit from having several versions on hand, however, by giving different extensions to files named *AUTOEXEC*. You can then activate an alternative version by using the COPY command.

12

In the extensions, you can use any character that DOS normally allows in file names. The extensions NEW, TMP, and 001 are just a few examples. By giving an AUTOEXEC file a unique name, such as AUTOEXEC.TMP, you can activate that AUTOEXEC file by copying it to AUTOEXEC.BAT. To make AUTOEXEC.TMP your current AUTOEXEC file, for example, type

COPY AUTOEXEC.TMP AUTOEXEC.BAT

Then to restore your normal AUTOEXEC.BAT file, copy your archive copy to AUTOEXEC.BAT as follows:

COPY AUTOEXEC.ARC AUTOEXEC.BAT

This method is handy if you want to include commands for special activities, such as automatically starting a monthly spreadsheet. When the monthly work is done and you no longer need the spreadsheet when you boot, you can reactivate your normal AUTOEXEC file.

Bypassing the AUTOEXEC.BAT File

Sometimes you may not want to activate the commands in the AUTOEXEC.BAT file when you boot your computer. DOS 6 enables you to perform a *clean boot*. A clean boot bypasses the AUTOEXEC.BAT file as if the file does not exist; it also bypasses the CONFIG.SYS file (see the next section).

To perform a clean boot, follow these steps:

1. Start your computer as you usually would.

2. Watch the screen as the computer performs its power-up routine. When you see the message Starting MS DOS..., press F5 .

DOS skips the AUTOEXEC.BAT file and the CONFIG.SYS file and displays the DOS prompt C>.

Understanding the CONFIG.SYS File

AUTOEXEC.BAT is not the only file DOS looks for when you boot your computer. Before DOS reads your AUTOEXEC.BAT file and, in fact, before DOS even loads the command processor, it looks for the *CONFIG.SYS* file, DOS's system configuration file.

Not only does DOS provide built-in services for disks and other hardware, it also extends its services for add-on hardware. The additional instructions that DOS needs to incorporate such outside services as a mouse and other devices are included in the CONFIG.SYS file.

CONFIG.SYS is also the location for naming the values of DOS configuration items that can be "tuned," which means that you can enter different values that affect the way the items work, without changing their basic function. Files and buffers, discussed in the next section, are two such "tunable" DOS items. CONFIG.SYS is a text file like AUTOEXEC.BAT that you can display on-screen or print. You also can change the contents of CONFIG.SYS with the DOS Editor.

DOS does not execute CONFIG.SYS as it does AUTOEXEC.BAT. Instead, DOS reads the values in the file and configures your computer to agree with those values. Many software packages modify or add a CONFIG.SYS file to the root directory. The range of possible values in the file is wide, but some common values you can include do exist.

Specifying Files and Buffers

When DOS moves data to and from disks, it does so in the most efficient manner possible. For each file that DOS acts on, an area of system RAM helps DOS track the operating details of that file. The number of built-in RAM areas for this tracking operation is controlled by the FILES command in CONFIG.SYS. The FILES command specifies how many open files you can have on-screen. (A command in the CONFIG.SYS file establishes the value of a system setting that can be modified.) If a program tries to open more files than the FILES command setting allows, DOS tells you that too many files are open.

Do not be tempted to set your FILES command to a large number just so that you always have room for more open files. The system memory for programs is reduced by each extra file included in FILES. As a rule of thumb, a safe compromise is 30 open files. To set the number of open files to 30, open the CONFIG.SYS file by using the DOS Editor, and edit the FILES line so that it reads

    FILES=30

The installation documentation for many programs tells you the minimum number you need to specify in the FILES command. Make sure that the FILES command is at least as large as the largest number a program requires. If one program requires 20 and another suggests 30, for example, use FILES=30. Do not add the numbers together and type **FILES=50**.

293

12

Similar to the FILES command is the BUFFERS command. *Buffers* are holding areas in RAM that store information coming from or going to disk files. To make disk operation more efficient, DOS stores disk information in RAM file buffers and then uses RAM, instead of the disk drives, for input and output whenever possible.

If the file information needed is not already in the buffer, new information is read into the buffer from the disk file. The information that DOS reads includes the needed information and as much additional file information as the buffer can hold. With this buffer of needed information, DOS can likely avoid constant disk access. The principle is similar to the way a mechanic might use a small tool pouch. Holding frequently used tools in a small pouch relieves him of having to make repeated trips across the garage to get tools from his main tool chest.

Similar to the FILES command, however, setting the BUFFERS command too high takes needed RAM away from programs and dedicates it to the buffers. The optimum number of buffers depends on the size of your hard disk and the type of application. The following list provides some general guidelines:

Hard Disk Size	*Number of Buffers*
Less than 40M	20
40–79M	30
80–119M	40
120M or more	50

Designating Device Drivers

You will recall that DOS works with peripherals, such as disk drives, printers, and displays. These peripherals are also called *devices*. DOS has built-in instructions, called *drivers*, to handle these devices.

Some devices, such as a mouse, are foreign to DOS. DOS lacks the built-in capability of handling such devices. To issue directions to devices that DOS doesn't recognize, use the DEVICE command in the CONFIG.SYS file. The syntax for this command is as follows:

DEVICE=*d:path/filename*

You replace *d:path* with the drive and path name to the file containing the device driver; then replace *filename* with the name of the file containing the driver. The device driver for a mouse, for example, might be in a file called MOUSE.SYS in the /UTIL directory on drive C. You would add the following command to your CONFIG.SYS file so that DOS understands how to use the mouse:

DEVICE=C:\UTIL\MOUSE.SYS

The DEVICE command tells DOS to find and load the driver program for the new device. This program enables DOS to control the device. If the device driver is not in the root directory, include the path to the device driver. A good place to put device drivers is in the \UTIL directory.

Many peripherals come with a disk that contains a device-driver file. This file contains the necessary instructions to control, or "drive," the device. The device-driver disk usually contains a provision to modify your CONFIG.SYS file to include the proper DEVICE command.

Some peripherals, especially nonstandard video adapters, come with diagnostic and other programs that you use to configure and control the peripheral. These programs and device drivers are often kept in their own directories. The DEVICE command must then include the path to that directory so that DOS can locate it.

Some device drivers also require additional parameters to work correctly on your computer. Always check your program and hardware manuals before experimenting with your system. Many installation programs provide prepared device drivers for you, but in some cases you have to enter the parameters yourself. A mouse driver may use COM1, for example, as the default serial port. If your mouse is attached to COM2, you may have to change the device driver as follows:

DEVICE=C:\UTIL\MOUSE.SYS /2

Note that if you miss this item in the installation instructions for your mouse, your mouse cannot operate.

Understanding Advanced DOS Configuration Options

A number of device drivers come with DOS. Some device drivers are added automatically to your CONFIG.SYS file during installation. These device drivers apply to the more advanced computers with a 286, 386, or 486 processor and extended memory. The normal memory that DOS and most programs use is called *conventional memory* and is limited to 640K. Extended memory is beyond the limit of conventional memory and can be used only in certain circumstances.

295

If you have a computer with a 386 or 486 processor and extended memory, you can configure your extended memory as expanded memory if it is needed by your applications programs. If you have a computer with extended memory, you can find more information in Que's *Using MS-DOS 6*, Special Edition.

If you have a computer with a 286 processor or higher, and you have extended memory, the DOS installation procedure adds the following commands to CONFIG.SYS:

DEVICE=C:\DOS\HIMEM.SYS

DEVICE=C:\DOS\SMARTDRV.EXE *nnn*

DOS=HIGH

HIMEM.SYS is the DOS extended memory manager, which allows DOS and applications programs to access extended memory.

SMARTDRV.EXE is a disk caching program that can speed up your disk operations, especially if you use database applications. A disk cache works a little like the BUFFERS command, but is much "smarter" and can speed up disk accesses much more than the BUFFERS command. The *nnn* is the amount of extended memory in kilobytes that DOS reserves for the disk cache.

DOS=HIGH tells DOS to load part of itself into extended memory and save more conventional memory for applications programs.

DOS 6 might add other commands to the CONFIG.SYS file. Although you do not have to understand the details of the commands added during installation, you should know where they came from if you see them in your CONFIG.SYS file.

Creating and Changing a CONFIG.SYS File

Because the CONFIG.SYS file is a text file, you can use the same methods to create, change, archive, and copy this file as with the AUTOEXEC.BAT file. Use the DOS Editor to create and change the CONFIG.SYS file. Make sure that you have a backup copy and an extra copy on a floppy disk before making changes. Note that errors in your CONFIG.SYS file cause your computer to hang more often than an error in the AUTOEXEC.BAT file. For this reason, having a floppy disk handy that contains the system files is especially important before you start making changes to the CONFIG.SYS file.

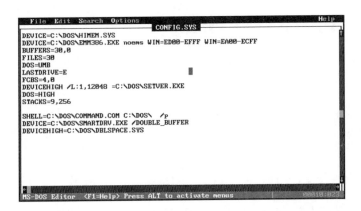

This screen shows a sample CONFIG.SYS file for a 486 computer with an 80M disk.

12

Your CONFIG.SYS file may contain other device drivers and DOS settings. Because the configuration of each computer can vary, the exact contents of the CONFIG.SYS file usually vary. If you want to explore configurations and device concepts in more detail, consult Que's *Using MS-DOS 6*, Special Edition. If you are unsure about the device drivers for new peripherals you buy, ask your dealer how to incorporate the new device.

Bypassing the CONFIG.SYS File

To bypass the CONFIG.SYS file, you can use the same clean boot procedure you use to bypass the AUTOEXEC.BAT file. When the Starting MS DOS... message appears during startup, press F5.

Alternatively, you can use the *interactive boot* to selectively activate the CONFIG.SYS values. DOS then boots without processing CONFIG.SYS, pausing to ask whether you want to load each device driver.

To perform an interactive boot, follow these steps:

1. Start your computer as you usually do.

2. Watch the screen as the computer performs its power-up routine. When you see the message Starting MS DOS..., press F8.

DOS skips the CONFIG.SYS file and prompts you to load each device driver individually.

Creating Sample Batch Files

12

If you are a beginner, you may benefit from entering sample batch files. Practicing with the following examples will make it easier to understand how to construct your own DOS batch files.

Remember that to use handy batch files, the directory that contains your batch files should be in your search path.

Using Batch Files To Execute Programs

One of the most common uses for batch files is to execute applications programs. The following sections discuss the methods you can use to set up batch files that execute programs.

Executing Programs from the Program Directory

Batch files are especially handy to use with programs, such as Lotus 1-2-3, that must be executed from the directory that contains the program files. If the 1-2-3 Release 2.4 program files are in the C:\123R24 directory, you must type the following commands from the command line to execute the program, or enter them in the Program Properties dialog box in the Shell:

```
C:
CD\123R24
123
```

This operation is an obvious candidate for a batch file. You can call the batch file 123.BAT, 123R24.BAT, R24.BAT, or anything else that you prefer. Use the DOS Editor to create this file, and put the file in your \BATCH directory.

If you call the batch file 123.BAT, aren't you breaking the rule about not naming batch files with the same name as a program file? Yes, but it works in this case because the 123 program directory is not part of the search path. If you are in any directory except the 123R24 directory, you execute the batch file. If you are in the 123R24 directory, however, you execute the program, which is all you want to do anyway; so the effect is exactly the same. A safer name choice for the batch file might be R24.BAT, to avoid any possible confusion.

When you execute 1-2-3, you can specify an alternate settings file. To enable this option with the batch file, add a replaceable parameter. You learned about replaceable parameters in Chapter 8. Replaceable parameters work in batch files exactly the same way they do in the Program Properties dialog boxes. To add a replaceable parameter to R24.BAT, type the file as follows:

```
C:
CD\123R24
123 %1
```

Then, to run 1-2-3 with a settings file named VGA43 and a 43-line display, type the following at the command line:

R24 VGA43

Whatever you type to the right of the space after R24 at the command line replaces the %1 in the batch file, and the final line of the batch file executes as though you had typed

123 VGA43

If you do not include anything to replace the %1, DOS ignores it completely. In the Shell, when you use a replaceable parameter, DOS pauses and presents you with a dialog box before it starts the program.

Using a Batch File To Run Programs from Associations

In Chapter 8, you learned how to run programs from the Shell by using associations. You associate a file extension with a program. Then when you open a file with that extension, DOS executes the program and tells the program to load the file automatically. As mentioned before, you cannot use this method with a program such as Lotus 1-2-3 Release 2.4 for two reasons:

- You have to start 1-2-3 from its program directory.
- 1-2-3 does not recognize the file name as a data file. Instead the program thinks that the data file is a settings file, and you get an error.

You can solve both of these problems with a batch file. The first problem is the easiest and applies to many programs. First, write a batch file, such as the R24.BAT example, and associate the file extension with the batch file, not the program. But in this case, the batch file will not work because of the second problem. To solve the second problem, you have to read the program manual and find out how to specify a data file to load when you start the program.

12

For 1-2-3 to load a worksheet automatically, you must type **-w** before the file name. To start 1-2-3 and load the SAMPLE.WK1 worksheet file without a batch file, for example, type this at the command line:

```
C:
CD\123R24
123 -wSAMPLE
```

Using the R24.BAT file to start the program, type

R24 -wSAMPLE

When you form an association in the Shell, DOS does not know about the -w prefix. DOS does not know that SAMPLE is a worksheet file.

To solve this problem, you need another batch file. Call this batch file R24A.BAT. The *A* means that the batch file is used in the Shell to start 1-2-3 from an associated file. The R24A.BAT file should look like this:

```
C:
CD\123R24
123 -w%1
```

Because DOS does not know to supply the -w prefix, the batch file supplies it.

To associate a file extension, select a file with that extension and choose **Associate** from the File menu. Then type the path and name of the batch file, including the BAT extension, and choose OK.

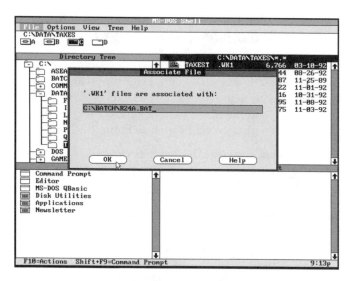

To execute 1-2-3 and automatically load a worksheet, double-click the worksheet file name, or highlight the worksheet and choose **Open** from the File menu.

Using Batch Files To Simplify the Search Path

Programs that must be executed from the directory that contains the program files are obvious candidates for batch files. But what about programs, such as Microsoft Word, that you can execute from any directory? You can use a batch file to tell DOS where to find the program. For example, the following one-line batch file tells DOS where to find Microsoft Word:

C:\WORD\WORD %1

Can you eliminate this batch file? Yes, if you put the C:\WORD directory in your search path. Then you just type **WORD**. This procedure works fine if you have only a few programs that you use and that you add to your search path. But if you use 10 or 20 different programs in different directories, your search path can get very long. A long search path can slow down processing because DOS has to search each directory in order every time you enter a command or program name.

If you use batch files to execute your programs, you can keep your search path short when you run programs from the command line. If you usually use the Shell to run programs, you do not need batch files to put the program directories in the search path. You just specify the complete path in the Program Properties dialog box when you set up the program in a program group, and DOS knows where to find the program. This procedure is discussed in Chapter 8.

Using a Batch File To Display Help Text

Using the batch file provisions of DOS does not mean that you can include only commands that do DOS jobs. You also can include commands that provide information for you or another user. In this example, text information is echoed to the screen. The text provides help for the COPY command. You can get help on the COPY command in the Shell, or by typing **HELP COPY** at the command prompt. A custom batch file, however, can display the exact help message you want.

Using the DOS Editor, create the following file, named COPYHELP.BAT, in your \BATCH directory:

```
ECHO OFF
CLS
ECHO *************** COPY COMMAND HELP INFORMATION ****************
ECHO * FULL SYNTAX:                                                 *
ECHO *                                                              *
Echo * COPY sd:\path\filename.ext dd:\path\filename.ext /switches  *
ECHO *    sd=source drive letter, dd=destination drive letter      *
ECHO *    /V=Verify switch                                         *
ECHO *                                                              *
ECHO * A space separates source and destination file parameters.   *
ECHO *                                                              *
ECHO *         FILES ARE COPIED FROM SOURCE TO DESTINATION.        *
ECHO * ? wild card matches any character and * matches all chars.  *
ECHO * Wild cards allow copying all files matching command line.   *
ECHO *                                                              *
ECHO *                   ---COPY EXAMPLES---                        *
ECHO * (1)COPY A:*.* C: (2)COPY\TEMP\MYFILE.123 \KEEP\YOURFILE.XYZ  *
ECHO * (3)COPY MEMO.DOC MEMO.BAK (4)COPY CON AUTOEXEC.BAT (re-      *
ECHO * direction using COPY CON)                                    *
ECHO *                                                              *
ECHO **************************************************************
```

To see the text entered in this file, type **COPYHELP** at the command line. You can substitute your own help text for other DOS commands by using the same method.

Lessons Learned

- The PATH command makes executing DOS commands and programs easier.
- The PROMPT command helps you keep track of where you are on a hard disk.
- Batch files are simple but powerful programs in the form of text files.
- Batch files personalize your computer to your own wishes.

■ The AUTOEXEC.BAT file is always executed by DOS after CONFIG.SYS to make your computer operate more efficiently.

■ The CONFIG.SYS file configures your PC.

■ Batch files can make executing programs easier, even when you use the Shell.

The next chapter teaches you some of the more advanced DOS commands.

12

12

More Advanced DOS Commands

The topics in this chapter may seem a bit exotic—
even unnecessary—but they are very useful tools in
certain circumstances. You may never have to recover a
damaged file, but if you do, it's nice to know that it is
possible.

This chapter covers DOS devices and redirection. The
section on redirection teaches you how to change both
the standard source and standard destination of input
and output.

As you gain mastery over DOS, you will use the command line more and more. You will learn how to use the
Doskey program to make the command line even faster
and easier to use.

Memory management may be important to you if you
have a 386 or 486 computer with extended memory
available. This chapter gives you only the most important information about these advanced topics. For more
information, consult Que's *Using MS-DOS 6*, Special
Edition.

Recovering
damaged files

DOS devices and
redirection

Pipes and filters

Using the command
line editor

Managing memory

13

Key Terms Used in This Chapter	
Bad sector	A sector on a disk that contains a bad spot in the magnetic coating where data cannot be read reliably.
Redirection	Taking input from some place other than the keyboard or sending output to some place other than the screen.
Device	A hardware component or peripheral that DOS can use in some commands as though that hardware were a file.
Console	The device DOS uses for keyboard input and screen output. DOS recognizes the console as CON.
Pipe	A method of taking the output of one command and making it the input for another command in DOS.
Filter	A method of processing the output of a command before displaying it.
Conventional memory	The main system memory used by DOS and programs. This memory is usually restricted to 640K.
Reserved memory	Memory between conventional memory and one megabyte that the computer hardware uses.
Upper memory blocks	Areas in reserved memory that are not used by the computer hardware.
Expanded memory	A special type of memory beyond conventional memory that can be used by some programs.
Extended memory	Memory above one megabyte on 286, 386, and 486 computers.
High memory	Refers to reserved memory or memory in upper memory blocks.

Memory-resident program	A program that remains in memory after you execute it, such as the DOS Shell. Also called *terminate-and-stay-resident program*, or *TSR*.
RAM disk	A portion of memory set up to act like a very fast disk drive.

13

Recovering Damaged Files

When you save a file in an applications program or copy a file with DOS, you expect that file always to be available when you need it. You learned in Chapter 10 that there are many potential threats to your data, so you must always have a backup copy of every important file.

One threat to your data is a bad spot on the disk itself. Data is magnetically recorded on a very thin coat of iron oxide. The high-speed manufacturing process that coats the platters of a hard disk is not perfect. Many hard disks have a few spots where the oxide coat is thin or imperfect and cannot record data reliably.

When you format a disk, DOS checks the disk surface and marks as "bad sectors" any sectors it cannot read. DOS makes sure that any bad sectors are never used to record data. You can find out the number of bad sectors on a disk when you format the disk or when you execute the CHKDSK command.

A few bad sectors on a hard disk are not a problem. A floppy disk with bad sectors may indicate a problem with the entire disk. Do not store important data on a floppy disk with bad sectors.

```
C:\>chkdsk a:
Volume Serial Number is 1B47-1CD3

   1213952 bytes total disk space
     15360 bytes in bad sectors
   1198592 bytes available on disk

       512 bytes in each allocation unit
      2371 total allocation units on disk
      2341 available allocation units on disk

    655360 total bytes memory
    534096 bytes free

C:\>
```

Even when only a small area of a floppy disk seems to contain bad sectors, any data stored on that disk is at risk.

13

DOS takes care of bad sectors automatically. Unfortunately, a spot on the disk may be marginal, or just good enough to pass the bad-sector test when you format the disk. As you read and write files, DOS may no longer be able to read data from this spot. A marginal sector has become a bad sector.

When DOS tries to read data from a bad sector, it returns an error. The error message is usually `Sector not found` or `Seek error`. The worst time to get this message is when you try to make a backup copy of the file.

If the unreadable file contains mostly text, such as a word processing file, you may be able to recover most of the data. The RECOVER command reads the file one sector at a time and restores the part of the file that can be read. The part of the file in the bad sector is lost, however. The format is as follows:

> RECOVER *filespec*

In most cases, you will replace *filespec* with the name of the file you want to recover. Although *filespec* can be a directory, or even an entire disk, you should recover one file at a time. No matter where the file started originally, RECOVER puts the recovered file in the root directory with the name FILE*nnnn*.REC, where *nnnn* is a sequential number starting with 0001. If you recover one file at a time, you can then rename the file to its correct name. If you try to recover multiple files at once, you will have to read through each FILE*nnnn*.REC to determine which file is which.

After you recover a file, use your word processor or the DOS Editor to determine what data is missing and then reenter the data. You may get an error message such as `Incomplete file` or `Invalid file format` when you try to open the file with a word processing program, because of the missing data. If the program refuses to accept the file, use the DOS Editor to delete all the nontext formatting information, and try again to open the file with your word processing program. You will have to reenter all format information.

If the recovered file is a database or a spreadsheet, you may be able to use the recovered file, or the program may just reject it, depending on which part of the file was lost. If the recovered file is a program, the recovered file is useless. Do not try to rename and execute a recovered program file. If you try to execute an incomplete program, the results are unpredictable and could be disastrous.

Considering DOS Devices and Redirection

In DOS, the term *redirection* means to change the source or destination normally used for input and output. The standard source of input is the keyboard. The standard output location is the screen display. When you use the keyboard to type a command, COMMAND.COM carries the text or messages and displays them on-screen. In DOS, the keyboard and display are the standard, or default, devices for messages, prompts, and input.

13

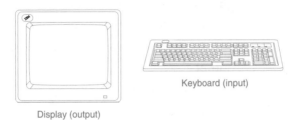

Display (output)   Keyboard (input)

DOS views devices as extensions of the main unit of the computer. Some devices send input and receive output. Other devices are used only for input (keyboards) or only output (video displays or printers). Disk drives are both input and output devices. Keyboards are input devices; displays and printer adapters are output devices. Serial adapters can send output and receive input.

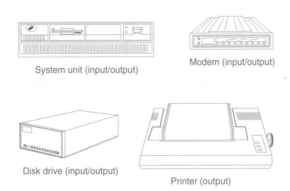

System unit (input/output)   Modem (input/output)

Disk drive (input/output)   Printer (output)

You can use device names in some commands (see table 13.1), as you do file names. In fact, DOS treats devices as if they were files. Device names are three to four characters long and do not contain extensions. You cannot delete device names or format them, but you can use device names in commands to perform some useful actions.

13

Table 13.1
DOS Device Names

Name	Device
CON	The video display and keyboard
AUX or COM1	The first asynchronous communications port
COM2	The second asynchronous port
COM3	The third asynchronous port
COM4	The fourth asynchronous port
LPT1 or PRN	The first line or parallel printer; used only for output
LPT2	The second parallel printer
LPT3	The third parallel printer
NUL	A dummy device (for redirecting output to "nowhere")

DOS controls devices through its system files and the special ROM BIOS files. Fortunately, understanding the details of how DOS handles devices is not essential to using them with DOS commands.

The COPY CON Device

A useful application for a DOS device is creating a file containing characters you enter directly from the keyboard. To do so, you use the familiar COPY command. This time, however, you copy data from CON, the *console* device. (You learned how to use COPY CON to create a batch file in Chapter 12.)

CON, as an input device, is DOS's device name for the keyboard. In this case, suppose that you want to create a file named TEST.TXT. Follow these steps to send characters directly to the file:

1. At the DOS prompt type the following command:

   COPY CON TEST.TXT

   This command specifies that you want DOS to copy data from the console and send the output to the TEST.TXT file.

2. Press ⏎Enter. The cursor drops to the next line and no DOS prompt appears.

3. Begin typing characters as the input to the file. For example, type the following text:

   This is a file copied from a device to a disk file.

4. Press ↵Enter. DOS writes the line that you typed in memory.

5. Type several lines, if you want, pressing ↵Enter after each line.

6. When you finish typing text, press F6 or Ctrl-Z. DOS recognizes either keystroke as the end-of-file character.

7. Press ↵Enter.

You have just entered a text file into your computer by using a DOS command and a device name.

```
C:\DATA>COPY CON TEST.TXT
This is a file copied from a device to a disk file.
^Z
        1 file(s) copied

C:\DATA>
```

When you press Enter after F6 or Ctrl-Z, DOS saves the information you typed as a new file and displays the message 1 File(s) copied.

You can create simple files quickly with this method. As the length of a file increases, however, COPY CON becomes more awkward to use. The DOS Editor or another text editor is more reliable. With COPY CON, you cannot go back to a previous line and correct it after you press Enter. If you notice that you typed an error on a previous line, you have two options:

- Hold down the Ctrl key and press the Break key. This ends the COPY CON operation. All the characters you typed are lost.

- If you see an error after you saved the file, delete the file and start over, or use a text editor to correct the mistake.

Remember to close your file by pressing F6 or Ctrl-Z. Until you close the file, DOS assumes that you are still typing characters into the file.

To verify that the file is correct, use TYPE to view the file.

Redirection

You must use special redirection symbols to tell DOS to use nondefault devices in a command. The following table lists the symbols DOS recognizes for redirection.

13

311

Symbol	Description
<	Redirects a program's input
>	Redirects a program's output
>>	Redirects a program's output, but adds the text to an established file if it exists

The < symbol points away from the device or file and says, "Take input from here." The > symbol points toward the device or file and says, "Put output there." The >> symbol redirects a program's output, but adds the text to an established file. When you issue a redirection command, place the redirection symbol after the DOS command, but before the device name.

Redirecting to a Printer

Wouldn't it be practical to get the output of a DIR or TREE command on your printer? You can, by redirecting output to the PRN device (the printer). Make sure that the printer is turned on and connected to your computer. Then type

DIR /W > PRN

When you press Enter, the output of the DIR command goes to the printer. The /W (wide display) switch lists the files in five columns. You can tuck such a printout into the sleeve of a floppy disk to identify the contents of a disk. If you entered text into the TEST.TXT file and your printer is ready, type the following command:

TYPE TEST.TXT > PRN

You now have a printed copy of the TEST.TXT file.

A more efficient way to print a text file is to copy the file to the PRN device. Type

COPY TEST.TXT PRN

Never try to redirect binary files to the printer. Redirecting binary data can result in paper-feed problems, beeps, meaningless graphics characters, and maybe a locked computer. If you get hung up, you can do a warm boot or turn the power switch off and then on again. If you must turn off your computer, wait about 15 seconds before turning it back on.

Redirecting to a File

When you use commands, such as DIR or TREE, the result displays on-screen and then it is gone; it is not stored for future use. As you just learned, you can easily redirect a listing to a printer for a permanent printed record. You also can redirect the listing to a file for a permanent record on your disk. To store a listing of all the directories on drive C in a file named TREE.TXT, use the following command:

TREE C:\ > TREE.TXT

You now have a permanent record of the structure of your hard disk at the time you created the file. To store a listing of all the directories and files on drive C in a file named TREEFILE.TXT, use the following command:

TREE C:\ /F > TREEFILE.TXT

Working with Pipes and Filters

Being able to manipulate the input and output of DOS commands to use them with other commands is sometimes useful. *Pipes* let you use the output of one command as the input of another command. *Filters* let you change the way data from a standard input is displayed. Together, pipes and filters give you a great deal of control over the results of basic DOS commands.

The pipe symbol (¦) presents, or "pipes," output from one command to another. For example, you can pipe the output, or result, of the DIR command so that it is used as input for one of the filter commands. (By the way, don't confuse the pipe symbol with the colon symbol. The pipe symbol is on the same key as the backslash. Books often print the pipe symbol as a single vertical dash (|), but on the keyboard and on your display the symbol is a pair of stacked vertical dashes.)

The FIND, SORT, and MORE commands are filters. A filter is a program that gets data from the standard input, changes the data, and then writes the modified data to the display. FIND, SORT, and MORE accept the output of a DOS command and do further processing on that output. FIND outputs lines that match characters given on the command line. SORT alphabetizes output. MORE displays a prompt when each screen of the output is full. The following sections discuss these filters in greater detail.

Using the FIND Filter

One handy way of using the FIND filter is to display a directory listing showing only the files that contain certain characters in their file names. To list just the files that contain TAX in their file names, for example, use the following command:

DIR ¦ FIND "TAX"

The FIND command filters the output of a DIR command. FIND displays on-screen only the lines that contain TAX. The ¦ symbol pipes the output of DIR to FIND.

```
C:\DATA\TAXES>dir

   Volume in drive C has no label
   Directory of C:\DATA\TAXES

.              <DIR>       11-08-92   11:39p
..             <DIR>       11-08-92   11:39p
TAXEST   WK1      6766 03-10-92    3:10a
INCOME   WK1      5822 11-01-92   12:13p
LOG      DOC      3587 11-25-89   11:25a
STATEMNT WK1     18944 08-26-92    2:47p
BUDGET   DOC     39416 10-31-92    6:21p
92TAXES  WK1      2395 11-08-92    9:49p
1992TAX  DOC      4375 11-03-92   12:56p
         9 file(s)       81305 bytes
                     100835328 bytes free

C:\DATA\TAXES>DIR ¦ FIND "TAX"
   Directory of C:\DATA\TAXES
TAXEST   WK1      6766 03-10-92    3:10a
92TAXES  WK1      2395 11-08-92    9:49p
1992TAX  DOC      4375 11-03-92   12:56p

C:\DATA\TAXES>
```

Using the SORT Filter

The SORT command is a filter that alphabetizes input. In the following command, the output of the TYPE command is piped to SORT:

TYPE NAMES.TXT ¦ SORT

The listing filtered by SORT displays on-screen in alphabetical order.

```
C:\DATA\DOCS>TYPE NAMES.TXT
DeFeis
Weisman
Lerner
Swaine
Flynn
Connors
Chamberlin
Fitzpatrick
Williams

C:\DATA\DOCS>TYPE NAMES.TXT ¦ SORT
Chamberlin
Connors
DeFeis
Fitzpatrick
Flynn
Lerner
Swaine
Weisman
Williams

C:\DATA\DOCS>
```

314

The main use for the SORT filter with earlier versions of DOS was to sort a directory listing. With DOS 6, to sort a directory listing by file name, use the /ON switch as follows:

DIR /ON

Using the MORE Filter

If a file is so long that the text scrolls off the screen, you can pause the display by pressing Ctrl-S (or the Pause key on Enhanced keyboards). If you have a fast computer, pressing the Pause key at the right time may be very difficult, and information can scroll off the screen before you can read it. The MORE filter provides a better solution to this problem. MORE displays information one screen at a time.

To see how MORE works, change to your DOS directory. (It is probably C:\DOS.) Enter the following command:

TYPE README.TXT ¦ MORE

```
++++++++++++++++++++++++++++++++++++++++++++++

For information about using applications with MS-DOS 6.0,
see the APPNOTES.TXT file.

The following topics are discussed in this file:

1. Readme Conventions
2. Notes on Setup
   2.1 Priam and Everex Disk-Partitioning Software
   2.2 SyQuest Removable Hard Disk
   2.3 Bernoulli Drive
   2.4 Disk Manager
   2.5 SpeedStor and Volume Expansion
   2.6 Novell Partitions
   2.7 Vfeature Deluxe
   2.8 Columbia Data Products Device Driver
   2.9 Incompatible Partition
   2.10 WYSE Partition
   2.11 286 Accelerator Card
   2.12 Bernoulli Cache
   2.13 AT&T 6300 Computer
   2.14 Western Digital SCSI Hard-Disk Controller
-- More --
```

MORE displays 23 lines of text and then pauses, displaying the message --More-- at the bottom of the screen. When you press any key, MORE displays the next screen of text.

If you want to read a long text file, using the DOS Editor might be easier. With the Editor, you can use the PgUp and PgDn keys to scroll the text. With MORE, after a screenful of text scrolls off the screen, you cannot scroll back to see it again. To read or edit README.TXT, use the following command:

EDIT README.TXT

Using Doskey, the Command Line Editor

13

One of the advantages of using the command line instead of the DOS Shell is that typing the command is usually faster than using the menus. The DOS Shell menus are much easier to use, however. The DOS Shell is the best way to learn how to use DOS commands.

After you are familiar with the common DOS commands, you may find yourself using the command line more often. When you use the command line, you find that you repeat many commands over and over, sometimes with slight variations. With the command line editor, Doskey, you can recall previous commands without retyping them. At times, you may type a long command and make an error. Whether you catch the error before or after you press Enter, you can correct the error without retyping the entire command.

Doskey is not built into COMMAND.COM. Before you can use Doskey's features, you must load it into memory. At the prompt, type **DOSKEY** and press Enter.

Doskey is loaded into memory with a 512-byte buffer. This buffer is a portion of memory where Doskey stores your commands. As long as a command is in the buffer, you can recall the command without retyping it. When the buffer fills up, every time you enter a new command, Doskey deletes the oldest command in the buffer.

You need to enter the DOSKEY command only once per session. If you plan to use Doskey regularly, you can put the command in your AUTOEXEC.BAT file. The AUTOEXEC.BAT file is covered in Chapter 12.

Recalling Previous Commands with Doskey

When Doskey is loaded, to recall the last command entered, press the up-arrow key. To recall an earlier command, continue to press the up-arrow key until DOS displays the command you want. If you press the up-arrow key too many times and go past the command you want, press the down-arrow key to recall the next command in the buffer. To clear the command line so that you can enter a command from scratch, press the Esc key.

Suppose, for example, that you entered the following commands:

```
C:
CD\DATA\TAXES
FORMAT A: /Q
COPY *.* A:
```

These commands make the DATA\TAXES directory the current directory, quick format a floppy disk in drive A, and then copy all the files from the DATA\TAXES directory to the floppy disk in drive A.

When the copy procedure is complete, DOS displays the DOS prompt. If you want to repeat this process for the DATA\DOCS directory, you can retype each command or use Doskey to recall the previous commands without retyping them.

13

```
Volume label (11 characters, ENTER for none)?

   1213952 bytes total disk space
   1213952 bytes available on disk

     512 bytes in each allocation unit.
    2371 allocation units available on disk.

Volume Serial Number is 2C34-16D4

QuickFormat another (Y/N)?N

C:\DATA\TAXES>COPY *.* A:
TAXEST.WK1
INCOME.WK1
LOG.DOC
STATEMNT.WK1
BUDGET.DOC
92TAXES.WK1
1992TAX.DOC
        7 file(s) copied

C:\DATA\TAXES>COPY *.* A:
```

When you press the up-arrow key once, you recall the last command entered: COPY *.* A:.

```
Volume label (11 characters, ENTER for none)?

   1213952 bytes total disk space
   1213952 bytes available on disk

     512 bytes in each allocation unit.
    2371 allocation units available on disk.

Volume Serial Number is 2C34-16D4

QuickFormat another (Y/N)?N

C:\DATA\TAXES>COPY *.* A:
TAXEST.WK1
INCOME.WK1
LOG.DOC
STATEMNT.WK1
BUDGET.DOC
92TAXES.WK1
1992TAX.DOC
        7 file(s) copied

C:\DATA\TAXES>CD\DATA\TAXES
```

When you press the up-arrow key three times, you recall the third-from-the-last command entered: CD\DATA\TAXES.

After you recall a previous command, you can press Enter to execute it again, or you can edit or change the command before you execute it. If you recall the command CD\DATA\TAXES and want to change it to CD\DATA\DOCS, press the Backspace key five times to erase the word *TAXES*. Then type **DOCS** and press Enter.

317

13

```
    1213952 bytes total disk space
    1213952 bytes available on disk

        512 bytes in each allocation unit.
       2371 allocation units available on disk.

Volume Serial Number is 2C34-16D4

QuickFormat another (Y/N)?N


C:\DATA\TAXES>COPY *.* A:
TAXEST.WK1
INCOME.WK1
LOG.DOC
STATEMNT.WK1
BUDGET.DOC
92TAXES.WK1
1992TAX.DOC
        7 file(s) copied

C:\DATA\TAXES>CD\DATA\DOCS

C:\DATA\DOCS>
```

The recalled command is CD\DATA\TAXES. The edited command makes DATA\DOCS the current directory.

To repeat the format command, press the up-arrow key three times. The first press recalls CD\DATA\DOCS, the second press recalls COPY *.* A:, and the third recalls FORMAT A: /Q. Because you do not want to change this command in any way, just press Enter to quick format another floppy disk.

To repeat the COPY command after the formatting is complete, press the up-arrow key three times. The first time recalls FORMAT A: /Q, the second time recalls CD\DATA\DOCS, and the third time recalls COPY *.* A:.

Because you do not want to change this command in any way, just press Enter to copy all the files from the DATA\DOCS directory to the floppy disk.

You use the up-arrow key when you want to recall a recently used command. Sometime you may want to recall a command that you used 10 or 20 commands ago. You could press the up-arrow key 10 or 20 times, but there is an easier way. The F7 key displays all the commands that are in the Doskey buffer.

```
    1213952 bytes total disk space
    1213952 bytes available on disk

      512 bytes in each allocation unit.
    2371 allocation units available on disk.

Volume Serial Number is 201E-16DA

QuickFormat another (Y/N)?n

C:\DATA\DOCS>COPY *.* A:
NAMES.TXT
        1 file(s) copied

C:\DATA\DOCS>
1: C:
2: CD\DATA\TAXES
3: FORMAT A: /Q
4: COPY *.* A:
5: CD\DATA\DOCS
6: FORMAT A: /Q
7: COPY *.* A:
C:\DATA\DOCS>Line number: 6
```

To recall any command from the displayed list, press F9 and type the line number of the command you want to recall. For example, to recall the quick format command, press F9, type 6, and press Enter.

```
    1213952 bytes total disk space
    1213952 bytes available on disk

      512 bytes in each allocation unit.
    2371 allocation units available on disk.

Volume Serial Number is 201E-16DA

QuickFormat another (Y/N)?n

C:\DATA\DOCS>COPY *.* A:
NAMES.TXT
        1 file(s) copied

C:\DATA\DOCS>
1: C:
2: CD\DATA\TAXES
3: FORMAT A: /Q
4: COPY *.* A:
5: CD\DATA\DOCS
6: FORMAT A: /Q
7: COPY *.* A:
C:\DATA\DOCS>FORMAT A: /Q
```

After you press Enter, DOS recalls the command at line number 6.

```
C:\DATA>
1: C:
2: CD\DATA\TAXES
3: FORMAT A: /Q
4: COPY *.* A:
5: CD\DATA\DOCS
6: FORMAT A: /Q
7: COPY *.* A:
8: cls
9: vol a:
10: cd \dos
11: type autoexec.bat
12: cd \
13: type autoexec.bat
14: type config.sys
15: cd \dos
16: type readme.txt | more
17: dir
18: cd \data
19: dir
20: type sample.txt
21: del test.txt
22: undelete test.txt
23: cls
-- More --
```

If the buffer contains more than 23 commands, the first 23 commands are listed when you press F7. Press any key at the --More-- prompt to scroll the display.

When DOS has displayed the entire list of commands, press F9 and type the line number of the command you want to recall. Then press Enter.

You have one more way to recall a command. Type one or more characters at the start of the command and press the F8 key. DOS searches the buffer, starting with the most recent command, for a command that starts with the characters you typed. If DOS finds a match, it recalls that command.

13

If you type just the letter *F* and press Enter, DOS searches for the most recent command that starts with an *F*.

```
 2: CD\DATA\TAXES
 3: FORMAT A: /Q
 4: COPY *.* A:
 5: CD\DATA\DOCS
 6: FORMAT A: /Q
 7: COPY *.* A:
 8: cls
 9: vol a:
10: cd \dos
11: type autoexec.bat
12: cd \
13: type autoexec.bat
14: type config.sys
15: cd \dos
16: type readme.txt | more
17: dir
18: cd \data
19: dir
20: type sample.txt
21: del test.txt
22: undelete test.txt
23: cls
-- More --
24: ver
C:\DATA>F
```

Here DOS recalls the most recent FORMAT command in response to your typing an *F* and pressing F8.

```
 2: CD\DATA\TAXES
 3: FORMAT A: /Q
 4: COPY *.* A:
 5: CD\DATA\DOCS
 6: FORMAT A: /Q
 7: COPY *.* A:
 8: cls
 9: vol a:
10: cd \dos
11: type autoexec.bat
12: cd \
13: type autoexec.bat
14: type config.sys
15: cd \dos
16: type readme.txt | more
17: dir
18: cd \data
19: dir
20: type sample.txt
21: del test.txt
22: undelete test.txt
23: cls
-- More --
24: ver
C:\DATA>FORMAT A: /Q
```

Table 13.2 lists all the commands you can use with DOSKEY to recall commands.

Table 13.2
Keys To Recall Previous Commands

Key	Action
↑	Recalls the previous command.
↓	Recalls the next command.
Esc	Clears the command line.
PgUp	Recalls the oldest command.
PgDn	Recalls the most recent command.
F7	Lists all commands in the buffer.
F8	Searches the buffer for a command that starts with the text you specify.
F9	Recalls the command at the line number you specify.
Alt-F7	Clears the entire Doskey buffer.

Editing Previous Commands with Doskey

After you recall a command, you can edit the command before you execute it. You already learned to use the Backspace key to erase characters at the end of the command. Doskey also provides a line editor that enables you to change any part of the command. Table 13.3 lists all the Doskey editing keys. Editing a command is similar to editing a line of text with the DOS Editor or a word processing program. The only difference is that you can edit only one line.

Suppose, for example, that you execute the following command:

    COPY *.DOC D:\BACKUP

You also want to copy all the files with a WK1 extension to the D:\BACKUP directory. Follow these steps:

1. Press ↑ once to recall the COPY command.
2. Press Home to move the cursor to the beginning of the command line.
3. Press → seven times to move the cursor to the *D* in *DOC*.
4. Type **WK1** in place of DOC.
5. Press ↵Enter to execute the command.

13

Table 13.3
Doskey Editing Keys

Key	Action
Home	Moves the cursor to the beginning of the command.
End	Moves the cursor to the end of the command.
←	Moves the cursor one character to the left.
→	Moves the cursor one character to the right.
Ctrl-←	Moves the cursor one word to the left.
Ctrl-→	Moves the cursor one word to the right.
←Backspace	Deletes one character to the left of the cursor.
Del	Deletes one character at the cursor position.
Ctrl-End	Deletes all characters from the cursor to the end of the command.
Ctrl-Home	Deletes all characters from the cursor to the beginning of the command.
Ins	Toggles between Overtype and Insert modes. In Overtype mode, everything you type replaces existing characters. In Insert mode, the cursor changes from an underline to a square block, and everything you type is inserted at the cursor.
Esc	Clears the command line.

Doskey has other features that are beyond the scope of this book. You can find out more about Doskey in Que's *Using MS-DOS 6*, Special Edition.

Managing Memory

A few years ago, managing memory was not an issue. Today, however, memory management can be a significant factor in using your personal computer efficiently.

If you have a PC or XT with an 8088 or 8086 microprocessor (or a compatible computer), you can skip this section; the amount and type of memory available for these computers does not require managing. If you have a 286 computer—a PC with an 80286 microprocessor, also known as an AT-class computer—memory management can affect you. If you have a 386 or 486 computer, memory management can be very important.

Memory management can be a very complex subject. This book covers only part of the topic of optimizing your computer's performance. You can find out more about memory management in Que's *Using MS-DOS 6*, Special Edition.

Types of Memory

You can have several different types of memory in your computer, as explained in the following list:

- *Conventional memory* is the main system memory that all personal computers use to run DOS and programs. It is sometimes called *DOS memory*. With DOS, conventional memory is limited to 640K. Almost all computers today have the maximum conventional memory. Many applications programs require or recommend a full 640K.

- *Reserved memory* is the 384K of memory between the 640K of conventional memory and 1M. All personal computers use the reserved memory area for the ROM BIOS, video memory, and adapter cards, such as disk controllers and network boards.

  Another name for reserved memory is *upper memory*. Although a 384K area is reserved, the computer does not use that entire area. Sections, or blocks, of memory in this area that are not used are called *upper memory blocks*. With 386 and 486 computers, you can use these upper memory blocks to increase the size of available conventional memory.

- *Expanded memory* is a special type of additional memory that enables some programs to use memory beyond the 640K limit of conventional memory. Expanded memory is sometimes abbreviated *EMS* for *Expanded Memory Specification*. To make use of expanded memory, you need a special expanded memory expansion board, special software known as an *expanded memory manager* that makes the expanded memory available to the applications program, and an applications program written to use expanded memory.

  Some computers come with expanded memory and do not require an expansion board. All 386 and 486 computers have expanded memory capability built-in, but require special software called an *expanded memory emulator* to activate it.

13

13

- *Extended memory* is memory above 1M. Only 286, 386, and 486 personal computers can have extended memory. Extended memory is sometimes abbreviated XMS memory. Because DOS, in general, was designed to operate with only conventional memory, most programs cannot use extended memory. DOS is evolving, however, toward using extended memory, and the most powerful applications now use it. Extended memory is faster and cheaper than expanded memory.

  Because extended memory support is not built into DOS, some programs require an *extended memory manager*. DOS 6 comes with an extended memory manager called HIMEM.SYS, which is added to your CONFIG.SYS file during installation if you have extended memory. DOS 6 also comes with EMM386, a memory manager that can simulate expanded memory for DOS-based applications that require it.

  Some DOS programs, such as Paradox 4 and Lotus 1-2-3 Release 3.1, have their own extended memory managers built-in.

In most cases, using conventional, reserved, and expanded memory is straight-forward and handled by DOS and your applications programs. The most important memory management issue is how to best use extended memory. Many personal computers have 3M or more of extended memory. How you use these megabytes determines how fast and how effective your computer is. One major goal of memory management is to free as much conventional memory as possible for applications programs.

DOS 6 comes with a memory-optimization program called *MemMaker*. If you have an 80386 or higher, you can use MemMaker to free conventional memory for DOS applications. MemMaker makes it easy to move device drivers and memory-resident programs into upper memory. This program takes a lot of the guesswork out of memory management and makes it simple even for beginning DOS users to get the best use of all the memory they have installed.

Using MemMaker

On 80386 and 80486 computers with extended memory, you can use MemMaker to load device drivers and memory-resident programs into the upper memory blocks in extended memory. To do this, MemMaker automatically changes your CONFIG.SYS and AUTOEXEC.BAT files.

13

To provide the most efficient memory configuration for your system, MemMaker must know which device drivers and memory-resident programs you usually use. Before you run MemMaker, you should take all commands that start unnecessary programs out of your CONFIG.SYS and AUTOEXEC.BAT files. (You learned how to change your CONFIG.SYS and AUTOEXEC.BAT files in Chapter 12.) Then you should start the hardware and the memory-resident software you usually use. For example, if you use a network, start the network software.

MemMaker offers you a choice of Express Setup or Custom Setup. The Express Setup automatically optimizes your computer's memory. The Custom Setup enables you to be more specific about which device drivers and TSRs are put into upper memory. Unless you have a good understanding of your computer's memory and feel comfortable manipulating it, however, you should stick with the Express Setup.

Use MemMaker if you use only DOS applications. If you use Windows applications, you should leave extended memory free and keep the device drivers and memory-resident programs in conventional memory.

To run MemMaker, follow these steps:

1. At the DOS prompt, type CD\ and press ⏎Enter to change to the root directory.

2. Type **MEMMAKER** and press ⏎Enter. The MemMaker welcome screen displays.

   MemMaker looks similar to the Anti-Virus and Backup programs, but you cannot use a mouse in MemMaker. From the welcome screen, you can press ⏎Enter to accept the default option (Continue); press the space bar to change the option; press F1 to display help; or press F3 to leave MemMaker and return to the DOS command line.

3. Press ⏎Enter to continue.

4. Press ⏎Enter to begin the Express Setup.

5. Press ⏎Enter to restart your computer using MemMaker. (If your computer usually loads into a menu program instead of to DOS, exit the program as soon as the computer starts so that MemMaker can continue.)

   MemMaker analyzes your system's memory during the startup procedure. The program determines the optimum configuration and adjusts your CONFIG.SYS and AUTOEXEC.BAT files to load device drivers and memory-resident programs into upper memory. MemMaker also makes backup copies of your original CONFIG.SYS and AUTOEXEC.BAT files so that you can undo the changes if necessary.

6. Press ⏎Enter to restart your computer again, using the new CONFIG.SYS and AUTOEXEC.BAT files. Watch the screen for any unusual messages indicating that your computer is not working correctly.

7. If your system appeared to boot properly, press ⏎Enter to select Yes. If not, press the **space bar** to select No, and then press ⏎Enter. You can undo the changes and revert to your original memory configuration.

   When MemMaker finishes optimizing your system memory, it displays a status report on the memory usage and availability.

8. Press ⏎Enter to return to DOS, or press Esc to undo the changes.

You can undo the changes made by MemMaker at any time. Type **MEMMAKER /UNDO** at the command line, and MemMaker restores your original CONFIG.SYS and AUTOEXEC.BAT files.

In the future, if you add devices or memory-resident programs, run MemMaker again to be sure that your system memory is still optimized.

Using the HIMEM Extended Memory Manager

If you have extended memory, DOS automatically adds the HIMEM device driver to your CONFIG.SYS file during installation. The standard statement is as follows:

> **DEVICE=C:\DOS\HIMEM.SYS**

If you add any other statements that use extended memory to CONFIG.SYS, make sure that you put them after the HIMEM device driver.

Some computers need special handling to manage their extended memory. These computers need a special /MACHINE:*xxx* parameter to operate properly, where *xxx* is the "machine code." A machine code defines the computers to DOS. The following table contains the possible values.

Machine code	Computer
AT	IBM AT
PS2	IBM PS/2
PT1CASCADE	Computer with a Phoenix Cascade BIOS
HPVECTRA	HP "Classic" Vectra
ATT6300PLUS	AT&T 6300 Plus

Machine code	Computer
ACER1100	Acer 1100
TOSHIBA	Toshiba 1600 or 1200XE
WYSE	Wyse 12.5 MHz 286 with Micro Channel
TULIP	Tulip SX
ZENITH	Zenith ZBIOS
AT1	IBM PC/AT (alternative delay)
AT2	IBM PC/AT (alternative delay)
CSS	CSS Labs
AT3	IBM PC/AT (alternative delay)
PHILIPS	Philips
FASTHP	HP Vectra
IBM7552	IBM 7552 Industrial Computer
BULLMICRAL	Bull Micral 60
DELL	Dell XBIOS

13

If you don't include machine code, HIMEM defaults to AT, which applies to most 286, 386, and 486 computers. If your computer is one of those mentioned (other than an AT), add the parameter to the HIMEM statement in your CONFIG.SYS file. If you have an IBM PS/2, for example, the HIMEM statement is as follows:

DEVICE=C:\DOS\HIMEM.SYS /MACHINE:PS2

If you have problems when you boot your computer with HIMEM, read the README.TXT file in your C:\DOS directory. This file may contain additional information regarding installation instructions for your computer.

Using EMM386

If you have a 386 or 486 computer with extended memory, you can use the EMM386 device driver in your CONFIG.SYS file to configure some or all of the extended memory as expanded memory. Expanded memory is slower than extended memory, but many applications programs cannot use extended memory.

13

If you use a program that can use expanded memory, such as 1-2-3 Release 2.4, you can build much larger spreadsheets if you make some extended memory available to the program as expanded memory. MemMaker automatically sets up EMM386 as an expanded-memory emulator.

The basic syntax to convert extended memory to expanded memory is as follows:

DEVICE=C:\DOS\EMM386.EXE *nnnn*

The *nnnn* parameter is the number of kilobytes to convert to expanded memory. To convert 512K of extended memory to expanded memory, for example, change the *nnnn* parameter so that the statement in your CONFIG.SYS file reads as follows:

DEVICE=C:\DOS\EMM386.EXE 512

EMM386 also provides access to the upper memory area so that you can run device drivers and memory-resident programs in upper memory.

Loading Drivers and Programs into High Memory

The term *high memory* refers to upper memory blocks in reserved memory. If you load some drivers and programs into high memory, you free conventional memory for other programs. MemMaker automatically configures your system so that device drivers and memory-resident programs run in upper memory.

If you have extended memory, DOS automatically adds the following statement to your CONFIG.SYS file during installation:

DOS=HIGH

With part of DOS in extended memory, you have more conventional memory for programs. In this case, HIGH refers to the *high memory area* (HMA), which is the first 64K of extended memory.

You can load drivers and programs into any available upper memory blocks. The size of upper memory blocks and whether they are available depend on your hardware configuration. The more adapter cards in your computer, the less upper memory block memory is available.

Enabling High Memory Support

Before you can load drivers and programs into high memory, you must have two statements in CONFIG.SYS. One involves the DOS=HIGH statement, and the other involves DEVICE=C:\DOS\EMM386.

A parameter that maintains upper memory support must be part of the DOS=HIGH statement. Add **UMB** (which maintains such support) to DOS=HIGH so that the statement reads as follows:

DOS=HIGH,UMB

The DEVICE=C:\DOS\EMM386.EXE statement is required, even if you do not want to convert any extended memory to expanded memory. Use one of the following procedures:

- If you do convert extended memory to expanded memory, add *nnnn* RAM to the statement (where *nnnn* is the number of kilobytes you want to convert to expanded memory) so that it reads as follows:

    DEVICE=C:\DOS\EMM386.EXE *nnnn* RAM

    The RAM parameter activates upper memory block support.

- If you do not convert extended memory to expanded memory, add **NOEMS** to the statement so that it reads as follows:

    DEVICE=C:\DOS\EMM386.EXE NOEMS

    The NOEMS parameter uses EMM386 to activate upper memory block support, but does not convert any extended memory to expanded memory.

With these statements in your CONFIG.SYS file, you can now load drivers and programs into high memory.

Using DEVICEHIGH

To load a device driver into high memory instead of conventional memory, change the DEVICE statement in your CONFIG.SYS file to DEVICEHIGH. Do not use DEVICEHIGH for HIMEM or EMM386.

You can load all device drivers that come with DOS by using DEVICE or DEVICEHIGH. Other device drivers that come with other hardware in your computer may or may not work. If DEVICEHIGH does not load the driver, use DEVICE. Here are some examples of DEVICEHIGH statements:

DEVICEHIGH=C:\DOS\EGA.SYS

DEVICEHIGH=C:\DOS\RAMDRIVE.SYS *nnnn* /E

If you have a mouse driver in the \UTIL directory, the following command should work:

DEVICEHIGH=C:\UTIL\MOUSE.SYS

When DOS runs out of high memory, it ignores the DEVICEHIGH statement and treats it as a DEVICE statement.

329

Using LOADHIGH

You can use a number of *memory-resident programs* with DOS. A memory-resident program is a program that remains in memory while you run other programs. Examples are the DOS Shell and Doskey. Another name for a memory-resident program is a *TSR*, or *terminate-and-stay-resident program*. After you execute a TSR program, it stays resident in memory.

To load a TSR into high memory, use the LOADHIGH command before the name of the program. To load Doskey into high memory, for example, use the following command:

LOADHIGH DOSKEY

You usually load TSR programs into your AUTOEXEC.BAT file.

You can load into high memory any of the TSR programs that come with DOS. Other TSR programs may or may not work. If LOADHIGH does not successfully load the program, just delete the LOADHIGH command and load the program into conventional memory.

If DOS runs out of high memory, it ignores the LOADHIGH statement and loads the program into conventional memory.

Using RAMDRIVE

RAMDRIVE is a device driver you put in your CONFIG.SYS file so that you can use a portion of your memory as a *RAM disk*. A RAM disk is a portion of memory set up to act like a very fast disk drive for DOS commands and programs. A RAM disk is assigned a drive letter, just like a real disk. You can use a RAM disk to read and write files, just like you can with a real disk.

Because access to a RAM disk can be 20 times faster than a hard disk, a RAM disk can speed up some operations significantly. Data stored on a RAM disk is temporary, however. When you turn off your computer or reboot, you lose everything in the RAM disk.

A RAM disk can be stored in conventional, expanded, or extended memory. Conventional memory is best reserved for applications. If you have expanded memory, you may need it for one or more applications. The best place for a RAM disk is extended memory.

330

The syntax to create a RAM disk with the RAMDRIVE device driver is

    DEVICE=C:\DOS\RAMDRIVE.SYS *nnnn* **/E**

or

    DEVICEHIGH=C:\DOS\RAMDRIVE.SYS *nnnn* **/E**

where *nnnn* is the size of RAMDRIVE in bytes (1024 creates a 1M RAMDRIVE). You put the command in your CONFIG.SYS file after HIMEM.SYS. The /E means to use extended memory. Use /A to store RAMDRIVE in expanded memory.

13

DOS assigns RAMDRIVE the next available drive letter. For example, if your hard disk is drive C, the RAMDRIVE is drive D.

Many programs need a place to store temporary files. These temporary files may be written and read many times while the program operates. When you tell the program to store these temporary files in a RAM disk, the program runs much faster.

These programs often look for the TEMP parameter in the DOS environment to tell them where to store temporary files. The DOS environment is like a bulletin board that any program can read to get information. You can store information in the environment with the SET command. If drive D is RAMDRIVE, the SET command is

    SET TEMP=D:

To find out how large your RAMDRIVE must be to hold all the temporary files for an application, check the documentation for the application.

If you read and write some files or execute certain programs frequently, you can speed up processing by copying these files to a RAMDRIVE.

Lessons Learned

- ◼ You can partially recover a damaged file.
- ◼ A device is computer hardware other than the main unit; for example, keyboards, video displays, and printers are devices.
- ◼ COPY CON enables you to create a file directly from your keyboard, without using a text editor.
- ◼ The PRN device enables you to direct printing from your keyboard to the printer without using a word processing program or text editor.

13

■ With Doskey, you can easily recall previous DOS commands so that you don't have to retype them.

■ If you have a 386 or 486 computer, you can convert extended memory to expanded memory for applications programs that can use it.

■ If you have a 386 or 486 computer, you can load drivers and programs into high memory and make more conventional memory available to applications programs.

■ MemMaker automatically optimizes your computer's memory.

■ You can use part of the computer's memory to simulate a very fast disk drive—a RAM disk.

The next chapter is a listing of the most common commands, including syntax and usage.

Common
Commands
and Your PC

This chapter is a command reference, encompassing the most frequently used MS-DOS commands. Each command is presented in the same format:

- The command name appears first, followed by the notation

  ⚹ Internal or 🖫 External

  which indicates whether the command is built into MS-DOS (internal) or is disk-resident (external).

- The entry then explains the command's purpose and shows the syntax required to invoke the command.

- Next are step-by-step instructions for using the command.

- Last are any cautions, tips, or notes about the command, often including a brief comment indicating the emphasis you should place on mastering the command.

DOS Commands by Purpose

Use the following list to determine which command to use for a specific task. Then refer to the command reference that follows the list for details about the use and syntax of that command.

If You Want To...	Use
Back up a hard disk	MSBACKUP, BACKUP (prior to DOS 6)
Copy or combine files	COPY
Change the current directory	CHDIR (CD)
Change the current disk drive	*d*:
Change the date	DATE
Change the name of a file	RENAME (REN)
Change the time	TIME
Clear the screen	CLS
Compare disks	DISKCOMP
Compare files	COMP, FC, MSBACKUP
Compress a hard disk	DBLSPACE
Copy between devices	COPY, XCOPY
Copy disks	COPY, DISKCOPY, XCOPY
Defragment a disk	DEFRAG
Display a text file on-screen	TYPE
Display batch file commands and text strings on-screen	ECHO
Display the amount of memory	MEM
Display the contents of a file	TYPE
Display the date	DATE
Display the files on a disk	DIR, CHKDSK, TREE
Display the free space on a disk	CHKDSK, DIR
Display Help text	DOSHELP, HELP
Display the subdirectories on a disk	TREE, CHKDSK

14

If You Want To...	Use
Display the time	TIME
Display the version of DOS	VER
Display the volume label	VOL, DIR, CHKDSK
Erase a character	⟨←⟩, ⟨◆Backspace⟩, or ⟨Del⟩
Fix a file	CHKDSK, RECOVER
Locate a string in a file	FIND
Make a new directory	MKDIR (MD)
Move a file	MOVE
Optimize system memory	MEMMAKER
Pause the display	⟨Ctrl⟩-⟨S⟩, MORE
Place DOS on the disk	FORMAT /S, SYS
Pipe the output between programs	⟨│⟩
Prepare a new disk	FORMAT
Prepare a hard disk	FDISK, FORMAT
Redirect the input of a program	⟨<⟩, ⟨│⟩
Redirect the output of a program	⟨>⟩, ⟨>⟩⟨>⟩, ⟨│⟩
Remove a file	ERASE, DEL
Remove a directory	RMDIR (RD), DELTREE
Restore files backed-up with DOS 6	MSBACKUP
Restore files backed-up with an earlier version of DOS	RESTORE
Scan for software viruses	MSAV
Set alternative directories for programs	PATH

14

continues

If You Want To...	Use
Set or change checks on file writing	VERIFY
Set or change the system prompt	PROMPT
Sort a file	SORT
Undelete a file	UNDELETE
Use a new device	DEVICE (CONFIG.SYS)

14

External Commands

Recall that you can issue DOS's internal commands from any disk drive or directory. Issuing external commands, however, is a bit more complex. To issue an external command, you have three alternatives:

- Change to the directory that holds the external command. External commands are best kept in a subdirectory containing all the other DOS files. On hard disks, the path is usually C:\DOS.

- Include the path name (disk drive and directory name, if necessary) every time you issue the command. This technique quickly becomes tedious.

- Add to your AUTOEXEC.BAT file a PATH statement that includes the subdirectory holding the DOS files. Then, when you issue an external command, DOS can find it and execute it no matter what directory is current. Make sure that the directory holding the external command is included in the PATH command.

If you issue a command and get a `Bad command or file name` message, you have not set the path with the PATH command or the command is not in the default directory on the logged disk drive. Remember the rule of currents for issuing commands:

- If you do not specify a disk drive name for the command, MS-DOS searches for the command on the current disk drive.

- If you do not specify a path, MS-DOS searches for the command in the current directory of the current drive (or the current directory of the specified disk drive).

336

A Note about Notation

In the command notation used in this chapter, *d:* is the name of the disk drive holding the file, and *path* is the directory path to the file. *filename* is the root name of the file, and *.ext* is the file name extension.

If any part of this notation does not appear in the syntax for the command, do not include the omitted part in the command. For example, the notation *d:filename.ext* indicates that you do not include path names in the command.

Commands that use source and destination drive parameters use *sd:* for the source drive name and *dd:* for the destination (target) drive name. Some other commands also use the *s* and *d* parameters.

14

APPEND

 External

Use APPEND to do the following:

> Open data files from a specified directory as if the data files were in the current directory.
>
> Start programs that are not in the current directory and not in the search directory specified by PATH.

Command Syntax

> APPEND *d1:path1;d2:path2 ... /switches*

Follow These Steps

1. Type APPEND and press the space bar once. You might need to precede the command with the drive and path for APPEND.EXE because APPEND is an external command.
2. Type the first search path, including the drive.
3. To search a second drive and path, type a semicolon (;) and then type the second drive and path. Repeat this step for additional search paths. A sample search path is

   C:\DOS;C:\DATA\WORDS;C:\DATA\ACCOUNTS
4. You can use any of the following switches:

/E adds the APPEND path to the environment. Use this switch only the first time you use APPEND after starting the computer. Use this switch with no other parameters.

/X:ON enables searching the appended directories for program files.

/X:OFF disables searching the appended directories for program files.

/PATH:ON enables searching the append path if a program with a specified path is not found.

/PATH:OFF disables searching the append path if a program with a specified path is not found.

5. Press ⏎Enter.

To delete the search paths, type the command APPEND;.

Caution: Do not use APPEND to search for a program's data files if the program writes a new file when a data file is modified (as do most word processors). Use APPEND only if the program modifies an existing file (as do database programs). Do not use APPEND with Windows or the Windows Set-up program.

ASSIGN

 External

Use ASSIGN to do the following:

Send the request for information from one drive to another drive.

Command Syntax

ASSIGN *d1:=d2: /STATUS*

Follow These Steps

1. Type ASSIGN and press the space bar once. You might need to precede the command with the drive and path for ASSIGN.COM because ASSIGN is an external command.

2. Type the name of the drive you want to assign (such as A:).

3. Type an equal sign (=).

4. Type the drive to which you want to assign that drive (for example, C:).

5. Press ⏎Enter.

14

The command ASSIGN A=C makes DOS read drive C when you specify drive A. Type **ASSIGN /STATUS** to view the current assignments. Type **ASSIGN** and press ⏎Enter to cancel the assignments.

ATTRIB

 External

Use ATTRIB to do the following:

Display a file's attributes.

Change a file's attributes.

Command Syntax

ATTRIB *attribs d:path\filename.ext /S*

Follow These Steps

1. Type **ATTRIB** and press the **space bar** once. You might need to precede the command with the drive and path for ATTRIB.EXE because ATTRIB is an external command.

2. After you press the **space bar**, type any of the following attributes:

    +R makes the file read-only so that you cannot modify the file.

    –R turns off the read-only attribute, enabling you to modify the file.

    +A makes the file appear as if it were new or changed by turning on the archive attribute.

    –A turns off the archive attribute.

    +S makes the file a system file by turning on the system attribute.

    –S turns off the system attribute.

    +H hides the file.

    –H turns off the hide attribute.

3. Press the **space bar** and then type the name of the file whose attribute you want to display or change. You can use the wild cards * and ? when you type the file name.

4. You also can use the following switch with the ATTRIB command:

    /S searches for files in subsequent directories.

5. Press ⏎Enter.

BACKUP

 External

Use BACKUP with versions of DOS earlier than 6.0 to do the following:

> Back up hard disk information to protect original programs and data in case of loss or damage.
>
> Back up files created or altered since a specific date or since the last backup.
>
> Copy long files that cannot be stored on one floppy disk.

Command Syntax

> BACKUP *sd:spath\sfilename.ext dd: /switches*

Follow These Steps

1. Type **BACKUP** and press the **space bar** once. You may need to precede the command with a drive and path for BACKUP.COM because BACKUP is an external command.

2. Type the drive name (*sd:*) of the hard disk you want to back up (for example, **C:**). To back up a directory or an individual file, type the path, file name, and extension; then press the **space bar**. You can use wild-card characters (* and ?) to designate groups of files.

3. Type the name of the drive (*dd:*) that will receive the backup files. (For example, to back up on a floppy disk in drive A, type **A:**.)

4. You can use any of the following switches:

   /S backs up the subdirectories as well as the current directory. If you start at the root directory, DOS backs up all subdirectories.

   The following switches are used in incremental backups:

   /F:*size* formats the target floppy disk to the size you specify (360, 720, 1.44, 2.88).

   /L:*d:path\logfile.ext* records the names of the backed up files to the file *logfile.ext*, located in *d:path*.

   /M backs up files modified since the last backup. Use the /A switch with the /M switch to avoid erasing unmodified files when restoring from the backup disks.

   /A adds files to the files already on the backup disk.

   /D:*mm-dd-yy* backs up files created or changed on or after the specified date.

/T:*hh:mm:ss* backs up files created or changed at or after the specified time.

5. Press ⏎Enter.

Caution: BACKUP is used only with versions of DOS prior to 6.0. To restore files backed up with the BACKUP command, use the RESTORE command.

As you back up your files, remember to number the backup floppy disks. If you need to use the RESTORE command to restore lost files, you use the disks in numeric order.

Backing up your hard drive reduces the chance of losing valuable information. You do not need to memorize every step, but you should be familiar with BACKUP's basic command and switches.

14

CHDIR or CD

✳ Internal

Use CHDIR or CD to do the following:

Change the current directory.

Show the name of the current directory.

Command Syntax

CHDIR *d:path*
    or
CD *d:path*

Follow These Steps

1. Type CHDIR or CD. CHDIR (CD) is an internal command that does not require a path.
2. Press the space bar once.
3. Type the drive name of the disk whose current directory you want to change (for example, A:, B:, or C:) and the name of the directory to which you want to change. If you don't specify a path, DOS displays the current path. Remember to use the backslash to separate the parts of the path.
4. Press ⏎Enter.

CHDIR is very important and simple to use; it is one of the commands you need so that you can navigate around your disk.

CHKDSK

 External

Use CHKDSK to do the following:

Checks the directory of the disk for disk and memory status. CHKDSK can display the following information:

- the number of files and directories on a disk
- the bytes used and the space available on a disk
- the presence of hidden files
- whether a floppy disk is bootable
- the total RAM and available RAM
- whether files are fragmented (noncontiguous)

Makes minor repairs.

Command Syntax

CHKDSK *d:path\filename.ext* */switches*

Follow These Steps

1. Type **CHKDSK** and press the **space bar** once. You might need to precede the command with the drive and path, because CHKDSK is an external command.
2. To check a disk on another drive, type the drive name, followed by a colon (:), after CHKDSK. For example, if your default drive is C and you want to check drive B, type **CHKDSK B:**.
3. You can use CHKDSK to determine the noncontiguous areas in an individual file by entering the path, file name, and extension. The file name and extension can contain wild cards.
4. You can use either of the following switches:

    /**F** repairs errors (use with caution).

    /**V** (verbose) displays paths and file names.
5. Press [⏎Enter].

Tip: CHKDSK informs you whether the files on your disk are contiguous. This command also reports errors it finds and can simulate the repair of errors. Using the /F switch with CHKDSK repairs the error, generally gathering fractured files and combining them in one special file in your root directory.

CHKDSK gives you more control of your computer. This simple command provides a quick analysis of your floppy disks and hard disks. You should use it once a week. For memory analysis, see the MEM command.

CLS

Use CLS to do the following:

Clear the screen whenever you are at the DOS prompt.

Command Syntax

CLS

Follow These Steps

1. Type **CLS**.
2. Press ⏎Enter. After DOS clears all messages on-screen, the DOS prompt and cursor reappear in the upper left corner.

You can use CLS to give your batch files a professional look.

COMP

Use COMP to do the following:

Compare two files to see whether they are the same.

Command Syntax

COMP *d1:path1\filename1.ext1 d2:path2\filename2.ext2 /switches*

343

Follow These Steps

1. Type **COMP** and press the **space bar** once. You might need to precede the command with the drive and path for COMP.COM because COMP is an external command.

2. Type the name of the first file you want to compare. You can include the drive and path of the file.

3. Press the **space bar** once.

4. Type the name of the second file you want to compare. You can include the drive and path of the file.

5. You can use any of the following switches:

   /D displays any difference using decimal numbers (rather than the default hexadecimal numbers).

   /A displays differences using ASCII characters.

   /L displays the line number of any difference.

   /N=*number* compares the specified number of lines in both files, starting at the beginning of each file.

   /C performs a comparison that isn't case-sensitive.

6. Press ⏎Enter.

After COMP finds 10 errors, the comparison discontinues. If you do not specify file names, COMP prompts you for the first and second files you want to compare.

COPY

 ⋇ Internal

Use COPY to do the following:

Copy one or more files to another disk or directory, or copy a file to the same directory and change its name.

Transfer information between DOS system devices.

Send text to the printer.

Create ASCII text files and batch files.

Command Syntax

The most common syntax for the COPY command is

COPY *sd:\spath\sfilename.ext dd:\dpath\dfilename.ext* /*switches*

Follow These Steps

1. Type **COPY** and press the space bar once.

2. Type the drive name and path of the source file (*sd:\spath*).

3. Type the name of the file you want to copy. You can use wild cards.

4. You can include the following switches for the source file:

   /A treats the source file as an ASCII text file.

   /B forces DOS to copy the entire file as though it were a program file (binary). Binary copying is the default.

5. Press the space bar.

6. Type the drive name, path, and file name of the target file (*dd:\dpath*). Skip this step if the file name is to remain the same as that of the source file.

7. You can include the following switches for the target file.

   /A places an end-of-file character (Ctrl-Z) at the end of the copied file.

   /B prevents an end-of-file character from being added to a copied file.

8. You also can add the /V switch to verify and check the accuracy of the COPY procedure

9. Press ⏎Enter.

Caution: COPY does exactly what you tell it to do. Before you use this command, make sure that you have planned well. When you copy to another directory or disk, COPY overwrites a file of the same name, so be sure to type the file names exactly, including directory names.

COPY is a very flexible command that you should know like the back of your hand.

DATE

Use DATE to do the following:

Enter or change the system date.

Set the internal clock on a computer with a battery-backed clock.

Check the current date stamp for newly created and modified files.

Provide control for programs that require date information.

Command Syntax

DATE *mm-dd-yy*

Follow These Steps

1. Type DATE and press the space bar once.
2. Enter the date in one of the following formats:
   - *mm-dd-yy* (for North America; this format is the default)
   - *dd-mm-yy* (for Europe)
   - *yy-mm-dd* or *yyyy-mm-dd* (for East Asia)

   mm is a one- or two-digit number for the month (1 to 12).

   dd is a one- or two-digit number for the day (1 to 31).

   yy is a one- or two-digit number for the year (80 to 99). DOS assumes that the first two digits of the year are *19*.

   yyyy is a four-digit number for the year (1980 to 2099).

   You can separate the entries with hyphens, periods, or slashes.
3. Press ⏎Enter.

If your PC doesn't have a built-in calendar clock, use this command every time you boot. Knowing when files were written or updated is good organizational strategy and aids you in being selective with MSBACKUP and XCOPY. Better still, cards containing battery-operated calendar clocks have become very inexpensive; you can purchase such a clock to eliminate typing the time and date every time you start your computer.

DBLSPACE

 External

Use DBLSPACE to do the following:

Compress existing files on a disk.

Install a device driver to manage the compressed files.

Display information about compressed drives.

Command Syntax

To start the DoubleSpace disk-compression program:

DBLSPACE

To display information about a compressed drive:

DBLSPACE *d:*

Follow These Steps

1. Type **DBLSPACE**. You might need to precede the command with the drive and path for DBLSPACE.EXE because DBLSPACE is an external command.
2. Follow the instructions that the DBLSPACE program displays on-screen.

Tip: DBLSPACE might take a long time. Use it when you have finished all of your other computer work for the day.

Caution: Do not run DBLSPACE if you use a third-party disk compression or disk cache utility.

Note: You also can use DoubleSpace to manipulate compressed disks. If you want to learn more about the DoubleSpace program, consult Que's *Using MS-DOS 6,* Special Edition.

14

DEFRAG

 External

Use DEFRAG to do the following:

Reorganize the existing files on a disk to optimize disk performance.

Command Syntax

DEFRAG *d: /switches*

Follow These Steps

1. Type **DEFRAG**. You might need to precede the command with the drive and path for DEFRAG.EXE because DEFRAG is an external command.
2. Press the **space bar** once and type the letter of the drive you want to defragment.
3. You can use any of the following switches:

   /F defragments files and ensures that the disk contains no empty spaces between files.

14

/U defragments files and leaves existing empty spaces between files.

/S:*value* sorts the files according to the value entered. If this switch is omitted, DEFRAG uses the current order on the disk. You can use any of the following values:

N sorts alphabetically by name A to Z.

N– sorts alphabetically by name Z to A.

E sorts alphabetically by file extension A to Z.

E– sorts alphabetically by files extension Z to A.

D sorts by date and time, earliest first.

D– sorts by date and time, latest first.

S sorts by size, smallest first.

S– sorts by size, largest first.

/B restarts your PC upon completion of defragmentation.

/SKIPHIGH loads DEFRAG into conventional memory instead of upper memory.

/LCD starts DEFRAG, using an LCD color scheme.

/BW starts DEFRAG, using a black-and-white color scheme.

/GO disables the graphic mouse and graphic character set.

/H moves hidden files.

4. Press ⏎Enter.

5. Select whether you want to optimize the disk or configure the optimization.

6. When the optimization is complete, select Exit to return to DOS.

Tip: The DEFRAG program has its own shell. You can use the keyboard or the mouse to make selections. Usually, the optimization method recommended by DEFRAG is sufficient to defragment the selected disk.

Caution: Do not use DEFRAG on network drives or drives created with the INTERLNK command.

DELTREE

 External

Use DELTREE to do the following:

Delete a directory and all of its files and subdirectories.

348

Command Syntax

> DELTREE *d:path*

Follow These Steps

1. Type DELTREE.
2. Press the space bar.
3. Type the drive and path of the directory you want to delete. You can use wild cards.
4. Press ⏎Enter. If you added the /Y switch, DOS prompts you to confirm the deletion before it deletes the directory.
5. If you are prompted to confirm the deletion, press Y and then press ⏎Enter to delete the directory and all of the files and subdirectories in it. Or press N and then press ⏎Enter to abort the DELTREE command.

Caution: DELTREE deletes all files and subdirectories in the specified directory. Use extreme caution with the DELTREE command.

DEVICE

 | Internal |

Use DEVICE in your CONFIG.SYS file to do the following:

> Support add-on peripherals.
>
> Install a block-device driver.
>
> Install a virtual (RAM) disk.

Command Syntax

> DEVICE=*d:path\devicedriver*

Follow These Steps

1. Using a text editor, open your CONFIG.SYS file. See Chapter 12 for information on the CONFIG.SYS file.
2. Type the following command on one line in your CONFIG.SYS file:
   > DEVICE=*d:path\filename.ext*

   d:path is the drive and path to the device driver, and *filename.ext* is the file name of the device driver. If you have a mouse driver called

MOUSE.SYS, for example, and it's located in the UTIL directory on drive C, you would add the line DEVICE=C:\UTIL\MOUSE.SYS to your CONFIG.SYS file.

3. Repeat step 2 until all desired device drivers are included in your CONFIG.SYS file.

4. Restart your system.

Note: Device drivers usually come with hardware you purchase. Check installation instructions for your device and driver.

Sooner or later, you will add the DEVICE command to your CONFIG.SYS file. The most commonly used device driver is ANSI.SYS, which provides additional control over your display and keyboard. If ANSI.SYS resides in C:\DOS, include the command DEVICE=C:\DOS\ANSI.SYS in your CONFIG.SYS file.

DIR

$\boxed{*\ \text{Internal}}$

Use DIR to do the following:

Display a list of files and subdirectories in a disk's directory.

List a specified group of files within a directory.

Examine the volume identification label of the disk.

Determine the amount of available space on the disk.

Check the size of individual files.

Check the date the files were last modified.

Command Syntax

DIR *d:\path\filename.ext /switches*

Follow These Steps

1. Type DIR and press the space bar once.

2. You also can type one of the following:

The drive name of the directory you want to display.

The path name of the directory you want to display.

The file name, if you want to limit the number and types of files listed. You can use wild cards to list groups of files.

3. You can use any of the following switches:

350

/W displays the directory in a wide format of five columns across. The /W switch displays only the directory name and file names. For large listings, also include the /P switch.

/P displays the directory and pauses between screen pages. This switch prevents large directories from scrolling off the screen before you can read them.

/A:*attrib* displays those files that have certain attributes on or off. If you leave off the attribute, DOS displays all files, including system and hidden. The attributes are as follows:

> **H** displays hidden files.
>
> **S** displays system files.
>
> **D** displays subdirectories.
>
> **A** displays files that have changed since the last backup.
>
> **R** displays read-only files.
>
> *–attrib* turns off the attribute.

/O:*sort* displays files in sorted order. The sort options are as follows:

> **N** sorts in alphabetical order by file name.
>
> **E** sorts in alphabetical order by extension.
>
> **D** sorts by date and time, earliest to latest.
>
> **S** sorts by size, smallest to largest.
>
> **C** sorts by compression ratio, lowest to highest.
>
> **G** lists directories before file names.
>
> *–sort* sorts in reverse order.

/S searches through subdirectories for files to display.

/B displays file names in the format FILENAME.EXT.

/L displays all file names and extensions in lowercase letters.

4. Press ⏎Enter.

DISKCOMP

 External

Use DISKCOMP to do the following:

> Compare two floppy disks on a track-for-track, sector-for-sector basis to see whether their contents are identical.
>
> Verify the integrity of a DISKCOPY operation.

Command Syntax

DISKCOMP *sd: dd: /switch*

Follow These Steps

1. Type DISKCOMP and press the space bar once.

2. Type the name of the drive that holds the source disk (for example, type A:) and press the space bar again.

3. Type the name of the drive that holds the target disk (for example, B:). If you have only one floppy disk drive, type A: again.

4. You can use either of the following switches:

   /1 compares only single-sided floppy disks.

   /8 compares only eight-sectored floppy disks.

5. Press Enter. DOS instructs you to place the source disk into drive A and the target disk into drive B. If you have only one floppy disk drive, DOS instructs you to place the source disk into drive A.

6. Insert the floppy disks requested and press Enter. DISKCOMP compares all tracks and issues any necessary error messages, indicating the track number and side of the floppy disk on which errors occur. If you have only one floppy disk drive, DOS then instructs you to exchange the source disk with the target disk. When DISKCOMP is finished, you are asked whether you want to compare more floppy disks.

7. Press Y and repeat steps 5 through 7 to compare more disks; otherwise, press N.

Tip: You might never use this command because you also can use the /V switch to verify as you use DISKCOPY.

DISKCOPY

 External

Use DISKCOPY to do the following:

Secure data against loss by duplicating a floppy disk. Note that DISKCOPY works only when copying floppy disks of the same size and capacity.

Command Syntax

DISKCOPY *sd: dd: /switch*

Follow These Steps

1. Type DISKCOPY and press the space bar once.
2. Type the name of the drive that holds the source disk (A:, for example). Press the space bar again.
3. Type the name of the drive that holds the target disk (B:, for example).
4. You can use either of the following switches:

   /1 copies only one side of the floppy disk (use only with single-sided floppy disks).

   /V verifies that the copy was performed correctly.
5. Press ↵Enter. Within a few seconds, DOS prompts you to place the source disk into drive A and the target disk into drive B. If you have only one floppy disk drive, DOS prompts you to place the source disk in drive A.
6. Insert the floppy disks requested and press ↵Enter. If you have only one floppy disk drive, DOS prompts you to exchange the source disk with the target disk.
7. When the copy is complete, DOS asks whether you want to copy another floppy disk.
8. Press Y and repeat steps 6 through 8 to copy another floppy disk; otherwise, press N.

Tip: DISKCOPY is for duplicating floppy disks, not hard disks. If a problem exists on the original (source) floppy disk, the same problem will appear on the duplicate floppy disk.

DISKCOPY is one of the basic commands that you need to understand completely.

DOSHELP

 External

Use DOSHELP to do the following:

Display summaries of DOS commands.

Command Syntax

DOSHELP *command*

Follow These Steps

1. Type DOSHELP and press the space bar once. You might need to precede the command with the drive and path for DOSHELP.EXE because DOSHELP is an external command.
2. Type the name of the command for which you want help. If you do not enter a command name, DOSHELP lists all of the commands.
3. Press ⌐Enter⌐.

Tip: The information displayed by the DOSHELP command is not as complete as the information displayed by the HELP command.

DOSKEY

 External

Use DOSKEY to do the following:

Load the Doskey program, which enables you to recall and edit commands typed at the command line.

Create custom commands (macros).

View macros and commands.

Command Syntax

DOSKEY *macroname=text /switches*

Follow These Steps

1. Type DOSKEY and press the space bar. You might need to precede the command with the drive and path for DOSKEY.EXE because DOSKEY is an external command.
2. You can use any of the following switches:

/REINSTALL installs a new copy of the Doskey program.

/BUFSIZE=*size* specifies the size of the buffer in which Doskey stores commands and Doskey macros. The default size is 512 bytes, but you can specify as little as 256 bytes.

/MACROS displays a list of all macros already created with Doskey.

/HISTORY displays a list of all commands that have been entered at the command line and stored in memory.

/INSERT inserts new text into old text rather than typing over it.

/OVERSTRIKE causes new text to overwrite old text instead of inserting it.

3. Press ↵Enter.

You can use DOSKEY to create macros that carry out one or more commands.

To create macros, follow these steps:

1. Type DOSKEY and press the space bar. You might need to precede the command with the drive and path for DOSKEY.EXE because DOSKEY is an external command.

2. Type the name you want to assign the macro. For example, type MACRO1.

3. Press =.

4. Type the commands you want the macro to perform. You can use the following meta-string characters, preceded by a $ to further define the commands:

   $G redirects output to a device or a file.

   GG appends output to the end of a file.

   $L redirects input to be read from a device or a file instead of from the keyboard.

   $T separates commands.

   $$ specifies to include a dollar sign.

   $1 – $9 represent any command-line information you want to specify at the time you run the macro.

   $* represents all command-line information you want to specify at the time you run the macro.

5. Press ↵Enter.

To run the macro, type the macro name, followed by any information you want to specify.

For example, to create a macro called MACRO1 that will check a disk in any specified drive and then quick format a disk in any specified drive, type **DOSKEY MACRO1=CHKDSK 1TFORMAT/Q $2** and press Enter.

To run this macro, type **MACRO1**, press the space bar, enter the drive on which you want to perform the disk check, press the space bar, and enter the

14

drive in which you want to quick format a disk. Then press Enter. For example, type **MACRO1 b: b:** and press Enter.

DOSSHELL

 External

Use DOSSHELL to do the following:

Perform DOS commands from menus.

Manage files and directories.

Manage and start programs.

Command Syntax

DOSSHELL /*switches*

Follow These Steps

1. Type DOSSHELL. You might need to precede the command with the drive and path for DOSSHELL.COM because DOSSHELL is an external command.

2. You can use any of the following switches:

    /**T**:*res* changes to a text display; *res* can be L, M, M1, M2, H, H1, or H2.

    /**G**:*res* changes to a graphical display; *res* can be L, M, M1, M2, H, H1, or H2.

    /**B** displays the DOS Shell in black and white rather than in color.

3. Press ⏎Enter.

Use the /T, /G, or /B switches to change the screen resolution only when you start the DOS Shell. Generally, you do not need to use these switches because the DOS Shell remembers the last screen resolution you used.

ECHO

 Internal

Use ECHO to do the following:

Display batch-file commands and text strings on-screen.

Control video output to the screen.

Debug batch files.

Command Syntax

To turn off the display of commands when you run batch files:

ECHO OFF

To turn on the display of commands:

ECHO ON

To display a message:

ECHO *message*

To display a blank line:

ECHO.

Notice that the period is directly after ECHO with no space.

ECHO is an excellent batch-file creation utility. If you understand how to use it, you can have fun personalizing your PC's operation.

EDIT

 External

Use EDIT to do the following:

Create or modify text files, such as a batch file or the CONFIG.SYS file.

Command Syntax

EDIT *d:path\filename.ext /switches*

Follow These Steps

1. Type **EDIT** and press the **space bar** once. You might need to precede the command with the drive and path for EDIT.COM because EDIT is an external command.

2. Type the name of the file you want to edit, including the drive and path of the file (if the file is not in the current directory).

3. You can use any of the following switches:

/B makes EDIT display in black and white rather than in color.

/G makes a CGA monitor update faster.

/H makes EDIT display in the maximum resolution of your video display.

/NOHI makes EDIT display in eight colors rather than the usual 16 colors.

4. Press ⏎Enter.

14 **ERASE or DEL**

Use ERASE or DEL to do the following:

Remove one or more files from the current disk or directory.

Command Syntax

ERASE *d:path\filename.ext* /P
   or
DEL *d:path\filename.ext* /P

Follow These Steps

1. Type ERASE or DEL and press the space bar once.
2. Type the drive name and path of the file you want to delete, unless the file is in the current directory.
3. Type the name of the file you want to delete.
4. You can use the following switch:

   /P prompts `filename Delete (Y/N)?` before each file is deleted. Press Y to delete the file or N to cancel the command.

5. Press ⏎Enter.

Caution: ERASE (DEL) is a deceptively simple command that can make your life easy or fill it with grief. Practice using this command and think carefully before pressing the ⏎Enter key. Be very careful when you use wild cards, or you might delete more files than you intend. To learn how to recover an accidentally deleted file, see UNDELETE.

FASTOPEN

 External

Use FASTOPEN to do the following:

> Remember the location of often-used files so that DOS can locate them quickly.

Command Syntax

> FASTOPEN *d1:=n1 d2:=n2 ... /X*

14

Follow These Steps

1. Type FASTOPEN and press the space bar once. You might need to precede the command with the drive and path for FASTOPEN.EXE because FASTOPEN is an external command.

2. Type the letter of the drive containing the files you want DOS to remember (for example, A:); then press =.

3. Type the number of files (*n1*) you want DOS to remember (type 40, for example, if you want DOS to remember the location of the last 40 files opened).

4. Repeat steps 2 and 3 for additional files you want DOS to remember.

5. You can use the following switch:

   /X places the storage area of often-used files in expanded memory.

6. Press ↵Enter.

If you use a program that opens the same files over and over again, such as a word processing or database program, FASTOPEN can speed up your program. If you use a program that reads files one at a time, such as a spreadsheet program, you get no benefit from the FASTOPEN command.

Caution: Do not use FASTOPEN when you are running Microsoft Windows. Do not run a defragmentation program when FASTOPEN is active.

FC

 External

Use FC to do the following:

> Compare two files or sets of files to see whether they are the same.

Command Syntax

FC */switches d1:path1\filename1.ext1 d2:path2\filename2.ext2*

Follow These Steps

1. Type **FC** and press the **space bar** once. You might need to precede the command with the drive and path for FC.EXE because FC is an external command.

2. You can use any of the following switches:

   /A displays the first and last lines of the section of a file that is different, rather than displaying the entire different section of the file.

   /B specifies that the files you are comparing are binary or program files, rather than text or ASCII files.

   /C performs a comparison that isn't case-sensitive.

   /L specifies that the files you are comparing are text or ASCII files, rather than binary or program files.

   /LB*n* changes the internal buffer for *n* number of lines you want to compare in a file.

   /N displays the line numbers of the differing lines when comparing text or ASCII files.

   /T does not change an ASCII file's tabs to spaces for comparison.

   /W condenses contiguous spaces and tabs into a single space during the comparison.

   /*xxxx* tells FC the number of consecutive lines (*xxxx*) that must compare as equal before FC considers the two files to be back in sync after mismatches. The default number of consecutive lines is 2.

3. Type the name of the first file you want to compare. If the first file you want to compare is not in the current directory, precede the file name with the drive and path of the file. You can use the wild cards * and ? in the file name.

4. Type the name of the second file you want to compare. If the second file you want to compare is not in the current directory, precede the file name with the drive and path of the file. You can use the wild cards * and ? in the file name.

5. Press ↵Enter.

FC is similar to COMP, but you can customize FC more.

FIND

⌈💾⌉ External

Use FIND to do the following:

Display lines that contain, or fail to contain, a certain group of characters. These characters are called a *string*.

Command Syntax

14

FIND */switches "string" d1:path1\filename1.ext1* ...

Follow These Steps

1. Type **FIND** and press the **space bar**. You might need to precede the command with the drive and path if FIND is not in the root directory or in a path governed by the PATH command.

2. You can use any of the following switches:

   /C counts the number of lines that contain the search string.

   /N displays the line number of each line that contains the search string.

   /V displays all lines that do not contain the search string.

   /I performs a non–case-sensitive search.

3. Type the string, enclosed in quotation marks ("*string*"). The string is the character set you want to find. FIND is case-sensitive; if you want to find uppercase characters, for example, type the string in uppercase letters.

4. If the file is not in the current directory, type the drive name and path of the file you want to search.

5. Type the file name and extension of the file you want to search.

6. Press the **space bar** and repeat steps 4 and 5 for each file you want FIND to search. You cannot use wild cards (? or *).

7. Press ⌐Enter⌐.

FIND is a very convenient command, becoming particularly important as your hard drive fills with files and subdirectories.

FORMAT

 External

Use FORMAT to do the following:

Initialize a floppy disk or hard disk to accept DOS information and files.

Command Syntax

FORMAT *d*: /*switches*

Follow These Steps

1. Type FORMAT. You might need to precede the command with the drive and path if FORMAT is not in the root directory or in a path governed by the PATH command.

2. Press the space bar once.

3. Type the name of the drive holding the disk you want to format (for example, B:).

4. You can use any of the following switches:

/V:*label* gives the formatted disk a unique, identifying volume label.

/S produces a bootable disk by placing the operating system on the formatted disk.

/4 formats (on a high-capacity drive) a single- or double-sided floppy disk for use in computers that use double-density disks.

/1 formats a floppy disk on one side. Use this switch to format floppy disks for older PCs and compatibles.

/8 formats a floppy disk with eight sectors per track rather than the default value of nine sectors per track. Use this switch to format disks for older PCs and compatibles.

/B creates an eight-sector floppy disk that reserves space for the operating system.

/F:*size* formats a floppy disk to a specific capacity, where *size* is one of the following values: 160, 180, 320, 360, 720, 1.2, 1.44, or 2.88.

/N:*xx* specifies the number of sectors (*xx*) per track on the disk. Always use this switch with the /T:*xx* switch.

/T:*xx* specifies the number of tracks (*xx*) on the disk. Use this switch with the /N:*xx* switch.

/Q performs a quick format on an already formatted disk.

/U performs an unconditional (nonsafe) format.

5. Press ⏎Enter.

6. DOS now instructs you to place a floppy disk into the drive you named in step 3. Insert the floppy disk you want to format and press ⏎Enter.

   In a few minutes, you see the message Format complete and a status report of the formatted floppy disk.

7. If you selected the /V switch, DOS asks you to enter the volume label, a name of up to 11 characters. Type the volume label and press ⏎Enter.

   DOS then asks whether you want to format another disk.

8. Press Y and repeat steps 6 and 7 to format another disk; otherwise, press N.

Caution: If you format a 360K floppy disk in a 1.2M disk drive, the formatted disk might not be readable in a 360K drive. Also, a 1.2M disk might look exactly like a 360K floppy disk, but you cannot use the higher density 1.2M floppy disk in 360K disk drive.

FORMAT is an absolute must to understand. This command is the heart of your disk maintenance system. If you accidentally format an already formatted disk, you may be able to recover the information by using the UNFORMAT command.

HELP

 External

Use HELP to do the following:

Display syntax help for a command.

Command Syntax

HELP *command*

Follow These Steps

1. Type HELP and press the space bar once. You might need to precede the command with the drive and path for HELP.EXE because HELP is an external command.

14

2. Type the command for which you want to get help (for example, FORMAT). If you do not enter a command name, HELP displays a complete command reference table of contents. You can select any command from the table of contents.

3. Press ⏎Enter.

Tip: The HELP program has its own shell. You can use the keyboard or the mouse to move through the Help screens.

14

JOIN

 External

Use JOIN to do the following:

> Attach a drive to a directory on another drive.

Command Syntax

To join two drives:

> JOIN *d1: d2:path2*

To break two joined drives:

> JOIN *d1: /D*

To list all currently joined drives:

> JOIN

d1: specifies the disk drive you want to attach, and *d2:* is the drive to which you want to attach it. *path2* specifies the directory path on the host drive (*d2:*) where you want to attach *d1:*. The /D switch cancels any previous JOIN commands for the specified drive (*d1:*).

The directory of the host drive must be empty and cannot be the root directory. If the directory of the host drive does not exist, JOIN creates the directory.

LABEL

 External

Use LABEL to do the following:

> Change or remove the electronic label stored on a disk.

364

Command Syntax

LABEL *d:label*

Follow These Steps

1. Type LABEL and press the space bar once. You might need to precede the command with the drive and path for LABEL.EXE because LABEL is an external command.

2. Type the drive for which you want to change the label, if that drive is not the current drive.

3. Type the new label. If you do not type a label on the command line, DOS prompts you for a label.

MEM

 External

Use MEM to do the following:

Display the current status of memory.

Display programs loaded into memory.

Command Syntax

MEM */switches*

Follow These Steps

1. Type MEM and press the space bar once. You might need to precede the command with the drive and path for MEM.EXE because MEM is an external command.

2. You can use any of the following switches:

/FREE lists the free areas of conventional and upper memory.

/MODULE *modulename* indicates how the specified module (*modulename*) is currently using memory.

/P pauses after each full screen of output.

/DEBUG displays programs and internal drivers loaded into memory, with the size and address if necessary. This switch also displays other programming information.

/CLASSIFY displays programs loaded into memory, specifying whether they are in conventional memory or upper memory. This switch displays the size of each program with decimal and hexadecimal values.

If you use MEM without any switches, DOS displays the status of your computer's memory.

3. Press ⏎Enter.

MEMMAKER

 External

Use MEMMAKER to do the following:

Make more conventional memory available by moving device drivers and memory-resident programs to upper memory.

Command Syntax

MEMMAKER /switches

Follow These Steps

1. Type MEMMAKER. You might need to precede the command with the drive and path for MEMMAKER.EXE because MEMMAKER is an external command.

2. You can use any of these switches:

   /BATCH runs MemMaker in batch mode, which means that MemMaker takes the default action on all prompts.

   /B displays MemMaker in black-and-white for monochrome monitors.

   /SWAP:*d:* specifies the letter of the drive that originally was your startup disk drive, if your startup drive has changed since you started your computer. *d:* is the current drive.

   /UNDO restores your original AUTOEXEC.BAT and CONFIG.SYS files.

   /W:*size1,size2* specifies how much space to reserve in upper memory for Windows' transition buffers. The default is 12K for each region.

   /T disables the detection of IBM token-ring networks.

3. Press ⏎Enter to start the MemMaker program.

4. Follow the on-screen instructions.

14

Caution: Do not use MemMaker when you are running Microsoft Windows.

Tip: In most cases, the Express Setup will successfully optimize your system memory. Use Custom Setup only if you have a very strong understanding of your computer's memory configuration. You must have at least an 80386 processor to use MemMaker.

MKDIR or MD

 Internal

Use MKDIR to do the following:

Create subdirectories to help organize your files.

Command Syntax

MKDIR *d:path\directory*
    or
MD *d:path\directory*

Follow These Steps

1. Type **MKDIR** or **MD** and press the space bar once.
2. If necessary, type the drive name and path of the new directory.
3. Type the directory name.
4. Press ⏎Enter.

If you have a hard disk drive, you need to understand this command.

MORE

External

Use MORE to do the following:

Display data one screen at a time.

Command Syntax

d:path\filename.ext ¦ MORE

Follow These Steps

1. Type the name of the file you want to display one full screen (23 lines) at a time, and press the space bar once. You may need to precede the syntax with a program name that acts on the file name; for example, TYPE filename.ext.
2. Type ¦ (the pipe symbol) and press the space bar.
3. Type MORE and press ⏎Enter.

    The video output pauses between pages, and DOS displays the message --More--.
4. Press any key to display the next 23 lines of data.

MORE is very convenient for reading files longer than one screen.

MOVE

 External

Use MOVE to do the following:

> Move one or more files to another disk or directory.
>
> Rename a directory.

Command Syntax

> MOVE *d:\path\filename.ext dd:\dpath*

Follow These Steps

To move a file:

1. Type MOVE and press the space bar once.
2. Type the drive, path, and file name of the file you want to move.
3. Press the space bar.
4. Type the destination drive and path. To rename the file when you move it, type the new file name after the drive and path.

    If DOS doesn't recognize the destination directory, it will ask you whether you want to create a directory by that name.
5. Press ⏎Enter.

To rename a directory:

1. Type MOVE and press the space bar once.
2. Type the drive, path, and directory name of the directory you want to rename.
3. Press the space bar.
4. Type the new directory name.
5. Press ⏎Enter.

You can move more than one file at the same time to the same destination. Separate the drive, path, and file name with a comma. For example, to move the TEXT.DOC and MEMO.DOC files from the current directory to the LETTERS directory, type **MOVE C:TEXT.DOC,MEMO.DOC C:\LETTERS**. When you move more than one file, the destination must include a directory name.

Caution: MOVE does exactly what you tell it to do. When you move a file to another directory or disk, MOVE overwrites any file of the same name, so be sure to type the file names exactly (including directory names).

MSAV

 External

Use MSAV to do the following:

Start the Anti-Virus for DOS program.

Scan your memory and drives for software viruses.

Clean viruses from your system memory and drives.

Command Syntax

MSAV *d1:path1\filename1.ext1 d2:path2\filename2.ext2 … /switches*

Follow These Steps

1. Type MSAV. You might need to precede the command with the drive and path for MSAV.EXE because MSAV is an external command.
2. If necessary, type the drive or drives you want MSAV to scan, as well as the path to any particular files you want to scan.
3. You can use any of the following switches:

   /S scans the specified drive but does not remove viruses.

14

14

/C scans the specified drive and removes viruses.

/R creates a report file called MSAV.RPT that lists the results of the scan.

/A scans all drives except drives A and B.

/L scans all drives except network drives.

/N turns off the display of information during the scan and displays the MSAV.RPT file upon completion of the scan.

/P displays a command-line interface instead of the graphical interface.

/F turns off the display of file names being scanned. Use this switch with /N or /P.

/VIDEO displays a list of the switches that affect the way MSAV is displayed.

/25 sets the screen display to 25 lines (default).

/28 sets the screen display to 28 lines (VGA only).

/43 sets the screen display to 43 lines (EGA and VGA).

/50 sets the screen display to 50 lines (VGA).

/60 sets the screen display to 60 lines (Video 7).

/IN uses a color scheme.

/BW uses a black-and-white color scheme.

/MONO uses a monochromatic color scheme.

/LCD uses an LCD color scheme.

/FF uses the fastest screen updating.

/BF uses the BIOS to display video.

/NF disables the use of alternate fonts.

/BT enables you to use a graphics mouse in Microsoft Windows.

/NGM uses the default mouse character instead of the graphics mouse character.

/LE exchanges the left and right mouse buttons.

/PS2 resets the mouse.

4. Press ⏎Enter to start the Anti-Virus program.

5. In the Anti-Virus program, follow the on-screen instructions.

Tip: Anti-Virus has its own shell. You can use the keyboard or the mouse to make selections and execute menu items.

Anti-Virus is an optional program you install by using the Setup program. For information on installing the optional programs, see Appendix A.

370

MSBACKUP

[💾] External

Use MSBACKUP to do the following:

   Start the MS Backup for DOS program.

   Back up hard disk files to floppy disks.

   Restore backed up files to a hard disk.

   Compare backed up files to the original files.

   Configure the MS Backup program for your hardware system.

14

Command Syntax

   MSBACKUP *setup file /switches*

Follow These Steps

1. Type MSBACKUP. You might need to precede the command with the drive and path for MSBACKUP.EXE because MSBACKUP is an external command.

2. Specify the setup file you want MS Backup to load. For example, type MSBACKUP DATA.SET. If you do not specify a setup file, MS Backup loads the default setup file.

3. You can use any of the following switches:

   /BW specifies a black-and-white color scheme.

   /LCD specifies a video mode compatible with laptop LCD displays.

   /MDA uses a monochrome display adapter.

4. Press ↵Enter to start the MS Backup for DOS program.

5. Select the function you want to perform: Backup, Restore, Compare, Configure.

6. Specify the files and disks you want to use for the current function.

7. Choose the Start button to start the function.

Tips: MS Backup has its own shell. You can use the keyboard or the mouse to make selections and execute menu items. Remember to store your numbered disks in order. The restore operation can be crucial, and you do not want to create unnecessary complications in the middle of this procedure.

Caution: The first time you use the MSBACKUP command, you will be prompted through configuration and a compatibility test. These features ensure that all of the backup functions will work with your hardware system. If you want more information, refer to Chapter 10.

MS Backup simplifies the task of backing up the files on your hard disk. It also makes it much easier to restore them in case of an emergency. Becoming comfortable with the MS Backup program and establishing a regular backup routine are vital. Without backups, all of your data is at risk.

MS Backup is an optional program you install by using the Setup program. For information on installing the optional programs, see Appendix A.

14

PATH

$\boxed{*}$ $\boxed{\text{Internal}}$

Use PATH to do the following:

> Access files not in the default directory without changing directories. PATH tells DOS to search specified directories on specified drives if it does not find a program or batch file in the current directory.

Command Syntax

> PATH *d1:\path1;d2:\path2;d3:\path3;...*

Follow These Steps

1. Type PATH and press the space bar once.
2. Type the drive name you want to include in the search path (for example, A:, B:, or C:). If you include the drive name with the path, DOS finds your files even if you change default drives.
3. Type the directory path you want to search (for example, \KEEP).
4. To add another directory to the search path, type a semicolon (;), and then type the drive name and path of the additional directory.
5. Repeat steps 2 through 4 until you type all the subdirectory paths you want DOS to search.
6. Press ↵Enter.

PATH is an important navigational aid you should understand fully. If you don't understand PATH, you don't understand the directory concept.

PROMPT

 Internal

Use PROMPT to do the following:

    Customize the DOS system prompt.

    Display the drive and directory path.

    Display a message on the computer.

    Display the date and time or the DOS version number.

14

Command Syntax

    PROMPT *promptstring*

Follow These Steps

1. Type PROMPT and press the space bar once.
2. Type the text string and the arrangement of parameters you want to display.
3. You can use the meta-string characters, preceded by $, with the PROMPT command to produce your own DOS prompt:

    $D displays the current date.

    $G displays the > character.

    $L displays the < character.

    $N displays the current disk drive name.

    $P displays the current drive and path.

    $Q displays the = character.

    $T displays the system time.

    $V displays the DOS version.

    $$ displays the dollar sign.

    $B displays the ¦ symbol.

    $H moves the cursor back one space, erasing the preceding character.

    $E displays a left arrow.

    $_ moves the cursor to the beginning of the next line.

    Any other meta-string character is ignored.

After you place PROMPT in your AUTOEXEC.BAT with the desired information, you may never refer to the PROMPT command again. PROMPT is used most frequently to extend the visual command line to display the path of your resident directory.

RENAME or REN

 Internal

Use RENAME to do the following:

Change the name of a file or group of files.

Command Syntax

RENAME *d:path\oldfilename.ext newfilename.ext*

Follow These Steps

1. Type RENAME or REN and press the space bar once.
2. Type the drive name and path of the file you want to rename.
3. Type the name of the file you want to rename. You can use wild cards (* and ?) to specify groups of files.
4. Press the space bar.
5. Type the new name you want to assign the file and press ⏎Enter.

Caution: Avoid giving files in different directories the same file name. You might accidentally delete the wrong file.

Practice this command. It has a million-and-one uses.

REPLACE

 External

Use REPLACE to do the following:

Replace files on a destination disk with the files of the same name from the source disk.

Copy files from the source disk that do not already exist on the destination disk.

14

Replace files on the destination disk with files from the source disk only if the source files have a later date than the destination files.

Command Syntax

REPLACE *sd:spath\sfilename.ext dd:dpath\ /switches*

Follow These Steps

1. Type **REPLACE** and press the **space bar** once. You might need to precede the command with the drive and path for REPLACE.EXE because **REPLACE** is an external command.

2. Type the drive name and path of the source file (*sd:\spath*).

3. Type the name of the file you want to copy. You can use wild cards.

4. Press the **space bar**.

5. Type the drive name and path of the target location (*dd:\dpath*).

6. You can use any of the following switches:

   /**A** copies files from the source disk that do not already exist in the destination directory.

   /**R** replaces files on the destination disk even if the files have the read-only attribute set on.

   /**U** replaces files on the destination disk that are older than the files on the source disk.

   /**P** prompts you before copying each file.

   /**S** copies specified files from the current directory and from subdirectories of the current directory.

   /**W** makes REPLACE wait before starting the copy so that you can insert the correct disks in the drive.

7. Press ⏎Enter .

RESTORE

 External

Use RESTORE to do the following:

Retrieve one or more files from a backup disk made with a version of DOS prior to DOS 6.

Command Syntax

RESTORE *sd: dd:\dpath\dfilename.ext /switches*

Follow These Steps

1. Type **RESTORE** and press the space bar once.

2. Type the name of the source drive that contains the backed up files. (For example, to restore files from drive A, type A:.) Then press the space bar.

3. Type the name of the destination drive. (For example, to restore files to a hard disk in drive C, type C:.) If you omit the drive name, the current drive becomes the destination drive.

4. To restore files from only one directory, type the path (directory name).

5. Type the name and extension of the file or files you want to restore. You can use wild cards to designate a group of files. (For example, type *.* to restore all files on a disk or subdirectory.)

6. You can use any of the following switches:

   /S restores all files in the current directory and subdirectories of the current directory, creating subdirectories when necessary.

   /P displays a screen prompt that asks whether you want to restore files that have changed since the last backup or that are designated by the ATTRIB command as read-only.

   /M restores only those files modified or deleted since the last backup.

   /N restores only those files that no longer exist on the target disk.

   /B:*mm-dd-yy* restores only those files modified on or before the specified date.

   /A:*mm-dd-yy* restores only those files modified on or after the specified date.

   /L:*hh:mm:ss* restores only those files that have changed at or later than the specified time.

   /E:*hh:mm:ss* restores only those files that have changed at or earlier than the specified time.

   /D displays the names of the files to be restored, without actually restoring the files.

7. Press ⏎Enter. When prompted, place a backup disk into the source drive and press ⏎Enter again.

8. Repeat step 7 until all backup disks are processed.

14

376

Tip: RESTORE can be used only with data backed up with the BACKUP command prior to DOS 6.

RMDIR or RD

 Internal

Use RMDIR to do the following:

>   Remove a directory.

Command Syntax

>   RMDIR *d:path*
>   >   or
>   RD *d:path*

Follow These Steps

1. Use the ERASE command to delete any files from the directory you want to remove. The directory can contain only the current (.) and parent (..) files.
2. Type RMDIR or RD and press the space bar once.
3. Type the drive name of the directory you want to remove.
4. Type the full path and name of the directory you want to remove.
5. Press ⏎Enter.

RMDIR is another essential command for maintaining a logical hard disk drive subdirectory system.

SORT

 External

Use SORT to do the following:

>   Read input data, sort it, and write it to an output device.

>   Sort and list directory information.

>   Display, arrange, and sort data alphabetically in ascending or descending order.

377

Command Syntax

SORT /*switch*

Follow These Steps

1. Type **SORT** and press the **space bar** once.
2. You can use either of the following switches:

   /R sorts in reverse alphabetical order.

   /+*n* sorts in alphabetical order, starting at column *n*.
3. Press ⏎Enter.

Example: SORT /R <PRESORT.TXT >POSTSORT.TXT

In this example, the SORT command sorts, in reverse alphabetical order, the contents of the file PRESORT.TXT and writes the sorted contents to the file POSTSORT.TXT.

SORT is not an essential command, but it is a useful command for visual control.

SYS

 External

Use SYS to do the following:

> Transfer the operating system files to another disk. SYS enables the transfer of operating system files to a disk that holds an applications program if the disk has enough space.

Command Syntax

SYS *sd: dd:*

Follow These Steps

1. Place the target disk (the disk to receive the operating system) into a disk drive.
2. Type **SYS** and press the **space bar** once.
3. If the operating system you want to copy is on a disk other than the disk from which you booted, type the name of the drive containing the operating system (for example, **A:**).

378

4. Type the name of the drive holding the target disk (for example, B:).

5. Press ⏎Enter. SYS transfers the operating system, including COMMAND.COM, to the floppy disk in the target drive.

Tip: You do not need to transfer the operating system to every floppy disk. Save disk storage space by transferring the operating system only to disks you want to use as boot disks.

In earlier versions of DOS, SYS was used to transfer the hidden system files without copying COMMAND.COM. Since DOS 5, the SYS command transfers COMMAND.COM as well as the hidden system files.

14

TIME

 Internal

Use TIME to do the following:

Enter or change the time used by the system.

Set the automatic clock on a computer with a battery-backed clock.

Establish the time that files were created or modified.

Provide control for programs that require time information.

Command Syntax

TIME *hh:mm:ss.xx* A|P

Follow These Steps

1. Type TIME and press the space bar once.

2. Enter the time in the format *hh:mm:ss:xx* or *hh.mm.ss.xx*.

   For *hh*, type the hour, using one or two digits from 0 to 23. For *mm*, type the number of minutes, using one or two digits from 0 to 59. For *ss*, type the number of seconds, using one or two digits from 0 to 59. For *xx*, type the number of hundredths of a second, using one or two digits from 0 to 99. It is not necessary to include more than the hour and the minutes.

3. If you use the 12-hour clock when you enter the time, type A to represent AM hours or P to represent PM hours. For the 24-hour clock, omit these identifiers. (For example, to indicate 3:13 PM, type 3:13P for the 12-hour clock or 15:13 for the 24-hour clock.)

4. Press ⏎Enter.

Use TIME with the DATE command. Including the correct time in a file may not be as important as including the date, but don't get into poor management habits. Better still, think about getting a battery-powered clock card for your PC to save time.

TREE

 External

Use TREE to do the following:

Display directory paths in hierarchical directories.

List the available files in each directory.

Find lost files within a maze of directories.

Command Syntax

TREE *d: /switch*

Follow These Steps

1. Type TREE and press the space bar once.
2. Type the name of the drive whose directory paths you want to display. The TREE command lists information about this drive.
3. You can use either of the following switches:

   /F lists the files in each directory.

   /A uses the characters ¦, –, \, and + to display the subdirectory structure (rather than using graphic line characters).
4. Press ↵Enter.

The TREE command is another way to monitor a hard disk drive's directory structure. As time goes on, you appreciate this command more.

TYPE

 Internal

Use TYPE to do the following:

Display the contents of a text file on-screen.

Send files to the printer.

380

Command Syntax

TYPE *d:path\filename.ext*

Follow These Steps

1. Type **TYPE** and press the **space bar** once.
2. Type the drive name, path, and file name of the file you want to display.
3. Press ⏎Enter.

To send the typed output to a device such as the printer (PRN), use the redirection symbol >, as shown in this example: TYPE TEXT.TXT > PRN

TYPE enables you to read a file without opening it in a word processing program.

UNDELETE

 External

Use UNDELETE to do the following:

Activate or deactivate deletion protection.

List files that have been deleted but can be undeleted.

Undelete files.

Delete the contents of the SENTRY directory.

Command Syntax

To activate deletion protection:

UNDELETE */switches*

To undelete files:

UNDELETE *d:path\filename.ext /switches*

Follow These Steps

To activate deletion protection:

1. Type **UNDELETE** and press the **space bar**. You may need to precede the command with a path for UNDELETE.EXE because UNDELETE is an external command.

381

2. Use any of these switches:

/LOAD loads the UNDELETE program into memory.

/UNLOAD unloads the UNDELETE program from memory, completely disabling UNDELETE.

/S enables the Delete Sentry level of protection against deletion. If you do not specify /S or /T, UNDELETE defaults to the MS-DOS level of protection.

/T enables the Delete Tracking level of protection against deletion. If you do not specify /T or /S, UNDELETE defaults to the MS-DOS level of protection.

/PURGE deletes the contents of the SENTRY directory.

/STATUS displays the active level of protection.

3. Press ⏎Enter.

To undelete files:

1. Type UNDELETE and press the space bar. You may need to precede the command with a path for UNDELETE.EXE because UNDELETE is an external command.

2. Specify the drive, path, and file name of the file you want to undelete.

3. Use any of these switches:

/LIST lists all deleted files, but does not recover them. This setting is the default.

/ALL recovers all deleted files.

/DOS recovers files protected with the MS-DOS level of protection.

/DT recovers files protected with the Delete Tracking level of protection.

/DS recovers files protected with the Delete Sentry level of protection.

4. Press Y for each file you want to undelete or N to cancel the process.

UNDELETE is an optional program you install by using the Setup program. For information on installing the optional programs, see Appendix A.

UNFORMAT

 External

Use UNFORMAT to do the following:

Restore a disk that was erased using the FORMAT command.

Rebuild a disk that has been corrupted by incorrectly using the RECOVER command.

Rebuild a corrupted disk partition table on a hard disk drive.

Command Syntax

UNFORMAT *d: /switches*

Follow These Steps

14

1. Type **UNFORMAT** and press the **space bar**. You may need to precede the command with a drive and path for the UNFORMAT.EXE file because UNFORMAT is an external command.

2. You can use any of the following switches:

   /L lists every file and directory found by UNFORMAT. If you do not specify this switch, UNFORMAT lists only fragmented directories and files.

   /TEST shows how UNFORMAT would re-create the information on the disk, without actually going through with the unformat.

   /P sends output messages to the printer connected to LPT1.

   /J compares the disk with its mirror files to verify that they are up-to-date, without actually unformatting the disk.

   /U unformats the disk without using its mirror files.

   /PARTN restores partition tables.

3. Press ↵Enter.

Caution: UNFORMAT cannot restore the disk if you used the /U switch with the FORMAT command.

Note: You cannot use UNFORMAT on network drives.

VER

Use VER to do the following:

Display the DOS version number.

Command Syntax

> VER

Follow These Steps

1. Type VER.
2. Press ⏎Enter. DOS displays the version number on-screen in a message such as the following:

       MS-DOS Version 6.00

The result of VER is infrequently used. This command is singularly limited in purpose.

VERIFY

Use VERIFY to do the following:

> Set your computer to check the accuracy of data written to a disk.
>
> Show whether the data has been checked.

Command Syntax

To show whether VERIFY is on or off:

> VERIFY

To set the verify status:

> VERIFY ON
>   or
> VERIFY OFF

Follow These Steps

1. Type VERIFY and press the space bar once.
2. Type ON or OFF depending on whether you want VERIFY on to check for accuracy, or off for fast disk-writing operation.

VERIFY provides absolute peace of mind, but requires twice as long to copy files. Many people are in the habit of using verification. If you have the time, you just might find it worthwhile.

VOL

✳ Internal

Use VOL to do the following:

> Display the volume label of the specified drive.

Command Syntax

VOL *d:*

Follow These Steps

1. Type **VOL** and press the **space bar** once.
2. Type the drive name of the disk that has the volume name you want to examine (for example, **A:** or **B:**), if that drive is not already current.
3. Press ↵Enter.

Some people never use this command, but (in fact) VOL is as important as labeling a disk.

XCOPY

 External

Use XCOPY to do the following:

> Copy files from multiple directories to another disk.
>
> Copy files with a specific date.
>
> Copy newly created or modified files.
>
> Copy subdirectories and files.

Command Syntax

XCOPY *sd:spath\sfilename.ext dd:dpath\dfilename.ext /switches*

Follow These Steps

1. Type **XCOPY** and press the **space bar** once. You might need to precede the command with the drive and path for XCOPY.EXE because XCOPY is an external command.

2. Type the drive name and path of the source file (*sd:\spath*).

3. Type the name of the file you want to copy. You can use wild cards.

4. Press the space bar.

5. Type the drive name, path, and file name of the target file (*dd:\dpath\dfilename.ext*). Skip this step if the file name is to remain the same as that of the source file.

6. You can use any of the following switches:

   /**A** copies files with the archive attribute set on and does not change the archive attribute.

   /**M** copies files with the archive attribute set on, but shuts off the archive attribute.

   /**D:***date* copies files that were created or modified on or after the specified date.

   /**P** prompts you before copying each file.

   /**S** copies specified files from the current directory and from subdirectories of the current directory, creating directories on the destination disk when necessary.

   /**E** copies empty subdirectories.

   /**V** verifies each copied file.

   /**W** makes XCOPY wait before starting the copy so that you can insert the correct disks in the drive.

7. Press ⏎Enter.

Caution: Like COPY, XCOPY does exactly what you tell it to do. Before you use it, make sure that you have typed the correct information so that you do not inadvertently copy over important files.

Errors Great and Small

Ending a book with a chapter on errors may make you wince, but don't lose heart. Error messages are DOS's way of telling you that you made a correctable blunder, or that DOS did. Error messages serve as reminders that both man and machine make mistakes.

Encountering Error Messages

Occasionally, you may issue a harmless but incorrect command or forget to close the door on a disk drive. DOS quickly points out such frailties with an error message, but you can correct and learn from these mistakes.

Some error messages appear when you start MS-DOS, and some appear while you use your computer. Most start-up errors mean that MS-DOS did not start and that you must reboot the system. Most of the other error messages mean that MS-DOS terminated (aborted) the program and returned to the system prompt.

Some error messages indicate a serious problem. Fortunately, you probably will never see those messages. Also, some potentially serious error messages can be caused by any of several problems; if you remain calm, you might discover an easy remedy.

Interpreting Error Messages

The following error messages are the ones that routinely appear on-screen. For easy reference, the messages are listed in alphabetical order with explanations of their most common causes. If you see an error message that isn't in this guide, refer to your computer's MS-DOS manual.

Access denied

You or a program attempted to change or erase a file that is marked as read-only or that is in use. If the file is marked as read-only, you can change the read-only attribute with the ATTRIB command.

Allocation error, size adjusted

This error is a warning message. The contents of a file have been truncated because the size indicated in the directory is not large enough for the amount of data in this file. To correct this problem, use the CHKDSK /F command.

APPEND/ASSIGN Conflict

This error is a DOS warning message. You cannot use APPEND on an assigned drive. Cancel the drive assignment before using APPEND with this drive.

Bad command or filename

The name you entered is not valid for invoking a command, program, or batch file. The most frequent causes are as follows:

* You misspelled a name.
* You omitted a needed disk drive or path name.
* You entered the parameters without the command name.

Check the spelling on the command line. Make sure that the command, program, or batch file is in the location specified (disk drive and directory path). Then try the command again.

Bad or missing Command Interpreter

MS-DOS cannot find the command interpreter, COMMAND.COM. MS-DOS does not start.

If this message appears when you start MS-DOS, COMMAND.COM is not on the boot disk, or a version of COMMAND.COM from a previous version of

388

MS-DOS is on the disk. Place in the floppy disk drive another disk containing the operating system, and then reboot the system. After MS-DOS starts, copy COMMAND.COM to the original start-up disk so that you can boot from that disk.

If this message appears while you are running MS-DOS, COMMAND.COM has been erased from the disk and directory you used when starting MS-DOS, or a version of COMMAND.COM from a previous MS-DOS has overwritten the good version. Restart MS-DOS by resetting the system.

If resetting the system does not solve the problem, use a copy of your MS-DOS master disk to restart the computer. Copy COMMAND.COM from this floppy disk to the problem disk.

15

Bad or missing filename

MS-DOS was directed to load a device driver that it could not locate, or an error occurred when DOS loaded the device driver. This message also might mean that a break address for the device driver is out of bounds for the size of RAM in the computer. MS-DOS continues to boot, but does not use the device driver.

If MS-DOS loads, check your CONFIG.SYS file for the line DEVICE=*filename*. Make sure that you spell the command correctly and that the device driver is where you specified. If this line is correct, reboot the system.

If the message appears again, copy the file from its original disk to the boot disk and boot MS-DOS again. If the error persists, contact the dealer who sold you the drive because the device driver is bad.

Bad or missing keyboard definition file

This error is a DOS warning message. DOS cannot find KEYBOARD.SYS as specified by the KEYB command. Solving this problem can take several steps. First check to see that KEYBOARD.SYS exists and that it is in the correct path. Then retype the KEYB command. If DOS displays the same message, KEYB.COM or KEYBOARD.SYS may be corrupted.

Bad Partition Table

This error is a FORMAT error message. While using FORMAT, DOS was unable to find a DOS partition on the fixed disk you specified. To correct this problem, run FDISK and create a DOS partition on the fixed-disk drive.

Batch file missing

MS-DOS could not find the batch file it was processing; the batch file was renamed or erased. MS-DOS aborts the processing of the batch file.

If the batch file was renamed, rename it again using its original name. If necessary, edit the batch file to ensure that the file name is not changed again.

If the file was erased, re-create the batch file from its backup file (if possible). Edit the file to ensure that the batch file does not erase itself.

Cannot CHDIR to path - tree past this point not processed

CHKDSK was unable to go to the specified directory. All subdirectories beneath this directory are not verified. To correct this error, run CHKDSK /F.

Cannot CHDIR to root

This error is a CHDIR error message. While checking the tree structure of the directory with CHKDSK, DOS was unable to return to the root directory and did not check the remaining subdirectories. To get rid of this message, try restarting DOS. If DOS continues to display the message, the disk is unusable and must be reformatted.

Cannot find System Files

While using FORMAT /S, you tried to use a drive that does not have the DOS system files in the root directory. Change to a drive that does have the system files in the root directory.

Cannot load COMMAND.COM, system halted

MS-DOS attempted to reload COMMAND.COM, but DOS did not find the command processor, or the area where MS-DOS keeps track of available and used memory was destroyed. The system halts.

This message can indicate that COMMAND.COM has been erased from the disk and directory you used when starting MS-DOS. Restart MS-DOS. If DOS does not start, your copy of COMMAND.COM has been erased. Restart MS-DOS from the original master disks and copy COMMAND.COM to your working disk.

Another possible cause of this message is that a faulty program has corrupted the memory allocation table where MS-DOS tracks available memory. Reboot and then run the same program that was in the computer when the system halted. If the problem occurs again, the program is defective. Contact the dealer or manufacturer who sold you the program.

Cannot load COMMAND, system halted

DOS attempted to reload COMMAND.COM, but DOS did not find the command processor in the directory specified by the COMSPEC= entry or the area where DOS keeps track of available and used memory was destroyed. The system halts.

This message can indicate that COMMAND.COM has been erased from the disk and directory you used when starting DOS or that the COMSPEC= entry in the environment has been changed. Restart DOS from your usual start-up disk. If DOS does not start, the copy of COMMAND.COM has been erased. Restart DOS from the DOS start-up or master disk and copy COMMAND.COM onto your usual start-up disk.

Another possible cause of this message is that a faulty program has corrupted the memory allocation table where DOS tracks available memory. Run the same program that was in the computer when the system halted. If the problem occurs again, the program is defective. Contact the dealer or manufacturer who sold you the program.

Cannot perform a cyclic copy

When using XCOPY /S, you tried to specify a target that is a subdirectory of the source. Depending on the directory tree structure, you might be able to overcome this limitation by using a temporary disk or file.

Cannot read file allocation table

You were attempting to regain data from good sectors in a bad or defective disk with the RECOVER command when DOS discovered that the file allocation table (FAT) is in a bad sector. Your disk is damaged, and recovering data from the bad sectors might be impossible.

Cannot recover . entry, processing continued

This error is a CHKDSK warning message. While using CHKDSK, this message means that the "." entry (the working directory) is defective and cannot be recovered.

Cannot recover .. entry,
Entry has a bad attribute (or link or size)

This error is a warning message. While using CHKDSK, DOS finds that the ".." entry (the parent directory) is defective and cannot be recovered.

If you specified the /F switch, CHKDSK tries to correct the error.

Cannot start COMMAND.COM, exiting

MS-DOS was directed to load an additional copy of COMMAND.COM, but could not. Either the FILES= command in your CONFIG.SYS file is set too low, or you do not have enough free memory for another copy of COMMAND.COM.

If your system has 256K or more of RAM, and FILES is less than 10, edit the CONFIG.SYS file on your start-up disk to use FILES=20. Reboot your computer.

If the problem occurs again, you do not have enough memory in your computer, or you have too many programs competing for memory space. Restart MS-DOS and do not load any resident or background programs you do not need. If necessary, eliminate unneeded device drivers or RAM-disk software. An alternative is to increase the random-access memory in your system.

Configuration too large

DOS could not load itself because you specified too many FILES or BUFFERS in your CONFIG.SYS file, or you specified too large an environment area (/E switch) to the SHELL command. This problem usually occurs only on systems with less than 256K memory.

Restart MS-DOS with a different disk and edit the CONFIG.SYS file on your boot disk. Lower the number of FILES and BUFFERS or the number after the /E switch in the SHELL command. Restart MS-DOS with the edited disk. An alternative is to increase the memory in your system.

Content of destination lost before copy

The source file for COPY was overwritten before the command was completed. This error occurred because the user typed the command incorrectly. Restore the source file from your backup disk; alternatively, you might be able to use UNDELETE to recover the file.

Current drive is no longer valid

You included the current path ($p) in the PROMPT command. MS-DOS attempted to read the current directory for the disk drive and found the drive no longer valid.

If the current disk drive is set for a floppy disk, you do not have a disk in the disk drive. MS-DOS reports a Drive not ready error. Press **F** to fail (the same as **A** to abort) or **I** to ignore the error. Then insert a floppy disk into the disk drive or type another drive designation.

An invalid-drive error also can happen if you have a networked disk drive that has been deleted or disconnected. In this case, simply change the current disk to a valid disk drive.

15

Data error reading drive x:

DOS could not correctly read the data. Usually the disk has developed a defective spot. You might be able to save the disk by using RECOVER or CHKDSK /F.

Disk boot failure

An error occurred when MS-DOS tried to load itself into memory. The disk contained IO.SYS and MSDOS.SYS, but DOS could not load one of the two files. MS-DOS did not boot.

Start MS-DOS from the disk again. If the error reoccurs, boot MS-DOS from a disk that you know is good, such as from a copy of your MS-DOS start-up or master disk. If this attempt fails, you have a hardware (disk drive) problem. Contact your dealer.

Disk unsuitable for system disk

FORMAT /S detected on the floppy disk one or more bad sectors in the area where DOS normally resides. Because DOS must reside on a specific position on the disk, and this position is unusable, you cannot use that floppy disk to boot DOS.

Reformat the floppy disk. Some floppy disks format successfully the second time. If FORMAT produces this message again, you cannot use that floppy disk as a boot disk.

Divide overflow

A program attempted to divide by zero. DOS aborts the program. The program was incorrectly entered, or it has a logic flaw. With a well-written program, this error should never occur. If you wrote the program, correct the error and run the program again. If you purchased the program, report the problem to the dealer or publisher.

Drive or diskette types not compatible

When using DISKCOMP or DISKCOPY, you specified drives of different capacities. You cannot, for example, use DISKCOMP or DISKCOPY from a 1.2M drive to a 360K drive. Retype the command using like drives.

15

Drive not ready

An error occurred while MS-DOS tried to read or write to the disk drive. For floppy disk drives, the drive door may be open, the disk may not be inserted, or the disk may not be formatted. For hard disk drives, the drive may not be properly prepared, or you may have a hardware problem.

Duplicate filename or File not found

While using RENAME (or REN), you attempted to rename a file to a name that already existed, or the file you attempted to rename does not exist in the directory. Check the directory for the conflicting names. Make sure that the file name exists and that you have spelled it correctly, and then try again.

Error in COUNTRY command

The COUNTRY directive in CONFIG.SYS is improperly phrased or has an incorrect country code or code page number. DOS continues its start-up, but uses the default information for the COUNTRY directive.

After DOS has started, check the COUNTRY line in your CONFIG.SYS file. Make sure that the directive is correctly phrased (using commas between the country code, code page, and COUNTRY.SYS file name) and that its information is correct. If you detect an error in the line, edit the line, save the file, and restart DOS.

If you do not find an error, restart DOS. If the same message appears, edit your CONFIG.SYS file again by reentering the COUNTRY directive and deleting the old COUNTRY line. The old line may contain some nonsense characters that DOS can detect but that your text-editing program cannot detect.

Error in EXE file

MS-DOS detected an error while attempting to load a program stored in an EXE file. The problem is in the relocation information MS-DOS needs to load the program. This error can occur if the EXE file has been altered in any way.

Restart MS-DOS and load the program again, this time using a backup copy of the program. If the message reappears, the program is flawed. If you are using a purchased program, contact the dealer or publisher.

Error loading operating system

A disk error occurred while MS-DOS was loading itself from the hard disk. MS-DOS does not boot.

Restart the computer. If the error occurs after several tries, restart MS-DOS from a floppy disk. If the hard disk does not respond (if you cannot run DIR or CHKDSK without an error message), your problem is with the hard disk. Contact your dealer.

If the hard disk does respond, use the SYS command to put another copy of MS-DOS onto your hard disk. You may need to copy COMMAND.COM to the hard disk also.

Error reading directory

MS-DOS encountered a problem while reading the directory during a format procedure, possibly because bad sectors have developed in the file allocation table (FAT) structure.

If the message occurs when DOS is reading a floppy disk, the disk is unusable and should be discarded. If the message occurs when DOS reads your hard disk, however, the problem is more serious, and you may have to reformat your hard disk. Back up your data files on a regular basis to prevent major losses if a problem reading the directory occurs.

Error reading (or writing) partition table

MS-DOS could not read from (or write to) the disk's partition table during FORMAT. This error message indicates that the partition table is corrupted. Run FDISK on the disk and reformat the disk.

EXEC failure

MS-DOS encountered an error while reading a command or program from a disk, or the value specified in the FILES= command of the CONFIG.SYS file is too low.

15

Increase the number of FILES in the CONFIG.SYS file of your start-up disk to 15 or 20 and then restart MS-DOS. If the error reoccurs, you may have a problem with the disk. Use a backup copy of the program and try again. If the backup copy works, copy it over the problem copy.

If an error occurs in the copying process, you have a flawed floppy disk or hard disk. If the problem is a floppy disk, copy the files from the flawed disk to another disk and reformat or retire the original floppy disk. If the problem is the hard disk, immediately back up your files and run RECOVER on the problem file. If the problem persists, your hard disk may have a hardware failure.

File cannot be copied onto itself

You attempted to COPY a file to the same disk, directory, and file name. This message usually indicates that you misspelled or omitted parts of the source or destination drive, path, or file name. This error also can occur when you use wild cards for file names. Check your spelling and the source and destination names, and then try the command again.

File creation error

MS-DOS or a program could not add a new file to the directory or replace an existing file.

If the file already exists, use the ATTRIB command to check whether the file is marked as read-only. If the read-only flag is set and you want to change or erase the file, use ATTRIB to remove the read-only flag, and then try again.

If the problem is not the read-only flag, run CHKDSK without the /F switch to determine whether the directory is full, the disk is full, or some other problem exists with the disk.

File not found

MS-DOS could not find the file you specified. The file is not on the disk or in the directory you specified, or you misspelled the disk drive name, path name, or file name. Check these possibilities and try the command again.

Filename device driver cannot be initialized

In CONFIG.SYS, the parameters in the device driver file name are incorrect, or the DEVICE line is in error. Check for incorrect parameters and for phrasing errors in the DEVICE line. Edit the DEVICE line in the CONFIG.SYS file, save the file, and then restart DOS.

FIRST diskette bad or incompatible

or

SECOND diskette bad or incompatible

One of these messages may appear when you use the DISKCOMP command. The messages indicate that either the source (FIRST) or the target (SECOND) floppy disk is unreadable or that the disks you attempted to compare have different format densities.

Format not supported on drive x:

The FORMAT command cannot be used on the drive you selected. DOS displays this message if you entered device driver parameters that your computer cannot support. Check CONFIG.SYS for bad DEVICE or DRIVPARM commands.

General failure reading (or writing) drive x:

MS-DOS uses this error message when DOS encounters an error it does not recognize. The error usually occurs for one of the following reasons:

- You are using an unformatted disk.
- The disk drive door is open.
- The floppy disk is not properly inserted in the drive.
- You are using the wrong type of disk in a disk drive, such as formatting a 360K disk in a 1.2M disk drive.

Incorrect MS-DOS version

The DOS utility program for the command you just entered is from a different version of MS-DOS.

Find a copy of the program from the correct version of MS-DOS (usually from the MS-DOS master disk) and try the command again. If the floppy disk or hard disk you are using has been updated to hold new versions of the MS-DOS programs, copy those versions over the old ones. If you have more than one version of MS-DOS on your hard disk, make sure that your PATH command refers to the directory with the correct DOS files.

15

Insert disk with batch file and strike any key when ready

DOS attempted to execute the next command from a batch file, but the disk holding the batch file is not in the disk drive.

Put the disk holding the batch file into the disk drive and press any key to continue.

Insert disk with COMMAND.COM in drive x: and strike any key when ready

15

MS-DOS needs to reload COMMAND.COM, but cannot find it on the start-up disk.

If you are using floppy disks, the disk in drive A probably has been changed. Place a disk with a good copy of COMMAND.COM in drive A and press any key.

Insufficient disk space

The disk does not have enough free space to hold the file being written. All MS-DOS programs terminate when this problem occurs, but some non-DOS programs continue.

If you think that the disk has enough room to hold the file, run CHKDSK to see whether the floppy disk or hard disk has a problem. Sometimes when you terminate programs early by pressing Ctrl-Break, MS-DOS cannot do the necessary clean-up work. When this happens, disk space is temporarily trapped. CHKDSK can free these areas.

If you have run out of disk space, free some disk space or use a different floppy disk or hard disk. Then try the command again.

Insufficient memory

The computer does not have enough free RAM to execute the program or command.

If you have loaded a RAM-resident program like SideKick or Doskey, restart MS-DOS and try the program or command before loading any resident program. If this step fails, remove any unneeded device driver or RAM-disk software from the CONFIG.SYS file and restart MS-DOS. If this action fails, your computer does not have enough memory for the program or command.

You must increase your random-access memory to run the program or command.

Insufficient memory to store macro.
Use the DOSKEY command with the /BUFSIZE switch
to increase available memory.

Your Doskey macros have filled the space set aside for them, and you cannot enter any new macros until you enlarge the memory area (the default is 1024 bytes). The BUFSIZE switch enables you to increase the amount of memory reserved for Doskey macros.

Intermediate file error during pipe

MS-DOS is unable to create or write to one or both of the intermediate files it uses when piping information between programs. The disk is full, the root directory of the current disk is full, or DOS cannot find the files. The most frequent cause is running out of disk space.

Run the DIR command on the root directory of the current disk drive. Make sure that you have enough free space and enough room in the root directory for two additional files. If you do not have enough room, create room on the disk by deleting—or copying and deleting—files. You also can copy the necessary files to a different disk.

Another possible cause of this error is that a program is deleting files, including the temporary files DOS uses. If this is the case, you should correct the program, contact the dealer or program publisher, or avoid using the program with piping.

Internal stack over flow
System halted

Your programs and DOS have exhausted the stack (the memory space reserved for temporary use). This problem usually is caused by a rapid succession of hardware devices demanding attention (interrupts). DOS stops, and you must turn the system off and on again to restart DOS.

The circumstances that cause this message usually are infrequent and erratic and may not reoccur. If you want to prevent this error from occurring at all, add the STACKS directive to your CONFIG.SYS file. If the directive is already in your CONFIG.SYS file, increase the number of stacks specified.

15

399

Invalid characters in volume label

This message is a FORMAT error message and label. You entered more than 11 alphanumeric characters or entered illegal characters (for example, +, =, /, \, or ¦) when you typed the disk's volume label (the disk name). Retype the volume label, following the proper procedure.

Invalid COMMAND.COM in drive x:

MS-DOS tried to reload COMMAND.COM from the disk in the specified drive and found that the file was of a different version of MS-DOS. DOS instructs you to insert a disk with the correct version and press a key. Follow those directions.

If you frequently use the disk that was in the specified drive, copy the correct version of COMMAND.COM to that disk.

Invalid COMMAND.COM, system halted

MS-DOS could not find COMMAND.COM on the hard disk. MS-DOS halts and must be restarted.

COMMAND.COM may have been erased, or the COMSPEC variable in the environment may have been changed. Restart the computer from the hard disk. If DOS displays a message indicating that COMMAND.COM is missing, the file was erased. Restart MS-DOS from a floppy disk and recopy COMMAND.COM to the root directory of the hard disk.

If you restart MS-DOS and this message appears later, a program or batch file may be erasing COMMAND.COM. If a batch file is erasing COMMAND.COM, edit the batch file. If a program is erasing COMMAND.COM, contact the dealer or publisher who sold you the program.

Invalid date

You entered an impossible date or used the wrong kind of character to separate the month, day, and year. DOS also displays this message if you attempt to enter the date with the keypad when the keypad is not in numeric mode.

Invalid device parameters from device driver

A FORMAT error message that DOS displays when it finds that the disk partition does not fall on a track boundary. You may have set the device drivers incorrectly in your CONFIG.SYS file or attempted to format a hard disk that was formatted with DOS 2.x (so that the total number of hidden sectors is not evenly divisible by the number of sectors on a track). As a result, the partition does not start on a track boundary.

To correct the error, run FDISK before performing a format, or check CONFIG.SYS for a bad DEVICE or DRIVPARM command.

Invalid directory

One of the following errors occurred:

- You specified a directory name that does not exist.
- You misspelled the directory name.
- The directory path is on a different disk.
- You didn't type the path character (\) at the beginning of the name.
- You didn't separate the directory names with the path character.

Check your directory names, ensure that the directories do exist, and try the command again.

Invalid disk change

The disk in the 720K, 1.2M, or 1.44M disk drive was changed while a program had open files to be written to the disk. DOS displays the message Abort, Retry, Fail?. Place the correct disk in the disk drive and press **R** for Retry.

Invalid drive in search path

A specification you entered in the PATH command has an invalid disk drive name, or a named disk drive is nonexistent.

Use PATH to check the paths you instructed MS-DOS to search. If you used a nonexistent disk drive name, use the PATH command again to enter the correct search paths. (Or, you can just ignore the warning message.)

Invalid drive or file name

You entered the name of a nonexistent disk drive; or you mistyped the disk drive, the file name, or both. Check the disk drive name and try the command again.

15

Invalid drive specification

DOS displays this message when one of the following errors occurs:

- You entered the name of an invalid or nonexistent disk drive as a parameter to a command.
- You entered the same disk drive for the source and destination, which is not permitted for the command.
- You omitted a parameter, and DOS therefore defaulted to the same source and destination disk drive.

Check the disk drive names; if the command is missing a parameter and defaulting to the wrong disk drive, explicitly name the correct disk drive.

Invalid drive specification
Specified drive does not exist,
or is non-removable.

One of the following errors occurred:

- You entered the name of a nonexistent disk drive.
- You named the hard disk drive when using commands intended only for floppy disks.
- You omitted a disk drive name, and DOS therefore defaulted to the hard disk when using commands intended only for floppy disks.
- You named—or DOS defaulted to—a RAM-disk drive when using commands for a true floppy disk drive.

Certain MS-DOS commands temporarily hide disk drive names while the command is in effect. Check the disk drive name you entered and try the command again.

Invalid media or Track 0 bad -- disk unusable

This message is a FORMAT error message. The disk you are trying to format may be damaged, but often a disk does not format the first time. Try to format the disk again; if the same message appears, the disk is bad and should be discarded.

Invalid number of parameters

You have entered too few or too many parameters for a command. One of the following errors occurred:

15

402

- You omitted required information.
- You excluded a colon immediately after the disk drive name.
- You put a space in the wrong place or omitted a needed space.
- You omitted a slash (/) in front of a switch.

Invalid parameter

or

Incorrect parameter

At least one parameter you entered for the command is not valid. One of the following errors occurred:

- You omitted required information.
- You omitted a colon immediately after the disk drive name.
- You put a space in the wrong place or omitted a needed space.
- You didn't add a slash (/) in front of a switch.
- You used a switch that the command does not recognize.

For more information, check the explanation of this message in the command reference in Chapter 14; see the command you were using when the message occurred.

Invalid parameter combination

When you entered an MS-DOS command, you typed parameters that conflict. Retype the command, using only one of the conflicting parameters.

Invalid partition table

When you started DOS from the hard disk, DOS detected a problem in the hard disk's partition information.

Restart MS-DOS from a floppy disk. Back up all files from the hard disk (if possible) and run FDISK to correct the problem. If you change the partition information, reformat the hard disk and restore all its files.

Invalid path

One of the following errors has occurred:

- The path name contains illegal characters.

15

- The path name has more than 63 characters.
- One of the directory names within the path is misspelled or does not exist.

Check the spelling of the path name. If needed, find a directory listing of the disk to ensure that the directory you specified does exist and that you have the correct path name. Be sure that the path name contains no more than 63 characters. If necessary, change the current directory to a directory "closer" to the file to shorten the path name.

Invalid path or file name

You entered a directory name or file name that does not exist, used the wrong directory name (a directory not on the path), or mistyped a name. COPY aborts when it encounters an invalid path or file name. If you used wild cards in the file name, COPY transfers all valid files before it issues the error message.

Check to see which files were transferred. Determine whether the directory and file name are spelled correctly and whether the path is correct. Then try the command again.

Invalid time

You entered an impossible time or used the wrong kind of character to separate the hours, minutes, and seconds. DOS also displays this message if you attempt to enter the time with the keypad when the keypad is not in numeric mode.

Invalid Volume ID

This message is a FORMAT error message. During the formatting of a fixed (hard) disk, you entered an incorrect volume label (the name of the disk drive). DOS aborts the format attempt.

To view the volume label of the disk, type **VOL** at the prompt and press Enter. Then try the command again.

Lock violation

With the file-sharing program (SHARE.EXE) or network software loaded, one of your programs attempted to access a locked file. First try **Retry**; if unsuccessful, try **Abort** or **Fail**. (If you choose **Abort** or **Fail**, however, you lose any data in memory.)

Memory allocation error
Cannot load COMMAND, system halted

A program damaged the area where MS-DOS keeps track of available and used memory. You must restart MS-DOS.

If this error occurs again with the same program, use a backup copy of the program. If the problem persists, the program has a flaw. Contact the dealer or program publisher.

MIRROR cannot operate with a network

MIRROR cannot save file reconstruction information because your computer's hard disk is currently redirected to a network. Get off the network.

Missing operating system

The MS-DOS hard disk partition does not have a copy of MS-DOS on it. MS-DOS does not boot.

Start MS-DOS from a floppy disk. Use the SYS C: command to place DOS and COMMAND.COM on the hard disk. If this command fails to solve the problem, back up the existing files (if any) from the hard disk, and then issue the FORMAT /S command to put a copy of the operating system on the hard disk. If necessary, restore the files you backed up.

No free file handles
Cannot start COMMAND, exiting

MS-DOS could not load an additional copy of COMMAND.COM because no file handles were available.

Edit the CONFIG.SYS file on your start-up disk to increase the number of file handles (using the FILES command) by five. Restart DOS and try the command again.

No room for system on destination disk

The floppy disk or hard disk was not formatted with the necessary reserved space for MS-DOS. You cannot put the system on this floppy disk without first copying all the disk's data to another disk and then reformatting the disk.

No paper

The printer is out of paper or is turned off.

No system on default drive

SYS could not find the system files. Insert a disk containing the system files, such as the DOS disk, and enter the command again.

No target drive specified

You did not specify a target drive when you typed a backup command. Retype the command, using first a source and then a target disk drive.

Non-DOS disk

MS-DOS does not recognize the disk format as a DOS disk. This disk is unusable. Abort and run CHKDSK to learn whether any corrective action is possible. If CHKDSK fails, an alternative is to reformat the disk.

Reformatting destroys any information remaining on the disk. If you have disks from another operating system, that disk was probably formatted under the other operating system and should not be reformatted.

Non-System disk or disk error
Replace and strike any key when ready

Your floppy disk or hard disk does not contain MS-DOS, or a read error occurred when you started the system. MS-DOS does not boot. If you are using a floppy disk system, put a bootable disk in drive A and press any key.

The most frequent cause of this message on hard disk systems is that you left a nonbootable floppy disk in drive A with the drive door closed and attempted to boot your computer. Open the door to disk drive A and press any key. MS-DOS boots from the hard disk.

Not enough memory

The computer does not have enough free memory to execute the program or command.

If you loaded a RAM-resident program, such as SideKick or Doskey, restart MS-DOS and try the program or command again before loading any resident program. If this method fails, remove any unneeded device driver or RAM-disk software from the CONFIG.SYS file and restart MS-DOS.

If this procedure fails, your computer does not have enough memory for this operation. You must increase your RAM to run the program or command.

Not ready

A device is not ready and cannot receive or transmit data. Check the connections, check that the power is on, and check whether the device is ready. For floppy disk drives, check that the disk is formatted and properly seated in the disk drive.

Out of environment space

DOS is unable to add any more strings to the environment from the SET command. The environment cannot be expanded. This error occurs when you load a resident program, such as DOSSHELL, MODE, PRINT, GRAPHICS, or SideKick, or when processing AUTOEXEC.BAT.

Out of memory

The amount of memory is insufficient to perform the operation you requested. This error occurs in EDIT, the DOS full-screen text editor. You might have to delete or remove memory-resident programs to free up memory.

Packed File Corrupt

A program file did not successfully load into the first 64K of memory. This error can occur when a packed executable file is loaded into memory. Use the LOADFIX command to load the program above the first 64K.

Parameters not supported

or

Parameters not supported on drive

You entered parameters for a command that do not exist, are not supported by MS-DOS, or are incompatible with the disk drive you selected. Check the command and retype the parameters.

Path not found

A file or directory path you named does not exist. You misspelled the file name or directory name, or you omitted a path character (\ ) between directory names or between the final directory name and file name. Another possibility is that the file or directory does not exist where you specified. Check these possibilities and try again.

15

407

Path too long

You entered a path name that exceeds the 63-character limit of MS-DOS. The name is too long, or you omitted a space between file names. Check the command line. If the phrasing is correct, change to a directory that is closer to the file you want and try the command again.

Program too big to fit in memory

The computer does not have enough memory to load the program or command you invoked. Type **EXIT** to ensure that you do not have another applications program in memory.

15

If you have any resident programs loaded (such as Doskey), restart MS-DOS and try the command again without loading the resident programs. If this message appears again, reduce the number of buffers (BUFFERS=) in the CONFIG.SYS file and eliminate unneeded device drivers or RAM-disk software. Restart MS-DOS. If these actions do not solve the problem, your computer lacks the memory needed to run the program or command. You must increase the amount of RAM in your computer to run the program or command.

Read fault error reading drive x:

MS-DOS was unable to read the data, usually from a hard disk or floppy disk. Check that the disk drive door is closed and that the disk is properly inserted.

Same parameter entered twice

You duplicated a switch when you typed a command. Retype the command, using the parameter only once.

Sector not found error reading drive x:

The disk drive was unable to locate the sector on the floppy disk or hard disk platter. This error is usually the result of a defective spot on the disk or defective drive electronics. Some copy-protection schemes use a defective spot to prevent unauthorized duplication of the disk. You might be able to recover the sector by using RECOVER or CHKDSK /F.

Seek error reading (or writing) drive x:

The disk drive could not locate the proper track on the floppy disk or hard disk. This error is usually the result of a defective spot on the floppy disk or hard disk platter, an unformatted disk, or drive electronics problems. You might be able to recover the sector by using RECOVER or CHKDSK /F.

SOURCE diskette bad or incompatible

The disk you are copying is damaged or is the wrong format (for example, a high-density, 5 1/4-inch disk in a double-density, 5 1/4-inch disk drive). DOS cannot read the disk. Specify the correct format for the disk you are using. If the disk is damaged, throw it away and use another one.

Syntax error

You phrased a command improperly, making one of the following errors:

15

- You omitted needed information.
- You entered extraneous information.
- You put an extra space in a file name or path name.
- You used an incorrect switch.

Check the command line for these possibilities and try the command again.

Target diskette bad or incompatible

or

Target diskette may be unusable

or

Target diskette unusable

This DISKCOPY message indicates that a problem exists with the target disk; MS-DOS does not recognize the format of the target disk in the drive, or the disk is bad.

Check that the disk is the same density as the source disk, run CHKDSK on the target disk to determine the problem, or try to reformat the disk before proceeding with the disk-copy operation.

Target media has lower capacity than SOURCE Continue anyway (Y/N)?

This DISKCOPY warning message informs you that the target disk can hold fewer bytes of data than the source disk. The most likely cause is a target disk with bad sectors. If you type a **Y** (Yes), some of the data on the source disk may not fit onto the target disk.

To avoid the possibility of an incomplete transfer of data, type **N** (No) and use a disk that has the same capacity as the source disk; or if you are not copying "hidden" files, you can use the COPY *.* command to transfer the files.

There is not enough room to create a restore file You will not be able to use the unformat utility Proceed with Format (Y/N)?

FORMAT has determined that the disk lacks sufficient room to create a restore file. Without this file, you cannot use the UNFORMAT command to reverse the format you are attempting. If you are willing to risk losing any data that may be on the disk prior to formatting, type **Y**. If not, type **N** and get a disk with sufficient room.

Unable to create directory

You or a program attempted to create a directory and one of the following errors occurred:

- A directory of the same name exists.
- A file of the same name exists.
- You tried to add a directory to a root directory that is full.
- The directory name has illegal characters or is a device name.

List the directories of the disk. Make sure that no file or directory with the same name already exists. If you are adding the directory to the root directory, remove or move (copy and then erase) any unneeded files or commands. Check the spelling of the directory and ensure that the command is properly phrased.

Unable to load MS-DOS Shell, Retry (Y/N)?

DOS could not load the Shell. You may have another program in memory, and the Shell won't fit into memory. Or, the DOS Shell program itself may be corrupted.

Exit the program and try to load the Shell. If the Shell still doesn't load, it is probably corrupt. Reboot your system and load the Shell. If the same error message appears, copy the Shell from a backup disk to your hard disk.

15

Unable to write BOOT

FORMAT could not write to the first (or BOOT) track or DOS partition of the disk you are formatting because one of these areas is bad. Discard the bad disk, insert another unformatted disk, and try the FORMAT command again.

Unrecognized command in CONFIG.SYS

MS-DOS detected an improperly phrased directive in CONFIG.SYS. The directive is ignored, and MS-DOS starts. Examine the CONFIG.SYS file, looking for improperly phrased or incorrect directives. Edit the line, save the file, and restart MS-DOS.

Unrecoverable read error on drive x side n, track n

MS-DOS could not read the data at the described location on the disk. (MS-DOS makes four attempts before generating this message.) Copy all files on the questionable disk to another disk and try the command again, first with a new disk and then with the backup disk. If the original disk cannot be reformatted, discard it.

Unrecoverable write error on drive x side n, track n

MS-DOS was unable to write to a disk at the location specified. Try the command again; if the same error occurs, the target disk is damaged at that location. If the damaged disk contains important data, copy the files to an empty, newly formatted disk and try to reformat the damaged disk. If the disk is bad, discard it.

Write fault error writing drive x:

MS-DOS could not write the data to this device. You may have inserted the floppy disk improperly or left the disk drive door open. Another possibility is an electronics failure in the floppy or hard disk drive. The most frequent cause is a bad spot on the disk.

Write protect error writing drive x:

You tried to write data to a write-protected disk. Use a different disk or remove the write-protection tab on a 5 1/4-inch disk or slide the write-protection tab to the write-enable position on a 3 1/2-inch disk.

15

411

15

Setup and Installation

This appendix tells you how to install, or upgrade to, MS-DOS 6. Why put this information at the end of the book if it's the first thing you must do? The answer is simple. Most computers are sold today with DOS already installed on the hard disk. Also, if you use your computer at work, you may have an Information Center or PC Support Group that installs DOS and other software on your hard disk for you.

If MS-DOS 6 is already installed on your computer, you can skip this appendix for now. Go right to Chapter 1 and start to learn about DOS from the beginning. You may need the information in this appendix later to help you upgrade to a new version of DOS.

Preparing to install MS-DOS 6

Making backup copies

Installing MS-DOS 6

Completing the installation

Restoring a previous version of DOS

Running Setup to install the optional programs

Preserving DOS Shell settings

Key Terms Used in This Appendix	
Low-level format	The process that physically prepares a hard disk so that DOS can use it. This process is not the same as the DOS FORMAT command and is not a part of DOS.
Boot	To start your computer and load DOS into the computer's memory.
Partition	A section of a hard disk set up so that DOS can use it. A partition can be all or part of a hard disk. Each partition has a separate drive letter and is considered a separate disk by DOS.
Working disks	Copies of the original DOS disks. If anything happens to your working disks, you can recreate them from your original DOS disks.
Uninstall	The process of reverting to your prior version of DOS if you have a problem after you upgrade to MS-DOS 6.

A

Preparing To Install MS-DOS 6

MS-DOS 6 can run on any PC with at least 256K memory. Virtually every PC sold since 1983 has at least this much memory. Computers sold since 1986 usually have the maximum of 640K conventional memory. If you plan to install MS-DOS 6 on a hard disk, you need at least 512K memory and 4 megabytes of available disk space.

If you are upgrading from a previous version of DOS, execute CHKDSK or DIR to determine the amount of available disk space. If less than 4 megabytes are available, use COPY or BACKUP to copy some or all of the files on the hard disk to floppy disks. Then delete enough files from the hard disk so that at least 4 megabytes are available.

If you plan to install MS-DOS 6 on floppy disks, you need a supply of blank disks that fit into drive A. If drive A is a 5 1/4-inch drive, for example, you need three 1.2M floppy disks. If drive A is a 3 1/2-inch drive, you need three 1.44M disks. If the floppy drive capacity of your computer is 360K or 720K, you need to order 360K or 720K Setup disks from Microsoft Corporation.

```
C:\>CHKDSK

  133971968 bytes total disk space
      81920 bytes in 2 hidden files
     319488 bytes in 39 directories
   34332672 bytes in 1060 user files
  103800832 bytes available on disk

       8192 bytes in each allocation unit
      16911 total allocation units on disk
      12671 available allocation units on disk

     655360 total bytes memory
     510448 bytes free

C:\>
```

This computer has over 103 megabytes of available disk space.

Making Backup Copies

If your computer has a previous version of DOS installed or you have another computer available with any version of DOS installed, your first step is to make backup copies of your new DOS 6 disks.

If you cannot copy the DOS disks and cannot successfully complete the installation because you get errors reading the DOS disks, contact your computer dealer immediately and get replacement disks.

To make backup copies of the DOS 6 disks, you need five or six 5 1/4-inch, 1.2M floppy disks or three 3 1/2-inch, 1.44M disks. If you have two floppy disk drives that are the same size, follow these instructions:

1. Type **DISKCOPY A: B: /V** and press `↵Enter`.

2. At the prompt Insert the SOURCE disk in drive A, put the original MS-DOS 6 disk labeled *Disk 1* in drive A.

3. You are prompted to insert the TARGET disk in drive B.

   If you have two 5 1/4-inch drives, put a blank 1.2M floppy disk in drive B, close the drive door, and press `↵Enter`. This disk does not have to be formatted.

   or

   If you have two 3 1/2-inch drives, put a blank 1.44M disk in drive B and press `↵Enter`. This disk does not have to be formatted.

4. When the DISKCOPY process is complete, remove the disks from both drives and label the new disk *MS-DOS 6 - Setup Disk 1*.

5. At the prompt Copy another disk (Y/N)?, press **Y**, press `↵Enter`, and repeat steps 2 through 4 for each original MS-DOS 6 disk. Be sure to label the disks in the correct order.

A

415

6. When you complete the DISKCOPY for the last original MS-DOS 6 disk, you are asked whether you want to copy another disk. Press N and then press ⏎Enter.

If you have only one floppy disk drive or drive A and drive B are different sizes, follow these steps:

1. Type **DISKCOPY A: A: /V** and press ⏎Enter.

2. When you are prompted, place the original MS-DOS 6 disk labeled *Disk 1* in drive A and press ⏎Enter.

3. At the prompt to insert the TARGET disk in drive A, remove the original MS-DOS 6 disk and insert a blank 1.2M or 1.44M disk into drive A and press ⏎Enter. This disk does not have to be formatted.

4. You may be prompted to remove the TARGET disk and insert the SOURCE disk again. You then are prompted to insert the TARGET disk again. Switch the same two disks as prompted until the DISKCOPY completes.

5. When the DISKCOPY process is complete, remove the disk from drive A and label the new disk *MS-DOS 6 - Setup Disk 1*.

6. At the prompt Copy another disk (Y/N)?, press Y, press ⏎Enter, and repeat steps 2 through 5 for each original MS-DOS 6 disk. Be sure to label the disks in the correct order.

7. When you complete the DISKCOPY for the last original MS-DOS 6 disk, press N and then press ⏎Enter.

If the DISKCOPY fails, repeat the process using a different blank disk. If you cannot successfully DISKCOPY each original MS-DOS 6 disk, contact your dealer for a replacement disk.

Store the original MS-DOS 6 disks in a safe place and use the copies. If you get any errors using a copy of one of the DOS disks, repeat the DISKCOPY process to re-create that disk. If you cannot make a copy of the disk to use for the installation, contact your dealer for a replacement.

In all subsequent instructions, any reference to an original DOS disk refers to the copy of the original that you just made. If you are installing DOS for the first time and do not have copies, you must use the original disks.

Installing MS-DOS 6

If you already have DOS Version 2.11 or greater installed on your hard disk, you can upgrade to MS-DOS 6 without having to partition or format your hard disk. The upgrade consists of running the MS-DOS 6 Setup program. Make sure that you purchased the MS-DOS 6 Upgrade package. If the DOS disks are not labeled *Upgrade*, contact your dealer before you attempt to upgrade your hard disk.

If you have a new hard disk or a hard disk with a DOS version prior to 2.11, you should install MS-DOS 6 as though your hard disk did not contain DOS. Refer to the manual that came with your computer to install MS-DOS 6. Also, make sure that you have the MS-DOS 6 OEM package instead of the Upgrade package. If you do have the MS-DOS 6 Upgrade package, you will not be able to boot your computer.

This section describes how to upgrade to MS-DOS 6 a disk that has a previous version of DOS installed. If you have a nonstandard disk that requires special device drivers in CONFIG.SYS, these procedures may not work. Also, you may want to change partition sizes if you are using a version of DOS prior to MS-DOS 4.0 and you have a hard disk bigger than 32 megabytes. In these cases, consult Que's *Using MS-DOS 6*, Special Edition, or the DOS manual for more detailed, technical information.

When you upgrade, you have data on your hard disk that you do not want to lose. Part of the upgrade procedure is to back up all the files on your hard disk and save your old version of DOS.

A

Preparing To Install

Before you start the upgrade procedure, make sure that you have two blank disks that fit into drive A. These disks are the disks that will enable you to revert to your old version of DOS in case you have problems after installing MS-DOS 6. If you use 360K disks, you might need two disks; label them *Uninstall #1* and *Uninstall #2*. If you use disks with a capacity greater than 360K, you will probably need only one disk; label it *Uninstall*. Uninstall disks can be formatted disks or unformatted disks. Existing data on the disks will be destroyed.

If your start-up drive (usually drive C) uses a disk-compression program, MS-DOS 6 will not be able to create an Uninstall disk for restoring your previous version of DOS. If you do use a disk-compression program, you should back up all of your data files before you run Setup, and create a system disk by copying the FDISK, FORMAT, and SYS commands as well as the system files of your current DOS version to a floppy disk.

In any case, it is a good idea to back up important files from your hard disk to floppy disks and to copy your AUTOEXEC.BAT and CONFIG.SYS files onto floppy disks before upgrading. If something goes wrong with the upgrade, you still have the most important data intact.

Some disk-caching, deletion-protection, and anti-virus programs may conflict with the MS-DOS 6 Setup program. You must disable or remove the start-up commands for any of these programs in your CONFIG.SYS and AUTOEXEC.BAT files before you start the upgrade procedure. To do so, type **REM** and press the space bar at the beginning of each command line that starts a disk-caching, deletion-protection, or anti-virus program. Then restart your computer before running Setup.

For example, if the command C:\VSAFE.COM is in your AUTOEXEC.BAT file, position the cursor at the beginning of the line, make sure that Insert mode is turned on (press the Ins key), type **REM**, and press the space bar. The new command is REM C:\VSAFE.COM. Save the AUTOEXEC.BAT file. You can read about editing your AUTOEXEC.BAT and CONFIG.SYS files in Chapter 12.

You also need to turn off automatic message services that print directly to your screen. For example, you must turn off network pop-up menus or printing notifications.

Installing on a Hard Disk

To upgrade DOS on your hard disk, follow these steps:

1. Copy your AUTOEXEC.BAT and CONFIG.SYS files to a floppy disk. You may need them later.

2. Exit any shell programs or task-switching programs such as DOS Shell, Windows, DESQView, or Software Carousel.

3. Place Disk 1 in drive A and, if applicable, close the drive door.

4. Type A: and press ⏎Enter to change to drive A.

5. Type SETUP and press ⏎Enter. The Welcome screen opens.

6. To begin Setup immediately, press ⏎Enter. To display Help information about the Setup program, press F1. To stop Setup, press F3.

7. Setup prompts you to label the Uninstall disks. It uses the Uninstall disks during Setup to save some of your original DOS files so that if Setup does not finish installing MS-DOS 6, or if you have problems after installing MS-DOS 6, you can restore your previous version of DOS.

A

418

8. Press ⏎Enter when you are ready to continue.

9. Setup prepares to install MS-DOS 6. It asks you to confirm the DOS Type, the DOS Path, and the Display Type. To accept the displayed values, press ⏎Enter. To change a value, press ↑ and ↓ to highlight the value and press ⏎Enter to display alternative values. Use ↑ and ↓ to select an alternative, and press ⏎Enter.

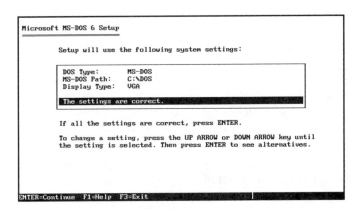

Press Enter to accept the displayed values.

10. Select any optional programs you want to install. To accept the displayed values, press ⏎Enter. To change a value, press ↑ and ↓ to highlight the value and press ⏎Enter to display alternative values. Use ↑ and ↓ to select an alternative, and press ⏎Enter. When the values you want are displayed, press ⏎Enter.

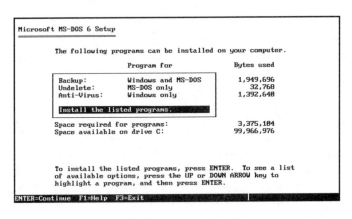

In this example, Setup will install Backup for both Windows and MS-DOS, Undelete for MS-DOS only, and Anti-Virus for Windows only.

419

If you do not install the optional programs now, you can do so in the future; however, you probably should install them now.

If you do not have Windows at this time, you cannot install the programs for Windows. When you get Windows, you can run Setup again and add the Windows programs.

11. If you are installing the Windows programs, Setup asks you to verify the Windows directory. Press ⏎Enter to accept the directory that Setup displays, or type in the correct directory and press ⏎Enter.

12. Setup is now ready to upgrade to MS-DOS 6. Press Y to begin the upgrade or press F3 to Exit.

13. Setup prompts you when it is time to insert a different disk in drive A. Remove the disk from drive A, insert the requested disk, close the drive door if appropriate, and press ⏎Enter. If you insert the wrong DOS disk, DOS tells you and gives you a chance to insert the correct disk.

14. During the upgrade, Setup copies your previous DOS files to a directory named OLD_DOS.1 on your hard disk. (If you already have an OLD_DOS.1, Setup names the directory OLD_DOS.2, and so on.) It also copies your AUTOEXEC.BAT and CONFIG.SYS files to the Uninstall disks. The copies are named AUTOEXEC.DAT and CONFIG.DAT.

15. Setup then copies the DOS files to the hard disk. Setup displays a horizontal bar that shows what percentage of the total installation process is complete. Setup displays the current activity in the lower right corner of the screen.

16. When the install process is complete, DOS prompts you to remove all floppy disks from the disk drives and press ⏎Enter.

17. Press ⏎Enter again to restart your computer with MS-DOS 6.

The upgrade process on the hard disk is complete.

Installing on Floppy Disks

If you do not have a hard disk, you can install MS-DOS 6 on floppy disks. Actually, you don't really upgrade your existing floppy disks to MS-DOS 6; you create a new set of DOS floppy disks. These disks will be your operating disks. You will use these disks to run DOS. After you complete this process, store the original DOS disks in a safe place and use the operating disks.

420

You will need three disks that fit into the drive on which you are installing
DOS. If you are using drive A, for example, and drive A is a 5 1/4-inch drive,
you need three 1.2M disks. If drive A is a 3 1/4-inch drive, you need three
1.44M disks. These disks can be unformatted; existing data on the disks will be
destroyed. (If you are using drive B, substitute *A* for *B* in the following steps.)

DOS gives you the option to continue or cancel the installation throughout
the installation process. If you cannot complete the installation for any reason,
press F3. You can start from the beginning at a later time.

To install DOS on floppy disks, follow these steps:

1. Turn on your computer. If your computer is already on, hold down
   Ctrl and Alt and press the Del key; then release all three keys. This
   action reboots, or restarts, your computer with your current version of
   DOS.

2. Place Disk 1 in drive A and, if applicable, close the drive door.

3. Type A:SETUP /F and press Enter.

   DOS loads and starts the Setup program.

4. Setup prepares to install MS-DOS 6. It checks your hardware configuration. Setup prompts you to label your floppy disks. Press Enter to
   continue.

5. Setup asks you to confirm the start-up drive and the Display Type. To
   accept the displayed values, press Enter. To change a value, press ↑
   and ↓ to highlight the value and press Enter to display alternative
   values. Use ↑ and ↓ to select an alternative, and press Enter. When
   the values you want are displayed, press Enter.

6. When you are prompted to insert a different disk, remove the disk,
   insert the requested disk, close the drive door if appropriate, and
   press Enter. If you insert the wrong disk, DOS tells you and gives you
   a chance to insert the correct disk.

7. Setup proceeds to copy the DOS files onto the three floppy disks. It
   displays a horizontal bar that shows what percentage of the total
   installation process is complete. Setup displays the current activity in
   the lower right corner of the screen.

8. When the installation process is complete, insert the Startup/Support
   disk in drive A and press Enter. This action reboots or restarts the
   computer by using the new working disk.

   The installation process on floppy disks is complete.

A

Completing the Installation

In most cases, after you complete the installation or the upgrade, you are ready to use your computer. In some cases, however, you must do some additional work so that you can improve the way DOS runs. For instance, you might have to modify the HIMEM command if you have one of the following computers:

- Abacus 386
- Chaplet
- Everex AT Plus 1800
- Everex Notebook ELX
- Excel Computer Systems
- OPT 386-25 Motherboard
- Pak 386SX
- PC Limited
- PC380/33C, PC350/33C, or PC300/33C BIOS revision 1.14

In the directory in which you installed DOS, such as C:\DOS, the README.TXT file contains additional information about DOS and the installation process. You should read this file to see whether any of the information applies to your computer system.

The README.TXT file contains up-to-date technical information about installing or upgrading MS-DOS 6.

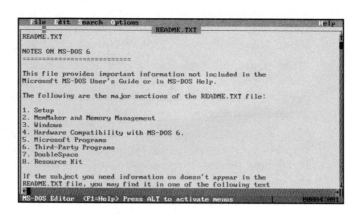

To read this file from the DOS Shell by using a mouse, follow these steps:

1. Point to the C:\DOS directory in the Directory Tree area in the upper left portion of the display, and click the left mouse button.

2. Point to the Editor in the Program List area in the lower left portion of the display, and double-click the left mouse button. If nothing happens, press ↵Enter.

3. In the dialog box, type **README.TXT** and click the OK button.

4. Read the information in the README.TXT file. Click on the up and down scroll arrows on the right side of the screen to see the entire file.

5. To leave the Editor, move the mouse pointer to the File menu at the top of the display and click the left mouse button. Then move the mouse pointer to the Exit menu choice and click the left mouse button.

To read this file from the DOS Shell by using the keyboard, follow these steps:

1. Press Tab⇆ until you highlight the Directory Tree area in the upper left portion of the display. Press ↑ and ↓ until you highlight the DOS directory.

2. Press Tab⇆ until you highlight the Program List area in the lower left portion of the display. Press ↑ and ↓ until you highlight the Editor in the Program List area; then press ↵Enter.

3. In the dialog box, type **README.TXT** and press ↵Enter.

4. Read the information in the README.TXT file. Use the PgUp and PgDn keys to see the entire file.

5. To leave the Editor, press Alt and then press **F** to display the File menu. Press **X** to choose the Exit command.

To read this file from the DOS prompt, follow these steps:

1. Type **CD \DOS** and press ↵Enter.

2. Type **EDIT README.TXT** and press ↵Enter.

3. Read the information in the README.TXT file. Use the PgUp and PgDn keys to see the entire file.

4. To leave the Editor, press Alt and then press **F** to display the File menu. Press **X** to choose the Exit command.

This file contains technical information about the installation that is outside the scope of this book.

Restoring a Previous Version of DOS

If you upgrade to MS-DOS 6 but cannot operate your computer, you can revert to your previous version of DOS by using the Uninstall disks created during Setup. You must use the most recently created Uninstall disk. If you try to use an Uninstall disk created during a previous installation, DOS prompts you for the most recent Uninstall disk.

To restore your previous version of DOS, follow these steps:

1. Insert into drive A the Uninstall disk (or Uninstall #1) that DOS created during the upgrade.

2. Restart your computer.

3. Uninstall tells you that if it can perform the restoration, it will remove the DOS 6 files and replace your original DOS files.

4. Press R to restore the original DOS. To stop the uninstall procedure, remove the disk from drive A and press E.

Under certain circumstances, you cannot restore your previous version of DOS. If, after installing MS-DOS 6, you do any of the following, your Uninstall disk will not work:

- Repartition or reformat your hard disk.
- Delete or move either of the two hidden MS-DOS system files (IO.SYS and MSDOS.SYS).
- Delete the OLD_DOS.*x* directory.
- Install DoubleSpace or any other disk-compression program.

Running Setup To Install the Optional Programs

If you did not install an optional program when you originally installed MS-DOS 6, or if you want to install another one or change a program's setup, you can run Setup just for that purpose. For example, if you did not have Windows when you first installed MS-DOS 6, you could not install Backup, Anti-Virus, or Undelete for Windows. If you now have Windows, you can run Setup to install those three optional programs.

To run Setup just to install the optional programs, follow these steps:

1. Insert Setup Disk 1 in drive A.

A

2. Type **A:** and press `⏎Enter`.

3. Type **SETUP /E** and press `⏎Enter`. The Welcome screen opens.

4. To begin installing the optional programs immediately, press `⏎Enter`. To display Help information about the Setup program, press `F1`. To stop Setup, press `F3`.

5. Select the optional programs you want to install. To accept the displayed values, press `⏎Enter`. To change a value, press `↑` and `↓` to highlight the value and press `⏎Enter` to display alternative values. Use `↑` and `↓` to select an alternative, and press `⏎Enter`. When the values you want are displayed, press `⏎Enter`.

6. If you are installing the Windows programs, Setup asks you to verify the Windows directory. Press `⏎Enter` to accept the directory that Setup displays, or type in the correct directory and press `⏎Enter`.

7. Setup prompts you when it is time to insert the other Setup disks in drive A. Press `⏎Enter` to continue.

8. When the optional programs have been installed, Setup prompts you to press `⏎Enter` to exit the Setup program.

Preserving DOS Shell Settings

At some point, you might need to uninstall and reinstall MS-DOS 6, even if the installation was completed without error. With any of the following situations, you may find it easier to reinstall DOS. For example, you may have a marginal sector on your disk that goes bad, causing part of DOS to be unreadable. If you change your video display, such as from EGA to VGA, you must follow a complex procedure to upgrade the DOS installation. You will find it much easier to reinstall MS-DOS 6.

Another reason to install DOS again is to upgrade to future new versions of MS-DOS 6. If you changed the DOS Shell settings or added program groups, this information is stored in a file named DOSSHELL.INI. After you reinstall MS-DOS 6 or install a future version of DOS 6, the DOSSHELL.INI file in the \DOS directory contains the original default settings. If the DOS Shell starts automatically when you boot DOS, you can see that you lose any customizing or program groups. To recover the custom settings, you must copy your customized DOSSHELL.INI file to the \DOS directory.

If you are in the DOS Shell, press F3 to cancel the Shell and return to the DOS command line. Then copy DOSSHELL.INI from the old DOS directory to the \DOS directory.

A

If your old DOS directory was renamed OLD_DOS.2 during the upgrade and your new DOS directory is DOS, enter the following command and then press Enter:

> **COPY \OLD_DOS.2\DOSSHELL.INI \DOS**

If your old DOS directory had a different name, substitute that name for OLD_DOS.2 in the command.

To return to the DOS Shell, type **DOSSHELL** and press Enter. The DOS Shell now reflects the changes you made to the Shell in the previous version of MS-DOS 6.

A

Optional Programs for Windows

MS-DOS 6 includes three programs for Windows users: Anti-Virus, MS Backup, and Undelete. All three are similar to their DOS counterparts, but you can use them from within Windows. These programs are powerful tools for preserving data security. Anti-Virus enables you to scan your memory and disk files for software viruses and to remove detected viruses. MS Backup lets you back up, restore, and compare your hard disk files. Undelete offers three levels of file-deletion protection.

These programs are optional, and you can install them with the Setup program, as described in Appendix A. When you set up MS-DOS and choose to install one or more of these programs, MS-DOS creates a new group named *Microsoft Tools* in Program Manager. Microsoft Tools contains the icons for the programs you choose to install.

This appendix provides instructions for using these programs. You do not need to read this appendix if you do not use Windows. If you do use Windows, however, or if you install Windows at a later date, you will find the information in this appendix valuable.

Anti-Virus for Windows

MS Backup for Windows

Undelete for Windows

Key Terms Used in This Appendix	
Software virus	Sets of computer instructions hidden inside program files. A virus can destroy your data.
Back up	To copy files from your hard disk to floppy disks.
Restore	To copy the backed up files from the floppy disks to the hard disk.
Catalog file	A file created during a backup that contains information about the backed up files and directories.
Undelete	To recover a file or directory that has been deleted.

Anti-Virus for Windows

B

As discussed in Chapter 10, software viruses are potentially deadly sets of computer instructions hidden inside program files. Viruses are often found in free software distributed through electronic bulletin board systems (BBS) and passed around on floppy disks. You should always be careful about using programs you obtain on disk from someone else.

To protect your computer from viruses, you can use the two anti-virus software programs that come with MS-DOS 6. *VSafe* is a terminate-and-stay-resident (TSR) program that continuously monitors your computer for signs of viruses. This program displays a prompt when it suspects the presence of a virus. Microsoft Anti-Virus for Windows lets you scan for, detect, and remove viruses from your computer's memory and drives.

Starting Anti-Virus for Windows

You install Anti-Virus by using the DOS Setup program. If Anti-Virus is not already installed, see Appendix A for installation instructions. When you install Anti-Virus for Windows, the Anti-Virus icon is added to the Microsoft Tools program group. To start Anti-Virus for Windows, first select the Microsoft Tools icon in Program Manager.

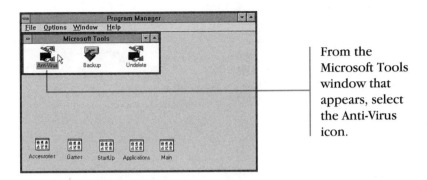

From the
Microsoft Tools
window that
appears, select
the Anti-Virus
icon.

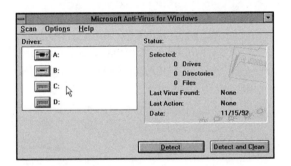

The Microsoft
Anti-Virus for
Windows screen
opens.

B

To scan for viruses, follow these steps:

1. Select the drive you want to scan by pointing at the drive icon and
   clicking the mouse. With the keyboard, use ↑ and ↓ to select the
   drive, and then press the space bar. To deselect the drive, click its
   icon or press the space bar again.

   Anti-Virus reads file information on the drive you select. Repeat this
   step to select additional drives.

429

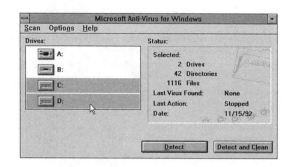

Anti-Virus for
Windows lets you
scan more than
one drive at a
time.

2. Choose the Detect button to begin scanning the drives. Anti-Virus
   prompts you when it finds a virus or detects any change in a file that
   might indicate the presence of an unknown virus. You can update the
   file, delete the file, stop the detection, or continue the detection.

   To scan the drives and remove viruses without prompts, choose the
   Detect and Clean button instead of Detect.

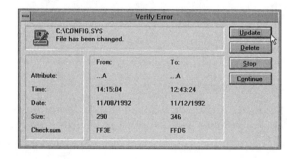

In this example,
Anti-Virus detects
a change in the
CONFIG.SYS file.

During the scan, Anti-Virus displays a status bar that includes information on
the files and directories being scanned, the last virus found, and the last action
taken.

B

430

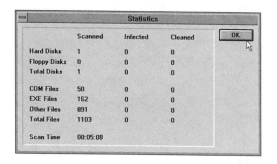

When the scan is complete, Anti-Virus displays a Statistics window that tells you how many disks and files it scanned and how many viruses it found and cleaned.

Specifying a Start-Up Command

You can specify a start-up command for Anti-Virus for Windows so that it automatically scans a specified drive when you start Windows.

To specify a start-up command, follow these steps:

1. Select the Anti-Virus for Windows icon from the Microsoft Tools program group.

2. Select Program Manager's File menu.

3. Select Properties. The Program Item Properties dialog box appears.

4. In the Command Line box, the file name MWAV.EXE is displayed. After the file name, type the letter of the drive you want Anti-Virus to scan.

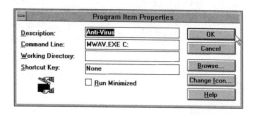

In this example, Anti-Virus for Windows will scan drive C.

5. Choose OK or press ◄Enter.

Getting Information about Viruses

Anti-Virus comes preset to scan your disks and memory for certain known viruses. You can see a list of the viruses and display or print out information about each one.

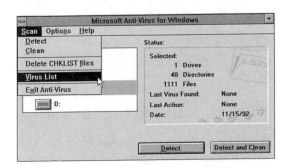

To see the list of known viruses, choose **Virus List** from the **Scan** menu.

B

To display information about a particular virus on the Virus List, use the mouse to click on the virus name, or use the keyboard to select it and press Enter.

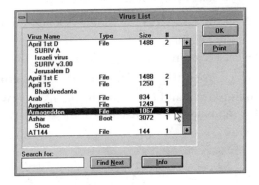

Setting the Configuration Options

The configuration options for Anti-Virus for Windows are preset so that, in addition to scanning for known viruses, the program scans for changes in executable files that may indicate an unknown virus. If the program detects a change, it displays a warning prompt. You can change the configuration options for Anti-Virus by turning the options settings on or off.

To change the default options settings, choose Set **Options** from the Options menu. To choose an option with the mouse, position the mouse pointer on it and click the left mouse button. To use the keyboard, highlight the option you want and press the space bar. To deselect an option, press the right mouse button or the space bar again. When you finish choosing the settings, choose OK.

432

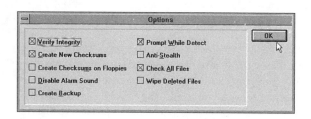

The selected
options settings
have *X*s beside
them.

The following table briefly describes each option:

Option	Description
Verify Integrity	Scans for changes in executable files. This option is selected by default.
Create New Checksums	Creates a checklist file for each directory scanned. If changes are detected in executable files, a warning message is displayed. This option is selected by default.
Create Checksums on Floppies	Creates checklist files on floppy disks.
Disable Alarm Sound	Turns off the audible alarm.
Create **B**ackup	Creates a backup file of any file containing a virus before the file is cleaned.
Prompt **W**hile Detect	Displays a dialog box when a virus is detected, giving you the option of cleaning the file, continuing the scan, or stopping the scan. This option is selected by default.
Anti-**S**tealth	Activates a deeper level of virus detection.
Check **A**ll Files	When on, all files are scanned. When off, only executable files are scanned. This option is on by default.
Wipe De**l**eted Files	Wipes out every cluster of infected files, rather than just deleting them.

B

433

Using VSafe with Windows

To use VSafe—a terminate-and-stay-resident (TSR) program—with Windows, you must load the VSafe Manager program and the VSafe program. To set up VSafe and the VSafe Manager program so that they are loaded into memory each time you start your computer, you must add the VSAFE command to your AUTOEXEC.BAT file and the LOAD command to your WIN.INI file.

To modify your AUTOEXEC.BAT file, follow these steps:

1. Use a text editor such as Notepad in Windows or the DOS Editor in DOS to open your AUTOEXEC.BAT file.

2. On a new line, type VSAFE.

3. Save the AUTOEXEC.BAT file and exit the text editor.

To modify your WIN.INI file, follow these steps:

1. Use a text editor to open your WIN.INI file, located in the Windows directory.

2. Change the LOAD= command so that it reads as follows:

   LOAD=MWAVTSR.EXE

   If you use Windows 3.1, you can place the VSafe Manager icon in the Startup group instead.

3. Save the WIN.INI file and exit the text editor.

   You must reboot your computer to load the VSafe program into memory. If you are in Windows, be sure to exit Windows first. To exit Windows, return to the Program Manager window. Choose Exit Windows from the File menu and then choose OK, or double-click the control menu box in the upper left corner.

4. Press Ctrl-Alt-Del to restart your computer.

MS Backup for Windows

MS Backup for Windows, like MS Backup for DOS, simplifies the routine of backing up disks and directories. With a few keystrokes, you can safeguard your data against hard disk failures, and you can restore and compare the backed up files without leaving the Windows environment.

In earlier versions of DOS, using MS Backup could get very confusing. You had to know which command switches to set and which parameters to use to backup the files you wanted in the way that you wanted. DOS 6 makes use of Windows' graphical format for its MS Backup for Windows program. You can select the options on-screen, and then save them in setup files you can use again and again.

With MS Backup for Windows, you can do the following:

- Back up an entire disk or directory structure.
- Back up files that are larger than the capacity of your floppy disks.
- Back up only those files that were created or changed since the last time you backed up.

MS Backup for Windows can copy files from your hard disk to the destination floppy disk or to another MS-DOS-compatible backup device, including network drives. The internal format of the backed-up file is different from normal files; therefore, you cannot use COPY to retrieve files stored on a backup disk. Your computer can use the files produced by MS Backup only after you run them through the Restore portion of the MS Backup program.

You can, however, use MS Backup for Windows to restore files backed up with MS-DOS 6's Backup for DOS. You cannot restore files backed up with an earlier version of DOS. You must use the DOS RESTORE command to do that.

B

For specific information on understanding the MS Backup program and the types of backup available, see the sections "Understanding MS Backup" and "Types of Backup" in Chapter 10.

Starting MS Backup

You must use the DOS Setup program to install MS Backup. If it is not already installed, see Appendix A. When you install MS Backup for Windows, DOS adds the Backup icon to the Microsoft Tools program group.

To start MS Backup for Windows, select the Microsoft Tools icon in Program Manager.

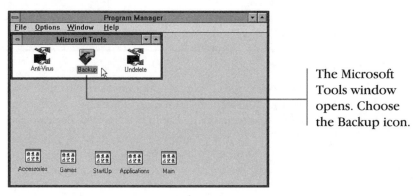

The Microsoft Tools window opens. Choose the Backup icon.

435

The Backup window opens. From this window, you can perform a backup, restore backup files, compare files that have been backed up to the originals, or reconfigure MS Backup.

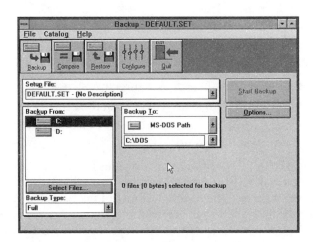

B

The first time you use MS Backup for Windows, it automatically sets the configuration for your hardware system. You should then run a compatibility test to make sure that MS Backup is compatible with your system. To change the configuration or start the compatibility test, choose the Configure button at the top of the main Backup window. The Configuration window opens.

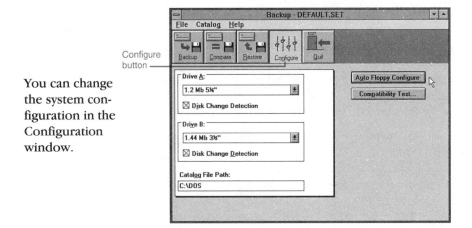

You can change the system configuration in the Configuration window.

You should reconfigure your drives if you install a new drive or use disks that have a different density than the currently configured drives. Choose the Auto Floppy Configure button to automatically configure the disk drives installed on your PC.

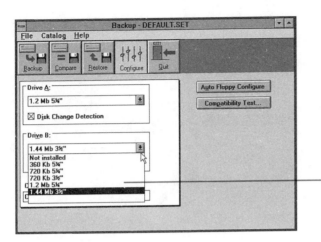

To enter the settings manually, select the drive you want to change. Select the correct size from the list that appears.

When configuration is complete, you can run a compatibility test. The compatibility test makes sure that MS Backup is correctly installed and configured to perform reliable file backups and restorations on your PC. The test consists of performing a small backup. You can skip the test, but then you cannot be sure that MS Backup works correctly.

Before you start the compatibility test, make sure that you have two blank disks available. They should be the correct size and density for the drive you are going to use. To run the compatibility test, follow these steps:

1. Choose the Compatibility Test button from the Configuration window. The Compatibility Test dialog box appears.

2. Specify the drive you want to use.

3. Choose the Start button or press ⏎Enter.

   During the test, MS Backup for Windows displays the Backup Progress dialog box and prompts you to insert the disks into the selected drive as they are needed.

   When the test is complete, MS Backup for Windows compares the backed up files with the original files.

When you are sure that your system is compatible with MS Backup for Windows, you can back up your files with confidence.

Backing Up Files

In the Backup window, you choose the type of backup you want to perform, the source drive, the destination drive, and the files you want to include or exclude.

B

The default
settings on the
backup screen,
shown here, are
for backing up all
of the files on
drive C to floppy
disks in drive A.

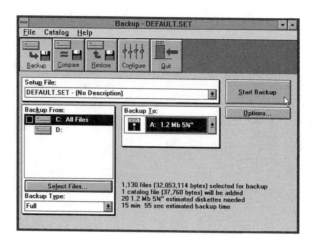

Performing a Full Backup

To perform the default backup, follow these steps:

1. Select the source drive in the Backup From box. To select all files on
   drive C, select the drive and then press the **space bar** or click the right
   mouse button.

   In the lower right corner of the Backup window, the MS Backup
   program displays the number of selected files.

2. Verify that the Backup Type box is set to Full. If it is not, choose the
   Backup Type box and choose Full.

3. Verify that the destination drive in the Backup To box is drive A. If it is
   not, choose the Backup To box and choose drive A. In the lower right
   corner, MS Backup indicates how many disks you will need and how
   much time the backup will take.

4. To verify the disk backup options, choose the Options button.

438

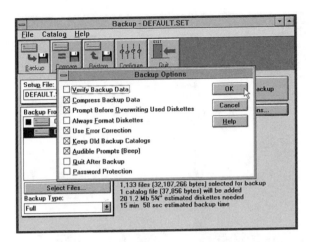

Options include
verifying data,
compressing
data, password-
protecting data,
using error
correction, and
pausing to issue
prompts.

5. To choose an option, click on it or highlight it and press the space bar. To deselect an option, click on it again or press the space bar again. When you have selected all the options you want, choose OK.

6. Choose the Start Backup button to back up the selected files. MS Backup prompts you to insert a disk into the correct drive. Always label the disks clearly, including the disk number, the files that were backed up, and the date the backup was performed. Put the backup disks in the proper sequence and store the disks in a safe place.

During the backup, MS Backup displays status information. When the backup is complete, the program displays a Backup Complete report.

Backing Up Selected Files

You do not have to back up every file each time you perform a backup. MS Backup is very flexible—you can select just one file. You can select files from different directories, or you can select entire directories.

To specify files individually or by groups, choose the Select Files button from the Backup window.

The Select
Backup Files
window lists your
files and directo-
ries so that you
can easily select
the files you want
to back up. To
change the way
the files and
directories appear
on the screen,
choose the
Display button
from the bottom
of the screen.

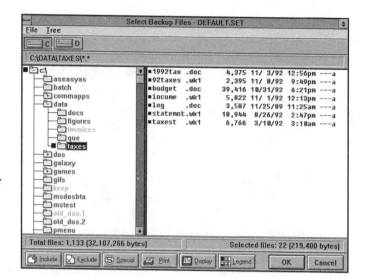

B

To select a directory or file, highlight it, and then press the space bar or click
the right mouse button. To deselect a directory or file, the process is the same:
highlight it and then either press the space bar or click the right mouse
button.

The **L**egend button displays a description of the icons used to specify which
files and directories are selected. The **P**rint button enables you to print drive
data.

The **I**nclude and **E**xclude buttons enable you to specify the path to individual files or to groups of files. Enter the path and file name and choose the
Add button. When all the files you want to include or exclude are listed,
choose OK.

The **S**pecial
button displays
the Special
Selections dia-
log box, which
enables you to
exclude files
based on their
attributes or
according to
the date they
were created
or modified.

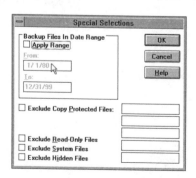

After you fill out the Select Backup Files window for the files you want to back up, choose OK to return to the Backup window.

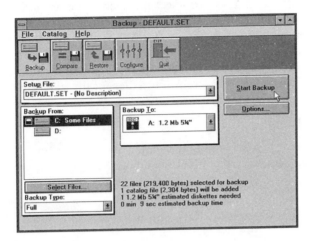

MS Backup displays the number of files you selected, the number and type of disks you will need to perform the backup, and the amount of time the backup will take.

B

In the Backup window, verify the type of backup, the source and destination drives, and the backup options, and then choose the Start Backup button to perform the backup.

Suppose that you want to perform an incremental backup of all of the files in your \DATA directory from drive C to drive A and that you want to use error correction and verify the backup data after the backup is complete. Use the following steps to set up this backup:

1. Choose the Backup icon from the Microsoft Tools window.
2. Select the source drive (C:) in the Backup From box.
3. Choose the Select Files button.
4. Select the \DATA directory from the Select Backup Files window. Press the space bar or click the right mouse button to include all of the files in that directory. Notice the icons that appear beside the selected files.
5. Choose OK.
6. Select Incremental from the Backup Type box.
7. Select the destination drive (A:) in the Backup To box.
8. Choose the Options button.
9. Select Verify Backup Data and Use Error Correction in the Backup Options window, and deselect the options you do not want to use.
10. Choose OK.
11. Choose the Start Backup button.

441

Using Setup Files

The Windows environment makes it easy to select the backup you want to perform, but MS Backup for Windows makes it even easier. You can save your backup settings into a setup file that you can use for future backups. That way, you can select a setup file instead of changing all of the settings whenever you perform a backup. The default setup file that MS Backup uses is called DEFAULT.SET. You can save up to 50 different setup files for the different types of backups you commonly perform.

To save the current MS Backup settings in a setup file, follow these steps:

1. In the Backup window, before you press the Start Backup button, choose Save Setup As from the File pull-down menu. The Save Setup File dialog box opens.

2. Enter an eight character file name in the File Name box; for example, type DATAFILE. MS Backup automatically enters the SET extension.

3. Choose OK.

To select a setup file to use it for a backup, follow these steps:

1. Select the Setup File box from the Backup window.

2. Select the file you want to use. MS Backup inserts the setup file information into the Backup window.

3. Choose the Start Backup button.

Catalog Files

Each time you perform a backup, the MS Backup program creates a Backup Set Catalog file and stores it on your hard disk and on the backup disk. If more than one floppy disk is used for the backup, the catalog file is stored on the last disk. On the hard disk, MS Backup for Windows stores the catalog file in the directory specified in the Configuration window. By default, MS Backup for Windows stores the catalog file in the \DOS directory. If you want to store it in a different directory, enter the directory name in the Catalog File Path box in the Configuration window.

The catalog file contains information about the files and directories that were backed up and the setup file that was used. You use the catalog file to compare files that have been backed up to the originals and to select the files you want to restore.

MS Backup uses a catalog file naming scheme that helps you know what the file contains. Each name includes the first and last drives backed up in the set;

the last digit of the year when the backup was performed, as well as the day and the month; the position in sequence of this backup if more than one backup was performed on the same day; and the backup type. For example, the catalog file for the first incremental backup from drive C on November 7, 1992 would be named CC21107A.INC. If it were the second full backup, the catalog file would be named CC21107B.FUL.

MS Backup also creates a master catalog file each time you back up. The master catalog file contains a list of each Backup Set Catalog file created using a particular setup file. A master catalog file has the same name as the setup file, but with a CAT extension. For example, DATAFILE.CAT is the master catalog file for the DATAFILE.SET setup file.

If you delete a catalog file from your hard disk, you can retrieve it from the backup set. If you cannot use the catalog file on your hard disk, you can rebuild it.

Catalog files are not necessary for comparing and restoring files, but they do make it easier.

B

Comparing Files

You can use the Compare function to verify that a backup set is identical to the original files and that it can be restored. You can also use Compare to find out whether changes have been made to files on the hard disk since the last backup. You can compare one file, selected files, or all of the files in the backup set.

Follow these steps to compare a backup set to the files on your hard disk:

1. Select the Compare button from the top of the main Backup window.

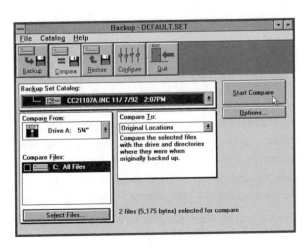

DOS loads the catalog file for the most recently completed backup. To load a different catalog file, choose the Backup Set Catalog box and select the catalog file you want from the drop-down list.

2. In the Compare Files box, select the drives or files you want to compare. Press the space bar or click the right mouse button to select all files on a drive. To select individual files, choose the Select Files button and select the files from the directory list.

3. To compare files to a drive or directory other than the original location, select Compare To and select the drive or directory.

4. Select Compare From and select the drive or device that contains the backup set.

5. Choose the Options button to turn audible prompts off or on and to set MS Backup to exit after the comparison is complete.

6. Choose the Start Compare button. The program prompts you to insert the disk containing the backup set into the correct drive.

When the Compare operation is complete, the program displays a status report.

B Restoring Files

MS Backup for Windows makes restoring files back to a hard disk or to a different computer easy. Like Compare, Restore uses the Backup Set Catalog files. The procedure for restoring files is the same as for comparing files.

Follow these steps to restore a backup set of files to your hard disk:

1. Choose the Restore button from the top of the main Backup window.

2. Load the catalog file for the backup set you want to restore.

   The MS Backup program loads the catalog file for the most recently completed backup. To load a different catalog file, select that file from the Backup Set Catalog drop-down list.

3. Select Restore From and select the drive or device that contains the backup set.

4. To restore files to a drive or directory other than the original location, select Restore To and select the drive or directory.

5. In the Restore Files box, select the drives or files you want to restore. Press the space bar or click the right mouse button to select all files on a drive. To select individual files, choose the Select Files button.

6. Choose the Options button to set restore options such as verification of data and whether or not you want the program to use prompts.

7. Choose the Start Restore button. The program prompts you to insert the disk containing the backup set into the correct drive.

When the Restore operation is complete, the program displays a status report.

Undelete for Windows

If you delete a directory, a file, or a group of files in error, you may be able to recover it by using the Undelete for Windows utility. Undelete is an optional program you install during setup. If Undelete is not installed, see Appendix A.

When you install Undelete for Windows, DOS adds the icon for the Undelete program to the Microsoft Tools program group.

To start Undelete for Windows, select the Microsoft Tools icon in Program Manager.

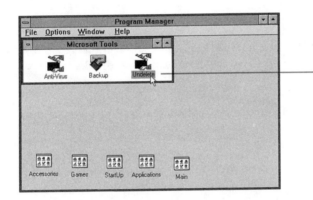

The Microsoft Tools window opens. Select the Undelete icon.

B

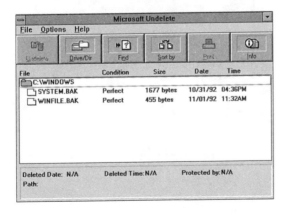

The Undelete window opens, displaying the names of the files you have deleted from the current directory.

The Undelete window displays the name of each deleted file, the condition of the file, its size, and its date and time stamp. The deleted file's condition can be Perfect, Excellent, Good, Poor, or Destroyed. You cannot use Undelete for Windows to undelete files in Poor or Destroyed condition. You can try to

445

undelete them by using Undelete for DOS, as explained in Chapter 10. If the file is in Good condition, you can undelete it by using Undelete for Windows, but you may not be able to undelete the entire file.

Undelete for Windows offers three methods of delete protection: *Delete Sentry*, *Delete Tracker*, and *None*. The default protection is None, but even with None, Undelete might be able to recover deleted files. You can assign a different method of protection to each drive.

Activating Delete Sentry

Delete Sentry is the highest level of protection. It creates a hidden directory called SENTRY, where deleted files are stored. In addition, the file allocation table is left unchanged so that a new file cannot be stored in its place. If you undelete the file, it is returned to its original location on the disk.

To activate Delete Sentry, follow these steps:

B

1. Choose Configure Delete Protection from the Options menu in the Undelete window.

The Configure
Delete Protection
dialog box opens.

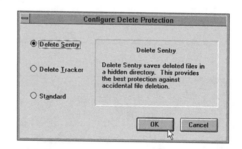

2. Choose Delete Sentry and then choose OK.

The Configure
Delete Sentry
dialog box opens.

446

3. Fill out the dialog box to specify which files Delete Sentry should save. You can select to save all files or specified files. If you select to save only specified files, enter the file names in either the Include or Exclude box. You can use the ? and * wild cards.

4. Set Delete Sentry to purge the files stored in the SENTRY directory after a certain number of days. The default is seven days, which means that every seven days, all of the files in the SENTRY directory are deleted. If you want to delete files from the SENTRY directory at any other time, select those files in the Undelete window and then choose Purge Delete Sentry File from the File menu.

5. You can reserve a certain amount of disk space for deleted files. If the files take up more space than you allocate, the Undelete program deletes them. The default amount of disk space is 20%.

6. Choose the Drives button.

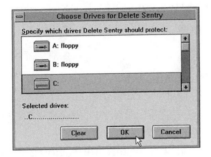

The Choose Drives for Delete Sentry dialog box opens.

B

7. Specify the drive or drives you want Delete Sentry to protect; then choose OK.

8. The Undelete Alert dialog box opens, telling you that you must reboot your computer to activate deletion protection. Choose OK.

9. Exit Windows (return to the Program Manager window and double-click on the Control menu box).

10. Press Ctrl-Alt-Del to restart your computer.

Activating Delete Tracker

Delete Tracker is not as thorough as Delete Sentry, but it is still an effective method of deletion protection. It records the location of deleted files in a hidden file, making it easier for Undelete to locate the file. However, even with Delete Tracker installed, the file allocation table is changed when you delete a file, which means that DOS can use the file's original space on the

447

disk to store a new file. If that is the case, you cannot recover the deleted file, or you might be able to recover only part of it.

To activate Delete Tracker, follow these steps:

1. Choose Configure Delete Protection from the Options menu in the Undelete window.

2. Choose Delete Tracker and then choose OK. The Choose Drives for Delete Tracker dialog box opens.

3. Specify the drive or drives you want Delete Tracker to protect, and choose OK.

4. The Undelete Alert dialog box opens, telling you that you must reboot your computer to activate Delete Tracker. Choose OK.

5. Exit Windows (return to the Program Manager window and double-click on the Control menu box).

6. Press (Ctrl)-(Alt)-(Del) to restart your computer.

B Undeleting Files

No matter which method of Undelete you choose, the procedure for recovering a file is the same. The directory that contains the deleted files must be the current directory. To undelete a file, first choose the Undelete icon from the Microsoft Tools window. Then follow these steps:

1. If the deleted files are not in the current directory, choose the Drive/ Dir button from the top of the Undelete window.

The Change Drive and Directory dialog box opens.

2. In the Change Drive and Directory dialog box, select the drive and directory that contain the deleted files. Choose OK to return to the Undelete window. The names of the deleted files are displayed.

   If you are not sure where the files are located, choose Find Deleted File from the File menu. Enter the file specification in the Find Deleted

Files dialog box. If you do not know the file name, enter a character string in the Containing box. Choose OK. Undelete searches the current drive and displays the names of any files that match the file specification or character string.

3. If a file you want to undelete is in Excellent or Perfect condition, select it. You can select more than one file at a time. (If the file is in Good condition, refer to the set of steps that follows this one.)

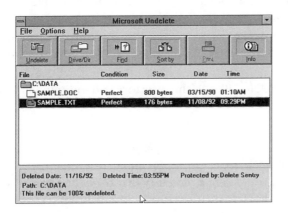

Information about the selected file is displayed at the bottom of the Undelete window.

4. To undelete the file, choose the Undelete button.

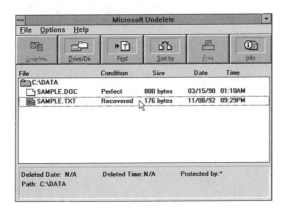

The condition of the undeleted file changes to *Recovered* in the Undelete window.

If you are not using the highest level of deletion protection, the first letter of the file name might be replaced by a question mark. When you choose the Undelete button, the Enter First Character dialog box appears. Enter the correct first letter of the file name and choose OK.

If the file you want to undelete is in Good condition, part of the file has probably been overwritten by a new file. Follow these steps to undelete the file to a different drive:

1. Make the directory containing the deleted file current.
2. Select the file or files you want to undelete.
3. Choose Undelete To from the File menu.
4. Select the drive and directory where you want the undeleted file stored, and choose OK.
5. If the first character of the file name has been replaced by a question mark, enter the correct first letter in the dialog box that appears; then choose OK.

File Manager stores the undeleted files in the directory you indicated in step 4.

Undeleting Directories

You may be able to use Undelete for Windows to undelete a directory you have deleted or removed. If you delete a directory that contained files you want to recover, you must undelete the directory before you can recover the files.

To undelete a directory, follow these steps:

1. If the deleted directory was not in the current directory, select the Drive/Dir button from the top of the Undelete window.
2. In the Change Drive and Directory dialog box that opens, select the drive and directory that contained the deleted directory. Choose OK to return to the Undelete window.

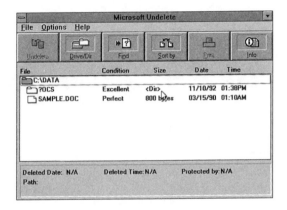

Undelete displays the name of the deleted directory, with <Dir> entered in the size column. This directory was deleted without Delete Sentry protection; therefore, the first character of the directory name is changed to a question mark. Undelete also displays any files that have been deleted in the current directory.

B

3. Select the directory you want to undelete.

4. Choose the Undelete button. If necessary, enter the correct first character of the directory name and choose OK.

    If Undelete can identify the entire directory, it undeletes the directory and lists it as *Recovered* in the Undelete window.

    If Undelete cannot identify the entire directory, the Directory Undelete dialog box opens. To undelete the directory, you must select the groups of files originally contained in that directory.

    The Directory Undelete dialog box displays each group of files in turn. If the displayed group was contained in the directory you are trying to undelete, choose the Add button. If it was not, choose the Skip button. When you have selected all of the groups of files that were contained in the directory, choose the Undelete button. Undelete for Windows undeletes the directory.

B

Index

Symbols

$ (dollar sign) in meta-strings, 277
% (percent sign) in parameters, 189
* (asterisk)
    file names, 238
    wild card, 214
+ (plus sign) file folders, 99
− (minus sign) file folders, 100
... (ellipsis), 75, 276
: (colon), 56
; (semicolon), 276
? (question mark)
    file names, 238
    wild card, 214
\ (backslash), 92
¦ (pipe) symbol, 313

A

/A (attributes) switch, DIR
    command, 202
accessing screens, 217
Active Task list (Task Swapper
    screen), 82, 182
adapters, 22
    display, 14
        CGA (color graphics
            adapter), 14
        colors, 15-16

EGA (enhanced graphics
    adapter), 14
Hercules, 14
monochrome, 14
resolution, 15-16
SVGA (super video graphics
    array adapter), 14
VGA (video graphics array), 14
XGA (extended graphics array
    adapter), 14
Add Program dialog box, 175-176
    Commands box, 175
    Password box, 176
    Startup Directory box, 175
address bus, 29
Advanced Properties dialog box, 192
All Files (Shell view), 86
allocation units (disks), 114, 124
alternative directories, 335
American Standard Code for
    Information Interchange, see ASCII
Anti-Virus for DOS, 369-370
Anti-Virus for Windows, 428-434
anti-virus programs
    Anti-Virus for Windows, 428
    installation, 418
    MS Anti-Virus, 230-231
    VSafe, 230-231, 428

M

M (megabytes), 9
Mace Utilities, 235
Macintosh, 10
macros, 354-356
Main Menu commands
    Detect, 231
    Detect & Clean, 231
    Options, 232
Main program group, 118, 169
    Command prompt, 169
    Editor, 169
    MS-DOS QBasic, 169
master catalog file, 251
math coprocessor, 22
MD command, 367
MDA (monochrome display
    adapter), 14
megabytes (M), 9
MEM command, 264, 365-366
MemMaker, 324-326
    Custom Setup, 325
    Express Setup, 325
    mouse usage, 325
MEMMAKER command, 366-367
memory
    availability, 264, 334
    conventional, 295, 306, 323
    disks, 264
    DOS, 323
    expanded, 306, 323
    extended, 296, 306, 324
        EMM386 device driver, 327-328
        HIMEM device driver, 326-327
        HIMEM.SYS, 296
    high memory, 306
        loading device drivers, 328-330
        loading programs, 328-330
    optimizing, 335
    programs, displaying, 365-366
    reserved, 306, 323

status, displaying, 365-366
    upper, 306, 323
memory management, 322-331
    see also MemMaker
memory-resident programs, 307, 330
    see also TSRs
menu bar, Shell, 68
menus, 356
    cancelling selections, 74-75
    options, selecting, 70, 232
    pull-down, 66, 72
    selecting options, 73-74
    Shell, 72-75
    View, 84
    see also individual listings
messages, error, *see* error messages
meta-strings, 274, 277-279
    $ (dollar sign), 277
    characters, 277-278, 373
microcomputers, 10
microfloppies, 24
microprocessors, 10
Microsoft Defrag utility, 267
Microsoft Tools, 427
minifloppies, 24
minus sign (–) file folders, 100
MIRROR program, 239
\MISC directory, 103
MKDIR command, 220, 367
modems, 9, 28
modifying
    AUTOEXEC.BAT file, 291
    program properties, 179
    text files, 357-358
monitor, 12
    see also display
monochrome display adapter
    (MDA), 14
MORE command, 367-368
MORE filter, 315
motherboard, 22